STRAIGHT AND LEVEL

Air Chief Marshal Sir Kenneth 'Bing'
Cross, KCB, CBE, DSO, DFC
with Professor Vincent Orange

STRAIGHT AND LEVEL

Air Chief Marshal Sir Kenneth 'Bing'
Cross, KCB, CBE, DSO, DFC
with Professor Vincent Orange

GRUB STREET · LONDON

Published by
Grub Street
The Basement
10 Chivalry Road
London SW11 1HT

Cross, Kenneth
  Straight and Level
  I. Title   II. Orange, Vincent
  940.54

ISBN 0 948817 72 0

Typeset by BMD Graphics, Hemel Hempstead

Printed and bound in Great Britain by
Biddles Ltd, Guildford and Kings Lynn

ACKNOWLEDGEMENTS

First and foremost to Brenda, who encouraged me throughout our life
together; Robin, Hugh and Adrienne, who never stopped urging; Vincent
Orange who convinced me that I should continue and John Davies for his
invaluable assistance; Henry Probert and Ian Madelin, and the staff at Air
Historical Branch, MOD, the experts always ready to help; and finally to
Roger Elmhirst, son of Tommy and a persistent supporter over the years.

Contents

CHAPTER I

EARLY LIFE

I WAS born on 4 October 1911 at East Cosham, a village a few miles outside Portsmouth on the road to Havant and Chichester. My father, Pembroke H. Cross, was a surveyor and estate agent with offices in Portsmouth. My mother, Jean Boyd, had been a school teacher in Portsmouth. Both were members of the Methodist Church and it was through their attendance at the same chapel that they had met. My grandfather on my father's side was a Methodist minister; he died when I was quite young and I hardly remember him. My mother was estranged from her parents and it was to be a good many years before I met my grandmother on that side of the family, my grandfather having died many years before.

We moved to a larger house called the 'Poplars' on the same road soon after I was born, and it was here that we lived until after the First World War. The house was a six bedroom and modern by contemporary standards, and certainly we needed a fairly large house because I already had three sisters, Jean, Baba and Joyce and a brother, Ian, arrived later. I was the second of the five.

The garden was also large so we were 'outdoor' children from as far back as I can remember. The War started just before my third birthday and I believe it must have been the intensity of the happenings that make them the earliest memories I have. Firstly our uncles all joined up and soon afterwards came the alarming news of Uncle Hugh being reported 'missing', followed by the tragedy of his brother, our 'Uncle Sharshay', being killed in the Royal Naval Division. Up to that time all seemed to be cheerful and gay amongst the many friends who visited for tea in the garden on Sundays, but now everything changed and even a very small boy noted the difference. I remember too the 'black out' and how one night my father came into the bedroom that I shared with my sisters. He took me to the bathroom and having extinguished the candle, pulled back the curtains and pointed to the searchlights. Four or five of them were holding a Zeppelin in the intersection of their beams. Although the Portsmouth guns were firing away the Zeppelin continued on its course and shortly left the searchlights behind. My father was not liable for military service but, by the second year of the war, decided that he must do his bit. He volunteered for the Navy, was accepted and given the rank of Lieutenant in the RNVR. He did his training at Portsmouth and on completion was posted to Dakar, in what was then French West Africa, so we were alone at home for the rest of the war.

Armistice Day came in November 1918 and I accompanied my mother and Mrs Petty (the vet's wife) to the Town Hall Square to hear the announcement at eleven o'clock. We went by tram from Cosham and when we reached the square the crowds seemed to me to be immense. When the cheering was over we found that the tramdrivers had decided to celebrate as well, so we had to walk the four miles home. But we didn't mind, all was smiles.

My father returned within a few months and wore his Naval uniform until he was demobilised. He found that his business, left in the care of his elder brother Conyngham, had more or less evaporated, so it was necessary for him to start again. Deciding that this time it would be in London and in partnership with a New Zealand friend called Crawshaw he set up offices in Lower Regent Street, where for a number of years he was very successful.

During the war I had attended a local nursery school with my sisters, but now it was decided that I should go to a boys' school and I was sent to Hilsea College, Portsmouth, a private school of about two hundred boys. I was thoroughly miserable from the first, as being rather a weakling as a youngster I was bullied unmercifully. It was only later on that I learnt to box by paying a shilling a lesson, once a week to an ex-Army PT Instructor. After a term or two I was taken away and joined my sisters at their day school in Portsmouth.

One day in the summer of 1921, a seaplane as we then called it, floatplane in today's jargon, forced landed in the bay and was left high and dry when the tide went out. Shortly afterwards a party of airmen appeared in a lorry with a trolley and hauled the seaplane up above high water mark. Apparently an engine change was needed; tripods were erected and work started, which took several days and was of the utmost fascination to us children. We went every day to see what progress was being made. The airmen were very friendly and explained their difficulties. It seemed that the replacement engine differed from the one they had removed, but one afternoon all was complete and the engine was started. The noise was greater than anything we children had ever heard before. After much consultation between the man in the cockpit and further 'running up' all was satisfactory and we gathered that the seaplane would be launched the next morning. We hurried home to give the news to my father who had found out that the take-off would be shortly after dawn and announced that we would all go to see it. This was a great adventure for us, particularly when we were called whilst it was still dark, and came downstairs to steaming hot cocoa which father had made specially. We walked the mile or so along the beach to where a considerable crowd had already gathered. It was light by this time and the engine was started up, run for a few minutes and then shut down. Shortly afterwards a car appeared pumping its way over the beachlands towards us. From it stepped a figure in a vast leather coat. Word went round that this was the actual pilot himself. He appeared to me to be an Olympian figure as he stood there and various airmen of the repair party reported to him. After much talk the pilot climbed aboard the seaplane, a companion got into the rear cockpit and the engine was started. Then the ground party, assisted by some of the bystanders, pulled the seaplane on its trolley into the sea. As they got into a few feet of water the seaplane floated off. The engine roared once more and soon it was streaking out to sea in a cloud of spray. Suddenly it was in the air and quickly disappeared towards the Isle of Wight. What magic for a boy of nine!

By 1923 the internal combustion engine was taking over from the horse in a big way. The baker's horse van was replaced by a motor van. My father bought a motor cycle and sidecar, a new Hudson that went well for a time, but once it started breaking down, it always seemed to be breaking down. We began taking our holidays at the seaside at Bonchurch in the Isle of Wight and Hayling Island, an unspoilt villagey place to the east of Portsmouth. We always took one of our daily maids with us and holidays were never less than a month, sometimes six weeks. The beaches at Hayling were superb and quite uncrowded but later, particularly when the motor car increased in numbers, the whole place became overcrowded.

By the mid-twenties, and with the onset of the 'Great Depression' my father's business in London began to decline and it was decided to sell our house at Cosham and move to Hayling. We children were delighted at this prospect, particularly as the house we were to move into, though smaller, was right on the beach. We moved and the Cross family lived happily at Hayling for many years. My father duly gave up his business in London and practiced in Hayling.

In 1926 he attended an Old Boys' anniversary of his old school—Kingswood, in Bath—marked by the presence of the Prince of Wales.

On his return he was determined that I should go there too. I was already fifteen which was a bit late to be going to a public school, but he swept aside all objections, though it must have meant a financial strain. Until then my sisters and I had attended the local High School in Havant, to reach which we cycled, in all weather, ten miles a day.

Kingswood School, John Wesley's foundation in 1748 for the sons of Methodist Ministers, was an austere place compared with contemporary public schools. It was small, with under three hundred boys including the junior house (preparatory school age), and the Governors had recently changed a long-standing policy to allow the admittance of a limited number of laymen's sons on a full fee-paying basis. Ministers' sons paid greatly reduced fees, the school being largely supported financially by the Methodist Conference. I was one of the first three laymen's sons to be admitted. My father went with me on the train to Bath for my first day in January 1927. In those days many boys travelled to and from school by train, so much so that the rail authorities at Bath made special arrangements for the transport of school trunks from the station to the School high up on Lansdown on the northern outskirts of the city. The school itself was to me a most impressive place. I had attended a succession of day schools in the Portsmouth area in which the corporate life of the school was virtually non-existent. We did have a football team at Havant High School which played on Saturday afternoons and likewise cricket in the summer, but those were the only occasions when we saw our school fellows outside the classroom. To me Kingswood had everything I could wish for, dormitories, House day rooms, gymnasium, swimming pool, library and School chapel. I thought, and still do, that it was a wonderful place for a boy to go to. When I arrived, I met the Headmaster, the renowned H A Wooten. I was to be in my father's old House, the Middle, and was placed in the Fourth Form. I was only to complete five terms at Kingswood, but this period of just under two years had a greater influence on setting my standards than any other similar period in my life.

Kingswood was a tough school in a good way. As might be expected, the whole of school life was conducted against a strongly religious background. We attended Chapel first thing every day, and twice on Sunday. Evening prayers were held for the whole school. Before bed a period of silence was called in the dormitory so that all could say their private prayers. In many ways Kingswood was way ahead of the contemporary public school; but in other ways it was well behind. As an instance of its 'advanced' thinking, fagging had been abolished years before I arrived, and caning was the prerogative of the Headmaster alone. We all agreed though, that what we lacked in quantity caning, Wooten made up in quality: a 'sixer' from him left the recipient in no doubt about his punishment.

The discipline in the school was strict which was a reflection really of Wooten's headmastership. I learned later that the Governors' brief to Wooten when he was appointed in 1925 was to "pull the place together". He, I believe, interpreted this by imposing a strict discipline which we all knew about and respected. Having been a Second Lieutenant in the Army and standing well over 6ft, he certainly was a formidable figure. We knew where we were and if we broke the rules and were found out punishment was automatic. Detention on half holidays was imposed by any master, with caning by the Headmaster for more serious crimes. I was something of a young prodigy when it came to games and quickly found myself as the youngest member of the school 1st XV at rugby football. I was fast and could tackle well. Unfortunately my academic performance did not match my athletic prowess, and consequently I often found myself in detention for unsatisfactory prep on the same afternoon that the School were playing their matches.

These were very important occasions on which virtually the whole school, masters and boys, turned out to watch. I had the choice: do my detention and miss playing for the School or cut detention and face the Headmaster next day. I never received any advice in making the decision. None of my team mates, many of whom were prefects, so much as indicated that they knew about my dilemma, let alone made any suggestions for resolving it. No, the decision was mine alone and of course I always cut detention. So the next day I lined up with other miscreants outside the Headmaster's study and when it was my turn went in. I was always greeted most civilly and generally we had a brief discussion about the game the day before. Then he would say: "Now let me see", looking at his list. "What are you here for? Ah yes, failing to attend detention. Bend over". But only four this time and at not much more than half throttle.

We also had a great respect for our House and School prefects. They really ran the School under the masters. We might take a liberty with a master, particularly a new one, but never with a prefect. They knew it all from personal experience and the chance of getting away with anything with them, was virtually nil.

In my first two terms the city of Bath was 'Out of Bounds'. To go there a chit was required from the Housemaster and would be granted only for very good reasons. Apparently the cafés in the town had become attractive for some of the older boys and some had actually been seen smoking and talking to the local girls! Similarly, when the Bath Races were on at the Lansdown Racecourse a mile beyond the

School, our programme was altered so that instead of games in the afternoon (our playing fields were not far from the course) we worked, and played our games in the evening. The Methodists weren't taking any chances with opportunities for sin!

Towards the end of my second school year at Kingswood it became apparent that my progress academically was insufficient to warrant elevation to the Upper Fifth and the Headmaster said so in a letter to my father. Would it not perhaps be best if I left? My father agreed. He was having a desperate time in his business in the slump and was, I believe, a little relieved at the prospect of reducing expenditure. I was bitterly disappointed not to be going back in September 1928 mostly because I would have been one of the few remaining members of the XV and would certainly have won 1st XV Colours.

Even before I had any idea that I would be obliged to leave Kingswood prematurely, my friends and I had discussed in a desultory fashion what we proposed to do when we left school. My particular friends, D G Butler and J G B Holmes (in those days we always used people's initials rather than Christian names), knew pretty well what their future was. Butler's home was in Leeds and it would be the wool business for him. Holmes, from Lincolnshire, would be going into his father's timber firm. For my part, I wanted nothing of the world of business. I had seen at close quarters the worry and misery brought about by the slump of the late twenties with my father, grey-faced, poring over his books and accounts late into the night. I wanted to belong to some secure organisation in which, even if the material rewards were small, there was some guarantee of permanence, and one in which the struggle to stay solvent was not the main aim. So I came to think of the Services. The Navy was out from the start, since I understood that entry to Dartmouth was at fourteen and I was already sixteen. The Army suffered in my mind from an overdose of the literature of the Great War with its awful concentration on the enormous loss of life in the muddy trenches of France and Flanders. This literature strengthened my belief in the general uselessness of war.

What about the Royal Air Force? This romantic new Service that flew aeroplanes? Kingswood had no military tradition whatever. It was, generally speaking, pacifist in outlook. Unlike most public schools, it had no Officer Training Corps so that any help and practical preparation for entry to the Services through this channel was denied us. On the other hand, a number of the masters had been in the Services during the Great War and, in particular, there were two who had served in the Royal Flying Corps as pilots. The first was A C Townend who taught us Geography. He was a short, rotund little man, but one to whom the exercise of authority came easily. No tricks with him. Silence was immediate when he entered the classroom. The other was F R Mangham, the gymnasium master. A quiet man, he was not easy to talk to. Townend however, liked to talk about the RFC. Incidentally both were fine cricketers: I understand Townend had played for Yorkshire as an amateur, and Mangham was still a formidable fast bowler and sometimes played for the School against the stronger club sides. So I got hold of the booklet on entry into Cranwell.

It was plain at the outset that the educational level required for entry was way ahead of my present standard. There was no possibility of staying at Kingswood to reach the required level; my father couldn't afford it anyway, and then there was the Headmaster's belief that I was not absorbing knowledge at the School and it would be better if I left. So regretfully Cranwell was out. But apparently there was another way of entering the Service as a prospective pilot: a Short Service Commission for which there was no entrance examination, only an application signed by two reputable referees followed by an Interview Board. My parents knew of a family, the Russels, whose son Edward was already serving on a Short Service Commission. So that was that. I left Kingswood at the end of the summer term in July 1928, when I was sixteen.

The lower age limit for entry on a Short Service Commission was seventeen and a half. I would be seventeen in October but then, just as I had obtained the necessary entry forms, the regulation was changed and eighteen became the minimum age limit. So I was therefore faced with a year before I could even send in my application. At first the prospect of a year doing nothing rather pleased me. Hayling Island was a delightful place to be living in. There was sailing, there were the beaches, a championship golf course and, with the winter coming on, I was about to join the Portsmouth Rugby Union Football Club.

However, a little thought soon convinced me that I should not spend a whole year simply amusing myself. Money being short in the Cross family, it would greatly help my parents if I earned some while waiting to see if the RAF would have me. Better still, I could learn something that would encourage the RAF to want me. I put this to my father. I thought I should try and learn about the internal combustion engine since this powered all the aeroplanes of the time. "Good", he said and bought me an excellent book couched in the most simple terms explaining how the internal combustion engine worked. Getting a job was going to be more difficult. Unemployment was running at over two million, but my father knew the owner of a garage which was one of the two Ford depots in Portsmouth. After some discussion, it was agreed that I would be taken on as a grease boy— way below the apprentices—straightaway. I was to work from eight in the morning to six in the evening with an hour for lunch, Saturdays eight to one: a fifty hour week for which I was to be paid ten shillings or fifty pence in today's currency. I was overjoyed at the prospect of actually being employed, though it was with some apprehension that I faced my initiation into the working world, which came very quickly the next Monday morning.

To reach the Works at North End Portsmouth by eight o'clock, my mother called me at six fifteen and, by the time I came downstairs, had prepared a hot breakfast. She never complained. Quite the contrary, she actually seemed to get pleasure in seeing her eldest son off to work. I left home on my bicycle at seven, cycled two miles to the Ferry at the western end of the island, paid my fourpence return fare and was ferried across to Eastney, the eastern tip of Portsmouth. I then cycled five miles to the Works. In the evening the reverse, so from home to home I was actually putting in an eleven hour day, except on Saturdays, a good introduction to the working world of which I considered myself fortunate and privileged to be a member.

Life was not easy in the Works to start with. On my first day the foreman said "Stand there", and that I did for a whole hour and was totally ignored by everyone. Then one of the fitters on the engine benches beckoned me, gave me a load of oily and very dirty engine parts and told me to take them outside and clean them. I was delighted. To be treated as if one didn't even exist was demoralising. George Reynolds, the fitter who gave me my first task, quickly saw that he was on to a good thing, an assistant to do all the dirty jobs, and at first I was very pleased to fill the role. Later, when very gradually I was being accepted as just another grease boy, I found ways and means of keeping out of George's way.

Percy Egerton, who had been an MT fitter in the RFC during the war and had just returned from five years in Canada, and Stanley Watkins the local ace on grass track motor cycling, became the two who took most interest in me. When I explained my need to know all about the working of the internal combustion engine, they did their best to teach me. At lunchtime it was the custom to go outside the Works and eat our sandwiches on the edge of a grass field adjoining our building. When the sandwiches were finished it was time for the apprentices and grease boys to amuse their elders and betters. This took the form of bare knuckle fights. I didn't mind this a bit. I had long since been taught the rudiments of the noble art of self-defence at Sergeant Spencer's gymnasium on Hayling Island and had little difficulty in holding my own, though some of the apprentices were pretty tough customers. In the end I was friends with everyone and learnt a lot about the Model T Ford and its more sophisticated successors.

I did find my engine knowledge useful later when I eventually joined the Royal Air Force, but what was even more valuable was the efforts I had to make to hold my own with the men and boys in the Works. Most of them were splendid people, hard working, fair minded and with a great sense of humour. I learnt a lot about human nature and the working man in particular during the year I worked at the Ford depot in Portsmouth. Time off except for strictly emergency or compassionate reasons was unheard of. I found this difficult because in the winter of 1928/29 I was playing regularly for the Portsmouth Rugby Club first team on Saturday afternoons and it was no end of a scramble to finish work at one pm, get cleaned up, change into some more appropriate clothes and still make the rendezvous for a match, if not on our home ground at Paulsgrove, then somewhere half way across Hampshire. Later, my father bought me a secondhand motor cycle and this eased the situation considerably. Out of my ten shillings pay I gave my mother half-a-crown, two shillings a week went on the Ferry, and the rest was mine. I saved money too, but once the motor bike arrived only the concession that we were allowed in buying petrol cheaply from the firm's pump made it possible to balance the books.

On my way to work in the early morning, I used to cycle past the Royal Army Ordnance Corps barracks at Hilsea. There I would see the soldiers doing their morning PT under the direction of a Physical Training NCO attired in his red and black ringed jersey. How I envied them and their laughing faces, when I was bound for oily overalls and the cleaning of dirty machinery! It reinforced my belief that it was the Services and flying for me. Consequently, I put in my application for a Short Service Commission on my eighteenth birthday, 4 October 1929. My referees were a Naval Captain friend of my father's and our local doctor.

Shortly afterwards, a letter arrived from the Air Ministry summoning me to an interview at Adastral House, Kingsway, London. My father decided to accompany me and we caught an early train from Havant. We reported. My name was taken and we were shown into a waiting room where a number of young men were waiting. Nobody said anything. I thought they were rather a scruffy lot, and they probably thought the same of me. My father departed, saying he would be back in an hour. Periodically a uniformed messenger would come in, call a name and off would go one of the others. Eventually my name was called. The interview board consisted of three elderly gentlemen in civilian clothes seated at a table and a younger man who

seemed to be preoccupied with pencil and paper. I was told to sit down
and then all three gentlemen asked me questions. What they were I
have not the faintest recollection. Anyway, after a time I was thanked
and the young man gave me a printed form. I went outside to where
the messenger was waiting. He took a look at the form I was carrying
and said: "Now for the medical, if you pass that you are in".

My father came back and we went to lunch nearby, returning for the
medical which seemed to take most of the afternoon. There was some
hitch and eventually I was given a chit telling me to return in three
weeks which I did. This time the examination was much shorter and
I was told I had passed, but it was not until January that I received
confirmation of this, when a letter arrived from the Air Ministry saying
that I had been "provisionally" accepted. Finally in March came a
further letter telling me to report to the RAF Depot at Uxbridge
before noon on 11 April 1930 for "a fortnight's preliminary course"
before proceeding to No 3 Flying Training School, Grantham, Lincs.

I was overjoyed. I had taken the first step.

CHAPTER II

JOINING THE ROYAL AIR FORCE

MY father drove my mother and me from our home at Hayling Island in the family Morris Oxford to Uxbridge railway station and, following the instruction in the Air Ministry joining letter, I put my suitcase on an RAF lorry that was standing there. A number of other young men were doing the same and, having said goodbye to my parents, I joined the others for a short walk to the RAF Depot. It was ten thirty am on 11 April 1930. So began for me the great adventure of joining the Royal Air Force. We were directed by a service policeman at the Guard Room to Station Headquarters, a one-storey building on the edge of the parade ground, and we followed on into a small classroom where we seated ourselves at desks facing a dais. There were twenty-five of us, twenty-one Englishmen, two New Zealanders and two Irishmen, one from the North and the other from the South.

As I looked round, I saw that most of my companions were older than myself. I was eighteen and only one or two seemed to be of that age. Some, I learned later, had already started and abandoned careers. We were a very mixed bunch varying from C P Dawson, aged twenty-nine who had actually been in the RFC in 1918 and was by profession a church organist, to J A S Brown and myself, at eighteen setting out on our careers as Short Service Commission Officers in the Royal Air Force. Amongst the others a New Zealander, L J Crosby, had been a ship's wireless officer. Some came from offices in the City. One, I remember, sported an Artists' Rifles tie. All, I discovered later, had one thing in common: a great desire to fly aeroplanes. After a few minutes an officer came in and we all stood up. Seating himself at the dais, he asked us to be seated and introduced himself. "I am Flight Lieutenant Harris, the officer in charge of your course whilst you are at Uxbridge."

Harris was the first officer in uniform with whom we had direct contact, and we could not have had a better introduction to the officer corps of the Service. He was, I suppose, in his thirties. He wore, beneath his pilot's 'Wings' two 1914/18 medals and he addressed us in a most friendly manner. From the start he conveyed the impression that as holders of the King's Commission we were something special, but that this status carried with it responsibilities, particularly as to our personal behaviour "at all times". He spoke to us in his quiet pleasant voice not as one much senior to us, but as a fellow officer, and he gave me the impression that we were already accepted, by him at least.

Much of his talk covered the programme for the two weeks we would be at the Depot. Drill would fill a large part of our day and we would also have lectures on the organisation of the Service, as it affected us. He spent some time on the etiquette of the Officers' Mess. Our category—Pilot Officers on Probation—entitled us to membership of the Mess but to help us learn the rules, many unwritten, we would be separated to some extent from the other members, the officers of the Depot. For instance, in the Ante Room (explained as the main public room in the Mess) the Short Service Courses were expected to keep to one end. This would also apply when we reached our Flying Training School. All this may seem slightly ridiculous in these allegedly enlightened times, but I believe that it was the emphasis on personal behaviour and personal responsibility that went with the possession of a Commission, that produced an officer corps that enabled the Royal Air Force (without the traditions of the older Services) to expand from 33,000 all ranks in 1930 to over a million all ranks in the Second World War.

Harris also explained about uniform. All items were made according to the Air Ministry "sealed pattern" by approved tailors, a list of whom would be provided for us. We could make our own selection and the programme allowed for three visits to London, one for measuring and two for fittings. The uniform list included tunic, breeches and puttees, slacks, full Mess kit, greatcoat, cap, gloves, ties, shirts (stiff and soft), socks and shoes, the whole lot to be provided within the then generous £50 uniform allowance from the Air Ministry.

Such was the competition between them that some firms on the list managed to do it for slightly less, thus providing a bonus for their customers. Gieves, Burberry, Alkit, Conway Williams and Moss Bros are some of those on the list that I remember. I chose Moss Bros because it was the cheapest and was reassured to find that Dawson, the eldest and most experienced member of our course, and Clarke, whose life up to then had been in business in South America, had done likewise. When Harris had finished his talk it was twelve thirty and time for lunch.

The Mess at Uxbridge was not unlike the Service clubs in London. The furniture in the public rooms was substantial and comfortable, the carpets deep piled. The servants, of whom there were many, were civilians, mostly pensioners and very good at their job. Their dress was a short blue and white jacket with dark blue trousers. On Guest Night dinners the senior waiters wore a special brass buttoned tail coat and striped waistcoat to indicate their higher status.

We occupied our end of the Ante Room and a few called for drinks which were eventually brought by the waiters. At this time, and indeed up to the outbreak of war in 1939, bars were unknown in Officers' Mess. Drinking, whilst not discouraged, was certainly not encouraged and the ordering of drinks—summoned by pressing the bells—caused a degree of delay that was probably intended to reduce the amount of drinking. When we went into lunch, we were guided to long tables running the length of the dining room. The permanent officers of the Depot sat at the top table.

After lunch, we returned to our classroom where we were met by Sergeant Major Snelling, one of those remarkable Non Commissioned Officers who, throughout its short history, have been one of the great strengths of the Royal Air Force. A man in his forties, he was clean shaven and as smart as paint in a rough blue uniform. He explained that it was his task to teach us enough drill during the next two weeks to enable us to take our place on parade with the rest of the station when we reached our Flying Training School. This was plainly a formidable task, for many of us had never done any drill in our lives. Some had in their OTCs at school but, as Sergeant Major Snelling said, "this would be Air Force drill" with the implication that it was different from, and superior to, that practiced in the Army. We then went outside, were put in two ranks by the Sergeant Major and marched off to the parade ground.   This was already occupied by numerous squads of airmen being drilled by NCOs, but part of it was kept clear and to this we were guided by Sergeant Major Snelling. Perhaps I should explain that at this stage in the development of the Royal Air Force, with its small numbers of officers and airmen, Uxbridge, though bigger, was very similar to any Army regimental depot in so far as the initial training of other ranks was concerned. The airmen drilling on the 'square' were recruits straight from civilian life who, like us, were learning their drill before going off to other stations to do their technical trade training.

The Sergeant Major kept us at it most of the afternoon. All was done in slow time and by the end of that afternoon, when we were dismissed, we knew what slow marching meant. Although we were by no means good at it, we also knew how to Halt, About Turn, Dress by the Right or Left, Wheel, Stand at Attention and Stand at Ease. Snelling was little short of a genius in getting the best out of such a diverse collection as our course provided. We were not the first lot of Short Service Officers that he had taught and his manner, which combined the asperity of the drill instructor with a small but positive show of respect for our commissioned rank, was just right. Secretly, most of us wished for his approval for we all stood in some awe of him.

After tea we were free until we assembled for dinner at seven thirty. Harris had explained that dinner was a formal affair, "a parade" in fact. We had to come into the Ante Room soon after seven thirty ("not before"), discern who was the senior officer present, go up to him and salute him by saying "Good evening, Sir". Having been acknowledged, one was then free to go to our end of the Ante Room and, if one felt like it, order a drink from a table set up for that purpose. Smoking was strictly forbidden before and during dinner.

Our rooms at Uxbridge were in two ground floor blocks flanking the Mess. Here we were attended by batmen, like the waiters in the Mess, civilians but old hands at the game. My man had already laid out my dinner jacket and had run a bath when I came to change. This really was treatment that I had never dreamed of as a schoolboy and, as I wrote to my mother later that evening describing the first day: "All this—and we actually get paid for it!"

The course proceeded. We were called at seven by the batman who brought tea. Breakfast at seven thirty and Colour-Hoisting Parade an hour later. We paraded in our civilian clothes of course, but were nevertheless placed at the head of the parade. The bugle, the flag hoisted, prayers by the Padre ("Fall out the Roman Catholics and Jews"), the march past the officer taking the parade, with the band playing. Another day had started. To me, an unsophisticated schoolboy, it was all very splendid.

Our lectures included one on the organisation of the RAF in the United Kingdom. We learned that flying training came under a formation called Inland Area, and that No 3 Flying Training School at Grantham was in a sub-formation called 23 Group which also had its Headquarters at Grantham, but not on the Station. Our uniforms were fitted and refitted. I made a special friend of J G B O'Hagan (always known as Brendan), a tall Irishman of about my own age. We had much in common, both being games players, and both with rugby as a speciality. At the end of the first week we were given 48 hours leave, and I went off home by train to fetch my motor cycle. Several others of our course did the same. We faced some difficulty here because we had been told in the course of our lectures that motor cycles were not permitted on the Station at Grantham for first-term pupils. Apparently it had been observed that Pilot Officers were not the most careful drivers of this type of vehicle. So much so that accidents had caused considerable interruption in flying training. It was decided therefore that motor cycles should not be allowed on the Station for the first term of six months. However, by this time the word had got back to Uxbridge that the operative phrase was "on the Station". Obviously this did not apply to keeping them in a local garage and previous first-termers had apparently found this a satisfactory arrangement. I intended to do the same.

When the time came to leave Uxbridge for Grantham, I teamed up with Dawson for the trip north. He had a 500cc P & M Panther which was marginally superior in performance to my 497cc BSA but I thought it a good idea to go in company because he knew the way, whereas I had never been north of London in my life. O'Hagan kindly agreed to take my luggage with him by train. Dawson and I set off after breakfast and, barring a slight diversion via Royston and Huntingdon when Dawson missed the Great North Road turning in Baldock, we arrived in Grantham in mid-afternoon. We left our motor cycles at a garage at the foot of the hill below the aerodrome and walked up to RAF Station Grantham, home of No 3 Flying Training School.

This aerodrome had been named Spitalgate during the First World War, and was to revert to that name after the Second, but in the 'thirties it was Grantham. It was one of five Flying Training Schools, the others being at Netheravon, Digby, Sealand and Abu Sueir in Egypt. These schools trained the bulk of the pilots required by the Royal Air Force, about two hundred a year, made up of Short Service Officers, the Sergeant Pilots recruited exclusively from volunteers from within the Service and the degree qualified entrants from the universities. The only other source of pilot training in the Service at this time was the Cadet College at Cranwell producing about thirty pilots a year.

Dawson and I made our way to the Officers' Mess, a much larger and more impressive building than the one at Uxbridge, where more than a hundred officers lived. The rest of the course had already arrived. Apparently there were no duties that day. We were taken in charge by the Senior Pupil from the course already in residence at Grantham, one Mahon who was to be in charge until our own leaders were appointed.

The course was designed to last a year, divided into two parts. We were all to spend the first six months, known as the junior term, learning to fly training aircraft, the Avro 504N, Avro Trainer and Hawker Tomtit. Those who mastered these aircraft successfully went on to become the senior term and were introduced to faster, heavier types—the Siskin and Atlas, both made by Armstrong Whitworth. At the end of both terms a graduation parade was held, 'Wings' awarded and the newly-qualified pilots posted to squadrons. Mahon, we learned, was the senior pupil of the senior term and he mustered us after tea in the card room to give us the form.

The daily programme from Monday to Friday began at seven with a PT parade outside the Mess taken by a Corporal. Breakfast was at seven thirty, Colour Hoisting parade at eight thirty, after which half the term would go to the hangars for flying and the others would receive instructions in ground subjects. After lunch the process would be reversed. We would always march as a squad from the Mess and as we moved about the Station. At the end of the first week our own senior pupil and his three assistants would be appointed and Mahon would return to the senior term. Work finished at four thirty but dining in Mess in full Mess kit at eight o'clock was compulsory on Monday, Tuesday, Thursday and Friday. Dinner on Wednesday was not compulsory and dinner jackets might be worn. At supper on Saturdays and Sundays, dark lounge suits were the appropriate dress.

The programme was plainly quite rigorous and Mahon emphasised the importance of punctuality, adding that it was one of his tasks to ensure it. Wednesday afternoon was allotted to organised games. These were compulsory; it was not an afternoon off. Saturday morning was normally devoted to ground work, and no weekend leave would be granted during the whole six months of the junior term. When Mahon had finished with us I went to my room and unpacked. My civilian batman appeared in order to help me. He looked after four of us and his comprehensive knowledge of what dress was required for which occasion went a long way to help me in keeping a secret resolve never to be late or incorrectly dressed. I was glad to see that O'Hagan had been allotted a room in the same corridor.

There was some time to spare before changing for dinner and I went for a walk, inevitably it seemed to me, down to the hangars. All was silent there, the hangars locked and only a patrolling sentry to be seen. The sheer size of the airfield impressed me, though by today's standards it would be judged small. After walking for a while, I returned to the Mess, changed into Mess kit and went in good time to the Ante Room. As at Uxbridge the staff officers occupied one end and the pupils the other. The senior term were very much the inhabitants in possession and were inclined to be patronising, but this didn't last long. I did not drink in those days but the older pupils on my term, and practically all the senior term, were enjoying their pre-dinner drink. At dinner the staff officers, mainly instructors, sat at the top table, the senior term on one leg of the U and the junior term the other. The same formality was observed as at Uxbridge and not until the port had been passed at the end of the meal and the King's health drunk, was smoking permitted. I went to bed soon after dinner. It seemed an age since I had left Uxbridge only that morning.

Next morning a bang on my door galvanised me into tumbling out of bed to dress in shorts, shirt and sweater and, half asleep, stumble down to the dining room where the duty cook had placed some very large pots of tea. Both terms trickled in and then, at five minutes to seven, Mahon gave the word and we moved outside. PT lasted fifteen minutes non-stop. The Corporal plainly was also a disciplinarian. I believe I would have quite enjoyed the exercise any other time but seven o'clock in the morning was a bit of a trial. After Colour Hoisting parade led by the Station voluntary band we, the junior term, were addressed by the Station Commander in our main classroom. Here we were joined by the Airmen Pupil Pilots who had been allocated to our course. There were fifteen of them, all of whom had already proved themselves in their various technical trades in the Service, and had survived a searching selection procedure since volunteering for flying training. Two became particular friends of mine, Leading Aircrafts-man Hooper, a very good rugby football fly-half, and Leading Aircraftsman Keill who, though a weight lighter than myself, gave me a boxing lesson every time I ventured into the ring with him.

The Station Commander, Wing Commander Jackson, addressed us as did the Chief Flying Instructor, Squadron Leader Johnny Leacroft, and then my half were off to the hangars. Three of us, Leftwich, LAC H Hobley and myself, were allotted to Sergeant F W Newman, a rather solemn flying instructor but, as I was to find out, a most con-scientious one. He explained the cockpit layout of the 504N to us, and later took each of us for a short 'air experience' flight. I had never flown before and was a bit apprehensive but enjoyed it, and certainly after we had landed was very keen to go again.

Sergeant Newman said that my first few trips would be in the 504N but then we would switch to the new Avro Trainers with which 'B' Flight was being re-equipped. The latter was a metal-framed machine—modern, but rather under-powered with a Mongoose five cylinder radial engine. Later it was to be provided with a Lynx engine and renamed the Avro Tutor. As such it was a fine training aeroplane. Newman said that the flying in the 504N would go down in our log-books as "passenger flying" and would not count in the total of dual flying instruction hours to first solo. There was great keenness amongst the instructors to bring their pupils up to the solo standard as quickly as possible, using no more flying hours than were strictly necessary to complete the syllabus, leading up to the magic Lesson 14 'Solo'.

I did three trips in the 504N before transferring to the Trainer and really starting instruction. There was intense interest amongst our term to learn who would be the first to go solo. The general consensus was that Dawson, the ex-RFC pilot, would be the one. But not so. That distinction went to Crosby, the New Zealander, who beat everyone to it after, I believe, seven hours dual. He was in 'A' Flight, flying the Tomtit. Dawson was the second and after that two or three were going solo every day.

My big day came on 24 June, six weeks after my first ever flight. I had completed just over 11 hours dual, which was about average. I was tested by the Flight Commander, Flight Lieutenant A L Duke. It seemed to be satisfactory for when we taxied back to the hangar he got out and, having had a word with Sergeant Newman, the joy stick was removed from the front cockpit and Newman said: "One circuit and landing" and I was off. There were of coure a great number of other aeroplanes taking off and landing so, as I had been instructed, I taxied with great care. It was exhilarating to be alone in the aeroplane, to know that I alone would decide just how to taxi, when to turn, where to position for take-off. Of course, I had completed so many take-offs, circuits and landings accompanied by Sergeant Newman that the procedure was by this time almost automatic. The take-off safely accomplished and the circuit completed, I was baulked on my final approach by another aeroplane and had to go round again which did not involve much risk as the airfield was so vast. I was clear the second time and the landing was a good one. Sergeant Newman seemed to be pleased but his pleasure was nothing to mine; this was the greatest thing in my life. Off I went to lunch in the Mess, not flying now, just walking on air.

Life at No 3 Flying Training School was, for me, delightful. I became a pilot by application rather than through natural flair and I fortunately had little difficulty in absorbing the lessons so carefully taught me by Sergeant Newman. However, there was always a residual fear that you wouldn't make it as a pilot. Some did not. And hence there was the thrill of, and relief at, success. But I also had another thing in my favour. Quite simply, I like flying.

Then there were the games. I had always been a bit of an athlete, making the School XV at Kingswood at the relatively early age of sixteen, and being in the House teams at athletics and cricket. In the Royal Air Force at that time, physical fitness was stressed as an essential for successful flying as a pilot and games were looked on as the main means of achieving physical fitness. This philosophy suited me fine. Most evenings I played tennis or squash or I was on the running track with the rest of the Station team, preparing for the Air Force Championships which were to be held at Uxbridge in a few weeks' time. Halfway between the Officers' Mess and the Airmen's Barrack Blocks was the gymnasium, a most convenient place to meet the airmen boxers. Our PT Corporal ran the gymnasium and saw that everything was conducted in an orderly fashion. He thoroughly approved of my frequent three rounders with LAC Keill. Though smaller than me, he was much faster and hit me about three times for every one I landed on him. I realised at this very early stage in my service life that games provided a unique opportunity to meet airmen of all ranks on equal terms and get to know them. The more I met and competed, the greater could be my respect for my fellow service-men at whatever level.

Trenchard, in his wisdom, had insisted on high technical standards and his Apprentices Schools at Halton and Flowerdown and Men's Technical Training Schools at Manston and Eastchurch produced artisans of very high calibre. It often occurred that the highly skilled tradesman was also the good games player and, in those days of the pure amateur, the three Services played a much greater part in the sport of Britain than now, when games at national level are dominated by the scramble for lucre. As an instance, the airmen's winter game was soccer. Grantham had a team that could take on almost any amateur team in the Midlands. The star of the side was the outside left, Aircraftsman Brown, who not only won his place in the RAF team against the Army and Navy but also finished up playing for England in the Amateur Internationals. Such success had an inspiring effect on the other airmen who did all they could to improve their skills with the resultant increase in success and deserved satisfaction.

In due course, the Station athletic team was selected and three of us junior termers found ourselves included: J A S Brown in the 880 yds, P Haynes in the 440 and myself in the 100 and furlong. Off we went to Uxbridge on our motor cycles, still technically illegal posses-sions! We didn't win the Inter Station Cup, but the experience of running against such stars as Don Finlay and R H Thomas, both AAA Champions, and rubbing shoulders with such as Sam Ferris, the great marathon runner, was heady stuff for an eighteen-year-old Pilot Officer on Probation.

The summer weather of 1930 was very good and our flying went on almost without interruption. Because there was no instrument flying, we flew visually and so night flying was not in the syllabus at Flying Training Schools at this time and flying ended each day at four thirty. Although in retrospect this omission was an obvious weakness of the syllabus, night flying was in fact a part of squadron training later on, by which time we had had more experience of flying *per se*, thereby minimising the risk of accidents in the dark. I normally took some exercise after tea and worked on my ground subjects after dinner. With one exception I could now compete better academically than I did at school because I was better motivated. The exception was that I found it very difficult to learn the transmission and reception of the Morse code. I never really mastered it, eventually scraping a pass in the examinations by, I believe, the charity of the examiners. Sadly, three of our term—Leftwich, Trappes-Lomax and Armitage—were unable to master the art of flying, despite exceptional measures taken by the instructors to overcome their inability. Trappes-Lomax was apparently unable to 'feel' the rudder even when he wore plimsoles in place of his normal uniform shoes and the others had problems co-ordinating the movements of the stick and rudder. It was no good: despite the instructors' best efforts and extra tuition, they simply couldn't make it and quietly departed.

One of our most important activities was practicing forced landings. The school had a large grass field away from the aerodrome for this purpose. We would arrive in its vicinity at about two thousand feet, where Sergeant Newman would throttle back the engine and then demonstrate how to land should the engine really fail. Whether the emphasis on forced landing practice was justified I don't know. Admittedly, the radial air-cooled piston engine of the time was not entirely reliable compared with the present-day jet engine, and there were a few forced landings by pupils, but I never had any engine trouble at Grantham. However, we practised and towards the end of the term there was a forced landing competition in which all pupils of the junior term took part. I see from my logbook that I finished 6th out of thirty eight which I was very pleased with indeed. Then the term was over. We had the graduation of the senior term, the end of term Ball, organised by O'Hagan and then we were sent off on a month's leave.

I had saved a large proportion of my pay (eleven shillings a day) during this six months' period mainly because I spent most of my spare time in activities on the Station, particularly games which, of course, were free. You were, in fact, limited in the amount you could spend in the Mess on drink — £3 per month rising to £5 on squadron. Some of the older pupils didn't find Station life so attractive and gravitated towards the local pubs in the evenings and wider afield at weekends. The result was that at the end of term several found themselves short of money to pay their bills. In the senior term several cars were therefore up for sale and I debated whether to take advantage of the bargains being offered. I decided to stick to my motor bike, but at the last moment a desperate senior termer offered me his Morris Cowley for five pounds. This was such a good offer that I changed my mind and bought it. So, at the end of September 1930, I set off on the two hundred mile journey home to Hayling Island in my new purchase. Fortunately another pupil, R G E Catt, lived at Bournemouth and offered to ride the BSA down on his way home.

I returned to Grantham at the end of October, legally in possession of a motor car, which was garaged in the Station's transport hangar. We had been given an opportunity before the end of the junior term to say which type we would prefer to fly in the senior term; the Siskin flight trained fighter pilots and the Atlas pilots for bomber, army co-operation, and flying boat squadrons. I had no doubt what I wanted to do. I wanted to be a fighter pilot and so I opted for Siskins. I now learned that I was one of the four officers and twelve airmen pilots who were to join the Siskin Flight. However, my first flying in the new term was with Sergeant Newman in an Avro trainer. Just thirty minutes to become acclimatised to the air again and then we were off down the tarmac to the Siskin Flight. Our pilots' room was a wooden hut on the tarmac outside the hangar housing the Siskins. We spent a good deal of our time in this room, and incidentally learned a lot on the technical side from the airmen pilots who were all qualified tradesmen.

The Flight Commander there was Flight Lieutenant H L P Lester who, of all the staff at Grantham, showed most understanding of the pupil pilot mentality—the fact that at this time we were little more than schoolboys not properly balanced or mature. My instructor was Flying Officer J W Duggan, a strict and conscientious teacher, but one who didn't unbend much. The other pupil officers were Brown, R B Clarke, H O Houghton, and two newcomers: K R Warton, a university entrant, and A E Clouston. The latter arrived with the new junior term, but after only two or three hours flying in Tomtits, was promoted to the senior term and on to Siskins. It transpired that Clouston, a New Zealander, had done a hundred hours' light aircraft flying in New Zealand. He was to become one of the exceptional pilots in the Service, as a man with most polished aerobatics, and was to serve with distinction in Coastal Command during the war. When he left the Service at the end of his five year commission, he went in for long distance record breaking flights in the original De Havilland Comet to South Africa and to New Zealand and back. Ken Warton also had previous flying experience in the Cambridge University Air Squadron. He was a quiet little man, a good pilot, but will best be remembered as an outstanding jazz pianist. The piano in the Mess at Grantham was in the entrance hall and most evenings Warton would play for us there. We were also fortunate in having two other competent pianists, C F Birks and Dawson, the organist.

The Siskin was a formidable proposition for a pupil pilot to tackle. It was at this time the standard front-line fighter in most of the RAF's fighter squadrons. There were still a few Gamecocks left and the Bristol Bulldog was shortly to replace the Siskin in some squadrons but at this time it was odds on that, if training was on the Siskin, then it would be a Siskin squadron that the embryo pilot would be posted to.

It was a heavy aeroplane, the first fighter to have an all-metal framed fuselage and wings. Its 400hp Jaguar engine was a tremendous increase on the 100hp of the Mongoose engine in the Tutor, but even so was only just sufficient to haul the metal airframe round the skies. It had an advantage over previous squadron types in that its engine was partially supercharged giving it an improved performance at altitude. Its enormous parasol top wing gave it a very quick take-off but its high angle of attack in the taildown position on the ground made it a very tricky customer to land. The classic way of landing any tail skid (or wheel) aeroplane was to glide in on the approach with the engine throttled right back and, on nearing the ground, 'hold off' the aeroplane in an approximate landing attitude just above the ground. As the speed decreased, the aeroplane 'stalled' and dropped the remaining few inches to land on all three points: the two wheels and the tail skid. That was the theory anyway, but it took most of us pupils some time to master the technique.

If the aeroplane was 'held off' too high and stalled, then it dropped one wing first which, if it caught the ground before the wheel, caused the aeroplane to cartwheel and it usually finished upside down. Needless to say, our instructors would never let us reach the stage of dropping a wing. If we were holding off too high we would be told and shown how to 'ease it down' and so adjust for the final stall. If we made a real mess of the approach then on would go the engine and round we would go for another try. Once the art had been mastered, bringing off a 'three pointer' in a Siskin was a most satisfying achievement. The tail skid dug into the turf (this was long before the advent of metal or tarmac runways) and the Siskin trundled to a halt in a few hundred yards.

As autumn turned to winter so learning to fly the Siskin became an increasingly rugged business. The open cockpits had no heating and, despite our padded Sidcot suits, wool lined flying boots and two pairs of gloves, we were frozen at the end of each flight. Nevertheless, the instructors often took two pupils in turn without themselves getting out of the cockpit. They certainly set us an example. One of the

Siskin's major shortcomings was its complete 'blindness' forward in the landing position. This made taxiing hazardous particularly on a busy aerodrome such as Grantham with its forty-odd aeroplanes. Even with your head craned out sideways from the cockpit it was impossible to see directly forward. So for safety's sake, taxiing had to be effected by weaving from side to side.

My progress was steady and unspectacular. Duggan was a patient instructor and one whom I could understand. After five hours' dual including a twenty-minute test with Lester the Flight Commander, I began my first Siskin solo at 10.30am on 18 December 1930, a cold and frosty morning. I see from my logbook that, following five minutes dual after lunch on that day, I again went solo during the afternoon, a rather unusual occurrence, but one indicating a certain confidence by the 'C' Flight hierarchy in young Cross's ability! Because of the relative power of the Siskin, to go solo was quite an experience. It was also difficult to land so the sense of achievement and pleasure on doing so safely on your own was something to savour.

Now that we were the senior term and had learned the ropes a bit, our off-duty pastimes became that much more enjoyable. The junior term produced some good games players and the Station rugby football team benefited accordingly. The team had one or two instructors and a few airmen in it, but the majority were pupils. We played other RAF Stations in Lincolnshire and some other Service teams on Wednesday afternoons, and civilian sides as far away as Nottingham on Saturdays. In Nottingham we would repair to The Black Boy, a very popular pub. As often as not, this would lead to going on to the Palais de Dance to dance with the local girls before driving back to Grantham in the early hours.

On one occasion in the The Black Boy we met some members of the Nottingham Rugby Football Club. We had played and beaten their 'A' team at Beeston during the afternoon. It was a convivial evening and, in discussion, one of our rather volatile players held forth on the defeat of the 'A' team ending with an assertion that we could do the same to the 1st XV if we were given the chance! The upshot was an agreement for a visit to Grantham by the full Nottingham side one evening at the end of the season. On that evening the whole Station turned out to see the bumptious young airmen given a hiding. Not so. The game was very hard but we beat the full Nottingham side by six points to three. Nottingham were not then among the most powerful Midland clubs but they weren't far behind and it was really something for a Station side to beat them.

Despite bad weather in January and February 1931, we flew regularly on almost every weekday. Though flights were short, half an hour being the average, we sometimes flew four times a day: at first more often dual than solo, but later nearly all solo with infrequent dual checks. I found as time went on that I could perform all the manoeuvres we had been taught with some competence. I had to admit though that my map reading and navigation were not so good, and this was fully disclosed when I got lost on a cross-country flight to Upper Heyford and finally landed at Halton near Aylesbury, almost out of fuel. This led to a dual cross-country exercise with another instructor, the hard man of 'C' Flight, Flying Officer Markby.

More than sixty years later I can still remember that flight. It was quite short, Grantham to overhead King's Lynn, Market Deeping and back to Grantham. I worked out the courses to steer on the Course and Distance Calculator using the wind speed and direction given me by the Met Officer. Markby, a large fairheaded New Zealander of few words, checked my work and handed it back to me without comment. We went to the two-seater or dual Siskin, strapped ourselves in and Markby started the engine. After taxiing to the take-off point he said, "Take off, climb to 2,000 feet over the aerodrome, then set course for your first turning point, King's Lynn. I don't expect to have to say anything," he added. I did as I was told. It was a fine day at the end of April with good visibility. I was quite looking forward to showing that getting lost on the cross-country exercise was a mistake unlikely to be repeated. I settled on the heading for King's Lynn at 2,000 feet and 110 mph reading, and read my map to check landmarks along the track. We had hardly been going a couple of minutes when there came a bellow from the backseat: "Watch your heading!"

Looking at the compass, I saw that I could not have been more than a couple of degrees off and that wasn't much for the compasses of those days, but I corrected as well as I could. A minute later, "Watch your height" came the bellow from the back. This really was something. Although I couldn't have been more than fifty feet from the prescribed two thousand feet, I corrected. "Watch your speed" echoed down the speaking tube. Surely, I thought, five mph is nothing to shout about? Not so, if I varied one iota then the bellow down the phones was instantaneous. "Watch your speed ... your height, your heading." It was my first experience of absolute concentration. Duggan, of course, had corrected me from time to time in our navigation exercises, but never to this extent. Gradually, by intense effort, I managed to keep my height, speed and heading dead on. When I did there was silence from the back, but the moment I erred, however slightly, then instantaneously came the bellow: "Watch your...".

We arrived over King's Lynn and set course for Market Harborough. Communication from the back was now less frequent and by the time we set course from Market Harborough for Grantham there was almost complete silence. We arrived over the aerodrome, the oracle said "All right, I have her" and proceeded to land. As we walked towards the instructors' office, Markby stopped and faced me unsmilingly. "Last leg wasn't bad", he said as he turned on his heel and walked away. What a lesson! In one hour I had been taught to concentrate on accuracy. If that was achieved and a check point on the map missed, no matter: the next was always near where one expected it to be, whereas if speed, compass heading and height were all over the place, the next check point wouldn't appear, and the pilot would be lost. I pondered this lesson. How well that hard man had summed me up as a rather hit-or-miss navigator!

There was absolutely no concession. Two degrees off heading and the bellow was immediate. It was the anticipation of the bellow that made me concentrate like mad. But I learned what could be done, what standards could be achieved, and all in one hour. No amount of reasonable explanation and advice could have had the same result. Later, I asked some of Markby's regular pupils what he was like as an instructor. "Does he shout at you?" No, they replied, none of them had been shouted at. The treatment had been specially for me and rightly so too. Nothing less would have had half the effect. Although Markby had me properly weighed up, I was surprised because I had hardly spoken to him before our memorable trip, either in the hangar or in the Mess. How did he know that the treatment he gave me was the only sort likely to be effective? I suppose he had spoken to Duggan and between them, as experienced instructors, they had agreed to sharpen me up. Anyway, I had cause to be grateful to them when shortly afterwards I completed my mandatory two cross countries successfully, the first to Sealand near Chester and the second to Upper Heyford near Oxford.

Thus far, everything was fine with my new career, subjects' examinations were over and I had done reasonably well. We were in the last week of the year. O'Hagan had made friends with a splendid local family, the Gardeners; their daughter Mary and her very pretty friend, Jill, were to be our guests at the end of term Ball; and then it happened!

I had completed what was supposed to be my last solo flight at Grantham and was so pleased with my landing that I decided to do just one more. I opened up the throttle, did a quick circuit and came in for my last landing. In my over-confidence I did not watch the ground as carefully as I should have done. Holding off too high, I let a wing drop; it touched the ground before I could do anything, the Siskin cartwheeled and finished upside down with me hanging on my shoulder straps. After all the noise of the crash the silence was complete. I wrestled with the safety pin of my Sutton harness, freed it and tumbled head first on to the airfield. As I stood up, the firetender arrived followed by an ambulance into which I was pushed though, as far as I could tell, I was quite uninjured. I was driven off to the sick quarters where the doctor examined me and pronounced me fit.

The crash was a terrible blow to my pride, to my confidence, but worst of all it came in the last few days of the term. What would happen? Would I be allowed to depart to a squadron with the rest of my term or would I be put back a term and stay at Grantham for another six months? No one in authority said anything and I was too frightened of an unfavourable answer to ask. Unknown to me, discussions had been going on, and here I was extremely fortunate to have Flight Lieutenant H L P Lester as my Flight Commander. I had flown with him several times recently and apparently he convinced everyone concerned that the mistake was quite uncharacteristic of my flying as a whole and that I should be tested again by him and, if I proved satisfactory, I should leave with the rest.

All other flying having been completed, one dual Siskin was wheeled out. Lester and I climbed aboard it and off we went. I had lost all confidence in my ability to land the aeroplane and Lester, with his immense experience, knew this. Off we went to four thousand feet, where he suggested we do some aerobatics. This surprised me because at the time landing was the problem. However, I went through all the routine loops, roll off the top of a loop, slow roll, spin and, most difficult of all, an upward roll. I had no undue trouble with any of these manoeuvres and Lester indicated that we should return to the aerodrome. I made the approach but when it came to the landing, I made an awful mess of it. I simply could not judge my height correctly for holding off to make a three-point landing. First, I would hold off too high, which had been the cause of my crash; then I would shove the stick forward too much and bang the wheels on the ground, causing us to bounce into the air in a stalled condition necessitating pretty quick opening of the throttle by Lester to prevent another accident. After three or four attempts, all unsuccessful, Lester took over and we climbed up away from the aerodrome for a breather.

"Now", he said, "I am going to show you a cast-iron way of landing the aeroplane safely. It is not in the book but you'll have to use it until you've got your judgement back again". We returned to the aerodrome and made a straight-in approach from a long way out with the engine partially on. This gave us a very flat glide and when we appeared to be undershooting the landing area, Lester opened the throttle a little and we literally motored to the spot he had selected to land on. When we got there, he eased the stick back just a little, letting the aeroplane land on its wheels with the tail still quite high in the air. This was very different from the classic tail down, three pointer that we had all been taught to aim at. However, it was certainly a safe way of landing the aeroplane because there was no stalling: the aeroplane still had minimum flying speed when the wheels made contact with the ground. The only disadvantage of this type of landing was that the aeroplane ran a far greater distance on the ground, but Grantham was a big aerodrome.

I did a couple of these landings successfully and then we taxied in. The pupils watching my performance from the tarmac were in fits of laughter. Such remarks as "Salisbury Plain not being large enough for you" and "What about a forced landing?" went right over my head. At least I knew how to get down thanks to Lester. Next day, the last day of term, I was sent solo. This was a great act of faith in me, but I got down safely—using my new method. We all then departed for four weeks' leave.

I had hoped to be posted to 43 Squadron at Tangmere in Sussex which was near my home. That squadron, with its aircraft carrying black check markings on the fuselage and wings, was then the RAF's most glamorous squadron, having topped the bill for two years at the Hendon Display. But it was not to be. Dawson got the one vacancy in that squadron and I was posted to No 25 Squadron at Hawkinge near Folkestone. Clouston, the embryo 'ace', was also posted there. Although disappointed, I was soon very happy in 25 Squadron and learned a lesson that stood me in good stead for the rest of my career: postings that did not at first appeal often turned out to have been very much to my benefit.

CHAPTER III

NUMBER 25 FIGHTER SQUADRON

HAWKINGE was a small grass airfield in the hills about three miles inland from Folkestone. As early as 1912 a field, now forming part of the airfield, had been used by pioneers to try out the very experimental machines that they themselves had built. In 1915 this field was taken over by the Royal Flying Corps and, with the addition of those adjoining, became Hawkinge airfield. Its boundaries, with minor adjustments, remained the same until its final demise in 1961.

When I arrived there in April 1931, it was that rarity amongst RAF stations in the United Kingdom, a single squadron station. It had no active flying unit other than 25 (Fighter) Squadron. There was a small storage organisation using some spare hangars on the far side of the airfield, but its only uniformed people were two elderly stores officers. All uniformed personnel who served at Hawkinge were posted to the Squadron. There were no divided loyalties and everyone worked wholeheartedly for their squadron.

I drove up the hill from Folkestone on the Canterbury road, turned off at the appropriately named Aerodrome Road past a large cemetery and came to the Officers' Mess, a wartime structure of one storey. At first, it suffered in my mind from comparison with the much larger and better equipped Mess at Grantham, but it proved very comfortable to live in which was fortunate because it was to be my home for practically the whole of the next three and a half years. In retrospect, these were probably the happiest years of my Service life.

It was Sunday teatime when I arrived and the Mess was empty except for the Orderly Officer (Pilot Officer Neil Daunt, as he introduced himself) and the Duty Waiter, one Bilborough. He became a legendary figure, not only at Hawkinge, but throughout the RAF because of his speed and efficiency. I was expected and Bilborough showed me to the room which I had been allocated. Daunt I knew of from the sporting pages of the newspapers. He had played rugby for the RAF against the Army recently, and had also had an Irish Trial. He made me welcome and called for tea, brought promptly to the Ante Room by the ubiquitous Bilborough. Apparently most of the living-in officers were on weekend leave and it would be Monday morning before everyone returned.

Here I should say something about the Service of which I was now a member. Though the government of the day had accepted the recommendations of General Smuts in his report of August 1917, resulting in the formation of the Royal Air Force on 1 April 1918, it was not until 1923 that a committee, under the chairmanship of Lord Salisbury, recommended the creation of a Home Defence Force, which led in turn to a new Command. The Air Defence of Great Britain was to consist of 52 squadrons, 35 bomber and 17 fighter. Such however was the cry for economy in the twenties that when I arrived at Hawkinge in 1931 only 13 of the 17 fighter squadrons had been formed. Though I was unaware of it at the time, the government was still following a policy that there would be no war for ten years (a period that began anew each morning). The reasons for this policy were unknown to us but its effect on our life in the Squadron was very apparent. We thought little of war. After all, if there wasn't going to be one for at least ten years, there would be plenty of time to prepare for it nearer the time. All our powers of concentration went on the flying efficiency of the Squadron and on improving the standard of training of the Squadron's officers, NCOs and airmen.

Quite as much importance was attached to our training as officers as to our training as pilots. In particular, we were never allowed to forget our responsibilities to the airmen. This meant acquiring a wide knowledge of all aspects of RAF organisation: its law, administration, specialisations and trade structure. In case we felt inclined to be idle, there were promotion examinations which included, according to rank, questions on all these subjects. To fail these examinations, as everyone was carefully warned, meant one could not be promoted. Even so, most Pilot Officers, myself included, regarded such work as something of a bore. It was the flying and training as a pilot that we were interested in, so it was just as well that our elders 'encouraged' us with the examination system. They understood their young men very well.

Our Commanding Officer was Squadron Leader H M Probyn, known throughout the Service as 'Daddy'. In 1931, he was in his 39th year and had been an airman since the Great War. This remarkable man would celebrate his 90th birthday in December 1981 by piloting an aeroplane he himself had built from his house near Kilimanjaro to the Nairobi Flying Club. We Pilot Officers were in some awe of Daddy Probyn; he was a strict disciplinarian and stood no nonsense from anyone. He had come to 25 Squadron from 2 Army Co-operation Squadron stationed at Manston across Kent near Ramsgate. As fighter pilots, we considered Army Co-op work rather dull stuff, but nevertheless we also had a pretty shrewd suspicion that the nature of the work made the Army Co-op pilot a very competent operator, particularly when it came to writing reports—an important part of Service life. When it came to flying, then of course we believed that the fighter pilot reigned supreme. We were told by one of the old hands that Probyn had certainly braced up 25 Squadron since his arrival six months previously. His hobby was light civil aviation and he owned a Westland Widgeon two-seater aeroplane, in which he and his wife flew all over Europe. But that was not his only hobby: in winter, when bad weather made civil flying unpleasant, Probyn went fox hunting. He was a member of the East Kent Hunt and we would see his pink clad figure departing for the Meet once a week during the season.

The Squadron was organised in three flights, each with four Siskin aircraft, and commanded by Flight Lieutenants—Swan of A Flight, Victor Beamish of B Flight and 'Tiny' Evans-Evans of C Flight. Victor was the eldest of four famous brothers who served in the Royal Air Force. Two, George and Charles, represented Ireland at rugby many times and Cecil played golf for his country. Victor himself was no mean sportsman: he played rugger for the RAF, and was a reserve for Ireland on more than one occasion.

As sometimes happens in a squadron, there had recently been a large changeover in flying personnel, both officers and airmen. Consequently, most of us were new boys learning and progressing together, which made for keen interest and no little rivalry. The emphasis in our flying training was on mastery of the aeroplane. The Siskins we were flying were heavier than those at Grantham because two Vickers machine guns were fitted and also a bulky and heavy radio telephone set. Aerobatics played a large part in our training, and was for most of us the most enjoyable part, but formation flying, 'Battle' climbs to altitude, pilot navigation, mock attacks against another aeroplane using a camera gun, and night flying were all included. Battle climbs were standard war training and regular procedure. You were despatched from the airfield to 16,000 ft (standard B-climb height) where you patrolled for imaginary enemy aircraft. Then twenty minutes later you returned. With Furies the height became 20,000 ft. It was very chilly indeed in an open cockpit. The results of these practices were recorded and successful completion meant qualification as a fighter pilot. There was great keenness amongst us newcomers to complete this syllabus so as to have our names on the 'qualified' list, since this opened the way to participating in many squadron activities not open to the unqualified.

I remember that my whole programme looked like coming to nothing because for various reasons, including bad weather, I had not completed my five hours' night flying. I had three hours and five minutes in my log book when the last opportunity came up before the end of the 'individual training period'. Though I needed one hour and fifty-five minutes, I was authorised for only one hour. Having completed the practices detailed for that one hour, I decided to get 'lost' for the next fifty-five minutes. Throttling right back for maximum fuel economy, I toured the bright lights of some Kentish towns—Dover, Deal, Ramsgate, Margate, Canterbury and Ashford— finally landing back at Hawkinge dead on one hour fifty-five minutes. I got a big ticking off from my Flight Commander, but it was well worth it for the magic word "qualified".

At the end of May 1931, the Squadron was due to go to Sutton Bridge, a training camp on the Wash, for three weeks air-to-ground and air-to-air gunnery practice. Daddy Probyn was extremely keen that the Squadron should show up well in competition with the other squadrons in Fighting Area. All aerobatics were therefore stopped; camera-gun exercises were stepped up and each pilot fired his guns repeatedly on the ground-firing butts. Any stoppages were imme- diately examined by the armourers with the pilot in close attendance on Daddy's instructions. We certainly learned about our guns in the weeks before Sutton Bridge. This three weeks' attachment of the Squadron away from its home airfield was something of an adventure for us newcomers. We flew up in squadron formation with Probyn in the lead, but landed by flights of three because the airfield was very small.

Sutton Bridge was truly a 'camp'. It had few permanent buildings, the hangars were of the Bessoneau type, canvas over a wooden frame as used in France by the RFC during the Great War. The domestic accommodation consisted of wooden huts. It was all pretty primitive, particularly the ablutions and sanitary arrangements, but we loved it. At Hawkinge, the married officers went home when work was over; here we were all together and revelled in it. We were to share the airfield with 23 Squadron from Kenley and during the afternoon they began to arrive piecemeal. Their aeroplanes were the new Bristol Bulldog, though they still had a few Gamecocks. The impression made on me by their ragged arrival was of a squadron that was neither well led nor fully together and that impression was fully confirmed in the weeks to follow. We started our firing programme on the second day after our arrival.

Targets ten foot square were set up on the edge of the Wash about ten minutes' flying time from the airfield. We were told to dive onto the target from about 1,000 feet, fire a short burst, pull out not lower than 200 feet, and repeat until the 200 rounds of ammunition carried in the Siskin were exhausted. It was plainly best to fire at the last possible moment, thus minimising the distance from the target. However, too low an approach would lead to a report from the Range Officer for dangerous flying and a deduction from one's score. I was a bit apprehensive at first—particularly in judging when to pull out of the dive—and found myself gasping for air several times after going in too low and pulling out just in time. Whether I hit the target or not I had no idea: there was a lot of mud splashing about, but that was all I could see. It was therefore gratifying (as well as surprising) to learn on return to base that I had scored 115 hits with my 200 rounds. There were only two higher scores in the Squadron, both by Flight Commanders. Some of the new boys were in the twenties and one failed to score at all. I knew that there were many better pilots than I in the Squadron and that my lead was unlikely to last long, but it was fun as a new boy to be up at the top of the list.

We continued on the ground targets for a while and were then given a new task: firing at a drogue towed behind a Fairey 111F biplane on a very long wire. With all the limitations dictated by safety regulations, this was the nearest we could get to serious practice for our main role, shooting at enemy aircraft. Hitting the drogue was more difficult than hitting the ground target. Our ring-and-bead sights were exactly the same as those fitted to fighters at the end of the Great War and judging the deflection necessary to allow for the target's speed was not easy. Some learned more quickly than others and one newcomer who joined the Squadron at Sutton Bridge, Flight Lieutenant Charles R Hancock, showed a remarkable aptitude. His first score was nil, but each subsequent shoot showed an improvement until towards the end of our stay he was by far the best air-to-air shot in the Squadron. Unusually, he came to us from a squadron in India and had won a DFC in operations on the North-West Frontier. He had no experience of fighter work, his previous squadron being Army Co-op, but he had a lot of flying experience (which, incidentally had initially made him slightly contemptuous of our work) and, on taking over C Flight from Evans-Evans, became a first-class leader in the air.

It was at this time, May 1931 at Sutton Bridge, that I first met Douglas Bader. He had joined 23 Squadron from Cranwell some eight months before. We met outside the Officers' Mess where we were both waiting for someone. He was indeed a most exceptional character and meeting him made such an impression on me that today, more than 60 years later, I remember the occasion as clearly as if it were yesterday. We introduced ourselves and, chatting about this and that, quickly found that our interests were very much the same, flying and games, most especially rugby. As he was already playing for the Harlequins at this time I remember much of our conversation centred round the 'great game'. My first impression was of a young man with complete confidence in himself and with absolutely no doubt that all his beliefs and opinions were correct. We started a friendship then which was to last until his death in 1982, although I didn't see a great deal of him until the war started.

At that time, as I have observed, 23 Squadron was a very poorly disciplined outfit being full of cliques and factions, which were encouraged by the CO, Henry Woollett, who had been something of an ace in the Great War and believed in the power of the individual. By 1931 his standard of shooting was distinctly average, and what is worse, he plainly regarded the detachment to Sutton Bridge as a routine move and had done nothing to prepare either his pilots or ground crews for it. This was disastrous because, being new in the Squadron, the ground crews were unfamiliar with the Bulldog's gun fittings, ammunition chutes and sight mountings. Consequently gun stoppages were endless during the early days of the detachment and even good shots were unable to score.

We in 25 Squadron pulled the legs of our opposite numbers unmercifully about their poor scores and Bader, in particular, was absolutely infuriated. Indeed we learned that three Gamecocks had been retained in 23 Squadron for one of the supporting items at the Hendon Air Display later that summer. This was the synchronised aerobatics by a pair of aeroplanes. Douglas was No 2 to his Flight Commander, 'Pricky' Day, a much older man and Geoffrey Stephenson, a friend of Douglas's from Cranwell days, was their reserve. They used to practice their programme between whiles at Sutton Bridge in front of a critical audience of 25 Squadron pilots. Although we secretly admired the aerobatic skill of Day and Douglas, we never admitted it when Douglas was around. In fact whenever he was in earshot there would be loud conversation about the irrelevance of aerobatics as compared with air gunnery. This made Douglas even more angry and one of his ways of expressing annoyance was to dive on the airfield in his Bulldog on return from the ranges and do a vigorous upwards roll starting at ground level. This was a continuing cause of amusement to us, but such manoeuvres were absolutely forbidden by regulations.

At about this time the Air Council, the highest authority in the Service, having become alarmed by the number of flying accidents resulting from low aerobatics, had issued an instruction that no aerobatics were to take place below 2,000 feet, except with the written permission of the Air Officer Commanding. This was a very big step since it removed authority from all lower commanders and indicated the Air Council's determination to put an end to what indeed could be very dangerous flying. For the sake of the Hendon Display, Day, Bader and Stephenson would of course have been given the AOC's dispensation, their aerobatics being performed mainly at 1,000 feet. But this dispensation related specifically to the Hendon programme, performed in Gamecocks, and in no way extended to normal flying in Bulldogs, a much heavier and less manoeuvrable aeroplane. Such niceties of definition were ignored by Douglas, who always interpreted regulations to suit his own convenience!

On one occasion, when pilots of both squadrons were gathered round the scoreboard watching the scores go up as they were telephoned in from the ranges, another indifferent performance by Douglas was posted. There were ironic remarks all round, not the least from some of his own Squadron. Just then, Douglas arrived overhead and guessing, I think, that he had not done very well, demonstrated his assumed indifference by a particularly spectacular upward roll. Daddy Probyn was watching with us and said quietly, "If that young man was in this Squadron I would put him under arrest and court martial him". We all looked at him, many of us in a disbelieving way because we all thought that Douglas knew what he was doing. Sensing our doubt, Daddy went on equally quietly: "I would probably be saving his life if I did". How wise a man he was. Only seven months later, on 14 December 1931, Douglas suffered terrible injuries in a crash after yet again disobeying the 2,000 feet rule and making a mess of a slow roll at ground level. He did not die, as many near him thought he would, and as maybe a lesser man would have done; he survived because of his unshakeable determination to live and his exceptional physical fitness.

What a pity that Douglas's own CO had not also foreseen the danger. Not only did Woollett fail to see it, but his methods of commanding the Squadron weakened the authority of Bader's immediate superior, Day, who did. When off duty at Sutton Bridge, we in 25 Squadron did almost everything together, but we noticed that Wollett took only Bader and Stephenson with him when he went out in the evening. It did nothing for the morale of the Squadron as a whole to see two Pilot Officers singled out in this way. Moreover, it undermined Day's authority in attempting to deal with an exceptionally strong-willed young man. From even our short acquaintance with Douglas Bader, we realised that he always knew best—in his own opinion. Having completed our air gunnery programme at Sutton Bridge we left for Hawkinge in squadron formation. True to form, 23 Squadron straggled away in ones and twos leaving behind several unserviceable Bulldogs. Thanks to the careful preparation insisted on by our excellent CO, we had performed as well as we could and later had the satisfaction of learning that only one squadron out of thirteen in the whole of Fighting Area bettered our record in 1931. 23 Squadron finished right down the list.

We arrived back at Hawkinge in good time to prepare for the annual Air Exercises. but before going on to describe these I should perhaps introduce the pilots who then manned our Squadron. 'Daddy' Probyn and Flight Lieutenant Swan had both joined the RFC and been granted permanent commissions in the RAF on its formation in 1918. Flight Lieutenant Hancock was a university entry from Cambridge. After Flying Training School he went straight to India, spent five years there and then joined 25 Squadron. Flying Officer H St G Burke was another Cambridge entrant but, unlike Hancock, had been a member of the University Air Squadron before going to Sealand for his service flying training. Because he had an engineering degree and more flying hours than the rest of us new boys, we could not match Burke either on the ground or in the air. Flight Lieutenant A C ('Tiny') Evans-Evans had been granted a permanent commission for passing a signals specialist examination. He was Squadron Signals Officer and commanded C Flight before Hancock's arrival. B Flight Commander (Flight Lieutenant F V Beamish) was a Cranwell graduate, had already served in a squadron, qualified as a flying instructor and then enjoyed an exchange posting with the Royal Canadian Air Force, before joining 25 Squadron. Flying Officer Brian W Knox was also ex-Cranwell and must at this time have been one of the most senior Flying Officers in the Service. Like Beamish, he was Irish—but they had little else in common. Although Knox had a reputation as an all-round athlete at Cranwell in the early twenties, he had done little other than represent the RAF against the Army and Navy in the shot putt since then. We never learned why he had been passed over for the relatively routine promotion to Flight Lieutenant. Whatever the reason, it had nothing to do with airmanship, for Knox could certainly handle an aeroplane. He lived with his wife in Folkestone and consequently we younger, single men scarcely knew him. On reflection, this was perhaps just as well because sooner or later one of us might have been tactless enough to ask embarrassing questions.

When I arrived at Hawkinge, Flying Officer Peter Heath (also ex-Cranwell) and Flying Officer Peter May (a Short Service entrant) were both in open arrest facing charges of unauthorised low flying. Apparently they had 'beaten up' a nearby girls' school and someone had noted the numbers of their Siskins, reporting them to Air Ministry. Because open arrest meant that both officers were confined to their rooms we saw little of them. I believe the charges were later dropped, but both men were nevertheless posted out of the Squadron and the rest of us tried to learn from their awful fate. The remaining officers all held Short Service Commissions: Garnons-Williams, Clouston, Douglas-Jones, Milsom, Daunt, Dunworth and myself. We therefore had pilots of varied origins: RFC, Cambridge University, Cranwell and Short Service Commissions. This diversity reflected Trenchard's determination to cast his net much more widely than did either the Army or the Navy in order to attract keen men from every level of society. He wanted men who were enthused by the new science of aviation, both for current service and future service should war come again. When war did return in 1939, many of those who had left the RAF on completion of their engagements were able to come back and pick up the threads quickly. Their success proved how imaginative and wise Trenchard's plans had been and, as he later remarked to me, gave him a sense of satisfaction.

Meanwhile, however, the Air Exercises of 1931 proved singularly unsuccessful from our point of view. We set up a Sector Operations Room on the edge of our airfield and received plots of 'enemy' raids from the local Observer Corps Centres, but owing to our location near the coast, we got insufficient warning from observers looking out to sea to get airborne and intercept before the 'enemy' was well on his way inland. The 'enemy' force consisted mainly of Fairey 111F and Hawker Horsley biplanes serving with squadrons in the Wessex bombing area. By the next year, a number of acoustical mirrors had been installed round our part of the coast facing out to sea. They were intended to pick up the sound of the approaching enemy aircraft before they could be seen, and so give us a better chance of getting airborne early enough to do something about them. These "mirrors" were actually huge concrete spheres. Their operators sat in huts alongside them and when sounds of approaching aircraft were detected, the bearing and estimated range were passed to the Sector Operations Room.

Even given the relatively slow speed of contemporary aeroplanes, these acoustical mirrors were unsuccessful in increasing our warning time. It was thought that perhaps the civilian scientists in charge of the mirrors might not appreciate the need for speed in passing information, so two well-qualified pilots were sent down to the site to see if they could improve things. Burke (the degree man) went from our Squadron, and Flying Officer Smythe (a New Zealander with a scientific background) went from one of the bomber squadrons. Although their work was supposed to be secret, we discussed the mirrors with them and it soon became plain that neither Burke nor Smythe believed the system had any value, actual or potential. Its range was simply too short to provide defending fighters with adequate warning of the approach of even the slow-moving bombers of the early thirties. On the other hand, its range was more than sufficient to pick up whispered conversations on the beach several miles away, particularly in the summer evenings when the beach and sand dunes were a favourite venue for courting couples. While extremely interesting, this facility was deemed of little military value.

In 1932 the Squadron, re-equipped with the Hawker Fury, was moved for a couple of weeks of exercises to Kenley a few miles south of London, which gave some fifty miles of Observer Corps warning of the approach of 'enemy bombers' to the airfield. The Fury was a welcome change to the Siskin, with its sharp-nose, modern sleek lines and state of the art Rolls-Royce water-cooled engine. It made the latter seem somewhat of a 'donkey'. Helped by the Sector Operations Room staff at Kenley, we enjoyed considerable success in intercepting 'enemy' raids on London by squadrons of Fairey 111Fs, Westland Wapitis and the new Hawker Hart day bombers. Years later in the 1950s when the part that radar played in winning the Battle of Britain was being exaggerated, I remembered this move back from the coast. In retrospect, this is an interesting indicator of the thinking of the "Powers That Be' then; namely that an area so many miles up from the coast would be 'abandoned' to enemy bombers while we had the chance to intercept them. I wondered then (as I do now) if we had had no radar in 1940, whether we could have fought the battle successfully by moving the fighters back even further, leaving Tangmere, Biggin Hill, Manston, West Malling, Detling and Hawkinge empty. We could have fought the battle from a ring of airfields such as North Weald, Hornchurch, Northolt, Halton, Heston and others about the same distance from the coast. This would certainly have faced the Germans with a considerable problem when attacking fighter airfields with escorted bombers (an essential part of their plan to eliminate Fighter Command) because the German fighters would have been at extreme range. The question can never be answered satisfactorily and would surely have been politically impossible, exposing as it would, the entire south-east to German bombers.

In 1931 with no war (if ever) anticipated for ten years the Annual Air Exercises were somewhat mundane, a tryout of existing techniques of air defence, rather than a test of the country's defences. The Air Defence of Great Britain (ADGB as it was known) consisted of bomber as well as fighter squadrons, it being a firm tenet of all 'air' thinking that in the air anyway it was doubly true that attack was the best means of defence. The thirteen fighter squadrons of Fighting Area, the defensive part of ADGB, were located on aerodromes in a curve round London starting at Duxford near Cambridge and continuing south and west to Upavon near Devizes in Wiltshire. Our thirteen squadrons were enough to try out, keep alive and practice the techniques of fighter interception which were to prove vital once the Luftwaffe appeared to threaten our defences. The semi-circle of aerodromes round London indicated to us that London was a priority target as it had been during the Great War, when German attacks in darkness and daylight inspired the creation of an air defence system that served as a model to meet the far greater challenge of 1940.

Kenley, Hawkinge, and Tangmere (near Chichester) were all located forward of the curve of the other fighter aerodromes and were near the coast, the idea being that the three squadrons located at these aerodromes would intercept the enemy before the main fighter force engaged further back. For this reason these squadrons at Hawkinge and Tangmere—25, 1 and 43—were known as 'Interceptor' Squadrons, which did not mean much when we were armed with Siskins but in 1932, when all three squadrons were re-equipped with the Hawker Fury powered by the new Rolls-Royce Kestrel engine, the term Interceptor really started to mean something.

Re-equipment began in February 1932, the first few aircraft being ferried from Hawker's aerodrome at Brooklands by our flight commanders because they were all very experienced pilots. On arrival at Hawkinge, they were thoroughly checked by the ground crews before the rest of us pilots were initiated into the new aeroplane's mysteries. At about this time, Victor Beamish was posted and replaced by Flight Lieutenant H I Cozens recently returned from Greenland where he had been attached to the Gino Watkins Arctic Expedition. Cozens was a rarity in the Service at that time: an 'E' Star grade engineer, the highest grade possible. A Short Service Officer, he had won a place on the Long Engineering Course at Hendon, finished top and thus qualified for a degree course at Cambridge. His arrival in the Squadron at this time was fortunate because the Kestrel engine had a higher degree of super charging than anything anyone had flown before and required careful handling; and his lectures on super charging were models of clarity.

We had no two-seater Fury equipped for dual instruction so that our ground initiation was all we had before being sent off solo. I flew this beautiful aeroplane for the first time on 1 March 1932, and my weekly letter to my mother started in capitals "I've flown a Fury". After a few more familiarisation flights I went to Brooklands to collect the Fury allotted to me. Here I met for the first time the renowned chief test pilot P W S Bulman, and his assistants Jerry Sayer and Philip Lucas. It was a proud moment when I opened the throttle for take-off and headed for Hawkinge. I was to fly this aeroplane for the next two and a half years and never ceased to enjoy it.

At the end of 1932, Daddy Probyn was promoted to Wing Commander and posted to Fighting Area Headquarters. His successor was Squadron Leader W E G Bryant, another World War 1 pilot who came to us straight from the Armament Specialisation Course. In those days, flying refresher courses were unknown: once a man was qualified as a pilot, the official view was that he could fly all aeroplanes, even after such a long lay-off from flying as Bryant had just experienced on the Armaments Course. Any rustiness, it was believed, could be polished away by a few days' practice. Bryant was certainly rusty but even making allowances for this, it was plain to all of us who flew behind him that he had serious limitations as a modern fighter pilot. However, in other respects Bryant was a good and conscientious Squadron Commander, concerned with all the Squadron's activities. Of these, organised games were a considerable feature.

Though the total of all ranks was only about 150, we produced teams that held their own with the best of the local civilians and with the Army units comprising the Shorncliff Garrison. In summer cricket, tennis and athletics were the most popular games and in winter soccer, rugby, squash rackets and boxing. It was taken for granted that all able-bodied officers would participate in and help organise as many games as they were qualified to do. The majority of the younger airmen also played one or more games. There was no compulsion, but the economics of the period meant that many of the airmen, though reasonably well paid by the standards of the day, could not afford to go away from the Station very frequently—nor were they encouraged to go away. There were also many economies imposed on us at Hawkinge—for example, no one could ring out on a Service call except the CO or Adj.

Service in the RAF was not regarded as a mere job with defined working hours, but as a way of life and therefore every station, at home and abroad, organised many activities outside flying and servicing the aeroplanes and equipment. As well as parades and church services, games played a very important part in everyone's life and officers were expected to set an example by organising and participating in them. Wednesday afternoons and Saturdays were routinely set aside for sport. I played most games but it was rugby in winter and athletics in summer that involved me most keenly.

We had great competition from soldiers in the Shorncliff Garrison, particularly those in young officers' courses at the Small Arms School at Hythe and the 3rd Battalion of the Royal Tank Corps at Lydd. I made friends in the Army at this time, some of whom I was not to see again until we met in the dusty wastes of the Western Desert during World War Two. Amongst our Saturday opponents were priests studying at St Augustine's, Canterbury, and miners (many of them Welsh) working at the two Kent collieries, Snowdon and Betteshangar. We often asked ourselves which were the toughest opponents, priests or miners, and agreed that the men of God had it by a short head.

The town of Folkestone, only two miles from Hawkinge, was a very pleasant place in the thirties. As well as a cross-Channel port, it was a holiday resort catering for the better-off sections of the populace. Its hotels and restaurants were excellent. When we were flush at the beginning of the month, we took our girlfriends to dine and dance at the Grand or Metropole, both very much four-star hotels. When it got towards the end of the month and pay was running out, then the Leas Cliff Hall, a dance place on the cliffs, would receive our patronage, particularly on 'Popular Nights'. All these places had good dance bands and to be able to dance a bit was reckoned essential if we were to retain the company of the best young ladies of Folkestone. In those days girls were companions, not serious involvements because for most people in the Service, marriage was not encountered until the age of 30 when you became eligible for married allowance.

Now that we had Furies, the RAF's most modern fighters, it was certain that we would be invited to appear at the Hendon Display of 1932. C Flight—of which I was a member—was detailed to carry out a demonstration attack on a Hawker Hart, the latest day bomber in service. It was an interesting experience performing before 150,000 people. The bomber 'shot down' one of our three Furies before being dispatched itself, streaming smoke from specially-installed canisters. In 1930, 43 Squadron had astonished everyone at Hendon by not only performing their aerobatics in squadron formation, but even more so by linking all their aeroplanes together with bunting and carrying out an elaborate programme without breaking a single connection. Rumour had it that a Fury squadron would be selected for this event, so it was with intense interest that we waited for the Fighting Area Headquarters decision to be given in January 1933; and it was with undisguised delight that we learned towards the end of the month that our 25 Squadron had been selected. Hendon represented the culmination of a year's training and it was a great honour to be selected.

1 Squadron at Tangmere was to provide the flight formation aerobatics with three aircraft. 43 Squadron, the third Fury squadron, was not included. There was speculation amongst us junior pilots as to who would lead the Squadron at Hendon. Though we did not say so out loud, we did not believe that Bryant was up to it. Of our Flight Commanders, we thought Hancock (as the most senior) was the man for the job, but of course what we thought didn't matter: no-one asked for our opinion.

The Hendon Display was scheduled for 24 June 1933 and during the early part of that year all three flights practised formation aerobatics assiduously, each with three aeroplanes. At the same time, we were expected to complete the various parts of the operational training programme laid down by Fighting Area for individual, flight and squadron efficiency. It is interesting to compare the policy of the thirties with that of today. Then it was maintained that formation aerobatics were within the competence of any suitably-equipped squadron, indicating what could be achieved in the normal course of Royal Air Force training. But in the 1990s, the need for operational war readiness precludes any such policy and so the Red Arrows represent the Royal Air Force and the country at air displays at home and overseas.

The question of the Squadron's leadership kept cropping up in conversation amongst us pilots. We agreed privately that either Hancock or Edwards could do it. Flight Lieutenant E C T Edwards was a university entrant from Oxford, where he had been a member of the Boat Race crew. A very good pilot, he came second one year in the King's Cup Air Race. Everything he did, he did well and we were astonished to see the accuracy of his shooting with the Colt automatic during our annual pistol shooting course. He several times put two rounds through the same hole on the target at twenty paces. Only our astute armament sergeant could detect such accuracy.

Then in March 1933 Bryant was posted after just a year in the Squadron. Apparently he had qualified as a Japanese interpreter some years before and was now required for the Air Attaché post in Tokyo. His replacement, who arrived the same month, was Squadron Leader A L (Tony) Paxton, also a First War pilot. Paxton was a quiet, gentle man with a bald head, whom we all liked instantly. However, the opinion of us flying officers was that he couldn't possibly learn about the new aeroplane and familiarise himself with formation aerobatics in time to lead the Squadron at Hendon in June. That bald head too! No: for our money Hancock was the man and the change of Squadron Commander reinforced our belief.

At the beginning of April, it was necessary to move on from independent practice by the three flights and join up into a squadron of nine aircraft. The day came for the first practice and we gathered in the Pilots' Room for the briefing. To our surprise, this was conducted entirely by the new CO and we were told quietly and precisely what the practice would consist of: no aerobatics for this first time; turns of varying steepness; changes in formation and positioning of the Squadron in relation to the airfield. We thought all this a bit elementary, but at least the old man seemed to know what he wanted and that was encouraging. Everything went very well in this first practice, as it did on succeeding days. Then came the first aerobatic venture: a squadron loop in flights of three, probably the simplest manoeuvre in the programme. I was in the right-hand Flight on the left of my leader looking outwards so I couldn't see what was going on in the rest of the Squadron, but Hancock was 'pumping' the throttle vigorously which was quite unlike him and I was having to work hard to keep any sort of station on him. As we came out of the loop, I was amazed to see a Fury way ahead of the formation. Afterwards I learned that this was not the only one to break formation. It was a shambles—as were subsequent attempts the same day. Not much was said at the post mortems we had after each practice, but us followers believed that our new leader wasn't up to it and that that was the main cause of the trouble.

Later, we realised that it was our own inexperience of formation aerobatics with nine aircraft that had been the main cause of our troubles and Paxton's leading was in fact excellent. In addition to being a very experienced pilot, he was a qualified Flying Instructor whose skills had been honed at the Central Flying School, the recognised authority on pure flying in the Service. Nevertheless, we pilots blamed what we believed was poor leading for our own failures until one day when the CO was absent. He had to attend a conference at Headquarters and the two practices scheduled for that day were due to be led by Hancock. Now we thought we'd see how the Squadron should be led! Alas, by the end of the day and two most unsatisfactory practices, we realised the truth. Paxton was a far more accurate leader; and it was he who decided that we would follow fashion and tie our aeroplanes together with light cords. These cords, if we could keep them unbroken, would show watchers on the ground how well we maintained formation in the air while performing the most complicated aerobatics.

Before the start of squadron practice, we in C Flight (Hancock, Burke and me) had debated the possibility of 'barrel' rolling three aircraft in formation. It had to be a barrel roll to maintain positive gravity throughout the manoeuvre because our carburettors only functioned under positive 'g' and to keep position on the Flight leader, continuous engine power was essential. We decided to try it because we felt that some variety from looping was required for the event at Hendon.

The first time we tried it, Hancock forgot for a moment about the positive 'g' and, as we reached the inverted position, pushed his joy stick forward to keep the nose above the horizon as for a normal slow roll. His engine cut out, as did ours, and the formation disintegrated. We reformed using sign language (the Fury had no radio at this time) and agreed on the mistake. Next time Hancock went into the roll with his aircraft nose high above the horizon and then, by gentle backward pressure on the stick all the way through the roll, kept his engine—and ours—running throughout. He finished with his nose well below the horizon, but we had at least maintained our starting formation—more or less. Even though this first attempt was so ragged, we were convinced that a formation barrel roll was possible. Eventually, after plenty of practice, we performed it. C Flight became the first unit in the RAF to roll three aircraft in formation. Our other flights, benefiting from our experience, also mastered the manoeuvre and thereafter it became commonplace.

During the working-up period we were visited by the Under Secretary of State for Air, Sir Philip Sassoon, Member of Parliament for the nearby constituency of Hythe. A most remarkable man, he was always stylishly if somewhat oddly dressed. On this visit, he wore a pink shirt, a superbly cut blazer, pale cream trousers and suede shoes. Sassoon had a most exceptional memory. Once introduced to him neither the person nor the name was ever forgotten. So phenomenal was his memory that he introduced the annual Air Estimates in the House of Commons without notes. I was told that the Opposition, scarcely believing such a feat possible, would deliberately interrupt him with questions. Sassoon always answered these courteously in detail and then proceeded without hestitation from the point of interruption in his speech. He was an immensely rich man. His home at 45 Park Lane and his lovely houses at Port Lympne near Hythe and at Trent Park in Hertfordshire were full of exquisite furniture and works of art.

He had a passion for golf and I was fortunate on his first visit to the Squadron to be asked to play with him at Hythe, which was the first of many such invitations. We played at Hythe or Folkestone when he was in residence at Lympne, or Trent Park where he had his own private course, when visiting him in London. Staying at Lympne or in Park Lane was an experience in itself. Philip was unmarried and his hostess was a cousin, Mrs Gubbay. The attention of the servants, the perfection of the food and all the arrangements for one's comfort were something I had never experienced before. The invitation to stay would come in Philip's own handwriting. Having arrived at Park Lane early in the evening, one would be faced with a great many questions over drinks about the Squadron and its flying. Sassoon would be assiduous in keeping in touch with events as seen through the eyes of a junior officer. He would then name the other dinner guests. I recall meeting such eminent persons as the Duke and Duchess of Kent, Anthony and Beatrice Eden, Lord and Lady Cholmondley, Lady Juliet Duff and a couple of auxiliary officers from 601 Squadron of which Philip was honorary Air Commodore. Dinner was always superb and the whole thing for me another world. Next morning, bright and early, we were off to Trent for golf—morning and afternoon. What a delight this all was!

Meanwhile at Hawkinge, the great day of 24 June was approaching, but first we were to unveil our act on the 16th at the annual Staff College Garden Party at Andover. We flew up that morning: a lovely one it was too with clear skies and a gentle breeze. Although our show went well, we were surprised at the sensation it caused amongst the spectators. In particular, the roll of three flights in line abreast startled even the experienced directing staff as well as the students. When we landed, one of the first to congratulate the CO was a breathless Under Secretary of State, Philip Sassoon, who left the VIP enclosure and rushed down to the aircraft parking area, such was his enthusiasm.

The Hendon Display itself was something of an anti-climax. The rehearsal the day before went well, but on the Saturday when 140,000 spectators were present the weather was very bad with low cloud and rain. The front that carried most of the weather was due to go through at about 3 pm, an hour before our event, but it was late. Before we took off at 4 pm, the CO said we would do the bad weather programme (straight and level formation and changes) but if the cloud base lifted, we would go into the full aerobatic routine. The cloud base did go up a bit and we managed a loop or two and the roll, but it was a most disappointing end to a day we'd been looking forward to (and sweating over) for months.

The next year, 1934, 25 Squadron was again selected to do the squadron formation aerobatics at Hendon. By then, some old hands had left the Squadron. We had lost Burke from C Flight but had a good replacement in Sergeant Pearson. Although B Flight were all right with Edwards, Clouston and Sergeant Upton, A Flight were weak and Garnons-Williams was moved from B Flight to make up the three with Paxton and Daunt. To our joy and relief, the great day this year was a beauty and everything went well except for the loop of nine aircraft in vee formation. In that, Daunt lost formation and broke his cord. Most of the Squadron went to London that night for a celebration party, but I felt slightly dispirited at this let down and joined one or two others who didn't feel the show deserved celebrating and returned to Hawkinge. I was fortunate in having a particularly nice girlfriend, named Pam, at that time to comfort me and so she and I celebrated quietly with dinner at the Esplanade Hotel, one of our favourite venues.

I was now in the fourth year of my five year Short Service Commission and the prospect of leaving was devastating. My only hope of a permanent commission was to take a specialisation examination and finish in the top 25 of about 120 candidates. I did my best, but it wasn't good enough: in those days, so it seemed, I could more than hold my own on sports fields, rugby grounds and in the cockpit—but not in the classroom. However, in 1934 the faintest war cloud, "scarcely bigger than a man's hand" was appearing over Germany and it was decided to retain some Short Service Officers on what was termed 'Medium Service', a second term of five years making ten in all.

I was advised by everyone from the CO downwards not to touch this offer—"Go out and start another career" was the gist—but I ignored them all. I loved the Service and if I could stay in it for another five years I'd gladly let the future look after itself. I applied for and was granted a Medium Service Commission. The purpose in retaining experienced pilots was to expand the RAF's capacity to train an increased entry of pilots and, in December 1934, I was therefore sent to the Central Flying School at Wittering near Stamford in Lincolnshire, for training as an instructor. I had been at Hawkinge since April 1931, three and a half happy years, and it was a wrench to leave. However, it had to be done, so I said goodbye to the girls in Folkestone, enjoyed my first Guest Night as a guest (rather than a host) and went off to Wittering in my latest car, a blue two-seater Morris Cowley. At first I missed Pam very much and for some time we wrote regularly to each other. But 'out of sight' eventually became 'out of mind' for both of us and our great romance died a natural death.

As I drove to London and then up the Great North Road to Wittering, I took stock of where I had got to. I was now an experienced pilot with more than 800 hours in my Flying Logbook. At 23, I already had nearly five years' service to my credit and had enjoyed the thrill of my first promotion (to Flying Officer, proudly wearing a slightly broader cuff-ring than a mere Pilot Officer). It was apparent to me as I drove along that I had learned a fair bit about life in general, and Service life in particular, during the years spent at Hawkinge. I had learned something from all three COs I had served under. From Probyn it had been discipline; from Bryant, the need to encourage the young, both officers and airmen (many of whom were away from home for the first time in their lives) and, from Paxton, I began to grasp the art of leadership: to give confidence to those led that they would never be asked to attempt anything I wouldn't attempt myself. Paxton not only led by example, he treated everyone of the 140 men serving under him as an individual. Even then, young as I was, I realised how fortunate I had been to serve under such men. I also learned a lot from those with whom I served in the Squadron. In any team—and a squadron is a team—the desire of each individual to be respected by his fellows is strong. I was pretty brash when I joined the Squadron in May 1931. Still only 19, I thought I knew everything, and was quite prepared to offer an opinion on any subject. The Flight Lieutenants and senior Flying Officers, having seen it all before, very quickly put me in my place. It would be better, said one "if you kept quiet and listened a bit more!"

At nineteen I knew little about the delights of alcohol, but dining in Mess four nights a week in full Mess kit meant that inevitably I was introduced to the merits of a well-stocked cellar. As an athlete I had often been warned of the dangers of alcohol, but as I learned from the others a glass of sherry before dinner, a little wine with dinner and a port to drink the King's health afterwards were not at all harmful. Spirits were not for us—they were for our elders—but we drank a lot of beer and this, too, did us no harm, for we also enjoyed plenty of vigorous exercise. However, one thing was very soon made apparent to us: that it was disgraceful to get drunk. Any officer who did so in the Mess was quickly led away to his room, to be faced in the morning by the President of the Mess Committee, his Flight Commander or both. When we went to a party, the weaker brethren (well known to us) were carefully watched and anyone who began to lose control was quietly warned. If he failed to heed a friendly word, he was taken home. I believe that the prospect of losing the respect of one's companions was the biggest deterrent to over-indulgence. If you couldn't drink and behave yourself at the same time, there was only one thing to do: stop drinking. I quickly learned my own capacity (as most of us did) and was careful not to exceed it.

These were some of the reflections that filled my mind as I sped up the Great North Road, leaving Hawkinge behind me for ever. Ah well, I was now for a new flying life. What would it be like to be an Instructor? I wouldn't know the answer to that question unless I passed the three months' course that I was about to begin. At long last—cold, tired and hungry—I turned my beloved Morris into the entrance of RAF Wittering, the home of the Central Flying School. It was 1 December 1934.

CHAPTER IV

FLYING INSTRUCTOR

IN 1934 it was quite a distinction to be selected for a flying instructors' course at CFS and there were a number of reasons for this. Most important was the prospect of possessing a category at the end of the course. In those days, it was the only pilot grading current throughout the Service. The annual assessment made by the squadron commander of 'Exceptional', 'Above Average', 'Average' or 'Below Average' appeared only in the pilot's own logbook, whereas the category awarded at the end of a successful instructors' course,—A1, A2, B, C—was held to apply throughout the RAF: it meant far more, good or bad, than the opinion of a single squadron commander. Most pupils were awarded Category B at the end of the course. However re-categorisation (up or down) was possible once one had had some actual experience of teaching. This would follow a test conducted by the CFS examining team during its annual visit to check the quality of instruction of flying training schools, the cadet college at Cranwell and the university air squadrons. There can be little doubt that Royal Air Force flying training at this time was the most thorough in the world and was probably the reason why its system was so widely adopted overseas.

I had been an 'Average' pilot on graduation from No 3 FTS at Grantham in 1931 and had improved this to 'Above Average' in 25 Squadron by May 1933, finishing up when I left the Squadron in November 1934, with the one and only 'Exceptional' I was to get in my whole service. I always believed that this was a present from Paxton (our bald squadron commander) in recognition of my efforts to justify 25 Squadron's selection to perform at two Hendon Displays, for I had no illusions about my flying. If I was above average in that Squadron, it was because I had more experience than most of my companions but my flying bore no comparison with some of the

'naturals' in the Squadron and some whom I met elsewhere in the
Service. The best 'natural' pilot in 25 Squadron whilst I was in it was
Flying Officer A E Clouston, the New Zealander with whom I had
trained at Grantham. There wasn't much that he couldn't do with an
aeroplane once he had familiarised himself with it. He was to demonstrate his exceptional flying ability after he left the Service in 1935, as
a civilian test pilot at Farnborough, and in record-breaking flights to
South Africa and to New Zealand and back. He became a very good
friend of mine then and we stayed in contact until he died.

Our course at CFS was 27 strong: 20 officers and 7 sergeants. They
were a congenial crowd full of an unobtrusive assurance that came
from some five or six years' experience in the Service. By the way they
tackled the course it was plain that they were keen to do well, though
none thought it necessary to say so. It was a relief in a way to be a
pupil again, and to shed the minor responsibilities of a junior officer:
Mess Secretary, Officer i/c Transport, Airmen's Messing Officer and
Squadron Adjutant, all of which I bore manfully at Hawkinge. But
here at Wittering I was a mere pupil again, in charge only of myself—
a relief for which I was most thankful.

Once again, the difference between the instructors and instructed
was indicated by them occupying one end of the Ante Room and we
the other. These CFS instructors, selected from all the flying training
units, were the best in the Service, but some stood out even in this
collection of high ability officers. My Flight Commander was Flight
Lieutenant Dicky Barwell, whom I later succeeded as commander of
46 Squadron. He was a splendid commander—firm, thorough and
conscientious and when I took over from him, I was not at all surprised
to find that Squadron so clearly stamped with his own mark. Among
the others, G R A Elsmie, G D Harvey and Waghorn, brother of the
Schneider Cup pilot, were outstanding. Not only were they experts in
the flying business and its academic side, they also excelled at games.
Elsmie was the squash racquets champion of the Service and both he
and Harvey played rugby football for the RAF. Sadly, but inevitably,
the outstanding quality of these officers meant that they were
committed to action against the odds in the first year of the war and
many lost their lives.

The Commandant of the school was Group Captain P C Maltby who
reminded me of my Headmaster at Kingswood, except that he was a
bit more approachable. We respected him from the beginning when
he addressed us on the first morning of the course. He particularly
stressed the responsibility we had for other pupils and not just for
ourselves. He was a squash player of about the same standard as
myself and we met on the court attempting to scale the Mess squash

ladder, so I got to know him perhaps better than many of the other pupils. In retrospect, my contact with people through sports was to be extremely important to me throughout my career. The Chief Flying Instructor, a man of great significance to us since it would be he who gave us our final 'make or break' flying test, was one Squadron Leader Harrison. A formidable man, we never quite lost our awe of him. 'Harrijohn', as the CFS instructors called him amongst themselves, had a hard visage and eyes which could become very angry at the slightest impropriety, let alone flying error, on the part of us pupils. However, when it came to the big day and the final test for a Category, we were one and all surprised to find that in the air 'Harrijohn' was a most fair and considerate examiner, though carrying out the test to the letter.

The pupils were divided into threes and allotted to an instructor. My companions were Flying Officer G N Snary from the Meteorological Flight at Duxford and Flying Officer D Mc Gordon from the flying boat base at Calshot and we were handed over to Sergeant Humphrey, a quietly spoken man who was to take us through the course with the minimum of fuss and the maximum of competence. As at Grantham, my instructor was to be a Sergeant Pilot. There had been some discussion at Grantham on the merits of an NCO as compared with an officer instructor. As youngsters, loyalty led us to maintain that whichever we had was best but, later in squadrons, opinions varied. Although I never had the opportunity of making comparisons because both my instructors were NCOs, I can certainly say that they were first class, taking endless care in seeing that I understood everything they were endeavouring to teach me.

Perhaps the most important part of our instruction was the 'patter'. This was the running commentary that described to the pupil the movement of the controls for manoeuvring the aeroplane, from ground taxiing to take-off followed by turns (medium, steep and gliding), spinning, aerobatics and landing. All these were demonstrated to me, one at a time, by Sergeant Humphrey and, while carrying out the appropriate manoeuvres, I also had to give him the appropriate patter. I was surprised to find out how little I actually knew about flying. When I arrived at CFS from the crack fighter formation aerobatic squadron, with some 800 hours in my logbook, I thought I knew everything worth knowing about flying. I quickly realised that, whereas there was little I couldn't do with an aeroplane, the analysis of each maneouvre for instructional purposes was quite another thing. It was fascinating to learn again.

Snary had had experience in a fighter squadron before so he and I had little difficulty with the actual flying. Not so Gordon, our third man. Flying Officer Gordon was a large, heavily-built man. On first acquaintance, he seemed a very solemn chap, and not surprisingly was quickly nicknamed 'Pixie'. Actually 'Pixie' had an acute sense of humour which was all the more effective for being hidden behind a deadpan face. He had a phenomenal memory which helped with the patter, but he had been away from small aeroplanes for a long time in his flying boats and found flying the Tutor rather difficult at first. Whereas his patter was perfection, he had difficulty matching his manoeuvres to it: with Snary and me it was the other way round. The procedure was for Sergeant Humphrey to instruct each of us in turn in one of the 27 lessons in the syllabus and then for us to practise on one another, taking it in turn to play the role of pupil. We progressed steadily. When not flying, we attended lectures on navigation, theory of flight and other subjects. Some of us fighter pilots were not too good at navigation but the experts on the course, Gordon and Rankin (another boat pilot), kindly coached us in the evenings so all was well. Although we worked hard during the week, almost everyone went off on leave at the weekends. It was quite a sight at 4.30 pm on a Friday to see the number of new and old sports cars turning on to the North Road, not to return until late on Sunday.

In my last year at Hawkinge, we played our usual match with the Small Arms School at Hythe in whose team was an old friend from Hayling Island, Howard Skinner, now a Lieutenant in the Duke of Wellington's Regiment which he had joined on coming down from Pembroke College, Cambridge. While we were enjoying a drink after the match, Howard asked me if I would like to be proposed for membership of the Harlequins of which he was already a member. I hesitated for a moment or two because I doubted whether I could afford to travel to London regularly, but the prospect was too dazzling to resist and I said I would. In due course, I was invited to play a few games for the club's A teams and was eventually elected a member. When I went to Wittering, I drove to London every weekend and towards the end of the 1934-35 season I made the first XV. This was rugby football at the highest club level and the skill of one's team-mates and opposition made playing all that more enjoyable.

The Harlequins were an exclusive club in those days, dominated by the legendary Adrian Stoop as the chairman of its committee. Unlike many London clubs which fielded as many as ten teams every Saturday, the Harlequins ran only three: the first fifteen and two A teams. It was understood that the A teams were stepping stones to the first XV and that if individuals in these teams were not candidates for first XV selection after a couple of seasons they should play elsewhere. Most players had an Oxford or Cambridge background and there were officers from all three services, the Army predominating. Two clergy-men—Peter Brook and Sammy Kemble—played in my time. The club was also different from other first class London clubs in not having an active social life after matches. Twickenham was not ours, it belonged to the Rugby Union, and after tea with the opposition we simply dispersed. This suited me, for I was keen to keep fit for football and flying and had little taste for the boozing common at some clubs.

Meanwhile at Wittering, I was enjoying the course immensely, despite the winter weather and the open cockpits. Many of us were introduced to the intricacies of instrument flying for the first time. It may surprise contemporary airmen that I amassed as many as 800 flying hours before even beginning to grasp instrument flying but, until we received the Fury in 1932 (which had a turn and bank indicator), the only flying instrument I had seen was a spirit level! This, a compass and and an air speed indicator were our only aids for flying in cloud. "Press the compass and follow the bubble" was the only instrument flying advice I received before going to CFS.

In the Avro Tutor we practiced cloud-flying 'under the hood'. The hood could be raised by the occupant of the rear cockpit to eliminate all visibility outside the forward cockpit and the pupil must then rely on his instruments, which were alarmingly primitive by modern standards: no artificial horizon, no rate of climb and descent indicator, only a turn-and-bank indicator. After much research and many trials, an instrument panel was produced at the CFS which became standard during and for long after the War; I have always thought that the production of this panel was one of the many greatest contributions CFS made to Service flying.

There were a number of 'characters' on our course. Geoffrey Stephenson, reserve pilot in the Day/Bader synchronised aerobatics event at the 1931 Hendon Display, was proving a very apt pupil. Physically small, he was strong for his size. We were short of a scrum half in the Station rugby team and though Geoffrey had never played the game (he was at Malvern, a soccer school), we persuaded him to have a go. Like everything else he attempted, Geoffrey quickly excelled. His friend, Reggie Gaskell (another ex-Cranwell cadet) came to CFS from the Fleet Air Arm. Always immaculately dressed in or out of uniform, Reggie had perfect manners and a courteous, almost olde worlde manner of speaking that made him a delightful companion: he was a real 'card'.

One of the small ways that the CFS staff had of indicating the differ-ence between themselves and the usual run of Service pilots was to wear breeches rather than trousers, with light blue woollen stockings instead of the usual puttees. In the whole Service, only those actually at the CFS were permitted to wear this dress. We pupils on the course were automatically accorded this privilege and I must confess that it pleased my vanity to wear stockings when visiting Stations and noting the respect accorded to this odd dress. Reggie protested at having to discard his perfectly cut slacks for what he described as "this cycling garb", but he quickly got used to it.

One trial which caused most of us some apprehension, was the obligation to give an hour-long lecture to the course in the presence of 'Harrijohn', the Chief Flying Instructor, and such other members of the staff as cared to attend. It was an occasion that few of us looked forward to; not only were one's fellows highly critical, but the awesome presence of 'Harrijohn' gave it an added tension. When my turn came, I described our trip from Hawkinge to Villacoublay when we flew in Tiger Moths as spectators to the World Aerobatic Championship during the summer of 1934.

At the end of the course, I had my test with Harrijohn and got through both it and the examinations in the ground subjects satisfactorily. Then came the final interview with the Commandant. Maltby was his usual friendly self and made several encouraging remarks about my work. He offered only one criticism: "Your voice", he said, "is a bit too loud. You should moderate it a little for the benefit of your future pupils!" Like most other members of the course, I had been awarded a 'B' category. Only Geoffrey Stephenson got an A2, a level which I later achieved.

The end of term Ball was a very lively occasion. Pam came up from Folkestone looking marvellous and then came the moment we had all been waiting for—the Posting List. I was to go to No 5 Flying Training School at Sealand, near Chester. I knew little of this place though it had been my destination for a cross-country flight from Grantham during my initial training. The few people on the course who knew it reckoned it "wasn't much of a place". However, as so often happens in the Service, postings that appeared unattractive at the outset turn out to be quite delightful in the event. Sealand was certainly one of these, though sadly going there meant that Pam, to whom I had intended to get married, and I drifted apart. I spent most of March 1935 on leave at home on Hayling Island and then drove up to Sealand at the beginning of April. Cruising speed of cars was much lower than it is now—forty mph was a good average, and I remember thinking what a long way it was. When I arrived on a nice spring evening I understood at once why Sealand was considered "not much of a place". The Station was about six miles north of Chester at the head of the Dee estuary and nearby was the Summers' Iron Works with massive chimneys belching smoke most of the time. The Station buildings were an odd mixture of old and new: some wooden huts put up during the Great War and some modern brick-built huts. Apparently money had run out before modernisation could be completed. The Officers' Mess was an instance of this: most of it was cheap, wartime construction but our bedrooms and bathrooms were brand new. However, Sealand was a cheerful, busy place and despite the mixture of buildings, a comfortable place to live in and work. I was to remain there for the next year and a half.

Shortly after joining the Bulldog Flight in April, I was promoted to Flight Lieutenant, and had to help clear a backlog of instruction caused by bad winter weather and was certainly kept busy: I gave dual instruction to no fewer than eleven pupils in one month. Then in May I was moved to one of the Tutor Flights commanded by Flight Lieutenant E A C Britton, an ex-RFC pilot whose face bore the scars of an aeroplane fire in France. We discovered that we had both been at Kingswood—rather remarkable, we thought, for two old boys to be in the same flight when so few from our school joined any of the services.

When the new junior term arrived, I was allotted three Acting Pilot Officers, Trumble, Fazan and Corder, and one airman pilot, Leading Aircraftsman Hornby. This was my first real test in instructing. The eleven pupil pilots that I instructed in the Bulldog Flight had already been sent solo before I took them on. These four had never flown before and I found it a most stimulating experience. I suppose teaching the young anything can be satisfying, but teaching them to fly adds a risk factor that greatly increases the satisfaction if they succeed. My four were all very keen and, if they had any fear of flying, showed no signs of it. They made steady progress and got through their first solos safely. Trumble had the greatest aptitude but the others weren't far behind. In a few weeks all had passed a Flight Commander's test and had been sent solo.

The Station Commander, Group Captain E W Norton, was a Welshman and very senior in the Group Captains' list. It may have been this 'bobbing on promotion' that influenced his behaviour, but he was almost nonsensically keen that every station activity should reach a superlative standard: drill and games as well as flying. I was, of course, keen to do my best, but Norton's unrealistic demands became wearisome.

By the time I arrived at Sealand, the rugby season was nearing its climax and the Station XV, having won its way through the numerous rounds of the inter-unit competition was about to appear in the grand final at Uxbridge. There was some talk of dropping one of the wingers to accommodate me with my Harlequin reputation, but in the end it was decided to keep the team that had won its way to the final. Rightly so, I thought. It was a great occasion. Sealand against Henlow: a small Flying Training School against the RAF's main engineering depot. Not only did Henlow have numerous players to choose from, but most of them were older and more physically mature. Sealand had fourteen young pupils, led by an instructor, W N McKechnie; Henlow had six older officers from the Engineering Course and nine NCOs or airmen from the Depot. McKechnie's captaincy of his young team was splendid. He capitalised on the speed and fitness of his players and kept the game going at a cracking pace. Henlow, the heavier and more experienced team, were quite out-manoeuvred and Sealand won with something to spare. After McKechnie, the greatest contributor to the victory was a young man destined to earn great fame as a sportsman and airman, Pilot Officer G A Walker, playing fly-half. He was a small man, but he had the courage of a giant. He was everywhere on the field and despite his small stature was a great tackler. Gus went on to play for the Royal Air Force, Blackheath, Yorkshire and England and, when war came, finished his service as an Air Chief Marshal.

I had one alarming experience while instructing on Bulldogs. The two-seat model had the fuselage lengthened to accommodate the second cockpit. For some reason that was never satisfactorily explained, the dual Bulldog occasionally became 'stable' in a spin; this meant that having started to spin the normal movement of the controls for recovery had no effect: the aeroplane just went on spinning. When I arrived at Sealand nobody had experienced this phenomenon, but I had heard rumours of its occurrence at Wittering and instructions had been issued to the effect that if it happened the 'immediate action' was to centralise the controls and commence the spin recovery procedure afresh. To allow plenty of height for this extra action to be tried as often as necessary, initiation of a spin was not permitted below 11,000 feet. I had demonstrated the spin and recovery many times to my pupils and they had also performed the manoeuvre satisfactorily themselves.

Then came the day when I went up with a pupil named Lerwill to practice spinning. When we got to 6,000 feet and being in something of a hurry (always a danger in the air!) I said: "This will do, spin to the right". Before obeying, luckily for us, Lerwill correctly turned the Bulldog to check the sky below. He spotted a Tutor immediately below and so I said, "Carry on climbing". On reaching 11,000 feet, Lerwill again checked the sky below, found all clear and spun to the right. After three turns I said "Alright, now bring her out". Lerwill used the controls correctly, but nothing happened: the aeroplane went on spinning downwards. "OK I've got her", I said and then repeated the recovery movements. Absolutely nothing happened: the aeroplane just went on spinning. I saw from the altimeter that we had lost 4,000 feet and were now at 7,000. I tried once more without result, by which time we were at 5,000 feet. There was nothing for it but to bale out and use our parachutes. I was just about to tell Lerwill to undo his straps preparatory to jumping when, with the controls all central and for no apparent reason, the aeroplane stopped spinning and continued downwards in a dive. I eased it out of the dive and once in level flight turned towards the airfield. I was slightly breathless by this time, but Lerwill appeared quite unperturbed. Such is the faith of the pupil in his instructor. I noted that when we flattened out from the dive our height was exactly 3,000 feet: how fortunate we were that a Tutor, innocently tootling along, prevented us from starting our spin at 6,000 feet!

Sealand was turning out to be an exhilarating posting. The flying was full of interest, with the progress of my pupils most satisfying. I realised too that constant practice was improving my own technique and this made instruction simpler. Off duty, Sealand was a games player's paradise. A sensible emphasis on the physical fitness required for flying meant that all—and particularly the pupils—were expected to participate in games and these were therefore well organised by the permanent staff. There were some splendid athletes amongst the airmen as well, so it was not surprising that the Sealand teams were of a high standard.

Our rugby team was particularly strong and attracted the attention of the Royal Air Force selectors. I was captain in the 1935/36 season (playing for Harlequins had sharpened me up considerably) and, to my great delight, was selected to play for the RAF against the Navy and Army at Twickenham that season. Our captain was Charles Beamish, third of the four remarkable brothers. The inter-service matches at Twickenham were always rugged affairs, but scrupulously fair, and I made lifelong friends amongst the sailors and soldiers that I played against.

I remember one memorable experience in Wales at Easter in 1936. Harlequins invited me to take part in a two-match tour, even though I had not been able to play regularly for them that season. We were to assemble at a small hotel in Caswell Bay on the Gower Coast on the Thursday before Good Friday; play Swansea on Saturday, Cardiff on Monday and disperse on Tuesday. The postcard I received instructed me to "bring golf clubs and dinner jacket". I was not a little thrilled at this invitation which I quickly accepted. I had never played in Wales—then, as now, a hotbed of the game—but I had heard many speak of the enthusiasm of Welsh teams and their spectators. I had recently purchased from a friend, Jeff Wilkes (one of the Wilkes brothers who ran the Rover Company) a very dashing six-cylinder open Sports Rover, painted bright red. Prototype for the standard model produced later, it was fast for those days and I was most proud of it. Sealand closed for Easter at mid-day on the Thursday and I set off for Caswell Bay in the red Rover that afternoon. The weather was fine and with the hood down I was able to enjoy the lovely scenery of mid-Wales. However, the journey took longer than anticipated and it was nearly midnight before I found the hotel: the only building in the bay and right on the beach. No-one was about, but a notice pinned in a prominent position read "Cross—Room 10". I found it and was soon in bed and asleep.

Apparently the Harlequins stayed in Caswell Bay every year for their two Easter games. When I went down to breakfast the next day, I was summoned to sit at Adrian Stoop's table. This remarkable man, most famous of all Harlequins, was then in his fifties and as club chairman went on the Easter tour. Adrian was intensely interested in rugby tactics. As England's fly-half from 1908 to 1914, his example had rejuvenated back play throughout the country. The Welsh had dominated British rugby for many years, but Adrian helped to change that. He emphasised the importance of good forward play as a foundation for backs to build passing movements and score tries. But he will always be remembered for his insistence on the correct methods of taking and passing the ball. Adrian taught players to take a pass at speed, run on hard and straight, steady themselves on meeting a tackle, and pass to the next man coming up in support by swinging the body away from the line of flight. If only there were a dominant figure in English rugby today to revive the art of back play! Nowadays, the ball is just shovelled along the line or, more often than not, kicked high in the air in the pious hope that the opposing team will make a mistake. 'Kick and hope' right up to international level. If occasionally a strong-minded centre stands back a little to allow himself room for change of pace, straightening and swinging away, he is instantly repaid by being missed out of the movement, the pass going to the next man in the line who is standing shallow, so shallow indeed that he is tackled with the ball or shovels it to his wing without going through any of the essentials for a good pass.

Enough of these grumbles: back to Easter 1936! At breakfast Adrian said we were playing golf that morning at Pennard, the local course. He and I would take on Hamilton-Hill, already an English international, and Robin Prescott, soon to be one. Nobody ever questioned Adrian so in due course we played. Pennard was a delightful seaside links and fun to play on. The club members were most hospitable and the long connection the Harlequins had with the club had led to a special competition played each Easter in which both Harlequins and club members competed. That year Hamilton-Hill won it.

Saturday came and after an early lunch we went off in a coach to St Helens, home ground of the Swansea club. I was taken aback at the crowds already making their way to the ground since we had arrived an hour before kick-off. We went to our dressing room under the stand and, shortly afterwards, singing started above us. A newcomer to Wales, I found it rather intimidating, but took comfort from the indifference shown by the rest of the team who were all very experienced in Welsh football at club or international level. Our back row of Bolton, Dunkley and Hamilton-Hill, all internationals, were quite unmoved and joked away as normal in any changing room before a game. I was down to play at left wing three-quarter. With about ten minutes to go before kick-off, I was nervously re-tieing my boot laces when the changing room door opened. In came a young man with fair curly hair wearing Swansea's all-white colours. He spoke with one of the Harlequins sitting by the door who pointed at me. The white-clad figure came over and said, in a lilting Welsh voice: "You are Flying Officer Cross, I believe?" I agreed, whereupon a cold smile appeared on his face and he said: "I am Aircraftsman Morgan and you took my place in the Air Force team this year. I see we are marking each other today, so *now* we shall see who is the better man!" He grinned at me again, turned and went out. With all the noise going on above us, my morale was not at its highest and now there was a personal challenge as well.

We were soon on the field and as it happened the Swansea forwards dominated ours at first, giving their backs plenty of ball. I realised quite quickly that I was not only bigger than Morgan, but marginally faster as well, and had no difficulty in tackling him whenever he got the ball. By half-time much of Morgan's assurance had departed. We beat both Swansea (3-0) and Cardiff (17-3) that Easter, both strong clubs and a rare feat for us.

An extraordinary incident happened before our game with Cardiff, however. As we came out onto the field, there was the usual desultory clapping that was the normal welcome from a Welsh crowd for English visitors but this suddenly gave way to loud cheering. The Cardiff team had not yet appeared and I was at a loss to understand what all the cheering was about. I soon realised that it was not for us, but for our touch judge, A L Gracie, a veteran Harlequin and a former Scottish International of a decade or more before. In the Wales versus Scotland match at Cardiff in 1923, he had scored a remarkable try well described by H B T Wakelam in his book *Harlequin Story*: "with the score at 8 points all Gracie, in an unlikely position, secured the ball. Head back and flat out, he fairly raced through the complete Welsh defence, beating man after man before hurtling over for three points which gave Scotland her victory and, when the final whistle blew a little later, the vast Welsh crowd burst the barriers, to carry the man who had defeated their country shoulder high off the field". Clearly the Welsh not only appreciated fine football, they also had long memories, for 13 years had gone by since Gracie's memorable try.

On Saturday night, Adrian had taken several of us to a neighbouring hotel for dinner and dancing. He and Fanny Marcroft, an old friend of his and something of a figure in Swansea society, arranged partners for us. My partner was 'Johnny' Farr, a slim, very pretty girl and a wonderful dancer. It was all the greatest fun. We went to Church next morning and played golf in the afternoon. Motoring back on Monday evening, I reflected that this had been one of the best Easters of my life.

Back at Sealand, we had a new Station padre posted to us, one Arthur Watson. An unusual man, he had been a contemporary at Oxford of Richard Temple Fisher (later Archbishop of Canterbury) and, like him, possessed a ready sense of humour. Watson had led a varied life since entering the Church: country vicar, naval padre and now service in the RAF. He preached sermons that I found electrifying and made Church Parade a pleasure. He never courted popularity, but both officers and airmen greatly respected and liked him. It was not surprising that anyone with a problem went first to Padre Watson.

Early in 1936, an event occurred that I had supposed impossible: the Air Ministry announced that, as an exceptional measure, permanent commissions would be awarded to selected officers holding medium commissions. The growing threat of war with Germany was about to cause a massive expansion of the RAF and, consequently, a greatly increased need for full career officers. So, despite the categorical assurance I was given at Hawkinge when accepting a ten-year medium service commission, that the term would not be extended, here was the possibility of achieving my dream: a permanent career in the RAF.

Six of us medium-service officers at Sealand applied for permanent commissions. We were interviewed initially by the Station Commander, who recommended five of us for the next stage, an interview with the Group Commander, Air Commodore C D Breese, at Grantham where I had started my service some seven years before. He was very formal in the interview until near the end when he seemed to relax a bit and we talked about rugby. Only then did I realise that he was chairman of RAF rugby! I felt when I came out that I had not done too badly.

On returning to Sealand I thought long and hard about my prospects: was there anything I could do to improve them? Many of us were accustomed to seeking Padre Watson's advice, so I went to see him. "Well", he said, "you have a pretty good record here and it will be your current performance which will probably be most important". I told him of the severe reprimand at Hawkinge for the taxiing accident, but he brushed that aside. "Technical, not disgraceful. I don't think you need worry about that". He thought for a moment and asked me if I knew anyone at the top of the air force. I didn't and said so, then suddenly I thought of Sir Philip Sassoon. "But he's a civilian", I told Watson, "and I couldn't possibly ask his help". "Pity", he replied "as Under Secretary of State for Air, he'll probably be concerned". As it happened, I visited London soon after this conversation and telephoned 45 Park Lane (as I had done since Hawkinge days) to tell Philip's secretary that I was in town. Although I was delighted when Philip invited me to dinner, I had resolved not to raise the matter of my permanent commission. As the guests were leaving, Philip said, "Wait a moment, Bingo, I want to speak to you". We went up to his study where he surprised me by saying "What about a permanent commission for you?" I told him that I had applied. "Good" he said—and nothing more. The list of those selected was published in Air Ministry Orders later that year. There were 150 names and—great joy—mine was among them. I went to tell Padre Watson at once. He was delighted for me and as I left said "You should remember, too, that the Service hasn't got a bad bargain either". These words, quietly spoken by a man for whom I had the highest regard, greatly encouraged me.

I spent the two months of June and July 1936 on attachment to the Cambridge University Air Squadron for its annual summer camp at RAF Abingdon. There were 75 undergraduates in all and they came in batches to spend a couple of weeks flying the Avro Tutor. I found teaching them most agreeable. Not only were they possessed of intelligence above the average, they were not—unlike many of the service entry—in any particular awe of their instructor. Although they respected me, they never hesitated to query anything I said if they thought it unsound and so I often had cause to bless Sergeant Humphrey for his thorough instruction at the Central Flying School.

The university air squadrons, brainchildren of Lord Trenchard, were unusual formations. The first two were at Cambridge and Oxford and their successful origin owed much to Sir Samuel Hoare's efforts during his time as Secretary of State for Air, efforts which are admirably described in his book *Empire of the Air*. Consultations with the universities had convinced both Trenchard and Hoare that in the prevailing climate the emphasis should be on flying, with no military instruction whatever: members of these squadrons were not liable for military service, wore no uniform and, though flying His Majesty's aircraft, were not subject to the Air Force Act. It might be thought that flying military aircraft without any military discipline would lead to all sorts of problems in an air force unit. In practice it was quite the reverse. It became a point of honour among squadron members to observe all rules meticulously. Not once had a member of either squadron been asked to resign, the sole sanction against indiscipline. Although there was no obligation for military service in exchange for being taught to fly, when war came in 1939 almost all past members of both squadrons promptly joined the RAF and many served with distinction.

Abingdon enjoyed exceptionally fine weather that summer and we flew hard. At the end of six busy weeks we went on leave. When I returned to Sealand at the end of August 1936, I learned that I had been posted permanently to the Squadron's home base, RAF Duxford, a few miles south of Cambridge. I was very pleased because I had enjoyed instructing the undergraduates during the summer camp and Duxford was on the whole a pleasanter place than Sealand. Also, being only a couple of hours drive from Twickenham, I would be able to resume playing for the Harlequins.

Duxford was home to 19 Squadron (equipped with Gloster Gauntlets) which would soon be joined by a new Squadron—66—because RAF expansion was now well under way. Both squadrons formed part of a new organisation named Fighter Command, created in July 1936 especially for the air defence of Great Britain against growing fears of German attack. Also at Duxford was a 'Station Flight' to which I was posted. This Flight, equipped with Avro Tutors, was responsible for teaching the members of the Cambridge University Air Squadron. Our CO, Squadron Leader Paul Chamberlayne, had the most magnificent array of initials ever to appear in the pages of the *Air Force List*: PRTJ MIC. Everyone called him 'Tanks', though not to his face, of course. I never knew why, nor did I ever quite summon up enough courage to ask him what all his names were. 'Tanks' started life as a page at the court of Emperor Franz Joseph in Vienna, emigrated to England and became a pilot in the Great War. A delightful man to serve under, he gave few orders and was himself a first class instructor. The other instructors, all Flight Lieutenants, were Rodney Wilkinson, John Fletcher and Dudley Lewis. Rodney and John were killed during the war, leading their squadrons.

One of my pupils was a young man named Kenneth Campbell, who was remarkable even among so many pleasant young men in that he always had a smile on his face. Only an average pupil, he was keen as mustard on his flying. In due course he went solo and his joy on landing was memorable. On 6 April 1941, now a Flying Officer in 22 Squadron, Campbell flew his Beaufort torpedo bomber alone into Brest harbour, probably the world's most heavily defended harbour at that time. Lifting his aircraft over the mole, he carried out a perfect attack, hitting the German battle cruiser, *Gneisenau*, with his torpedo and severely damaging her. Almost immediately the Beaufort was shot down by concentrated gunfire. Kenneth and all the other members of his gallant crew were killed. His posthumous Victoria Cross was one of the best won in the war.

In 1937 the expansion of the newly-formed Fighter Command meant that Duxford was transferred from No 11 Group, defending London and the south-east to No 12 Group, responsible for the defence of the east coast and the midlands. Our Air Officer Commanding in 11 Group had been Air Vice-Marshal Gossage, a quiet unobtrusive man whom, on the rare occasions that we met him, we all liked. Our new AOC in 12 Group was a very different character. Air Vice-Marshal T L Leigh-Mallory was a man of some eminence in his rank. A graduate of the Imperial Defence College, he had been an Army Co-operation pilot in France in the First World War and since then had filled many important appointments, mainly on the staff. His determination to make 12 Group a thoroughly efficient fighting force was apparent to us at Duxford within a very short time of his taking command. It had been my experience up to this time, that the senior commanders kept very much to their HQ with infrequent visits to the Stations. Not so Leigh-Mallory: he made many visits to his Stations, sometimes four or five times a month and he was intensely interested in the training and operational state of the squadrons. As a training unit, we were not part of his command but he nevertheless took an interest in the Station Flight and I met him, and spoke with him, on several occasions.

As the threat of war increased in 1937, so did the tempo of Service life, but we in the Cambridge University Air Squadron were largely insulated from it. While the fighter squadrons at Duxford were taking part in numerous exercises, some even at night, our life in the Station Flight went along placidly, governed entirely by the short university terms. It was frustrating to be on the sidelines, as it were, but at least I was able to keep in regular flying practice, if only in training machines, and take my full leave allowance of 61 days. My golf improved wonderfully during these easy days, the easiest I would enjoy during my entire career. Kenneth Ferguson, the Squadron

Adjutant, was a Scot and a very good player. We played several evenings a week at nearby Royston and it was here that I met E E 'Bev' Beverley, the assistant professional, who became a lifelong friend. Bev was a fine teacher and helped me get my handicap down to three, making me eligible for the English Amateur Championship. I got to the third round, I remember. I also played in the RAF Championships and at one of these met Denys Field who was to become my closest service friend and who tragically died in 1940 in a Hampden over Hamburg. Denys was a scratch golfer who won the Air Force Championship in 1938.

Away from the golf course, I was working to pass an examination that would qualify me for promotion to Squadron Leader. Denys was doing the same. He was stationed at Hendon and I joined him there for a week's cramming for the exam, which was to be held nearby at RAF Northolt. Although working all day and far into the night, we always managed at least a few holes of golf each evening. This mixture seemed to work as we both passed and on 1 October 1938, three days before my 27th birthday, I was delighted to find myself promoted to the rank of Squadron Leader, having been made Acting Sqn Ldr at the end of 1937. I was less delighted, however, to find myself posted to Station Headquarters at Duxford as Station Administrative Officer. I did not fancy this one bit: all the domestic problems, from failure to collect garbage to complaints about airmen's food, would find their way to my desk. However, we now had a new Station Commander, Wing Commander H L P Lester, the same man who had been so understanding when I had crashed the Siskin in 1930. Although he sympathised with my opinion that Administrative Officer was hardly the thing for a brand-new Squadron Leader, Lester told me firmly that "one must take the rough with the smooth" and, to be honest, I had had a very smooth time in the Cambridge University Air Squadron. I therefore did my best, but was mightily relieved when a totally unexpected signal arrived, posting me to the staff of Leigh-Mallory at 12 Group, Hucknall near Nottingham. I was to be the rather grandly entitled Auxiliary Liaison Officer. There would be no more agitation for me over garbage or meals – and no more regular flying either: I was about to start a new career as a Staff Officer.

CHAPTER V

STAFF OFFICER AT 12 GROUP HEADQUARTERS

I ARRIVED at Hucknall on a wet, dank day in early November 1938. My beautiful red Rover had gone by then and I was reduced to a Hillman Minx, the best I could do in a part-exchange deal. Hucknall seemed an uninspiring place in the gloom of a winter evening. On one side of a main road lay some Great War hangars and buildings housing 504 (Auxiliary Air Force) Squadron. There were also two hangars where Rolls-Royce conducted engine test-flying. On the other side of the road, a sprawl of single-storey wooden buildings was the HQ of 12 Group, Fighter Command. Fortunately, the Officers' Mess proved surprisingly warm and comfortable and I even found someone I knew who told me something of the local routine.

Next morning, I reported to the Senior Personnel Staff Officer, Wing Commander Parker. The Air Force has a custom of bestowing nicknames diametrically the opposite of what would be appropriate. Thus, this Wing Commander had been dubbed "Lovely" Parker and as I stood before his desk I could easily understand why. He glowered at me. Apparently I had been selected for the post of Auxiliary Liaison Officer by the Air Officer Commanding personally and this plainly rankled with 'Lovely', who explained that such appointments were normally his prerogative. He told me I was to share an office with Squadron Leader F K Damant, an old war horse who had been doing my new job up to now: Damant would put me "in the picture".

Later that same morning I was sent for by Leigh-Mallory who greeted me kindly. He was 46 when I joined his staff, a man of medium height, stocky build and robust health. He kept himself fit by playing tennis, cricket and golf enthusiastically. A markedly patriotic Briton, he was proud of his brother George Mallory, killed in an attempt to climb Mount Everest. He warmly approved George's reply, "because it's there", when asked why he risked his life in such a venture, and it pleased LM that this remark had become part of British folklore. His energy was prodigious: working seven days a week for long periods was no burden to him. He was popular with his staff, who could accept a slightly pompous manner that was easily compensated for by his immense enthusiasm. On the other hand, he was less popular with his Station commanders because LM was over-whelmingly ambitious and tended to reserve all decisions for himself.

Leigh-Mallory told me that the Group's eight auxiliary squadrons had recently converted from bombers to fighters and consequently had much to learn about their new duties. It was much to ask, he thought, of the civilian volunteers who manned these squadrons and flew only at weekends and on summer evenings. Moreover,they were soon to be re-equipped with Hurricanes and Spitfires, new monoplane fighters that were much more demanding than the dear old biplanes on which we had all trained. My job, said Leigh-Mallory, would therefore be a very important one: to go round the auxiliary squadrons and advise on training. My boss would be none other than my old and much-respected CO at Hawkinge, 'Daddy' Probyn, now a Group Captain and head of training in 12 Group. The job was so important, concluded Leigh-Mallory, that he intended to visit each squadron in turn at weekends and required me to accompany him. So much, then, for my hopes of playing regularly for Harlequins in what proved to be the last pre-war rugby season! And yet, as I listened to Leigh-Mallory, I knew that we were in for a more serious game than any played with an oval ball. I was delighted to be a member of what promised to be the first XV, no longer stuck on the sidelines as for so long I had been at Duxford.

I also realised as I listened what immense responsibilities Leigh-Mallory had at this time. Until shortly before the outbreak of war, his Group was responsible for preparing all the elements of an air defence system for the whole of Great Britain north of a line through Leicester. This meant the individual and collective efficiency of the RDF (radar) chain, the Observer Corps, the fighter airfields and their associated Sector Operations Rooms, the Group Operations Room, nerve centre of the whole business, the multiplicity of communications connecting each and every part, and last and most important, some twenty-odd fighter squadrons. It was a vast task and unlike 11 Group in the south, where the system had been installed for some years, all was new in the midlands and the north. Indeed, the radar chain was still being extended northward when the war began and personnel for the Observer Corps were still being recruited in 12 Group's area.

Although he was a senior group commander, Leigh-Mallory had no aircraft allocated for his personal use and on a Friday afternoon he and I would travel by rail or car to Newcastle, Edinburgh or Glasgow to visit the auxiliary squadrons near these cities. The next weekend it might be Liverpool and Birkenhead to be followed in turn by Leeds and Doncaster, with the local Squadron (504) being visited on our return to Hucknall. These exhausting weekends usually ended most pleasantly with Leigh-Mallory inviting me home for supper. His wife and daughter Jacqueline (then 21) were both delightful women who always made me very welcome.

On these visits, Leigh-Mallory would inspect almost all aspects of a squadron's work and would then finish by addressing the assembled pilots, explaining in lucid language what they had to achieve in training. These auxiliary pilots had mostly joined for the fun of flying. Some were rich young men with plenty of spare time, but the majority were professionals with a living to earn. It was not surprising therefore that there was apprehension at the extra burdens Leigh-Mallory was proposing for them. Even in the winter of 1938-39, after the calamity of Munich, many people recalled the beating Germany took in the Great War and were reluctant to believe that she would be foolish enough to start another war. So it was with some scepticism that the sophisticated young gentlemen of the Auxiliary Air Force listened to Leigh-Mallory.

Nevertheless, his rigorous programme meant more flying and this suited everyone, so training was taken very seriously indeed. Early in 1938, Leigh-Mallory had decided that all the auxiliary squadrons would spend their annual camp at their designated war station, to exercise with the regular squadrons based there and also to take part in Fighter Command's major exercise that year. There was some opposition to this decision from those who preferred their old seaside camps, but Hitler's aggression was sufficiently obvious in 1938 to convince most that those carefree days were over and the time for realistic training had arrived.

However, my life was not entirely dominated by work even in that dark winter, for I had a new girlfriend: Lesley Brook, an actress in the Shakespeare company at Stratford and, after work on weekdays, I would sometimes drive the 60-odd miles from Hucknall to watch her perform and afterwards take her to supper. This meant not getting to bed until 2 or 3 am next morning, but naturally I never let that petty consideration deter me! It certainly increased my prestige to have an actress as a friend, but I enjoyed the plays immensely. We have remained firm friends ever since and she has shown me great kindness during the recent premature loss of my dear wife.

During my time at Hucknall I gradually learned to be a competent staff officer, largely thanks to Daddy Probyn's excellent tuition.

At first, drafts of my reports to Leigh-Mallory came back covered in red ink comments with whole sections cut out or rearranged. I was furious, but Probyn only laughed and bit by bit I learned the need for brevity, clarity and accuracy. Eventually my drafts came back initialled, without comment: I expected no higher praise from my mentor. The pace of expansion since 1936 had been so rapid that many staff posts in all RAF headquarters were filled by officers such as myself who had not been trained at the Staff College. Recognising my weakness in this respect, I had begun to study for the qualifying examination at Duxford as soon as I passed the examination for promotion to Squadron Leader. I used what little spare time I had at Hucknall to continue this work, under the guidance of a well-known coach, Colonel Plummer at Aldershot, but war came before I could sit for it.

A major air exercise was to be held in Fighter Command from 8-11 August 1939, and on the morning before it started I learned that I was no longer an Auxiliary Liaison Officer but something apparently far grander: a Chief Intelligence Officer. This was to be my job both for the duration of the exercise and in the event of an outbreak of war. To say I was flabbergasted would be an understatement, for I had no experience of intelligence duties whatever. The officers and airmen comprising my new staff were all reservists and knew even less than I did. The only person who could help us was a very able civilian clerk: he had been through two previous exercises and so we hung on his every word. It was a complicated job. We were responsible for reporting to Fighter Command Headquarters at Bentley Priory with summaries of 'enemy action' at the end of each phase of the exercise, and of 12 Group's response to it. These summaries were supposed to be dispatched within an hour of the completion of the phase. In fact, our first summary went off some ten hours late, but we improved with each succeeding report and, in the end, nearly made the one hour deadline. Overall, 12 Group's system functioned fairly well in this, its first test. Although mistakes were legion, they were recognised and corrected and, if we had not been a matter of weeks away from the outbreak of war, the results of the exercise would have been encouraging. As it was, we were indeed fortunate that the so-called "Phoney War" granted us a breathing space to exercise everything continuously and reach a much higher level of operational efficiency.

Meanwhile, however, the head of Fighter Command, Air Chief Marshal Sir Hugh Dowding (widely known as 'Stuffy') flew up to Hucknall on 11 August and went straight to the 'Bridge' in the Operations Room where he had a long discussion with Leigh-Mallory. He then said, "Now send for your Chief Intelligence Officer". I was already there, standing with other staff officers at the back of the 'Bridge' so when Leigh-Mallory looked round I stepped forward. "Now young man!", said Stuffy, "your reporting to my Headquarters has been lamentable. Do you think we are playing at this business?" Leigh-Mallory, bless him, tried to explain that I had taken over the job at short notice, but he was waved aside and I was given a lecture on the importance of prompt reporting. Despite the apparent injustice, I did not feel a bit badly about it, quite the reverse if truth be told. Plainly, the C-in-C needed to know what had happened in one phase before the next phase started, so I hurried off to the Intelligence Section, assembled the entire staff and told them how important the C-in-C thought their work was. The exercise over, Stuffy held a large conference of all concerned at Bentley Priory: airmen, soldiers, civilian observers and scientists.

He began with a long monologue going through the exercise in detail, drawing attention to failures and mistakes, but also emphasising the remedies that were found. When he had finished, he asked his two group commanders if they had anything to say. Leslie Gossage, head of 11 Group, wisely shook his head but Leigh-Mallory started what he intended to be a long speech. Stuffy cut him off abruptly and the meeting ended. It was the first time I had seen Stuffy in action and he made a great impression on me. I left Bentley Priory feeling that the Commander-in-Chief had a complete grasp of the business and that there could not be the slightest doubt of his competence to command. A few days later, I went with Leigh-Mallory to inspect an auxiliary squadron at Manston in Kent. That morning, 24 August 1939, I had read in the newspapers that Germany had signed a non-aggression pact with Russia and Leigh-Mallory told me: "This pact makes war certain". The certainty of his pronouncement startled me, but he was obviously quite right.

The Operations Room at Hucknall was crowded at 11 am on 3 September to hear Chamberlain make his famous broadcast. Although the Prime Minister sounded dreadfully depressed, our commander wasn't. Far from it: in fact, Leigh-Mallory was in his element and had his Group on a war footing even before war was formally declared. But nothing happened that day. No plots of enemy aircraft appeared on the Operations Room table and so, after a while, I returned to my office. When I went outside, I looked up at the blue September sky, so peaceful, and wondered what it held for us. Would it soon be filled with German bombers? Meanwhile, the Operations Room was manned continuously and all squadrons came to readiness at first light, maintaining various degress of alert throughout daylight hours. At night, our Blenheim squadrons took over. Reservist officers and airmen joined Group Headquarters in ever-increasing numbers and were soon hard at work. Among them was Harold Rothery who joined my intelligence section. An old RFC man, Harold had for years headed a family firm in Leeds and quickly earned the respect of staff and squadrons alike.

Not much did happen in the 12 Group area for the first few days, then sporadic attacks were made by single enemy aircraft, mostly He 111s and Ju 88s on coastal shipping. These raids were difficult to intercept owing to the limited time of warning from the radar stations and the inaccuracy of the plotting at all levels in the system. In a very short time standing patrols were initiated over the convoys. There was one notable interception by a flight of 46 Squadron from Digby led by the Squadron Commander, Dicky Barwell, against a formation of He 115 floatplanes off the Lincolnshire coast, when five of the enemy were shot down without loss.

As the weeks passed, it seemed to me that a comfortable billet at Group Headquarters was hardly the place for a Squadron Leader 28 years old (on 4 October 1939) so I asked Leigh-Mallory about my prospects of moving to a flying job. He smiled and said: "I have anticipated your request". Something called an Operational Conversion Unit was to be started at Aston Down in Gloucestershire, he told me, to instruct pilots in air fighting before they went to squadrons. Until then, individual squadrons had been responsible for this instruction, but they were now fully committed to operational duties. Leigh-Mallory thought my background in fighters and training fitted me admirably for the post of Chief Instructor at this new unit. I had hoped to go to a squadron but at least I would be flying again. I therefore hid my disappointment as well as I could, thanked Leigh-Mallory for his consideration and left it at that.

Within a few days, all was changed. The CO of 46 Squadron, the same Dicky Barwell who had been my Flight Commander at CFS, was promoted to Wing Commander and would be posted away. Leigh-Mallory sent for me, told me 46 needed a CO at once and that I was to go to Digby, only a few miles east of Hucknall, and far away from Aston Down. I was overjoyed, the more so because at that time 46 Squadron was recognised as perhaps the best in 12 Group and was one of the few in the whole command that had actually been in action. I gladly handed over my intelligence section to Harold Rothery and was honoured by a farewell dinner party at Leigh-Mallory's home. He said some appreciative things about both me and the Squadron and then I was off. Although at times I found LM a bit pompous, working with him at that stage of my career was the best education in the Service I could have had.

CHAPTER VI

WARTIME SQUADRON COMMANDER

I ARRIVED at Digby on 28 October 1939 and having reported to the Station Commander, the suave Wing Commander Rogers, went to the Squadron hangar and there met Dicky Barwell. I see from a pocket diary I was keeping at the time that I spent the afternoon in the air flying one of the Squadron's Hurricanes. Barwell agreed to remain a week before handing over officially. A few days after I arrived, we were inspected by the King accompanied by the Chief of the Air Staff, Sir Cyril Newall, and Leigh-Mallory. The King spent a good deal of time speaking to the pilots and his visit greatly encouraged everyone.

The winter of 1939/40 was particularly severe. There was snow on the ground from December until March and, as Digby was a grass airfield, keeping strips clear for take-off and landing was a big task. In peacetime we would not have flown at all in such weather; the hangar doors would have remained firmly closed but now, in wartime, it was the enemy who dictated when we flew. If plots of enemy or unidentified aircraft appeared on the Operations Room table, then willy nilly off we went. Normally we went forward from Digby at dawn as a squadron of 12 Hurricanes to North Coates, an airfield right on the coast near Grimsby.

I always led when the whole squadron was involved. If a flight of 6 aircraft only was ordered forward, then one of my flight commanders would lead. The flight commanders in 46 were Flight Lieutenants Pat Jameson and David Stewart. Both were competent leaders, but Jameson was also an exceptional pilot. Whenever a convoy crossed our front, we normally covered it with a section of three aircraft on constant daylight patrol. This was an attempt to counter sneak attacks by single raiders coming in at such a low altitude that radar could rarely give us much warning. Constant patrol was the only answer, backed by the rest of the Squadron at North Coates, ready to help within a few minutes of being summoned.

Sitting in the crew room all day in flying kit, I was able to get to know my pilots well. There were 19 of them—13 officers and 6 sergeants—and a splendid lot they were, mostly in their early twenties and only two married. As pilots they were very experienced, most having several hundred hours on Hurricanes alone. All were quietly confident of their ability to deal with anything the enemy could send against them in our sector. However, from the various scrambles in which I took part during the next six months, it became apparent that our system for guiding fighters to intercept the enemy bombers suffered from severe limitations in equipment, organisation and training. This was hardly surprising since it was the first such system in the world.

The radar stations, responsible for early warning, were only able to track aircraft approaching over the sea. Once those aircraft reached the coast, radar was helpless. Worse still, at that time radar's only reliable information concerned range. What it told us about the height, position or number of approaching aircraft was not reliable. Plotters in the Filter Room at Fighter Command Headquarters, receiving information by landline from all radar stations, did their best to plot the track of intruders. They then broadcast that information, again by landline, to group and sector operations rooms. Very good tracks were plotted, but unfortunately several minutes passed between the moment of the initial reading at a radar station and the moment when information appeared on the tables of operation rooms. Consequently, the aircraft in question were actually miles ahead of the position shown on the tables.

Our controllers (directing fighters by radio) became quite clever at overcoming equipment deficiencies in their efforts to guide us to the right place in the sky to intercept intruders. They had to estimate speed and height and guess when or where course changes might be made. Not the least of the controllers' problems was the fact that they had no way of telling whether a blip on the radar screen represented an enemy or friendly aircraft. Many were therefore designated as 'unidentified' but they all had to be intercepted in case they turned out to be enemy aircraft. In fact, as we quickly learned, most of them were our own bombers or reconnaissance aircraft returning to England. However these false alarms gave all parts of the system such excellent practice that it was working well by the Battle of Britain in the summer of 1940.

46 Squadron patrolled over the North Sea on most days. 611 (an auxiliary squadron flying Spitfires) had joined us at Digby from Speke, near Liverpool, but their 'amateur' pilots, being much less experienced than we 'regulars', could not handle the awful weather we had

that winter and were left to train at Digby while we went forward to North Coates. Another squadron (229, flying the Blenheim) was forming at Digby for night fighting. At times we were overworked and Group Headquarters would then reinforce us with a squadron from an adjoining sector, to help out with the convoy patrols. On one occasion, we were relieved by 19 Squadron from Duxford, then commanded by my old friend, Squadron Leader Geoffrey Stephenson. I was delighted to see him again and was busily shaking his hand when who should come climbing out of the next Spitfire but Douglas Bader! I had no idea that he was back in the Service so I was greatly surprised to see him, for I had not thought it possible for a man with wooden legs to return to any kind of active duty, let alone to the most physically demanding of all. We had an hilarious few minutes before Geoffrey and his pilots went off to be briefed on the task for the day. Douglas had not been court-martialled for his stupid act which resulted in his losing both legs, mainly because it was thought he had suffered enough.

Although the enemy never crossed our coast in daylight, they did occasionally fly inland at night without bombing, so early in the New Year of 1940 we received instructions that one of our flights was to operate at night. These instructions were thoroughly unpopular with everyone in the Squadron since the Hurricane was quite unsuitable for night fighting. They were particularly unpopular with me because I felt that, as CO, I must be around whenever the Squadron was flying and consequently I would now be around day *and* night. Despite practising hard, our success on night interception was virtually nil. The theory was that the searchlights would illuminate enemy aircraft for us to shoot down. Unfortunately, the theory ignored certain practical difficulties. Firstly, on only the rarest occasions were searchlights able to locate and (more important) hold the enemy aircraft in their beams. Secondly, flying a single-seat Hurricane in blacked-out winter conditions meant flying almost entirely on instruments with one's head in the cockpit. Outside, all was black, with only the occasional searchlight waving about and generally failing to locate anything—except a Hurricane.

One reason for the introduction of the unsound policy of using day fighters on night work was the almost complete absence of any flying experience in modern aircraft by those in authority over us. Leigh-Mallory, for instance, never flew a Hurricane or Spitfire by day, let alone at night. The same applied to most of his staff. Their judgement was influenced by the success of fighters in the Great War operating against Zeppelins when searchlights easily held such large, slow-moving target in their beams. It was very different nowadays with enemy aircraft travelling at least three times as fast—and, moreover, the blackout was much more complete. Even taking off from a grass airfield with its glim lamp flarepath was a hazardous business. It had to be done visually because the bumpy surface made the flying instruments jump about so much that they were useless as a reference until the wheels left the ground. Most pilots managed somehow but one, Terry Scott, lost control on take-off, crashed and was killed.

Shortly after this tragic accident, we were taken off night-flying— to our great relief—and sent to Acklington, north of Newcastle. Until the outbreak of war, Acklington had been a gunnery practice camp for fighter squadrons and its facilities, both technical and domestic, were rudimentary. We had been sent to reinforce the newly formed 13 Group, which had taken over from 12 Group responsibility for the air defence of northern England and Scotland. The group commander was Air Vice-Marshal Richard Saul, whom I had met at Hucknall prior to moving north to Newcastle. He was a thick-set, rugged man with the reputation of being a bit of a bully, but I did not find him so. He visited us within two days of our arrival and confirmed that attacks on coastal shipping had been more frequent off his Group front than off those further south. We secretly hoped this 'trade' would continue. There was another Hurricane squadron in residence when we arrived, the famous (infamous my chaps called it!) 43 Squadron from the 11 Group station at Tangmere. It was commanded by Squadron Leader George Lott and he, like myself, had two outstanding flight commanders, Caesar Hull and Peter Townsend. We quickly established a superiority complex over 43 since we had been in action, whereas they had not encountered a single enemy aircraft to date.

If anything, the weather was more of a trial than even that at Digby during what turned out to be the worst winter for many years, with the snow fall the heaviest this century. The grass airfield was muddy and our arrival coincided with a period of no enemy activity. We spent most of the day sitting in our cockpits on the edge of the airfield, waiting. We had the occasional scramble by a section of three aircraft to investigate unidentified aircraft off the coast, which invariably turned out to be our own bombers or Coastal Command aircraft. Finding the airfield after these sorties in the weather we were having was something of a hazard. The Controller in the Sector Operations Room at Newcastle helped us to intercept the unidentified aircraft and then gave us a course to steer for base, but thereafter we were on our own. There was no homing device at Acklington and we learnt from bitter experience that the 'course to steer for base' given us by the Controller could be very approximate indeed. Therefore, we usually let down to below cloud level well out to sea (where there were no hills) and turned left or right after sighting the coast until we recognised a landmark that would guide us home. It was all very hit-or-miss, but our training and self-reliance were such that few accidents occurred. Even so, after a month of this rigorous life, we were glad to be ordered back to Digby.

When the war started, the other regular Hurricane squadron at Digby, 73, went to France as a part of the Advanced Air Striking Force (AASF). They were at an airfield near Metz and the Air Head-quarters itself was at Rheims. In November 1939, I was told that we had been nominated as the AASF's first reinforcement squadron and must be prepared to move at short notice to France if ordered. This decision meant a considerable increase in the size of 46 Squadron: more officers, men, equipment and transport. Early in 1940 we learned that we were to go to an airfield called Auberive near Rheims and I was to inspect it beforehand. I decided to take Pat Jameson and David Stewart (my two flight commanders) with me and we were met at Rheims by an old friend, Harry Burke, whom I had known at Hawkinge. Harry was now a Squadron Leader on the Staff at AASF and drove us to Auberive which was not far away. I was startled to see that it was nothing more than a large field with no buildings what-soever. Landlines were being laid, said Harry, but we'd get nothing else.

Since we were in France I got permission for us to visit 73 Squadron at Metz. We knew from the newspapers that the Squadron had been in action against German fighters and one pilot in particular, Flying Officer 'Cobber' Kain, shot down several Messerschmitt 109s. We were naturally eager to get a first-hand impression of aerial combat because, at this time, no single-engined German fighters had yet been seen over England. 73 was commanded by J W C 'Hank' More: a great character and sportsman, always full of fun and bubbling over with good spirits. Not surprisingly, the Squadron's morale was high. The general opinion was that though the Me 109 had a superior performance to the Hurricane, the latter was more manoeuvrable and, in dog fights so far, they had just about held their own. As for 'Cobber', he was an exceptional pilot and doing much better than that.

One thing all pilots agreed on was that Fighter Command's instruction for the alignment of the eight wing-mounted machine-guns was no good for fighter versus fighter combat. The eight guns fitted in the Hurricane and Spitfire were a revolutionary part of Operational Requirement F5/34 which had been issued to the British aircraft industry by the Air Ministry five years before the war. Even before that Sidney Camm, of the Hawker Aircraft Company, and Reginald Mitchell, of Supermarines, had been invited by Sir Hugh Dowding in his capacity of Director of Technical Development in the Air Ministry to produce a design for a monoplane fighter embodying all the innovations appearing at the time, among them the enclosed cockpit, retractable undercarriage and the variable pitch propellor, but no mention was made in Dowding's specification of the armament for this fighter. It was not until F5/34 was issued later that eight guns mounted in the wings and outside the arc of the propellor, became a part of Camm and Mitchell's designs.

The need for eight guns was the far-sighted conclusion of a thirty-five year old Wing Commander, Ralph Sorley, then occupying a post in the Operational Requirements Department in the Air Ministry. He realised that, with the increase in speed of all aircraft, the time the fighter pilot had to aim and fire his guns, was likely to be very small and after much thought, calculation and practical experiment, he came to the conclusion that this time period would be just about two seconds. He realised immediately that the accepted practice of mounting two or at most four Vickers guns in the cockpit with their slow rate of fire, further limited by the interrupter gear for firing through the propellor arc, was no longer acceptable. At this time, he was fortunate to learn that the faster-firing American Browning gun was available. This gun had a rate of fire of 1,200 rounds per minute as compared with the Vickers 600 rounds per minute, and it had other advantages over the Vickers gun. Its more compact shape facilitated it being mounted in the confined spaces in the wing, and its greater reliability removed the necessity for the pilot to have to attend to it in the air, which in turn removed the need for it to be mounted in the cockpit as with the Vickers. Sorley therefore specified these guns in the F5/ 34 requirement. Service theorists (either in the Air Ministry or at Fighter Command HQ) had decided that the guns fitted to both the Hurricane and Spitfire should be splayed to give the average pilots a good chance of hitting an enemy bomber.

This thinking made sense before the war when it was expected that any aerial attack on Britain must come from bases in Germany. (France was our ally and would, we believed, prove as steadfast in this war as she had in the last; no-one anticipated the German conquest not only of France, but of *all* the coasts closest to Britain.) Since no single-engined fighter had the range to reach Britain and return to Germany, the attack must therefore be carried out by unescorted bombers. These, it was rightly thought, would prove vulnerable to attack by Hurricanes and Spitfires, whose pilots must therefore be given every chance to score as many hits as possible. The Luftwaffe, recognising this situation as clearly as the RAF, produced a twin-engined fighter (the Me 110) with sufficient range to escort bombers all the way from Germany to Britain and back, but fortunately for us it lacked the manoeuvrability to match our fighters.

In France 73 Squadron had quickly learned that combat meant fighter versus fighter. The Me 109E against the Hurricane 1. The 109 was a much smaller and more elusive target than any German bomber and even the Squadron's best found that, with the guns aligned according to command instructions, too few hits could be achieved to cause significant damage. So, being outside the authority of Fighter Command and finding that Advanced Air Striking Force Headquarters had no opinion in the matter, Hank More decided to realign the eight guns so that all converged on a point 250 yards ahead of the Hurricane. By concentrating the impact of their fire in this way, 73's pilots found that they could at last do real damage. Kain told me that, with his guns re-aligned, he had been able to destroy an Me 109 with a single burst. The short burst he fired hit the 109 in the wing root, large pieces broke off and the pilot baled out. We returned to Rheims that evening and were taken out to dine by Harry Burke and his friends from the AASF Headquarters. It was strange for us used to drinking beer, to be drinking nothing but champagne the whole evening and we realised the difference next morning when we exported three substantial headaches back to Digby!

We resumed our routine convoy patrols but saw no action. During this relatively quiet spell in early April 1940, my young brother Ian— a Wellington pilot at Marham in Norfolk—telephoned to say that he had a day's 'stand down' coming up shortly and what about a day's golf at Woodhall Spa? He would bring a chum, 'King' Bowman, an England international golfer now serving in the Army. My old RAF team-mate, Denys Field, and I played them and we had a great day on one of the finest inland courses in England. Ian had the longest handicap but played the best golf and he and King Bowman beat us quite comprehensively. I remember that day so well because we four would never be together again: Ian would soon be lost to us in circumstances that I will describe later; Denys, my best friend, would be shot down and killed over Hamburg on 6 August and, as for me, the war was just about to start in earnest.

On 25 April, I received an unexpected signal ordering me to report to Air Vice-Marshal Sholto Douglas, the Assistant Chief of Air Staff (Operations) at the Air Ministry. I reported next morning and met Douglas for the first time. He was a burly figure whom, very much later, I heard described as "the Goering of the RAF": there was at least a *physical* resemblance. He told me that it was intended to send my Squadron to central Norway to replace 263 Squadron. That Squadron, equipped with Gladiators, had been almost completely destroyed by German bombing while attempting to operate from a frozen lake at Lesjeskog, near the fishing village of Andalsnes. It was now apparent that the lake was unsuitable as an airfield, but an open space had been found nearby.

Douglas told me that he wished me to go to Andalsnes and decide whether it was possible for Hurricanes to operate from that open space. I was to go to Invergordon, where a Sunderland flying boat would be waiting to take me there: I was to return as quickly as possible and report to Douglas personally, who impressed on me the need for secrecy about my mission. I returned to Digby and, next morning at first light, flew my Hurricane to Dyce near Aberdeen, the nearest airfield to Invergordon. The CO of the squadron based there was an old friend, Finlay Crerar, who loaned me a car to complete my journey. I was met by Flight Lieutenant R Craven, who introduced himself as Captain of the Sunderland which was to take me to Andalsnes. We were due to start early next morning. He discussed the flight with me and I was impressed with his knowledge of the Norwegian coast and his obvious competence. There had been no "Phoney War" at sea, where the Navy and Coastal Command had been hard at it since 3 September 1939, and I sensed that Craven and his crew were fully 'operational'.

We went aboard the Sunderland anchored in the Firth during the night and took off at first light in weather so bad that "even the birds were walking": low cloud base and very poor visibility. The weather did not appear to affect Craven or his crew at all. We flew nearly all the way at a few feet above the sea. After a time, the weather cleared and the mountainous Norwegian coastline appeared. We made a good landfall at the entrance to Romsdalfjord and as soon as we entered it, again just above the surface of the sea, had to turn 90 degrees to port to follow the fjord for the next 50 miles to Andalsnes. A few minutes later, I saw my first signs of war: a village of wooden houses almost all in flames. Ahead was a convoy of five small ships escorted by a destroyer flying the white ensign. There were some messages flashed by Aldis lamp between the destroyer and ourselves and then Craven told me he was going to land beside the destroyer which would take me up to Andalsnes. He would accompany me to the destroyer to find out the situation at Andalsnes and whether it was reasonable to take the Sunderland into the narrow part of the fjord there.

We landed, a whaler came away from the ship and we transferred to it. I scrambled up the side of the destroyer, quickly followed by Craven and the boat's crew. No sooner were we aboard than some Ju 88s appeared at about 8,000 feet and proceeded to bomb the convoy. There was a sharp order from the bridge and the whaler was cut adrift as we went full speed ahead in a wide circle to rejoin the convoy. As we did so, a stick of bombs blew the whaler we had just abandoned clean out of the water. The Sunderland, flown by the second pilot, had already taken off and was attacked either by a Ju 88 or an Me 110 that was shot down for its pains by the gunner in the rear turret.

We went up to the bridge and spoke to the Captain. He told us he hoped to make Andalsnes well before nightfall, but advised that the Sunderland should not land there until last light because the place was under continuous daylight bombing. A wireless message to that effect was sent to the Sunderland.

All that afternoon, as we progressed slowly up the fjord, we suffered repeated bombing. Each time a raid was reported approaching, the ship's gun crews went through their drill for opening fire, but each time the gun captain was obliged to call out: "Unable to bear". The guns on this old ship could not elevate above 30 degrees and were quite useless as anti-aircraft weapons. Even so, my admiration for the gun crews increased by the hour. Never once did they fail to carry out their drill as each bomber approached, only to hear yet again the words "unable to bear". I couldn't understand why the Ju 88s didn't dive-bomb us: with no guns to put them off, they could hardly have missed. Instead—and greatly to my relief—they persisted in their level bombing from much too high an altitude and hit only the unlucky (but empty) whaler. At about 4 pm, we reached Andalsnes safely. Craven stayed aboard the destroyer to await the arrival of the Sunderland at last light. His final words to me were: "We must be out of here by first light tomorrow".

I found my way to the office of Wing Commander L T Keens who was the senior RAF officer in that area, though I had not been told about him at the Air Ministry. He knew about my task but seemed disinterested. A lorry would take me to Setnesmoen, the open space I was to vet. It was only a mile or so to the place, which turned out to be a grass plateau enclosed on three sides by sheer-faced mountains; the open side faced the fjord. A single Gladiator stood on the edge of the field, looking rather lonely. I walked across the field, noting that it was so soft that even the relatively light Gladiator had left deep ruts and quickly concluded that Setnesmoen would be no good for the heavier Hurricane. Returning to Keens' office, I slept on the floor until after midnight when I was called to go down to the Sunderland. I was ferried out in the pitch blackness by some Norwegians to find Craven. He was as alert as ever, minding the aircraft while the crew slept. I sat talking to him for an hour or so until he roused his crew to start carrying out their checks. At the first signs of dawn, the engines were started and we taxied quietly out into the fjord. When we were well clear of Andalsnes, we took off and had an uneventful trip back to Invergordon, arriving mid-morning. I got a car and drove to Dyce where my Hurricane was waiting. On checking the weather for the flight south, I learned it was bad and would get worse. I had to refuel once en route to my destination (Northolt) and Acklington seemed to be the furthest I could get before the weather closed in entirely, so I settled for that.

Soon after take-off, my radio went dead and no amount of juggling produced a sound. There was nothing for it but to fly below cloud level in visual contact with land or sea. Luckily I could get most of the way to Acklington over the sea (where there were no unexpected hills): after crossing the entrance to the Firth of Forth the cloud base got lower and lower until I was flying only a few feet above the water. Later the coast appeared as a dark shadow on my starboard side. Thanks to our stay at Acklington in the year, I was familiar with this coast and eventually spotted a landmark I knew. Turning inland, I scraped into Acklington, mightily relieved to be down, safe and sound. I checked the weather again. It was quite hopeless, so I got a car to take me into Newcastle, where I caught the night train to London.

I reported to Sholto Douglas bright and early in the morning, 29 April. He thanked me for my efforts and then said "It's irrelevant anyway, because the Government has decided to evacuate central Norway". I realised afterwards that this decision had been taken while I was in Norway, so my 'epic' flight from Dyce had been quite unnecessary and could have been avoided if a message had been sent to me at Invergordon. I returned to Digby the same day. Everything was fine in '46' under Pat Jameson's command. The pilots were keen to know about Norway and disappointed to learn that we were not to go to Andalsnes. Little did we guess that very soon we were in for an even more distant adventure.

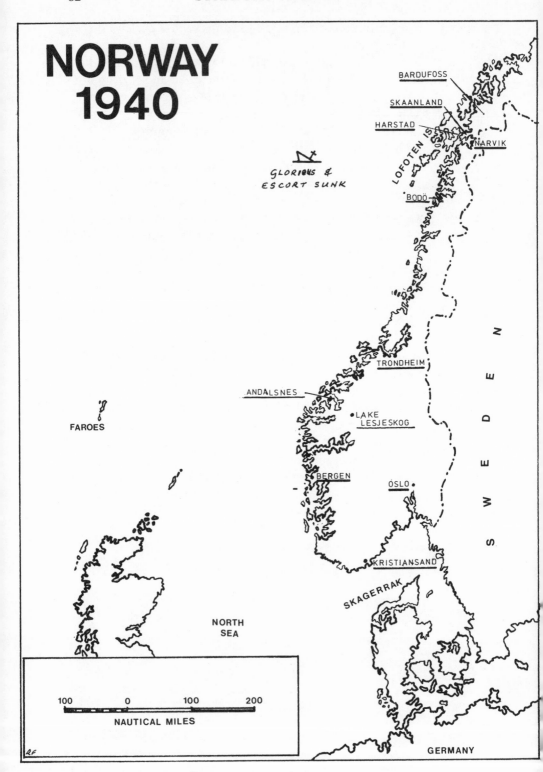

NORWAY 1940

BARDUFOSS

SKAANLAND

HARSTAD

NARVIK

LOFOTEN IS

BODÖ

GLORIOUS &
ESCORT SUNK

TRONDHEIM

ANDALSNES

LAKE
LESJESKOG

FAROES

BERGEN

OSLO

S W E D E N

KRISTIANSAND

SKAGERRAK

NORTH
SEA

100   0   100   200

NAUTICAL MILES

GERMANY

CHAPTER VII

NARVIK

THE signal we had been warned to expect from Fighter Command HQ arrived on 9 May 1940 and gave the details "received from Air Ministry for immediate action, embarkation of sixteen Hurricanes of 46 Squadron in the *Glorious* now anchored in Clyde," and concluded "first aircraft to be at Abbotsinch airfield in readiness to load early morning of 10 May", the next day. We left Digby in squadron formation in the early afternoon of a lovely spring day, a great contrast to the weather we had suffered the whole winter. Everyone was in high spirits at the prospect of action in northern Norway, which we understood was to be our ultimate destination. There was also a sense of relief, of escaping from incessant convoy patrols, for a more adventurous theatre of war. One hour and twenty minutes later, we landed at Abbotsinch and dispersed the aircraft for the night.

During the next two days, we taxied our Hurricanes one by one through the fields to Blackburn's wharf on the Clyde where a number of powered barges awaited us. The Hurricanes were hoisted aboard by crane, one per barge, and then went down the Clyde to Greenock where the aircraft carrier, HMS *Glorious*, was anchored. Pilots accompanied their aircraft and this turned out to be a sensible precaution because the bargee's estimate of wing-tip strength was greatly exaggerated and they had to be persuaded to go alongside very gently. The *Glorious's* crane did the rest, depositing the Hurricanes neatly on the flight deck. My pilots wondered why we hadn't saved hours of time and a great deal of labour by simply flying on to the flight deck as we believed possible, small as it was, but Air Ministry had ordered it done this way, and who were we to argue? Apparently trials on a measured strip at Farnborough had convinced the test pilots there that the landing speed of the Hurricane without arrester hooks was too fast for a safe landing on so short a flight deck. Hence the hoisting aboard.

I accompanied my aircraft in the first barge and as soon as it was safely on the flight deck, I went aboard and was welcomed by the Commander Flying, Commander John Heath, a Fleet Air Arm pilot. He was a friendly man and, from the first, made me feel welcome. We discussed where to stow the Hurricanes. The lifts, fore and aft in the flight deck, gave access to the two hangars, upper and lower. It was agreed that we were to be stowed in the lower of the two hangars as this would cause the least interference with the carrier's own squadrons: one of Swordfish torpedo-bombers (used also for reconnaissance duties) and the other of Gladiator fighters (to protect them). We then went to call on the Captain. I had very little knowledge of the Navy at this time, never having been in a warship before. I had made some naval friends playing rugby against the Navy at Twickenham, but that was about the extent of my contact with the Senior Service during ten years in the Royal Air Force. We entered the Captain's cabin, Heath removing his cap and placing it under his arm. (I was to learn that this is the naval way of saluting indoors.) I kept my cap on and saluted, as was our custom. Captain Guy D'Oyly-Hughes was a formidable-looking man, at least six feet tall and squarely-built. He was also a legendary figure in the Navy. While a lieutenant in the Great War, he had swum from a submarine in the Dardanelles, pushing ahead of him a raft loaded with explosives which he used to blow up a stretch of railway track behind Turkish lines before calmly swimming back to his submarine. By the end of that war, he had won the DSO and Bar and the DSC. He kept us only a few minutes and I noted that his manner with Heath was somewhat off-hand and very formal. Knowing no better, I assumed that this was the way the Navy conducted its affairs and thought little about it at the time.

It took two days to load our 18 aircraft and then, on 12 May, we sailed—only to be recalled. Whilst waiting at Greenock we got to know many of the ship's officers and I found that the Gunnery Officer, Lieutenant Commander Kit Wells, was the brother of a friend of mine, Jimmy Wells, then serving in 604 Squadron. Wells went ashore one day and told me that Jimmy was reported missing from a sortie over Holland. We eventually left the Clyde on 16 May and sailed up the west coast of Scotland in a slow convoy with an escort of four destroyers. Next day, we entered Scapa Flow where the *Glorious* refuelled. I had never seen so many warships together before, the whole of the Home Fleet. We learned that we were to leave on the 19th and, in the meantime, no-one was to go ashore. We were sailing with another carrier, HMS *Furious*, which had aboard a reconstituted 263 Squadron (still equipped with Gladiators) as well as its own Fleet

Air Arm squadrons. Six destroyers escorted us and we reached our flying-off position 40 miles west of the northern tip of the Lofoten Islands on 21 May. On passage, we learned all we could about how the Fleet Air Arm squadrons operated, knowledge which later proved useful. Commander Heath always kept a pair of Swordfish on anti-submarine patrol during daylight hours, one ahead over the horizon and one within visibility distance, circling the ship. The Naval Gladiator was the same as its RAF counterpart except that it was equipped with a landing hook for engaging the arrester wires which stretched across the flight deck.

On 21 May, when we reached the take-off point, the weather was really foul: low cloud, rain and a very rough sea. Nevertheless we prepared for take-off, but just before our aircraft were raised to the flight deck, a signal arrived from military HQ at Harstad (on the north-east corner of the Lofotens) to say that our airfield at Skaanland was not ready. What an anti-climax: but also, in such awful weather, what a relief! Bardufoss, the destination of 263 Squadron, was alright but was supposed to be too short for our Hurricanes. However, we remained in company with the *Furious*. Both carriers turned into wind and we watched 263's Gladiators take off. The weather was really appalling, the aircraft seeming to go into cloud almost as soon as they were airborne. One Gladiator did a quick circuit and landed again; another (so we later heard) flew into a mountain.

Later that day, we left the *Furious* to return to Scapa Flow and refuel. One of my difficulties as Squadron Commander was not being able to find out what was intended so that I could keep my chaps informed. Heath did his best, but did not appear to be in the Captain's confidence and was therefore short of information himself. We reached Scapa Flow on the 23rd, refuelled and left next day on our return to the take-off point.

On the evening before we were due to leave the *Glorious*, a signal arrived from the senior RAF officer at HQ in Harstad telling us that we were to fly to Skaanland in twos and threes. I read the signal several times, and liked it less each time because twos and threes wouldn't be able to handle serious opposition. Also we could be picked off on the ground before we'd had a chance to refuel, as happened to 263 Squadron at Andalsnes. Having discussed the signal with Jameson and Stewart, who agreed with me, I went to see Heath and told him of our misgivings. "Have you an alternative plan?" he asked. "Of course", I replied. My plan was to fly to Skaanland in three separate formations of six aircraft at carefully calculated intervals. I would lead the first; land; refuel quickly, and come to 'Readiness'. Before we landed, Jameson would have the second six over the airfield to guard us whilst we refuelled. Once my flight had come to 'Readiness', Jameson's six would land and be replaced overhead by Mike Mee with the third six.

By these means we would never have less than two thirds of the Squadron ready for action. "Seems sense to me", said Heath. "We'll go and see the Captain". Heath, bless him, explained to D'Oyly-Hughes my objections to HQ's plan and my alternative. We got a frosty reception together with a lecture on the theme of "junior officers thinking they knew better than their seniors" and "those at a distance knowing better than those on the spot". I was thoroughly disconcerted. My brief experience in central Norway convinced me that many of the officers sent on that expedition had little or no modern operating experience, such as we had gained during the previous hard winter, and the plan proposed by those at Harstad reinforced my opinion that here was inexperience speaking again.

We were disconsolate when we left D'Oyly-Hughes. At the time I did not realise how much harm Heath was doing to himself by speaking up on my behalf. Only afterwards did I learn that there was constant disagreement between D'Oyly-Hughes and Heath over the operation of the ship's aircraft. But all Heath said as I went off to my cabin was: "Leave it to me". Next day, our D-Day, he told me that he'd sent a signal to Harstad advocating my plan. Some hours later, it was accepted in full. Great relief throughout the Squadron! We had a quick squadron conference, went over every point again and began our final preparations. Being so far north, we had no darkness to help or hinder us: twenty-four hours of daylight would be our lot from now on.

The carrier's flight deck had one amazing fault: the front part was about a foot higher than the rear and the two were joined at a point one-third of the way from the stern by a ramp up which the Hurricanes would have to ride. The length of our propellor blades allowed little clearance over this ramp once our tails were up in the take-off attitude. But if we kept our tails down, the aircraft would not accelerate so quickly and we needed all the surge we could get with only 800 feet to use when we were accustomed to 800 yards! A dilemma. Never mind, we would raise the tail just a little, hold this attitude until we were over the ramp, then the stick hard forward, full throttle, and hope for the best.

By take-off time at 8.30 pm, the first six aircraft were ranged in threes at the extreme rear end of the deck. Unfortunately, the wind had dropped to zero and we were in a flat calm. This meant no help on take-off from extra wind flowing over the deck. As Squadron Commander, I had the doubtful privilege of being first off. It would be the first-ever Hurricane take-off from an aircraft carrier—unless, of course, I failed to make it! The six of us got into our flying kit in silence and went to our respective aircraft. The *Glorious* was full steam ahead and the wind over the deck was a gale despite the calm. I was sitting in my Hurricane with the engine running and with five minutes to go, when I saw a somewhat portly figure in a pair of clean brown dungarees staggering down the gale-swept deck towards us. He spoke to a mechanic who pointed at my aeroplane. He then came round the tail and clambered up to the side of the cockpit.

It was Lieutenant Commander D E Smeeton, the engineering officer who had helped us beguile many an idle hour during the past fortnight by showing us round the ship. Now he put his mouth close to my ear and, over all the noise of the engine and the gale, bellowed: "She is going faster than she's gone since 1928". I didn't know then— and I don't know now— the significance of that year, but it greatly encouraged me to realise that he shared my paramount concern of the moment: that the wind speed over the deck should be as high as possible. Smeeton then let go of the cockpit edge and was almost blown off the aircraft.

I looked at my watch. About a minute to go. A final check round the cockpit. Trims OK. The override boost plug pulled. Third flap down. Eyes then on the Naval Dispatching Officer positioned ahead and to port. He dropped his flag. This was it. I opened the throttle about three quarters and, as I began to move, pushed the stick forward to raise the tail just off the deck. Here came that damned ramp. I was on it in a moment, then full throttle, stick further forward and to my surprise I was airborne almost before I started to ease the stick back— with still a third of the deck to go. Bonzo! A piece of cake!

Having raised the undercarriage and third flap and changed into coarse pitch, I turned in a slow turn to port on to the heading for Skaanland. I looked back. The second Hurricane was already airborne and the third accelerating down the deck, but what a sight the ship was, "fastest since 1928". To me, the *Glorious* looked like a great big speed boat with her bow wave and white wake spreading for miles behind. Smeeton had certainly done his stuff.

I steadied on course and climbed to 4,000 feet, by which time the others were in the agreed loose formation behind me. After about fifteen minutes flying I should have been seeing land, but none appeared. We were observing radio silence, so I didn't know if anyone else had seen anything. I scanned the horizon ahead, really concentrating, but saw only sea. I checked the compass heading and my watch and then suddenly, looking up away from the sea, there was the most wonderful sight: a row of snow-covered mountain peaks. Lower down,

I suppose, the grey of the land merged with the grey of the sea and this was why I couldn't see the coastline: certainly it was several more minutes before I did.

Our maps were very poor, but at least the shape of the fjords was accurate and within the hour we were overhead Skaanland. All looked peaceful, with the empty landing strip running parallel to the edge of the fjord and close to it. If our timing was right, Jameson and his six should be here in a few minutes. We did a couple of wide circuits so that everyone could have a good look at the place and then, sure enough, there was Jameson waggling his wings to say he had seen us and was ready to take over top cover. I waggled in reply and let down in a left-hand turn to bring me in line with the runway. While landing, I saw that the surface was Summerfield Track (a wire mesh over coconut matting) and, as I began to slow and weight came onto the wheels, I felt them dragging. As the end of the runway was coming up, I couldn't give the engine a burst to provide extra slipstream to keep the tail down; I could only keep the stick hard back and hope for the best. I had almost come to a stop when the wheels dragged again and I tipped gently forward, just touching the propellor on the track, before settling back again and stopping. I taxied gingerly off to one side and switched off. Only then did I realise that I had bent about two inches of propellor tip on each of the three blades.

Dismay was followed quickly by anger. The surface was too soft and would not take the weight of a Hurricane. As I climbed out, an elderly Squadron Leader approached. "The airfield isn't fit", I shouted. "Was it tested?" To my surprise and embarrassment, he burst into tears and I got no coherent answer to my question. Then a Group Captain came over and introduced himself: he was Maurice Moore, Senior Air Force Officer Norway. I told him the runway wasn't fit for Hurricanes but, at that moment, the second Hurricane landed safely. So did the third. Moore's eyebrows went up a shade as he looked at me, indicating plainly that he thought the Squadron Commander at fault, rather than the runway. Just then David Stewart came in. He touched down safely but, as he ran on, a slight fore-and-aft rocking caused a wheel fairing to catch in the tracking and fling the Hurricane on to its back. We ran over to lift the aeroplane and release Stewart who was more angry than shaken. "It's not fit to land on" he shouted, as his aeroplane was dragged clear of the runway.

This really was a pretty kettle of fish. There were still two to land from my six and twelve more using up petrol in the air. Fortunately, my last two landed successfully, but what was to be done with the rest? We could not risk any more accidents at Skaanland. "They will have to go to Bardufoss," I told Moore and he agreed. "What's more," I added, "We're going to break radio silence to tell them". He was a bit dubious at first because he wanted to conceal our arrival from the enemy but soon realised there was no alternative. I climbed into my Hurricane, called Jameson and told him. He acknowledged and set off north-eastwards for Bardufoss. I hoped he would find the place with such inadequate maps, but if anyone could find it Jamie would: a natural pilot, he was quite unflappable and didn't query my order for a moment, even though (as he later told me) it gave him the shock of his life! Mee arrived shortly after with his six and was similarly diverted. Again, no query: he just did as he was told. Our discipline in 46 was excellent.

Moore and I had a brief discussion. Now we knew what the runway was like, I thought we would be able to avoid accidents, but even so I also thought we should only operate from Skaanland on receipt of confirmed reports that enemy aircraft were in the area. Our ground crews and spare pilots had crossed to Norway aboard a Polish liner, reaching Skaanland on 18 May. They should now go to Bardufoss, I said, and as soon as they arrived I would join them there with the remaining Hurricanes. Moore didn't like my suggestions. Apparently the ground and sea attack to recapture Narvik had been delayed pending our arrival. Bardufoss was twice as far from Narvik as Skaanland and consequently our time on patrol over the assault area would be reduced. However, he recognised that the experiment of laying matting on marshy ground and covering it with Summerfield tracking was a failure. He agreed that we should go to Bardufoss as soon as the ground crews could be moved there—which might take some time, given the absence of paved roads and shortage of sea transport.

By now the four serviceable Hurricanes had been laboriously refuelled from two-gallon tins stacked round the so-called airfield and the pilots were standing by. The five pilots with me were Flight Lieutenant Stewart, Flying Officers Frost, Bunker and Lefevre and Flight Sergeant Shackley. We had a quick council of war standing by one of the aircraft. The Squadron Engineer Officer, Warrant Officer Simpson, reported that Stewart's aircraft was unrepairable with the limited equipment we had on hand. That Hurricane (serial number L1892) was therefore dismantled and returned to England, where it was rebuilt and came to its final end in the Battle of Britain. My Hurricane, Simpson was already repairing. He had no spare airscrews but he was straightening the blades by judicious use of a couple of large hammers. It was after eleven o'clock at night and still broad daylight before we were ready. In the weeks to come we were to realise just how much extra effort was required to be able to operate throughout the twenty-four hours of daylight. I decided to keep three of the four aircraft on 'Readiness', and told the other three pilots to get some sleep. Stewart, Frost and Shackley were to take the first watch and myself, Bunker and Lefevre would take over in the early morning. We slept in our clothes in a disused house on the edge of the airstrip.

We relieved Stewart and his two at 6 am on 27 May and a few minutes later were airborne, or at least Lefevre and I were. Bunker had runway trouble and somersaulted as Stewart had done. Two aircraft gone already. I silently cursed that runway. We saw 3 Heinkels way above us and, having set the Heinkel wing span on the reflector sight, started the long climb up to their altitude. Unfortunately, cloud increased before we got near them—they disappeared into it and we lost them. After searching unsuccessfully for a short time we returned to Skaanland. We had anxious moments landing but by minimal use of the brakes and much holding of breath we both met with success.

We had no news of the rest of the Squadron at Bardufoss and spent the day at Readiness but were not called. At about 4 pm I got a message from Harstad to say it was OK for us to go to Bardufoss. The four of us left soon afterwards. It was about sixty miles across snow-tipped mountains and very rugged country to our new airfield and, despite the poor maps, I had no difficulty in finding the place: a rock strip running east to west on a table land surrounded on all sides by mountains. We circled and I saw that the best approach was from the east over the Barduelva river and, as there was no wind, we landed that way. The runway was about six hundred yards long, but work was in progress at the eastern end and, by the time we left Norway, it had been increased to over eight hundred yards. There were no taxi-ways off the strip, just lanes leading to dispersal pens.

I was met by Jameson and the Station Commander, Wing Commander R L R Atcherley. The latter's dress was unorthodox, tunic over a rollnecked sweater and dark blue ski trousers stuffed into flying boots. I had not met this famous air force character before but knew of him, as did everyone else in the Service, from his membership of the team that won the Schneider Trophy in 1929. He greeted me in the most friendly way and then left driving off in a thirty-hundred-weight truck. Unfortunately, I was to find that Dick Atcherley, though an artist with an aeroplane, had no grasp of operational requirements and was thoroughly unreliable in his judgement. The upshot was that J W Donaldson, CO of 263 Squadron (equipped with Gladiators), and I tended to run the operations ourselves. I asked Jameson what the form was, and he said that we had been instructed by HQ at Harstad to maintain a standing patrol of three aircraft over Narvik from 19.30 hrs that evening when a bombardment by cruisers was due to start as a preliminary to an assault aimed at capturing the place. This patrol was to be provided entirely by 46 Squadron as 263 Squadron were busy with aircraft maintenance, having been at it non-stop since arriving on 21 May, earlier than us as they could land on a shorter runway, ours still being constructed. In addition to the Narvik patrols, 46 would also be responsible for the defence of the airfield, which meant keeping aircraft at Readiness at the end of the runway. I asked how long we were to maintain this 'state' and was told until further orders. This was going to be a pretty strenuous commitment for our twenty-one pilots, none of whom had had much sleep for thirty-six hours. But the prospect of action banished all weariness and everyone was eager to get started. I told Jameson to make out a programme with myself leading the first patrol at 19.30 hrs. It was then about 17.30, so I had time to have a look around.

Bardufoss in peacetime had been merely a summer landing ground offering minimal facilities in a district with a very small population. Now, with a great deal of Norwegian help, Atcherley had seen to the clearance of several feet of snow, dozens of trees, masses of dense bush and the laying of tons of gravel. Two runways had been lengthened and widened, taxiways and blast pens constructed for aircraft, shelters for men and numerous drains dug to deal with the effects of thaw. A road leading for twenty miles to the nearest fjord had been cleared and repaired. This immense amount of work had been deemed worthwhile because the nearest German base was at Trondheim, some 400 miles to the south and beyond the range of German single-engined fighters. The two RAF squadrons were dispersed among pine trees and tents had been pitched nearby. As I looked around, I realized we had a very good set up.

It was the evening of 27 May and the weather was like a mild English winter. Jameson had already established an Operations Tent on the edge of the runway with a field telephone to the Station Operations Room in a school on the road leading away from the airfield. The Squadron cooks had a field kitchen going and produced a delicious stew and tea, so we had our first hot food since leaving the *Glorious* almost forty-eight hours before. Everything was satisfactory and, when we had finished our meal, it was time to get ready for the first patrol over Narvik. The two pilots in my section, Lefevre and Bunker, and myself had a discussion on how we should play it. Jameson had wasted no time since his arrival the day before and had found out from 263 Squadron that the opposition was mostly Heinkel 111s and Ju 88s which bombed from 8-10,000 ft, so we decided to fly just below that height and about a couple of miles out in the fjord on the likely line of the enemy approach. We flew below the anticipated height of the enemy hoping to see them against the sky, since we certainly could see little against the dark background of the mountains. We checked our aircraft and were airborne in good time, to be over Narvik on schedule.

It was some fifty miles to Narvik, and when we arrived the bombarding cruisers were already in a semi-circle round the town. Shortly afterwards the bombardment commenced. By some trick of the light in the fjord the gun flashes had a greenish tinge. We kept a sharp lookout but no enemy aircraft appeared and an hour later we were relieved by the next section and returned to Bardufoss, landing at 21.00 hrs. There were no reports of enemy aircraft in the Operations Tent and, having checked that all was going well and that my next patrol was at 03.30 hrs, I went to my tent and fell asleep at once.

I was called at 02.00 hrs with a cup of boiling hot tea. The Duty Officer in the Operations Tent reported no enemy aircraft. All our patrols had been on time and uneventful; the later patrols had seen the assault go in and, as far as they could see, it had been successful. We were airborne again at 03.00 hrs and were soon near Narvik, taking over from the previous patrol. We had not been there long when we saw fog forming away to the east. Visibility was excellent at our altitude and we could see the fog spreading across the country towards Bardufoss. This created a problem. There was no ground radio at Bardufoss, not even airfield control, so we would have to make our own decision as to when to return. There was no alternative airfield. I watched the fog spreading and eventually waggled my wings (we were again on radio silence) and turned for base. When we got to Bardufoss the fog was almost up to the edge of the airfield and, within minutes of landing, visibility was zero. The next patrols were unable to take off and the fog lasted until 08.30 hrs when it dispersed quite quickly and we resumed patrols. We heard later that day that the only appearance of the Luftwaffe was during this break and that they had attacked the ships at Narvik hitting one, the cruiser *Cairo*. Maddening!

I was on patrol again shortly after 09.00 hrs and by this time we were all just about out on our feet. One section intercepted some Ju 88s and Jackie Lydall shot down 46 Squadron's first enemy aircraft on Norwegian soil. Later Jameson, Knight and Johnson caught two four-engined Dornier flying boats on the water in Rombaksfjord and sank both of them. At midday 263 Squadron took over and some very tired pilots fell into their tents and were soon fast asleep.

From then on operations settled down into some sort of pattern. I talked with 'Baldy' Donaldson, one of three flying Donaldson brothers and a man who certainly had his wits about him, on sharing the load between the two squadrons. They had lost one or two Gladiators in combat in addition to the aircraft that had crashed into the mountain in the fly-in from the *Furious*. They had learnt a lot in the weeks they had been at Bardufoss. With so few aircraft, it was impossible to maintain standing patrols throughout the twenty-four hours of daylight, as we had done over Narvik—which he agreed was a special case. The most likely targets were ships, Harstad, Tromsoe, Narvik and our airfield. Apparently very few orders came through from the Headquarters at Harstad—the Narvik assault cover was an exception—so Donaldson had tried to guess the time and place of German attacks and covered the targets as well as he could. This was not complete guesswork because, according to Donaldson, the Huns always followed the same route from their base at Trondheim, flying up the coast to the southernmost tip of the Lofoten Islands and then up Vestfjord before heading for whichever target area they had selected. What is more, the Norwegian coastguards were still manning a lighthouse 180 miles south, and reported the passage of these aircraft to Harstad who then repeated these messages to us at Bardufoss. Thus the element of guesswork was considerably reduced.

From experience, Donaldson had become quite expert in estimating the time of arrival of the Luftwaffe and covered the main targets on this basis. I was incredulous. Surely the enemy wouldn't use the same route every time? But Donaldson was emphatic. 263 had brought off several interceptions using this assumption. Later in the war, in other theatres, I was to recognise time and time again the German weakness of doing things from habit. Now, for want of anything better, I decided to use the 263 method. Though 46 never made a calculated interception, we and 263 managed to cover the main targets whenever enemy aircraft were reported coming up the coast. We shot down 13 unescorted enemy bombers in the next nine days and these successes can in some degree be attributed to the system worked out by Donaldson and 263 Squadron. Incidentally, I flew almost twice as many times as anybody else and never saw an enemy plane until the last morning, the first time I was to fire my guns.

Another thing Donaldson suggested was that we should patrol in pairs, rather than in sections of three aircraft. This was contrary to all Fighter Command practice at the time but, with so few aircraft and with so much daylight to cover, it was obviously sensible for reasons of economy and we adopted this formation soon afterwards.

With so few fighters on our side—never more than thirty odd against a Luftwaffe strength of approximately 300 (according to Intelligence) at Trondheim—our main aim was to prevent the uninterrupted bombing of the main targets in our area and, by spreading the resources of the two squadrons however thinly, we managed to achieve a fair degree of success in this. Few ships were sunk after the unlucky cruiser *Cairo* was damaged in the assault on Narvik. In this period 46 Squadron alone shot down 6 Ju 88s, 1 Fw 200 Condor (a four-engined bomber), 3 He 111s, 1 Ju 87 and sank two Dornier flying boats. Two of our pilots (Lydall and Banks) were killed and Drummond was shot down whilst attacking a Heinkel 111, but baled out and landed in his parachute in a fjord fortunately near one of our destroyers, HMS *Firedrake*, which quickly picked him up. This was very fortunate as survival in those icy waters was very rare. We had no news of him at first, so there was great joy when he walked into the Operations Tent two days later.

Someone discovered that the ground security for the airfield area was provided by the French Alpine Chasseurs and it seemed a good idea to invite them to supper. It was thought that, with our limited gastronomical resources, inviting them to a guest night dinner would be overstating things a bit. However our admirable sergeant cook said that he had a good line in tinned meat balls put by for just such an occasion and, what with one or two other things he had managed to obtain locally, he had no doubt that he could provide a spread worthy of the occasion. The three Chasseurs appeared in their dark blue uniforms and, despite not speaking a word of English between them and our French being of strictly fourth form variety, we had a wonderful evening.

Then, on 31 May, we were honoured with a visit by the Crown Prince of Norway, later King Olav. He was accompanied by Ole Reistadt, now Acting CO of the Royal Norwegian Air Force, whom I had known back in 1932 when he had been attached to 25 Squadron at Hawkinge. The Prince was keenly interested in our operations and also in the Hurricane, for he spent some time in the cockpit whilst Jameson explained it.

Unbeknown to me, a decision had already been made in London on 24 May to evacuate north Norway altogether as the result of the deteriorating situation in France. At the same time it was decided that, despite this decision, Narvik should be captured and the railway to Sweden and the iron ore plant destroyed. So, even before 46 Squadron had arrived in Norway, the decision to evacuate had been taken. Despite the fact that the concept of going to Norway in the first place was unsound, in retrospect one can only marvel at the high degree of security that kept this knowledge from the soldiers, sailors and airmen actually doing the fighting.

The six faces of Bing Cross, 1930-1940

1: Number 5 Short Service Officers' Course, April 1930;
2: C Flight, 3FTS, Grantham 1930;
3: 25 Squadron, Hawkinge 1933;
4: 44th Flying Instructors Course, CFS Wittering, 1935;
5: Cambridge University Air Squadron, Abingdon 1937;
6: 46 Squadron, April 1940.

Top: Family snap in front of 'The Poplars', 1915 - the first home I can remember.
Bottom left: My mother, Jean Boyd.
Bottom right: My father with Joyce and self - Southsea beach 1913.

Top left: With Uncle Jack, on leave from Chinese Maritime Customs, 1919. Jack has Joyce (left) and Baba on his knee and Jean is behind Baba.

Top right: D.G.Butler (Full back), Self (Wing 3/4) at Kingswood School.

Bottom: Avro-Trainer Mongoose - the actual aircraft I went solo on, 27 June 1930.

Top left: Qualified pilot at last! Hawkinge 1931.

Top right: Siskins flying over Hawkinge airfield, 1931. This was the first operational type that I flew. Note the airfield's name chalk in the foreground. Every airfield adopted the same method of displaying its name, a practice which ended in WWII.

Bottom left: Late-night reading in my room at Hawkinge.

Bottom right: Scoreboard at Sutton Bridge, 1931. My elevated position was not maintained!

Top left: From left to right F/O Douglas-Jones, Self, F/O Clouston - 25 Squadron 1932.

Top right: Snap of myself taken by F/O Clouston from the front seat of a Fairey Fox. The goggles weren't for decoration, I'd just lifted them up for the shot.

Middle: Final instructions by Squadron Leader A.L. Paxton, prior to take-off at Hendon 1933. From left to right: Hancock, Upton, Pearson, Self, Douglas-Jones, Blackwood, Clouston and Daunt.

Bottom: The complete 25 Squadron team take off for their display at Hendon 1933. My aircraft is third from the left.

OFFICIAL PROGRAMME

THE ARMY	REFEREE : Mr. R. J. JONES (Wales)	ROYAL AIR FORCE
15 Gent.-Cadet S. I. HOWARD-JONES *Royal Mil. Coll.*	**Full Backs**	15 *F.O. R. H. PRATT* *Odiham*
	Threequarters :	
11 Lieut. E. R. M. BOWERMAN *The East Yorks. Regt.*	L. Wing R. Wing	11 P.O. P. J. HALFORD *Odiham*
12 *Lieut. H. P. L. GLASS* *The Sherwood Foresters*	L. Centre R. Centre	12 P.O. A. V. ROGERS *Upper Heyford*
13 Lieut. R. LEYLAND *Army Educational Corps*	R. Centre L. Centre	13 F.Lt. K. B. B. CROSS (Captain) *Duxford*
14 Lieut. J. H. MARRIOTT *The Leicestershire Regt.*	R. Wing L. Wing	14 F.O. J. M. THOMPSON *North Weald*
	Half Backs :	
10 *Lieut. F. J. REYNOLDS* *The Duke of Wellington's Regt.*	Stand-off	10 P.O. W. G. MOSEBY *Abingdon*
9 Lieut. G. J. DEAN (Captain) *Royal Tank Corps*	Scrum	9 P.O. R. H. SPENCER *Upper Heyford*
8 Lieut. W. M. INGLIS *Royal Engineers*		8 P.O. H. D. JONES *Lee*
7 Lance Sergt. C. R. OWEN *The Welch Regt.*		7 Sergt. L. FOX *Felixstowe*
6 Sergt. A. T. BOAST *The Welsh Guards*		6 F.O. R. H. WATERHOUSE *Lee*
5 Lieut. H. J. SAYERS *Royal Artillery*		5 Cpl. C. W. SHEPPARD *Grantham*
4 Lieut. C. L. MELVILLE *The Black Watch*	Forwards	4 P.O. J. A. RONCORONI *Upper Heyford*
3 Lieut. J. H. H. WHITTY *Q.O.Royal West Kent Regt.*		3 Sergt. W. F. GASCOIGNE *Upper Heyford*
2 Lieut. G. TAYLOR *The West Yorkshire Regt.*		2 F.O. P. S. HUTCHINSON *Uxbridge*
1 Lieut. J. H. BOWMAN *The Coldstream Guards*		1 A.C.I. J. HOLLAND *Hendon*
* INTERNATIONAL		* INTERNATIONAL

Top: The RAF Rugby team to play the Army, 1936.
Left to right from back row: Craven, Reynolds, Sheppard, the legendary 'Jimmy' Lawson, Coslett, Self, Greaves; Holland, Thompson, Walker, Beamish (capt), Barker, Gascoigne, Ashton; Strong, White.

Bottom: An ambition achieved "to captain the RAF at Twickenham."
Saturday April 3, 1937.

Top left: The "one off" red Rover at Duxford 1937. Rover decided to make an open sports car and this was the prototype model. The production model was different so my car, purchased for £75, was totally unique.

Top right: Greenock, May 1940. Tests at Farnborough had shown that the flight deck of *Glorious* was too short for a Hurricane to land on. The aircraft were therefore hoisted aboard by crane.

Middle: Telegram from Philip Sassoon - Under Secretary of State for Air and a personal friend.

Bottom left: Narvik - June 1940. Note the snow, still deep and lying on the ground.

Bottom right: Bardufoss, Norway, May 1940: Hurricane Mk. I of 46 Squadron is standing in front of a wooden shelter. Aircraft seems to have the squadron letters "PO-M". Second aircraft is visible on the taxiway. The aircraft in the foreground is painted half white, half black underneath.

Top: HMS *Glorious*, too short for the Hurricanes to land on according to the test pilots - but we proved them wrong.

Bottom: Telegram sent from hospital on Thorshaven in the Faroe Islands to my parents.

CHAPTER VIII

EVACUATION

The first I knew of the decision to evacuate Norway altogether was on 3 June when Atcherley told me that we were to "thin down" the numbers of ground officers and airmen in the Squadron. So as not to alarm the Norwegian military and civilians this thinning down was to be done unobtrusively. The next day the first party of fifty left at 3 am under our Equipment Officer, Pilot Officer Westcott, and later that day a second party under the Medical Officer, Flight Lieutenant Peock, also departed.

With these departures it was no longer possible to conceal from the pilots what was to happen, and I called them together and told them of the decision to evacuate Norway altogether. As good professionals they showed no surprise or regret; they were accustomed to obeying orders however inexplicable. There was not, nor could be, any sorrow for the Norwegians left to their fate. We just had to get on with the job. Later, when the meeting was over and we were discussing the situation in the Low Countries and France, (news of the evacuation through Dunkirk was beginning to come in) several said that it seemed to be illogical to evacuate north Norway where we had been successful in capturing Narvik and pushing the Germans back up to the Swedish border, unlike France where we had been beaten. We were short of news about the defeats in France and quite unable to grasp the magnitude of the failure or its implications. We assumed we would continue to fight elsewhere in France, little realising that the complete collapse of France was only two weeks away, with the Petain/Weygand Government suing for peace on 16 June. At this stage we had no information as to how the Hurricanes and Gladiators of the two squadrons were to be disposed of. It seemed from talking to Atcherley that we would cover the evacuation by sea until the last moment and do our best to prevent attacks on the ships. This we understood—but what then?

Eventually, on the afternoon of 4 June, Group Captain Moore came over to Bardufoss in a Naval Walrus from Harstad and Atcherley, Baldy Donaldson and I met him on the runway. He said that 46 Squadron would be the last to leave; 263 Squadron would leave a few hours before us and would fly onto the *Glorious* which was once more operating off the coast. As for 46, there was a choice. We could fly to the extreme north of Norway to a landing ground called Lakselv (at the head of Porsangerfjord) on the coast where it was hoped to arrange for a tramp steamer to be positioned. We could then dismantle the Hurricanes and stow them in the tramp's hold. Alternatively, after the last patrols, we could burn the Hurricanes at Bardufoss. Needless to say, neither of these proposals appealed to me at all. The first was too far-fetched even to contemplate, and nobody seemed to know for certain where Lakselv was! Again, dismantling the aircraft without any ground equipment or cranes just wasn't on, even if we as pilots were capable of doing it, which was extremely doubtful. As for burning the Hurricanes, well really! I said at once, "What about us having a shot at landing on the *Glorious*?" Moore said, "I'd hoped you would say that, but what about the Air Ministry report that says it's impossible for a Hurricane to land on the deck?" I replied that taking off had proved to be much simpler than forecast and maybe landing would prove to be the same. "Right" answered Moore, "I will arrange for you to fly out to *Glorious* in a Walrus tomorrow to talk it over with the Navy."

I went back to the 46 Squadron dispersal area and told Jameson and Stewart what I had let the Squadron in for. Both were keen to try the landing and Jameson, who had clearly anticipated this possibility, said, "Might it not be a good idea to put some ballast in the tail bay of the fuselage so that we can use more brake than normal?" This was obviously a sensible move because our Hurricanes were slightly nose heavy anyway, as the result of being fitted with metal three-bladed, variable-pitch propellors which were heavier than the wooden two-bladed propellors that had been standard when the Hurricane entered the service. I asked him to do some trials on the runway as soon as possible. Pat did his trials and came to the conclusion that a fourteen-pound sandbag in the tail bay was about the heaviest that we could take and still keep the aeroplane reasonably manageable in normal flight. So we settled for that.

I then called all the pilots together in the Operations Tent and told them what the proposal was and asked for volunteers to try and land on the carrier. They all volunteered, so it was decided on seniority in the Squadron, which meant that two of the Sergeant Pilots, Shackley and Taylor, were included in the ten pilots required. We were down to ten aircraft by this time: we had lost two aircraft at Skaanland, three shot down by the enemy in combat, and another three were damaged, unrepairable in Norway. Next day, the Walrus arrived flown by a Naval pilot but with a Wing Commander Keary aboard. I had met him before and knew he was Fleet Air Arm trained. He said that the *Ark Royal* was also off the coast with the *Glorious* and that we would go to her after we had been to *Glorious*. So off we went at a cruising speed of 80 knots.

It took us about an hour and a half before we saw the flashing lights of the two carriers, which were about one hundred miles from the coast. When we were overhead I had a good look at the two decks. The *Ark Royal's* was the longer, but both looked microscopic to me. We got the OK to land from the *Glorious* and the Walrus with its low landing speed came on like a bird. We were met by Lieutenant Commander W H Parkin whom I remembered as Commander Heath's deputy on our trip out. We went straight to the bridge and saw the Captain.

D'Oyly-Hughes was surprisingly cheerful, knew about the proposal for us to try to land on, and seemed to think nothing of it. I explained the need for three Hurricanes to come out in advance of the main party so as to spread the load if it proved to be a difficult process. He accepted this and agreed a signal should be sent to Bardufoss signifying success or failure. When we left the bridge I asked Parkin where 'Wings' Heath was. He was evasive and I still didn't know what had happened to Heath when we left the ship to fly over to the *Ark Royal*, landing easily on what was a very long deck compared with that of the *Glorious*.

We went straight to the 'island', that is to say the superstructure on the port side of the ship, and at once I couldn't help noticing the cheerful bustling activity of all ranks manning this modern carrier. It was in stark contrast to that of the carrier we had just left. The Captain and 'Wings' of the *Ark Royal* seemed to know all about our operation and were full of encouragement. "If you can't get down on the *Glorious*, come over here" the Captain said, "we have a hundred feet more deck and, though our lifts won't take you (they were built for aeroplanes with folding wings), we'll saw off your wings and save the fuselages anyway." It was most encouraging to me to experience such enthusiasm, and I felt a lot happier as I flew back to Bardufoss.

The next day we got our precise orders. We were to cover the evacuation points with 263 Squadron during the day. By 00.15 hrs on 8 June, 263 would leave. We would leave half an hour later at 00.45. Swordfish would be overhead at these times to lead us to the *Glorious* whose position was not divulged to us ashore. Our ground troops would be further reduced during the day leaving just enough to see us off after midnight. All this would of course, take place in broad daylight. We were also told that all petrol stocks were to be destroyed during the day, and that when we left shortly after midnight our rear party was to help in blowing holes in the runway.

7 June started early for me. I was asleep in my tent when I was awakened by the sound of a Hurricane section taking off. It was just 3 am and I thought this was rather early for the Germans, and wondered whether the enemy had at last got wind of the evacuation. I got up, put my flying overalls over my pyjamas and walked over to the Operations Tent. Mee was the Duty Operations Officer and I asked him what the flap was all about. "Enemy aircraft reported in the area", he said, "and the Readiness Section has gone to cover Harstad". "Right, I'll do the next Readiness, call Pete Lefevre."

Lefevre was my number two at this time and he joined me as I walked over to my aircraft. I told Pete what I knew and we got aboard and taxied down the runway to the take-off end. When we got there and turned to be ready for take-off, I was alarmed to see a formation of 4 He 111s in a shallow dive for the airfield and only a few miles away. Pete saw them at almost the same time and, slamming the hood shut, I opened up to full throttle and took off straight towards the approaching enemy aircraft. As we became airborne, the Heinkels turned away to the south and started to climb. I put the firing button on 'Fire', switched on the reflector sight and turned after them with Pete close behind me. We were about a thousand feet below and, despite full throttle, it seemed an age before we reached their altitude.

The enemy had tightened his formation a bit and I selected the starboard aircraft. Pete was on my left in a good position to engage one of the others. As I got within range I fired and immediately my target's undercarriage dropped down and his starboard engine started smoking. Almost simultaneously the perspex on the port side of my windscreen disintegrated and smoke filled the cockpit. I turned away quickly, cursing inwardly that I had been too deliberate in my attack and had been hit by the rear gunners of the Heinkels. I opened the hood and the smoke cleared a bit. A quick look round the cockpit showed me I had no oil pressure and already the coolant temperature gauge was going off the clock. There was nothing for it but to try to get back to the airfield. I was able from the height we had climbed, 4,000 ft, to glide back and, thank goodness, the undercarriage came down when selected so I landed safely. I ran gently off the runway and cut the switches.

As I got out of the cockpit my ground crew came running up and we went round the Hurricane together. I had been hit in the port oil tank, which was blown to pieces, and also in the radiator. The bullet that had hit the side of the perspex of the windscreen had gone through the armour plate directly behind where my head would have been, if I had been strapped in. Luckily, because of the hurry on take-off, I had been unable to do up the straps and had been crouching forward over the control column to steady myself. A narrow escape. Corporal Willers, one of the Armament NCOs and who is still alive today, found the strengthened core of this bullet and recorded the incident in a personal diary he was keeping.

It was still only 4 am when I completed my examination of the Hurricane. Warrant Officer Simpson was confident that it could be repaired in a few hours which was fortunate because, being our last day in Norway, we anticipated it might be very busy and that all the ten aircraft we had left would be required. In the event, this last day was no different from the rest with only light enemy air activity. In the evening Mee and Drummond, on patrol over Narvik, engaged 4 He 111s and claimed two shot down and two damaged. Jameson, their Flight Commander, thought that this was an exaggeration. I detailed Jameson to take out the first three Hurricanes to the *Glorious* at 6 pm. He was by far the best pilot in the Squadron and everyone had confidence in his judgement. If he and his section landed successfully, I told him that I had arranged for the Captain to send us a signal.

Dead on 6 pm, a Swordfish appeared over Bardufoss and Jameson, Knight and Taylor, who were waiting in their cockpits, took off and followed the Swordfish westwards. By midnight the majority of our ground troops had left and those looking after our seven Hurricanes had their kit packed and by them at the end of the runway. They were limited to what each man could carry. They were to go to a nearby fjord as soon as we departed to embark in a destroyer. Corporal Willers gives the following account in his diary:

> "After having seen the aircraft take off, the runway was blown up. I thought we had to flee to Sweden when the pilots left. We left Bardufoss in a lorry bound for Sorreisa. The lorry stopped half a mile past the jetty and was destroyed, whilst we marched back and embarked on a Norwegian fishing vessel (*Puffer*). Later we were met by a destroyer, D27/HMS *Walker*, and climbed a ladder on to its deck. A couple of minutes later the air raid warning sounded and we were packed below so tightly that we had to leave the rifles on deck. The destroyer made 28 knots and, at 09.00 hrs, we were transferred to the troopship *Andora Star* and sailed in Group 2, the last convoy to leave Norway".

No signal came from Jameson but at forty-five minutes past midnight the faithful Swordfish appeared over Bardufoss. We seven, Cross, Stewart, Mee, Cowles, Frost, Bunker and Shackley, were all sitting in our cockpits ready and, signal or no signal, there was nothing to do but go! Dick Atcherley appeared at the last moment to wish me good luck and then we were off.

Keeping behind the Swordfish was a problem. It was cruising at 90 knots and we had to remain in fine pitch and put down 20 degrees of flap to go slowly enough. Even then we had to tack from side to side. We crossed the mountains for the last time and headed out to sea. Normally, flying over the sea in a single-engined aircraft was not a pastime I enjoyed but this was different; the sea belonged to us, whereas the land we had just left would shortly be in enemy hands. We were going home *and* with our aircraft. The sea looked friendly this time. After about an hour's flying we saw the flashing lights and a few minutes later were overhead the *Glorious*. The *Ark Royal* was comfortably close on the port side. I got a green light from the *Glorious* and started my approach.

We had discussed many times amongst ourselves, and with the naval pilots, the method of approach and landing. There were no batmen in those days to indicate that the approach was too high or too low. Everything was left to the judgement of the pilot. I believe each individual pilot in 46 Squadron had decided just how he would do it, but kept his method to himself. I decided that the classic approach, a fairly steep glide with the minimum of engine, required the fine judgement that I did not possess as a novice in this area. I settled for what the Fleet Air Arm pilots called a "round down crawler", not the most elegant way of approaching the flight deck but in my opinion easier to judge. It meant making the approach slightly below the level of the deck and then, with a burst of engine, lifting the aircraft over the 'round down' onto the extreme rear end of the deck, which ensured the maximum length of deck for braking. This I did, arriving with a thump almost tail first on the deck. I applied full brakes just as soon as I had slowed a little and came to a halt not more than two thirds of the way up the deck.

I found out afterwards that thumping the tail on the deck had broken the tail wheel strut, but I was assured that the Navy would have no difficulty in repairing that. I was waved forward to the front lift, cut the engine and the Hurricane was being lowered into the hangar before I could get out of the cockpit. My aircraft was parked with the three that had already landed and the 263 Gladiators behind them. It was all smiles amongst the ratings in the hangar as I hurried up on deck to see the arrival of the others. All came on safely though one required two attempts. I went up to the bridge to report to the Captain who was pleased but said we had taken rather a long time to complete the manoeuvre! Captain Guy D'Oyly-Hughes true to form. Anyway shortly afterwards we got a signal from Vice-Admiral Wells (commander of both carriers, but flying his flag in the *Ark Royal*) which read: "Manoeuvre well executed"—so he at least appreciated our endeavours!

Pat Jameson appeared from below rubbing the sleep from his eyes, —it was after all four o'clock in the morning. He said he had sent a signal and was surprised and disconsolate when I told him it had not arrived. We all went below to the wardroom for hot cocoa. Only then did we realise how tired we were: indeed it was more than twenty-four hours since we last slept. We found out where we were sleeping and turned in. It was 4.30 am on 8 June.

I woke at three o'clock in the afternoon and, having removed two days' growth of beard, went up to the flight deck and forward to the 'island'. I went first to the plot room located immediately below the Bridge and realised then that we were not the only tired ones. Except for those actually on watch, most were catnapping wherever they could stow themselves. I had a look at the chart and a word with the Duty Navigator. Our track was a straight one from a point 150 miles west of the northern tip of the Lofoten Islands to Scapa Flow. I was told that we could not sail further west (and so avoid the danger of attack by German bombers based at Trondheim) because of a shortage of fuel. This was not true, but of course I had no way of knowing this at the time. I was very concerned. True, the *Glorious* had her own Gladiator fighters but we had an escort of only two destroyers, *Ardent* and *Acasta*, and the *Ark Royal* was no longer with us as she had gone with the main convoy to the Firth of Clyde.

I asked the Duty Navigator about the ship's air patrols and was astonished to learn that none were being flown. This surprised me because on the way out, when Heath was in charge of flying, we had always had one Swordfish patrolling over the horizon ahead of the ship and another on close anti-submarine patrol within visibility distance. The Duty Navigator must have sensed my surprise because he said "there is no need for an anti-submarine patrol because no sub could position to hit us at the speed we are travelling -17 knots". I left the plot soon afterwards reflecting that the Navy probably knew their business best, but wishing we had a bit more sea between us and the Norwegian coast.

I went below and saw one or two of my pilots in the wardroom; the others were still sleeping. We had no duties in the *Glorious*, and hence there was no point in disturbing them, so I went for some tea.

I suppose the time was about 4 pm. I had hardly started tea when "Action Stations" sounded over the ship's public address system and the wardroom emptied in a rush. I assumed that this was another of the many practices such as we had participated in on the way out and, because I had been allotted no Action Station, went to my 'Abandon Ship' Station on the quarter deck. As I passed my cabin I remembered how cold it could be standing about on deck and put on my fleece-lined Irvine jacket and, for some reason I can't recall, took a file containing the Squadron's flying and operational records and my logbook and stuck them inside my jacket. It a was only a matter of seconds before I was on the quarter deck.

There was the usual bustle of the ship going to 'Action Stations' but those on the quarter deck were staring at a couple of patches of smoke on the horizon astern of us. Just then, three columns of water appeared in the sea about forty yards away on our starboard quarter and I realised that this was no practice. I had a nasty sinking feeling in the pit of my stomach due as much as anything to the uncertainty of the whole business. As a professional airman, almost every situation one was likely to be involved in had at least been imagined and the corollary, the action to be taken and one's part in it, became second nature. But this was entirely different; here we were in action and me with no part to play. There was nothing to do and so nothing to take my mind off the apprehension I felt. It was no good worrying or standing about on the quarter deck, so I decided to go up to the bridge to see how things were being handled from there.

I noticed as I left that only one destroyer was now with us and she was making smoke on the port side. I learned afterwards that the other destroyer, the *Ardent*, had been ordered to investigate the smoke when it first appeared and had already been sunk. The *Acasta* continued to put down a smoke screen between the *Glorious* and one enemy ship but, as they were now positioned one on each stern quarter, the screen was only half effective. I climbed the stairs from the quarter deck level on the outside of the starboard side of the ship. As I stepped on to the flight deck there was a crash and a hole appeared in the metal deck about fifteen feet from me. Looking back I saw that the stairs I had just stepped off were now a mass of twisted metal. Not so good. The superstition that "everything happens in threes" crossed my mind. First there had been that bullet through the armour plate where my head should have been, and now this narrow escape. What would the third be? I walked forward to the island. The Swordfish were being raised from the upper hangar with every indication of haste.

When I got to the island, I realised that all was not under control as I had assumed. There was nothing but tense faces staring at the smoke patches on the horizon. I decided that I would only be in the way up here on the bridge so I walked across the flight deck to the undamaged stairs on the port side to make my way back to the quarter deck. As I passed the Swordfish now ranged on deck I saw that they were armed with anti-submarine bombs which were being hastily removed, whilst torpedoes on their trolleys were being brought up on the forward lift. I passed Bertie Knight, the quiet one in the Squadron, calmly sucking an empty pipe as he watched the horizon. We grinned at each other as I passed. Bertie was the only one in the Squadron that I saw during the action.

The bombardment continued. As I went down the stairs there was a crash and then another, as I stepped on to the quarter deck. The public address system was now out of action and someone said that the bridge and the wireless flat had been hit. I had escaped again by not staying on the bridge. Later I heard that D'Oyly-Hughes had been killed by this salvo, and that Commander Lovell was now in command.

The quarter deck in the *Glorious* was at the extreme stern of the ship and the lowest deck level, about ten feet above the sea. I could see the flashes on the horizon and moments later would come the crash. The noise on impact was a great tearing sound like the tearing of calico many thousands of times magnified. Soon the hangars were on fire, and a passing naval pilot said, "Bad luck, your Hurricanes got it with the first salvo". The built-in drenching apparatus put out the fire in the hangar but, at about this time, the ship began to list to starboard, and this was accentuated by the violent zig-zag which we had been doing since the action started. We were still going quite fast and I feared she might roll over.

How long this went on I have no idea. No aircraft were able to take off from the ship. The crews of the anti-aircraft guns stood by their weapons but the enemy was never within range. It was just a matter of 'taking it' with no reply possible. The small arms ammunition in the Swordfish began to explode on the flight deck and every now and then there were those rending explosions as another salvo hit. And yet I recall vividly the calm, business-like conduct of the crew during what were obviously the final minutes of most of their lives. Crashes and explosions were now continual with fires raging out of control and billowing clouds of black smoke enveloping the carrier. The PA system had long ceased to function and the word to abandon ship was passed from man to man.

Now, from all parts of the ship, carley floats began to be launched. These were rather like inflatable aircraft crew dinghies, except that they were larger and the buoyancy part was of metal. They were oval in shape and the centre was a wooden grid secured to the buoyancy by rope. Soon there was a trail of the floats and other wreckage for some way behind the ship. There was no panic at any time, but sailors began to jump into the sea from the flight deck, a drop of some fifty feet. I saw few wounded during the action and I suppose that this was because I was at the extreme end of the ship and not being hit. Nevertheless, I thought it was about time I left.

I enquired of my naval friend 'Ginger' Marmont who was standing nearby if there were any special points to be observed in abandoning ship. He replied: "No, nothing special—except that it'll pay to jump pretty soon after a float gets dropped or you'll be facing a long swim because the ship's still doing a fair speed." I thanked him and removed my shoes. As the next carley float went over the side I jumped. I hardly went under at all, so effective was the Mae West I had on, and in a few strokes I reached the float and hauled myself aboard. I was one of the first in the float and one by one others joined, and then great joy, who should come swimming along using an impeccable New Zealand crawl but Pat Jameson! "Permission to come aboard, Sir" he called and I replied, "Certainly, Jameson." He did so and then almost at once plunged back into the sea to grab hold of a young marine he knew as Geordie who had been struck on the head by a raft as soon as he jumped. Pat had spotted Geordie struggling some 20 yards away and towed him to the carley. At the same time, he retrieved a floating oar which he thought might come in handy.

It is difficult to estimate from sea level, but the *Glorious* seemed to stop about a mile away with a heavy list to starboard and then the two enormous German ships, which we now know were the *Scharnhorst* and *Gneisenau*, came past quite close to us. I thought they would be certain to pick us up so I threw my file of squadron records and my logbook into the sea. Alas, I need not have worried about security. The German ships didn't stop and, having passed us, turned away and were soon out of sight. I did not see the *Glorious* actually sink as I had my back to her at the time. Our hopes were now pinned on the remaining destroyer, the *Acasta*, which was in sight but soon afterwards disappeared. We know now that she was sunk after gallantly attacking and hitting the *Scharnhorst* with a torpedo.

So now there were no ships, either of our own or the enemy. All around there were carley floats, rafts and wreckage with figures clinging to them. The sea was rough and very cold—we were after all about 100 miles inside the Arctic Circle. We had thirty-seven on our float but they began to die one by one within a few hours.

Strangely, it was some of those who looked physically toughest who went first. A stoker, partially unclothed, gradually became unconscious and slipped into the well of the float. We held his head above the water but he died soon afterwards. There was nothing for it but to push him over the side. This sad proceeding was repeated at intervals. Men would slide into the well, we would then pick them up and push them over the side. Again and again. Most of the deaths took place in the first few hours, due rather more to people giving up hope than to wounds or lack of clothing. Owing to the perpetual daylight we had no idea of the passage of time, but periodically it got colder and we assumed that this was night. It was real misery and the rough sea and wind meant we were constantly wet through and very cold. Our companions continued to die and after some time I said to Pat: "How long do you think we can stick this?" He thought for a moment and then said "About four days". Considering that half our complement had died already in hours rather than days, I thought it was a rather optimistic estimate, but it was to be this prognostication that kept me going!

One man dozed off and fell backwards into the water. Being unable to swim, he panicked and his wild thrashing carried him further from the float. Pat wanted to go after him, but I dissuaded him. Those still in the float were by now too weak to pull two men aboard and though Pat agreed, it was terrible to hear the man's last despairing cries. Later, another man slid over the side, but Pat grabbed him just before he was swept out of arm's reach. He struggled violently, fearing that those aboard did not wish to save him. Pat spoke to him sharply, then slapped him hard across the face. He relaxed and we were able to haul him back into the float.

Some time later the wind began to drop and the seas became less rough, and this improvement continued until we were in a flat calm which remained for the rest of the time we were on the float. Sadly only seven now remained, and surprisingly one was Geordie, the marine, who had nothing to keep him warm but his tunic. Our party now consisted of Geordie, a Warrant Officer RN, three sailors, Jameson and myself. There was now plenty of room, but the snag with the carley float was the wooden grid, so rigged that, with our feet on it, it was permanently under water. So our feet had already been under water for some hours. I suggested to Pat that if we could cut out the grid and place it the narrow way across the oval of the buoyancy tank, then at least we could keep our feet out of the water. Pat thought this was a good idea and produced a penknife from his pocket. The rest agreed with the suggestion and we took it in turns to saw away at the ropes holding the grid in position. It was slow work, with some of it under water, but eventually the grid was free and we hoisted it up and placed it athwartships instead of fore and aft. The party split, four on one side and three on the other. Someone thought we ought to have a mast and so we set up the oar Pat had found and tied a shirt to it as a sail.

There was no food or water in the carley float and we all got very thirsty. The Warrant Officer produced from his pocket a small Oxo tin full of brown sugar which was passed round, each of us taking a pinch. We organised a watch order which ensured that one of us was always on look-out. The sky was covered the whole time with high grey clouds, and we heard the sound of high flying aircraft several times. There was some discussion on how long it would be before we would be rescued, and it was thought that it would take some time for the Navy to come to us from Scapa. Once, on the far distant horizon, we saw what we thought were ships and aircraft searching for us but, if they were, they were looking the wrong way for not long afterwards the horizon was empty again.

We didn't talk much. With the exception of the one on watch, we tried to sleep. Jameson in particular had no difficulty in this. He had always been a bit of a dormouse, curling up and going to sleep wherever he was and had time to kill, whether it was the crew room, at dispersal, or in the back of a car. I envied him, he had obviously made up his mind that there were at least four days to go and so what better way was there of passing the time than sleeping? I had, and maintained, a strong feeling that we would be picked up eventually. Surely three ships, the *Glorious*, *Ardent* and *Acasta*, couldn't have disappeared without one of them transmitting a sighting report and our position? Anyway, I had an 'automatic' belief in God, as many did in those days, and I was also sure that he had us under surveillance and, if we could stick it out and thus do our part, he would see that everything would be alright in the end.

On one occasion when everyone was awake we had a discussion about the progress of the float. Having tied a shirt to the mast we had rigged, it was plain that we were moving, however slowly. One of the sailors was adamant that, though it might take a long time, we were bound to get somewhere. Nobody disagreed with him. It was the thirst that was our main problem. One of the sailors tried seawater which didn't seem to help much, and for which he was to pay later. I had a bone collar stud which I sucked most of the time— at least it kept my mouth moist. The glassy nature of the sea which had come with the flat calm meant that we could see a long way down through the centre hole of the float. I was contemplating the depths during my watch period whilst busily sucking my stud when, carelessly, I let it fall out of my mouth into the water, and I could see it descending fathom after fathom. I let out a curse and woke the whole float up. I explained the reason for my agitation whereupon the Warrant Officer said, "I shouldn't worry Sir, they don't bother much how you are dressed in these circumstances!"

Then, one day when hope was drifting away, I was on watch when one of the sailors on the other side of the float pointed behind me and said quite quietly, "there's a ship". I looked round and sure enough one, two or even three miles away was a ship. Everyone woke up, some stood up holding onto the shoulders of those sitting. We all began to shout until we realised that we couldn't possibly be heard. Then all was silence, with all eyes on the ship. She was either approaching us or going away because most of the time the masts were in line. When they weren't, we watched with unspoken anxiety. But gradually she got larger and then came the ecstatic moment when she was so near that we knew she must have seen us. We all started shouting our heads off again and waving anything we could lay our hands on. We forgot entirely our thirst and the pain in our feet. At last she stopped right by us, a rope was thrown, seized and we were pulled alongside where a rope ladder was hanging. I seem to remember that I was first up and was grabbed by willing hands at the top. Soon we were all aboard and led away to resting places. The day turned out to be Tuesday, 11 June and the time was about 3.15 pm, so seventy hours had passed since the *Glorious* went down about 5.30 pm on Saturday, 8 June. All seven of us had survived, though one died later in hospital of gangrene.

The ship was the SS *Borgund*, a small Norwegian fishing vessel of some seven hundred tons. She was making for the Faroe Islands having left Tromsoe when the Allies evacuated the place. I found this out later, but in the meantime Pat and I were led down to the engine room where it was warm. All accommodation was already packed with survivors, for the *Borgund* had sailed right through the area where those remaining from the three ships were drifting. Once below, reaction set in. We both felt so weak. I was given the metal work bench to lie on, which was much too small to stretch out and the vice was in the middle of my back, but I have never been more comfortable. Pat lay on the metal grill over the big-end. The Norwegian engineer understood our needs perfectly. It was water, water and more water. He had a little metal mug the size of a teacup which he filled about half full and would then hold to our lips for a sip or two. He had no English but when we indicated we wanted more, much more, he shook his head slowly, and nothing would move him. He rationed us to a few sips every half hour or so. Some of the others drank too much, too soon, and made themselves quite ill.

We were forty-eight hours in the *Borgund* and, on the second day, I was moved to a bunk in a cabin at deck level. We had recovered pretty well in twenty-four hours except for our feet which were agony. I think we had a sort of mixture of frostbite and 'trench feet' from having them in the water for such a long time. The Captain, a large taciturn man who spoke a little English, came to see me. He said gloomily that we had just been reconnoitred by a German aeroplane, "and in a few hours" he added, "we shall be attacked". I listened but was beyond caring. He said he had forty-one survivors aboard.

We weren't attacked and, on the following day, we reached the Faroes and entered the harbour at Thorshavn. Shortly after tying up to the quay, ambulances appeared and we were put on stretchers to be taken up to the hospital which overlooked the harbour. We were put to bed and looked after like royalty by delightful fairheaded Danish nurses. One of our seven died en route to Thorshavn and another died in hospital there. But the rest of us improved rapidly, except that our feet got worse rather than better. The doctors did their best but said there wasn't much they could do. They were confident that our feet would recover but it was matter of time. The doctors could speak English and were very pessimistic about the news from France. "France is beaten, England's turn next", they said. "Don't you believe it", we replied, "You'll see". Most of the staff in the hospital spoke pretty good English, and we were glad to hear after a couple of days in the hospital that we were to be taken to Rosyth in a destroyer but, in the meantime, we had a touching visit from the old Captain of the *Borgund*. He didn't know what the future held for himself or his ship, but he was happy that we were safe.

On 15 June we were given some new clothes and taken down to the harbour in ambulances to be put aboard HMS *Veteran*, the ship of Commander J E (Jacky) Broome, a remarkable man in any company. He met us at the gangway dressed in a pair of flannel trousers that had seen better days, an old uniform jacket over a roll-necked sweater, and plimsoles. He gave us a cheerful welcome and soon we were tucked up in bunks below. It was plain that the *Veteran* was a happy ship. From the Captain down to the stewards all were happy and cheerful; the latter couldn't do enough for us, though they explained that they were short on variety in their rations as they had been at sea for some days and had been unable to buy much in Thorshavn. We couldn't have minded less, we were amongst our own people again and on our way home. I discovered that there were five officer survivors all from the *Glorious*: Lt Cdr Rupert Hill, a tea planter from Ceylon and a Naval reservist who had returned to the

Colours; Sub Lt I V MacLachlan and Mdspm (A) E Baldwin, both Fleet Air Arm aircrew from 825 Swordfish Squadron, and Jameson and myself.

The next day the ship's doctor thought it would be good for us to spend some time on deck in the sunshine and so we were carried up. The *Veteran* was escorting a small convoy of Norwegian ships and submarines down to the Firth of Forth. We were off the coast of Scotland when an RAF Sunderland appeared and circled the convoy. We saw that the bridge was having an aldis lamp conversation with the flying boat and then Commander Broome came down to where we were sitting and said, "I told him I had Air Force survivors from the *Glorious* aboard, and would he watch the convoy whilst I go and get some fish for them—and he has agreed willingly". The *Veteran* had by now turned at right angles to the convoy and was off at speed towards a trawler a few miles away. The Commander produced some pound notes. Apparently the trawler's skipper refused to take any payment.

We arrived at Rosyth on 18 June, and were told we were to go to the Gleneagles Hotel. As a golfer I knew of this superb place in Perth, with its two lovely courses and its four-star hotel. Though we were in considerable pain, the thought of bright lights and cocktail bars cheered us up a lot. We said goodbye to the ratings and we, the five surviving officers, went off by ambulance to Gleneagles. Alas, when we arrived we found that the hotel had been turned into a military hospital: no bars, cocktail or otherwise. The five of us were put into a small ward on our own. Everyone was very kind to us but there was not much anyone could do. As in the hospital in the Faroes, we were told that time would be the cure. However, the doctors did relent a bit when the pain was at its worst and we were given morphia injections which helped us sleep.

As we slowly got better we discussed endlessly the reasons for the loss of the *Glorious*, and the failure to rescue the survivors once the ship and the two destroyers had been sunk. We were agreed that not having a Swordfish patrol over the horizon was the reason why the *Scharnhorst* and *Gneisenau* had surprised us. For this omission Captain D'Oyly-Hughes must bear the responsibility. Captain S W Roskill, an official historian, wrote in *The War at Sea*, vol. 1 (HMSO, London, 1954) p. 195: "it seems strange that no patrols were flown at this time for her own protection, nor a striking force kept prepared", speculating that the reason for this failure was that "she had, in the small hours of the previous morning, successfuly completed the *difficult* task (my italics) of flying on the last of the shore-based Royal Air Force Hurricanes and Gladiators—none of whose pilots had ever before made a deck landing". This is really no excuse at all. The task was not difficult for the *Glorious* and its officers and crew. The ship had only to be turned a few degrees into the prevailing wind and speed increased a bit—the Gladiator and Hurricane pilots did the rest. Nor can the accommodation of 10 Gladiators and 10 Hurricanes have impeded the operation of the naval aircraft. Our twenty aircraft still left space for twenty-five others. The truth is that the captain believed that the only threat came from submarines and that, at seventeen knots, we were invulnerable to this type of attack. Jameson and I came to the conclusion that D'Oyly-Hughes's concept of how the ship's aircraft should be used was very different from John Heath's. Flying patrols was an elementary precaution and one that had previously been routine.

Captain Roskill went on to say that the *Glorious* had been ordered to proceed home independently because she was low on fuel and therefore obliged to run direct and lightly escorted for Scapa Flow. This is not true, as Roskill later learned. He published his revised version in *The Sunday Times*, London, on 15 June 1980. The true reason why the *Glorious* was caught virtually alone is that Vice-Admiral Wells gave D'Oyly-Hughes permission to go ahead for no better reason than to begin court martial proceedings as soon as possible against John Heath. I knew that D'Oyly-Hughes's relations with Heath were poor, but I did not know they had become so bad that D'Oyly-Hughes put him ashore at Scapa Flow to await a court martial before sailing north on his last voyage. Consequently, Heath avoided the disaster that would almost certainly have cost him his life and we would meet again in West Africa (see Chapter X).

The other topic we discussed at length was why no help arrived to pick up the hundreds of survivors on rafts and carley floats after the *Glorious*, *Ardent* and *Acasta* had been sunk. Even taking into account that the wireless flat in the *Glorious* had been destroyed early on in the engagement, surely some message must have been transmitted by one of the ships in the interval of more than an hour between first sighting and all three being sunk. Captain Roskill wrote that the *Glorious* did broadcast a message and that it was received by Admiral Cunningham in the cruiser *Devonshire*, some 100 miles to the west. It used to be said that this signal was received only in a "garbled" form as a "cryptic whisper". But that is not true. Cunningham decided, ruthlessly but realistically, that the risk of further loss outweighed the benefit of a rescue attempt. Later, when it was learned that the German ships had gone into Trondheim, efforts were made to find survivors. Aircraft from the *Ark Royal* searched the area, but saw nothing. The Germans left us to our fate because they believed that the torpedo which badly damaged the *Scharnhorst* had been fired by a submarine and preferred not to offer it any sitting targets. In fact, the torpedo came from the *Acasta* just before she went down. In September 1972 a letter appeared in the correspondence columns of the *Daily Telegraph* giving particulars of the passengers and cargo embarked in HMS *Devonshire* and also, in a final paragraph, said: "A few hours after leaving Tromsoe we intercepted the very last radio enemy report from the aircraft carrier HMS *Glorious*". The letter was signed "T T Jenkins, Newport, Mon." I saw this letter and wrote to Mr Jenkins who, in 1940, had been a Petty Officer Telegraphist in the remote control office on the bridge of the *Devonshire*. He was an experienced man of some nine years' service. I asked him, "was the description given in the official history of a 'cryptic whisper' and a 'garbled message' accurate?" He replied, "One of my operators called out and he and I read the enemy report from the *Glorious*. It was a full enemy report prefaced 'Most Immediate'. The report gave bearing, position, course, speed and time of origin". Jenkins continued, "It was transmitted in clear and, when repeating it for the second time, the transmission ceased abruptly. I realised she had been hit".

Jenkins was quite categoric about this message: "as an experienced operator I can assure you two of us did not dream up this report. I knew that the *Glorious* was evacuating RAF from the Harstad area, that she had two 'A' Class destroyers as escort which were sunk. The position given in the report was plotted on the *Devonshire*'s chart because I saw it done and, immediately afterwards, Admiral Cunningham and his Flag Lieutenant came in to the RCO and took the Operator's Log and all copies of the signal. Neither questioned the accuracy of the signal".

It is now known that a signal was also picked up by a duty officer in the Admiralty's Operational Intelligence Centre. He failed to realise its significance because, in the interests of secrecy, he had not been informed that British ships were in that area. No doubt many more of us could have survived if other ships had been risked sooner in the area. But the fact remains that the *Glorious* and her gallant escorts should not have been in those waters and given that they were, they should not have been caught by surprise. Altogether, only 45 of the 1,474 men aboard the three British ships survived and so I must regard my life since June 1940 as a rare bonus.

The doctors were right about time being the only cure for our feet. We were mobile in wheel chairs after a while, and then were walking with sticks. Hill, the old warrior, discovered that the bar in the Golf Club was still functioning at lunchtime and, by careful planning and organisation, managed to visit it most days without the staff finding out. We were visited by the Flight Commanders of 263 Squadron, Flight Lieutenants Mills and Caesar Hull. Both had escaped the trip home in the *Glorious* because of injuries that had necessitated an early return to England. Their squadron was reforming for the second time at Drem airfield near Edinburgh. We also heard that 46 Squadron was reforming at our home airfield, Digby. Out of the twenty-three pilots that left Digby in May, two—Lydall and Banks—had been killed in combat in Norway, and eight—Stewart, Cowles, Frost, Knight, Mee, Bunker, Schackley and Taylor—were lost in the the *Glorious*. Jameson and I were unserviceable at Gleneagles, so only eleven of the most junior pilots were left to help in reforming the Squadron. Of these eleven, five survived the war.

We were six weeks in Gleneagles Hospital before being released on sick leave on 1 August. Our feet were better but we still could not wear shoes. Carpet slippers were the most we could bear and these, with a couple of sticks, made us fairly mobile. We went down by train to Grantham where a car awaited to take us to Digby. I only stayed one night for there were too many ghosts, and then went off home to Hayling Island. My mother and father fussed around a bit and I sat on the lawn in the sunshine, watching the aerial battles going on overhead. We were now some four weeks into the Battle of Britain and the sight of the Hurricanes from nearby Tangmere going out to sea made me very restless.

Slowly, as the feet got better, I could put enough pressure on them to drive a car, and got my Riley out of store. The doctors had told me to report to the Central Medical Establishent at the end of August, but the urge to get back into the swim became overwhelming. I went on 16 August over to Tangmere where I had many friends and spent a sunny morning catching up on the war. I was just leaving at lunchtime to go over to the satellite airfield, Westhampnett, when the alarm went and a shower of Ju 87s descended on Tangmere, causing considerable damage. When I reached Westhampnett, the Squadron located there were just returning from intercepting another raid. This experience made up my mind for me.

I hobbled off to the Air Ministry and asked for employment. As I was unfit for flying, I was attached to Training Command HQ at Reading and sent round recruit depots to tell new arrivals about the war. It was an absurd mission because the airmen were rightly absorbed in their training and did not relish interruptions such as mine. The end of August came and the Medical Board having passed me fit for 'Light Duty', the postings people told me I was to go to 12 Group HQ at Watnall as a Group Controller. I saw the hand of my old master Air Vice-Marshal Leigh-Mallory in this move and, having obtained some petrol coupons from the Air Minsitry Unit, I packed my kit in the Riley, said goodbye to my family at Hayling and headed for Nottingham. I arrived at the beginning of September, the Battle of Britain was now in full swing and, from the 'Bridge' of the 12 Group Operations Room, I was to have a clear if remote view of the rest of the battle.

CHAPTER IX

BATTLE OF BRITAIN

WHEN I arrived at Hucknall in early September I discovered that 12 Group HQ had moved to a new location, a hutted camp two miles away at Watnall, and that the underground Operations Room there, completed several months previously, was now in full use. There had been many changes in the staff but there were still a fair number of familiar faces. I called in on the Intelligence Section next morning on my way to report to the AOC, and got a great welcome from Harold Rothery and my old staff who, when I left the previous October had been newcomers and somewhat bewildered. Now they seemed confident in their work. I was shown round and marvelled at the progress that had been made in the intervening year. Knowledge of the Luftwaffe, its equipment and organisation, was extensive, and I was assured that all this was readily available to the Stations and squadrons. It was not for nothing that Rothery had been a fighter pilot on the Western Front in the Great War, as he never forgot those now in the air. The section had been given an extra task by Leigh-Mallory: to provide a report of every engagement by 12 Group squadrons operating in the 11 Group area. This was in addition to routine and pilots' combat reports. They showed me some, and I noticed that the name of my old friend, Douglas Bader featured fairly frequently. He was now a Squadron Leader, commanding 242 Squadron at Coltishall.

I asked how the air defence system as a whole was coping but the Intelligence staff were the wrong people to answer this question. They knew all about the Luftwaffe and our activity in the air, but little about radar, the Observer Corps, the problem of identification, the Sector Operations Rooms, ours at Group HQ or that at Fighter Command. I was interested in all these aspects since, apart from 1935 and 1936 when I was a flying instructor at Sealand, I had spent all my service life from 1931 on fighter stations. On these, I had been involved continuously in air defence organisation, initially for three years at Hawkinge as a pilot in 25 Squadron during which we participated in most facets of the developing system. Before RDF we had used acoustical mirrors on the coast near Hythe, the limitations of which had impressed on all of us the need for early warning of aircraft approaching over the sea. Then there had been the numerous tracking exercises conducted by Wessex Bombing Area with its Virginia bombers to practise and test the ability of the Observer Corps. Each pilot would be given the pinpoint of an Observer Corps post and we would go off, locate it, and stay with it for the duration of the exercise to assess the ability of the observers to recognise, identify and track the 'raids'.

In the Sector Operations Room at Hawkinge we had learned, mostly from a well-informed Signals Warrant Officer, about the ground organisation of air defence. How the Observer Corps 'plots' as we called them, were transmitted and displayed on the Sector Operations Room table, the functions of the Controller and the other officers and NCOs manning the room, and the instructions to the fighters to 'scramble' and by Radio Telephony (R/T) to guide them to an interception. The theory was impeccable but in practice the technical means were inadequate. Our High Frequency (H/F) radio sets in the aeroplanes were very unreliable and limited in range. The time taken to pass the 'plots' took so long that even with the slow speed of contemporary bombers, the information on the sector table was so far behindhand as to be almost useless for planning an interception. Nevertheless, the experience we had gained was invaluable for an understanding of the requirements of air defence and helped enormously later on, when we were responsible for making the developed system work.

Of course the greatest step forward of all in air defence had been the introduction of the RDF stations in 1936. RDF was so secret that it was not until 1938 when I went to 12 Group on Leigh-Mallory's staff that I began to learn of it, but not about it. In retrospect it is plain that the super security surrounding RDF was a great advantage in denying a knowledge of our capabilities to the Germans, but this also had its disadvantages. Few of us in the executive branch of the Service knew enough to make the best use of the information the RDF screen provided. I never even did a radar (as RDF was renamed when the Americans entered the war) course until I returned to the UK from the Mediterranean in 1944. During my time in the Middle East and Mediterranean I was to command Wings, Groups and the Air Defence of Egypt, all involving the extensive use of radar, but I just had to learn as I went along.

In Britain, France and Norway in 1940 the pilots doing the actual fighting knew very little about the air defence system and during the Battle of Britain some of the least informed amongst the squadron commanders complained at what they believed were avoidable failings by those manning the system on the ground. Some of it was justified but most not: the system was very prone to error. The Intelligence staff I was chatting with that day in September 1940 did mention an attack in the Group area that occurred on 15 August when, for the first time since the opening days of the war, the Luftwaffe had crossed the North Sea unescorted and had attacked targets on land. I was all agog to hear about this since it was precisely the type of attack we had anticipated before the war. We always assumed that France would survive as an ally as she had done in World War I and that therefore the nearest enemy fighter airfields would be in Germany and out of reach of the 12 Group area. There seemed to be a reluctance amongst the Intelligence staff to discuss 15 August, but from what little they did say, I got the impression that the Group had not shown up too well. Anyway, it was now time for me to go to my appointment with the AOC.

Leigh-Mallory was most welcoming and I believe, pleased to see me back on his staff. He congratulated me on my DFC, which had been Gazetted on 13 September and recommended I believe by him, and expressed his sorrow at the loss of so many good chaps in 46 Squadron. Then he gave me a run down on the state of affairs in the Group. Most parts of the system were working well and there had been a considerable improvement in reporting and control, but the raid on 15 August had shown a weakness, he said, right here in the Group Operations Room. He was referring to the competence of the Group Controllers. When the raid occurred he was on a visit to Wittering, was told about it at once, and decided to return to the Group Operations Room in his Proctor communications aircraft, landing at Hucknall. This took about an hour and by the time he arrived at Watnall the raid was over. "If I had stayed at Wittering I might have been able to control the action from there despite the incomplete information available in the Sector Operations Room. As it was, it was too late when I got here." He then described what had happened.

A large formation had been detected and plotted well out to sea opposite the most northern of the Group's sectors, Kirton in Lindsey. The raid turned out to be fifty unescorted Ju 88s of Air Fleet 5 from Denmark. Simultaneous raids had been made on the 13 Group area further north and had been dealt with satisfactorily by that Group's squadrons, despite being escorted by Me 110s, the German twin-engined long-range fighter. The fifty Ju 88s entered the 12 Group area, split into two raids and attacked the bomber airfield at Driffield and the fighter airfield at Leaconfield. These raids had been intercepted by twelve Spitfires of 616 Squadron and six Hurricanes of 73 Squadron. I was astonished when I heard this because there were fourteen squadrons in the Group at this time and six at Wittering, Digby and Kirton in Lindsey within easy range.

Leigh-Mallory's chagrin was easy to understand. He was the first appointed of the AOCs in Fighter Command. Park at 11 Group, Saul at 13 and Brand at 10 had all joined their groups after him. He was advocating that the battle in the south be conducted differently and then when he had the opportunity to demonstrate the efficiency of his own Group in its planned role—to attack unescorted bombers—the result had been failure. Apparently the Group Controller on whom all depended to initiate action against the raids was one Wing Commander Woods, a 'hostilities only' officer, who had been the head of the civilian RAF Education Service before the war. He was not a pilot, had no flying experience and when faced with the situation on 15 August had acted entirely defensively, sending the fighters to patrol over what he thought would be the priority targets, the major cities such as Sheffield and Nottingham, where of course they saw nothing. Leigh-Mallory now realised that there was rather more to controlling at group level than watching the counters on the Operations Room table.

The name Group Controller did not completely describe the function of the post. When he was on duty he was acting commander of all group forces in the absence of the real commander, Leigh-Mallory himself. Plainly the life of a school master was no training for conducting an air battle. Therefore, Leigh-Mallory decided to replace his present controllers by flying people with a knowledge not only of the air defence system but if possible with actual experience of recent operations in the air. I was the first of the new category to be appointed, and I found myself on watch "under instruction" later in the day.

The new underground Operations Room was an excellent place to conduct operations from. Everything had been done to make the troglydite existence bearable for those who worked the eight-hour shifts. The air-conditioning was very good and the decoration, usually bright whites, was toned down with a touch of green to minimise eye strain. I commented on this and was told that Wylie, the marine artist, who had been attached to the Group as a war artist, had also recognised the need for great care to be taken in the decor of the Operations Room, which was then nearing completion. He virtually appointed himself to the job with the most beneficial results. The WAAF, now completely accepted, predominated in the manning of the place and I recognised some faces I had known back in September '39. These women, then newly recruited, had worn civilian clothes, but were now all in uniform.

I now settled into the job of Group Controller in war. In truth, there was little happening in the 12 Group area in clear contrast to further south where 11 Group seemed to be busy most of the day. I dispatched squadrons to reinforce when requested. Mostly the requests were for squadrons to patrol the airfields that the 11 Group squadrons had left in order to intercept enemy aircraft approaching the south-east. This limited role did not suit Leigh-Mallory at all and he would come into our Operations Room and fret, enquiring repeatedly of the Operations Rooms at Duxford and Wittering whether there was any news of our squadrons being in action.

Leigh-Mallory's desire to be more actively involved in the battle rather than accepting the role of reinforcement and guarding the northern flank of 11 Group, led to some strain between him and Park (who commanded 11 Group), and this inevitably spread to the staff of our two key Operations Rooms. I escaped most of this 'feeling' because I found that two of my opposite numbers as 11 Group Controllers were personal friends of mine, John Willoughby de Broke, an auxiliary officer, and 'Tommy' Thompson, an ex-Squadron Commander with whom I had played in the RAF three-quarter line against the Navy and Army before the war. It was noticeable that the difficulties that existed between 11 and 12 Groups did not occur between 10 and 11 Groups since Brand appeared to accept his supporting role to 11 Group, even though he had a front of his own across the western end of the Channel. I knew of these difficulties because at this time, with the GPO subservient to Fighter Command, we had the freedom of the airwaves. I could pick up the phone at any time and speak to other groups to see what was going on and I frequently did.

In his efforts to be more actively involved Leigh-Mallory found a ready supporter in Douglas Bader, the newly promoted Squadron Leader who, despite his almost complete ignorance of the air defence system and its capabilities, was ever ready to tell anyone who would listen, how the battle should be conducted. He sold Leigh-Mallory the idea of operating 'Big Wings' with up to five squadrons with of course himself in the lead. Up to this time the squadron of twelve aircraft was the normal intercepting force, though for sometime 11 Group had been scrambling two squadrons together, generally a Hurricane squadron to attack the bombers and a Spitfire squadron as top cover to protect the Hurricanes from the escorting fighters. This arrangement had worked well enough and complied with Park's over-riding priority for speed both off the ground and in climb to operating height, because warning time was so limited. But Douglas 'always knew better' and in the few interceptions he had made so far with 242 Squadron when reinforcing 11 Group it occurred to him that if he had been leading many more aircraft then the probability was that many more enemy aircraft would have been shot down. The consideration that arranging for the collection of a formation composed of three or five squadrons would take so long that most interceptions would be missed, was waived aside.

Douglas was so headstrong, always had been, even after his terrible accident in 1931 which resulted in his losing his legs. Now he was one of fifty-four squadron commanders in Fighter Command and because of his 'broken service' between 1932 and 1939 one of the least experienced. When it came to discipline Douglas ignored the word. It was axiomatic with him that any order or procedure with which he disagreed need not be obeyed or conformed with. He was a great trial to his immediate superiors and later to those who served under him, but all were prepared to put up with him mainly because of their respect for his courage in overcoming his disability.

However, in late September 1940 in one of my periods off duty in the Operations Room, I went to visit my old Station, Duxford. I was still unfit for flying and so travelled by car. When I arrived I went to the 242 Squadron dispersal on the east side of the airfield. The Squadron had been warned that it was likely to be required to patrol North Weald. Although there was a lot of banter amongst the pilots I sensed also some apprehension, but certainly none in Douglas and it was here that he was at his best, and I did recognise his great value as a Squadron Commander. He simply didn't know the meaning of fear; far from being apprehensive he was positively looking forward to anything that might occur. This attitude of his had a great effect on his pilots and whatever their inward feelings, they were certainly going to conceal them from their Squadron Commander. Douglas looked doubtfully at my feet still encased in carpet slippers but suggested that I might like to come along. I declined, believing I would be a liability, and I think he was relieved that I had not taken up his offer. It was his utter fearlessness that was so valuable in 242 Squadron and to a lesser effect on the other squadrons at Coltishall and Duxford, but contrary to much post-war writing about the Battle of Britain, his influence was not widespread in Fighter Command. He was hardly known at all in 11 Group where the real fighting was taking place.

The position of Group Controller soon began to pall with me and I longed to be back on flying. My feet were improving and the medicos thought that another month would see them all right for a medical board inspection. One morning in November when I came on watch at eight the off-going Controller said, "Coventry caught it last night". I asked, "How long did it go on?" and he replied, "Most of the night" as he left the bridge. Reading the log of the night's activity (14/15 November) I discovered that Wittering, in whose Sector was Coventry, had flown their Blenheim night-fighters all night with precious little success. But I also learned that some of the day fighters, Spitfires and Hurricanes, had been airborne, though unfortunately none had achieved any success.

This was the first time there had been a concentrated night attack in the Group area and it fully exposed the known weakness of air defence at night. Our night-fighters, without airborne radar and without ground radar to direct them, simply could not find the enemy aircraft. Later in the war this would not be a problem, with the introduction of the GCI (Ground Control Interception) radar stations and the AI (Airborne Interception) radar, but that was not to come for many months. Furthermore, at Coventry the anti-aircraft gun defences were not numerous enough to deter the bombers or interfere seriously with their attack. This bombing was very destructive with much of the centre of the town being destroyed. One remarkable detail emerged, however: the only contact the group Operations Room had with Coventry was the Observer Corps Centre in the city. Many times during the night land line communication was broken by the bombing, but never for more than a few minutes because the GPO engineers in the town constantly performed miracles of switching to restore contact. Fortunately, the Centre itself was not hit.

Leigh-Mallory spent a great deal of time on the bridge in the Operations Room always occupying the Controller's chair. When he came in I moved to the Staff Officer's chair next to him and assisted him in any way I could. One of his practices was to have the Staff Officer monitor all his telephone conversations and make notes for him. This led to us Staff Officers having a pretty complete knowledge of Leigh-Mallory's relationships with his subordinates, with his fellow AOCs Park, Saul and Brand, and with the Commander-in-Chief, Dowding. I formed the opinion at this time that Dowding and Park were realistic and practical in facing the tremendous problems that beset 11 Group. It was clear that they were in close touch with each other and that both were entirely preoccupied with the battle. Neither seemed to be much impressed with Leigh-Mallory's theories. Park in particular was a practical airman and fighter pilot with a great record from the Great War. He flew Hurricanes in the battle area, listening to the R/T and went to the airfields on which squadrons recently in action were landing. His judgements were made on first-hand experience. Leigh-Mallory had never been a fighter pilot and never flew the Hurricane or Spitfire; nor was he in any way an original thinker. It was not unusual for a staff officer to recognise a pet idea retold later by Leigh-Mallory as his own. In this respect, he was a 'gift' for Douglas with his Big Wing ideas.

In October another voice joined in the discussions with Leigh-Mallory on the bridge, that of Air Vice-Marshal Sholto Douglas, Deputy Chief of the Air Staff. He seemed to be critical of the way the battle was being conducted in the south though it was not clear to me on what this criticism was based. Whether Dowding and Park, the two commanders responsible for the conduct of the battle, were aware of the critical attitude of Douglas was not apparent from the conversations I was instructed to listen to. Later in the month, on 17 October, Sholto Douglas chaired a meeting at the Air Ministry to which he invited the C-in-C Dowding, and the three AOCs, Park, Brand and Leigh-Mallory to discuss "Major Day Tactics in the Fighter Force". Also attending this meeting were Air Marshal Sir Charles Portal (CAS designate) and Douglas Bader.

Bader's presence at the meeting was engineered by Leigh-Mallory but the chairman, Sholto Douglas, must have acquiesced. His being there was of course absurd on two counts. Firstly, Bader's inexperience of the real battle, not being in 11 Group and secondly, to have the views of just one squadron commander was bound to give a one-sided impression. Park represented the view of the squadron commanders who mattered: those in 11 Group really fighting the battle. Leigh-Mallory was simply using the opinion of one inexperienced but voluble squadron commander to cast doubt on the way Park was conducting the battle. In light of what happened later, Douglas succeeding Dowding and Leigh-Mallory succeeding Park, coupled with all that I had heard in the various telephone conversations, I believe this meeting was just part of a move to discredit the two principal figures fighting the battle with a view to the takeover later. Though not recognised at the time it was altogether a disgraceful episode and highly discreditable to Douglas and Leigh-Mallory. Bader of course was just a pawn in the game. Incidentally, the success of the system, which I explained earlier, is one of the reasons why the part played by its commanders, particularly Dowding and Park was not given full credence. The system dominated and whilst of course it was known that the commanders played a leading role, the feeling in the command and to a lesser extent outside it, was that the system did not require any special genius to operate it. Certainly at squadron level when Dowding and Park were removed, it was regarded as normal posting procedure for two officers who had acquitted themselves well. Much later, in Dowding's case, there was full recognition which led to his Peerage, while Park went on to other commands in Malta, Cairo and South-East Asia.

It was unfortunate that Portal as CAS Designate had no authority at this time or, considering his preoccupation with Bomber Command which he had just left, little knowledge of the background to the meeting. He was a man of the utmost integrity and completely impersonal and must surely have queried the presence of just one squadron commander, if he had been in office as CAS at this time. It is significant, I think, that in later years he looked after Park very well indeed!

The telephone conversations between Sholto Douglas and Leigh-Mallory continued until one evening Sholto Douglas confirmed that he was to replace Dowding as C-in-C of Fighter Command. Leigh-Mallory congratulated him and said, "I am glad that I am to be closely associated with you in my next appointment". Shortly afterwards he was appointed to succeed Park as AOC of 11 Group.

I was passed fit for flying in mid-November and at about this time Leigh-Mallory sent for me together with Rupert Leigh, a squadron commander from 10 Group who came to us as Wing Commander Training, and we were told, "You two know most of the squadron commanders in Fighter Command so I want you to produce a list of all those you believe to be potential wing leaders". We duly produced a list putting our own names at the bottom and gave it to Leigh-Mallory, but I never learned what happened to this list because within a few weeks I had left 12 Group and Fighter Command. I was glad in later years that I had left before Douglas and Leigh-Mallory took over because I missed what proved to be an absurd period in the command's history which started in the spring of 1941 and which warrants some description.

Throughout the winter of 1940-41, we assumed that daylight attacks would recommence in the spring of 1941 and so measures were taken to strengthen the day fighter force as well as the now much-needed night-fighter force. To our surprise (and relief), the Luftwaffe did not resume regular, large-scale operations over south-east England in daylight and when Hitler began his attack on Russia in June 1941, it should have been apparent that the forces that won the Battle of Britain were adequate for the air defence of the country, augmented by additional night-fighter squadrons to meet a resumption of night bombing when autumn came. But the 54 squadrons that Dowding won the battle with were considered insufficient and by the summer of 1941 the total had risen to 79 and by September 1942 to 111—over double the number needed to win the battle in 1940! In the absence of a second Battle of Britain in the summer of 1941, what was this vast fighter force supposed to do?

It was decided to go over to the offensive despite the fact that neither the Spitfire nor the Hurricane had the range to reach German targets. The military aim was never clear. The policy, as expressed in official terminology, was to "lean forward into France" and "force the enemy to battle under conditions tactically favourable to our own fighters". The "enemy" in this context was the reduced Luftwaffe fighter force of Me 109s left behind in northern France when the main body of the German Air Force accompanied the Wehrmacht in its move east to attack Russia. So the aim was to bring these remaining fighters (which posed very little threat to anyone) to battle under "conditions tactically favourable to our own fighters".

The initial Big Wing sweeps (known as 'Circus' operations) over occupied France failed to bring the Luftwaffe to battle, however. The sweeps were doing no harm so why should the Luftwaffe risk taking on superior numbers? It was then decided that heavily-escorted Blenheim bombers were to bomb the German fighter airfields and thus force the Luftwaffe to try and intercept; the Blenheims in addition acting as 'bait' for the Me 109s. Neither of these strate-gems proved successful. The Germans quickly discovered that the relatively light bomb load of a squadron of Blenheims coupled with the inaccuracies imposed by the bomb sights employed at that time, did not damage their airfields much, so that the bait was not worth taking. The canny Germans waited therefore until the 'Circus' was forced by fuel considerations to turn for home and then picked off stragglers. The conditions far from being "favourable to our own fighters" were favourable to the enemy. Not surprisingly we lost more Spitfires than the Luftwaffe lost Me 109s, and unlike the Battle of Britain those pilots forced to bail out over France were with few exceptions lost as prisoners of war. The conclusion, in retrospect, must be that not only were these operations a failure in achieving their specified aim but that they also served very little military purpose.

The futility of these operations was not lost on many of the pilots taking part. But to the wing leaders it was an opportunity to increase their personal 'score' of enemy aircraft shot down and any questioning as to the military value of such operations by the rank and file pilots was quickly quelled. Later when some of the pilots reached us in the desert we learned of the feelings in the wings at this time. Billy Burton for example, who commanded 616 Squadron in Bader's Wing at Tangmere, maintained that by the time Bader was shot down in August 1941, the Wing was in a state of mutiny brought on by his reckless leading in an effort to increase his own score.

Worse even than the fact that these operations were virtually useless from a military viewpoint was the fact that they dominated all thinking about fighters. The critical shortage of long-range fighters at home and overseas from 1941 onwards might have been remedied—if the *need* to remedy it had been recognised early enough in the Air Ministry, at Fighter Command HQ or in the great airframe and engine companies. Superb short-range interceptors were produced, but these were not suitable for war-winning offensive operations.

Moreover, the effect overseas of this concentration on Fighter Command was disastrous. No worthwhile air defence system was set up in the Middle East Command or in India or Singapore. What a difference it would have made if the Air Ministry had insisted from June 1941 onwards that Fighter Command's strength be strictly limited and resources sent overseas! By then, the Spitfire in its successive ranks was widely recognised as a match for the best German fighters. Yet it was not until late 1942 that Spitfires began to appear in North Africa. Until then, the squadrons of the Western Desert Air Force had to make do with Hurricanes, Tomahawks, Kittyhawks and even Gladiator biplanes, all inferior to the best German fighters. During this entire period, so critical for Allied fortunes in the Mediterranean and North Africa campaigns, there were hundreds of precious Spitfires in Fighter Command, virtually unemployed. By the end of 1941, with Barbarossa stalled and the Americans now in the war, Fighter Command could well have been pruned, if Douglas had not resisted so vehemently and if Portal had pressed him harder.

When I had been passed fit, I started with the Magister light aircraft in the Group Communications Flight which was delightful fun. I went down to Bassingbourne, a bomber training station, where my brother Ian was instructing. He had just completed a tour in a Wellington squadron and considering some of the hair-raising tasks he had been given, reckoned he was fortunate to survive. It was the last time I was to see him, as he was shot down in the Channel in February 1942 while attacking the *Scharnhorst* and *Gneisenau* when they made their dash for home from Brest. A wind from the north blew the dinghy which he and his crew had managed to launch ashore in Holland and he was taken prisoner by the Germans (see Chapter 13). So both Ian and I had been clobbered by the *Scharnhorst* and *Gneisenau*.

But I *had* to get back to operational flying. It was all very well living in comfort at Watnall and even the Operations Room had its compensations—it was staffed by beautiful WAAFs—but it was not the war. Nor did I welcome the thought of returning to a post in Fighter

Command with its tightly controlled operations. I had had enough of form filling—the dreaded Form 'D' especially, which specified exactly what Ops were to take place next day. If the weather changed another form had to be filled out, and so on. I wanted freedom. Norway, where we had made our own plans and carried them out, had given me a taste for independent command and if I wanted to repeat the experience, then overseas service was the only answer. I would have to be careful about how I tackled this because I was clearly earmarked to go to 11 Group with Leigh-Mallory. When it was quiet one day in the Operations Room I rang Pat Hutchinson, an old friend from Harlequins, Hawkinge and Duxford days and now in the Air Ministry Postings Department, and asked, "Can you get me out of this, Pat?". There was a short pause then Pat said, "Well, I can try. Where do you want to go?" I said, "They seem to be having a decent little war in the Middle East. What about that?" "Leave it with me" he said.

Consequently, in early December a signal arrived at 12 Group from Air Ministry, posting me to the staff of the Air Officer Commanding-in-Chief Middle East, Air Chief Marshal Sir Arthur Longmore. Leigh-Mallory was upset and offered to intercede and have the posting cancelled, but did not pursue the suggestion when I showed no enthusiasm for it. I left Watnall a couple of days later in my Riley car for a brief leave at Hayling with my parents before going to Egypt. My people found me a dry garage in which to store the car (it was in first-class shape four years later on my return in 1944) and on 18 December 1940 I duly reported to the Air Ministry for instructions on how to proceed to Cairo.

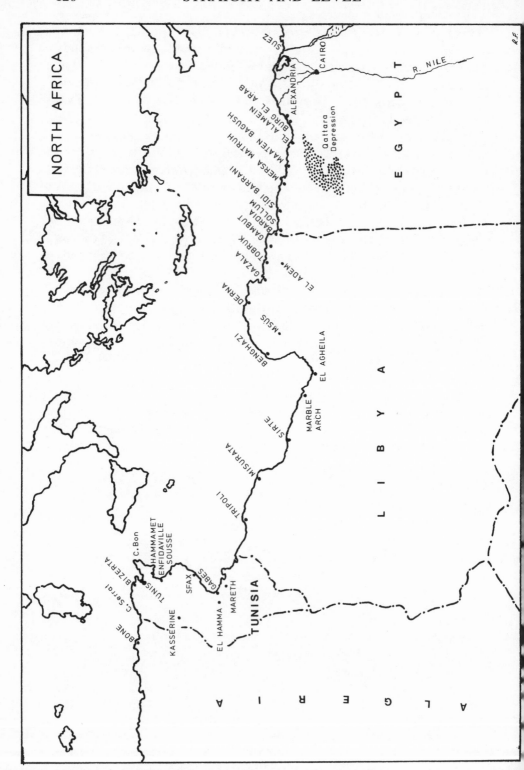

CHAPTER X

OVERSEAS AGAIN

I WENT to Adastral House in London and called first on Pat Hutchinson who explained that the AOC-in-C Middle East had requested as a matter of urgency the posting to his staff of an officer with current experience of all aspects of the air defence system in the United Kingdom. It was considered that, more or less, I had the qualifications for the post and was to proceed forthwith. Because of the urgency I had visions of flying through the night in a Sunderland via Gibraltar and Malta but when I reported to the Movements Department in the basement of Adastral House I got a shock. The civil servant there pulled a file towards him from the many on his desk and said "You are to go in the aircraft carrier HMS *Furious* in Convoy WS5A to West Africa in charge of a consignment of 40 Hurricanes and see them dispatched from Takoradi in the Gold Coast (now Ghana) en route to their destination Heliopolis in Egypt."

I asked how I was to get to Egypt from Takoradi and he replied, "There are some Blenheims used as guides for the Hurricanes and you can travel in one of them." I was told that the *Furious* was in Liverpool but her date of sailing was unknown to the movements staff. I was given a railway warrant to Liverpool and told to report to the ship the next day, Thursday 19 December. I phoned Hayling from the RAF Club and told my parents that I was off to Egypt at once but not how. In the train I reflected about my passage. The *Furious* was the third carrier of her type, all converted cruisers. Of the other two, *Courageous* had been sunk by a German submarine in September 1939, and the *Glorious* in June. I did not fancy being in a 'hat-trick' of sunken aircraft carriers!

It was raining when I arrived in Liverpool and I was fortunate to get a taxi to the docks, which was a dismal scene in the rain with the light failing and the great grey hulk of the *Furious* alongside. I made my way up the companionway and a marine orderly showed me to a cabin on the starboard side of the ship. I stowed my kit and then went to the wardroom where I met some of the RAF officers who had been detailed to fly the Hurricanes. They were all Flying Officers or Pilot Officers and it was a sign of the enormous turnover in pilots since I had left Fighter Command seven months before, that I did not recognise any of them. None of those gathered in the wardroom had been told before leaving their various Stations that I was to be in charge of the party, but my acting Wing Commander's stripes (I was promoted while controlling in 12 Group) gave me instant authority and I believe the pilots were glad to have someone experienced in command. None of them knew me but when, in conversation, it emerged that I had already flown on and off a carrier in a Hurricane I was accorded more respect than due my rank from those discerning young men. I heard that our Hurricanes were not the only cargo: there was also a flight of Fleet Air Arm Fairey Fulmars bound for Alexandria and the Mediterranean Fleet. Its commander was a Marine Lieutenant, 'Skeets' Harris of whom I saw a great deal during the voyage. In addition, the ship had six Blackburn Skuas for its own protection.

There were numerous air raid alarms whilst we were tied up alongside in Liverpool though no actual attacks, but I was still very relieved when we sailed in the early afternoon. We had an escort of destroyers and very soon after clearing harbour were ordered to Action Stations. Rumour had it that we were expecting an attack by Focke Wulf Condors from Bordeaux, but nothing came of it. In contrast to the *Glorious*, all us RAF passengers were allocated duties for Action Stations. I was attached to the Vickers .303 machine gun on the port side of the ship at flight deck level and level with the bridge. I was sent for by the Captain during the afternoon and so made the acquaintance of C P Talbot.

During the afternoon there were a number of alarms and rumours of impending air and submarine attacks but nothing came of any of them. When it was quite dark we were released from Action Stations and I went below to join the others in the wardroom. There were other RAF passengers in the ship in addition to the Hurricane pilots. They were mostly Poles and their senior officer was a grey-haired Squadron Leader by the name of Rolski who spoke good English and to whom I took an instant liking. I found out later that Ryski had been the head of the Polish Air Force when the Germans invaded Poland without warning on 1 September 1939 and that he had paid the price for the alleged failure of the Polish Air Force when it was overwhelmed in a surprise attack by a vastly numerically superior Luftwaffe. Now here he was, a full General dressed as a Wing Commander and bound for Takoradi to become a ferry pilot taking Blenheims across Africa to Egypt. What a man. I spent hours talking and listening to him about the war and the air's part in it. We had plenty of time for chat because various diversions (of which more later) kept us in the ship for twenty days.

On 20 December we joined Convoy WS5A bound for the Cape and Egypt, of which we were to be part until we reached West Africa. That was a quiet day but on the next we were called to Action Stations at first light to hear that one ship in the convoy had been torpedoed during the night, but there was no confirmation of this rumour. We also learned that the convoy was being shadowed by a U-boat and for some reason unknown to us the *Furious* left the convoy for a time but rejoined it later in the day. On Sunday 22 December, we were again warned of an expected attack by Focke Wulf Condors from Bordeaux, and the Skuas were brought to 'Readiness' on the flight deck. Later, after some work had been done on the 'passenger' Fulmars, Skeets Harris and his five pilots were also brought to Readiness, but nothing happened. Nevertheless it was a definite relief when darkness came and from then on alarms became less frequent. We were then joined by another convoy and in addition to our destroyers three cruisers joined the escort, the *Berwick*, *Bonaventure* and *Dunedin*. We were well out into the Atlantic by now and Christmas Eve was uneventful except for a large poker party in the wardroom that I prudently did not join. I went to my cabin and was sound asleep when at about 07.00 hours, when it was still quite dark, I heard a loud bang outside the ship, and which seemed near my cabin. "That's no wave!" I said to myself, leapt out of my bunk and dressed hurriedly. Almost at once Action Stations sounded on the ship's intercom so I hurried up to my post on the machine gun.

It was still very dark but as it became lighter I saw that the *Furious* was entirely alone except for one destroyer, which in response to much flashing on the signal lamp came in close on our starboard quarter. I learned from the sailors crewing the machine gun that the convoy had been attacked just before dawn by what was believed to be the *Admiral Scheer*, and that the convoy had been ordered to scatter. Our position at this time was some 700 miles west of Cape Finistere and we leaned much later that it was another German heavy cruiser, the *Admiral Hipper*, that had attacked the convoy. The present situation of the *Furious* and one destroyer alone with German warships in the vicinity was horribly reminiscent of that I had experienced with the *Glorious* six months earlier. I also reflected again that the *Furious* was the third and last of her class, the *Courageous* and *Glorious* having already been sunk. However, the horizons were empty and perhaps this time we would be lucky. All six Skuas were ranged on deck, armed with one 250 lb bomb each and two were dispatched to search for the German cruiser. *Furious* then turned onto the heading of the last sighting of the enemy and we set off in pursuit.

Captain Talbot then came on the intercom and told us it was his intention to find and attack the enemy ship with bombs from the Skuas. I thought that this was unrealistic because even if all six two-fifty pounders hit the enemy ship (a most unlikely occurrence) such small bombs would hardly put the ship out of action, let alone sink it. Also, was not the aim of the exercise to deliver the forty Hurricanes and six Fulmars to Takoradi? Fortunately the two Skuas failed to locate the enemy ship and when they returned the chase was abandoned and we were told that *Furious* and her one destroyer were putting into Gibraltar. We were encouraged to learn that Force 'H' (consisting of the battleship *Hood* and an aircraft carrier), was coming out to meet us so my fears that the *Furious* might suffer the same fate as the *Glorious* were to some extent allayed. When darkness came at last and we were released from our Action Stations, the cooks, bless them, produced turkey for dinner. So ended Christmas Day 1940.

We met Force 'H' the next day, which was a great sight, and went into Gibraltar harbour together. Captain Talbot performed the seemingly remarkable manoeuvre of turning the *Furious* completely round before coming alongside the quay. Apparently his efforts were not appreciated by the admiral in charge of the port for I was told that that was the reason for the numerous messages flashed from high up on the Rock. I was invited to dine with the Captain that evening when despite his frosty welcome he seemed to be in very good spirits. No shore leave was permitted, but we were able to send letters home. I sent one to Hayling and Lesley Brook.

We sailed at mid-day on 29 December with bands playing after morning service on the flight deck. We now had a full destroyer escort and, having joined up with a convoy the next day, continued our way round Africa. By this time I had got to know the pilots who were to fly the Hurricanes across Africa from Takoradi to Cairo in Egypt. I learned from the Poles that the practice was for one Blenheim with a navigator aboard to lead a formation of six Hurricanes. I had made up my mind from the outset that I would lead the first flight of six and by careful questioning and examination of their logbooks I selected six more leaders. Then came the task of dividing the remaining pilots into flights and in the process of doing this I learned something of how these pilots had come to be allotted this task.

Apparently a signal had gone to all squadrons in Fighter Command instructing them to detail "experienced" Hurricane pilots for a special operational posting. Despite the wording of the signal some squadrons saw this as an opportunity to shed some of their weaker members, and hence some of the "experienced" pilots now in the *Furious* had less than thirty flying hours on the type. I picked four pilots whose records from their logbooks seemed to be good, but I thought it only fair to take one of the weaker brethren to make up my six. He was a Sergeant Pilot with just thirty-five hours on Hurricanes and was destined to give me grey hairs during the three thousand six hundred miles trip to Cairo.

We had many discussions amongst the forty-one of us. I assured them that the take-off from the deck would be easy and quoted my experience of the *Glorious*. Finding Takoradi airfield might be a problem since there would be no navigating Swordfish to guide us in, such as we had had in Norway, and again the maps of the African coast were very small scale. Though nobody voiced an opinion, it was clear to all of us that the operation could fail at the outset, since there would not be much in the way of fuel reserve in the Hurricane to carry out a prolonged search for Takoradi once we hit the coast of Africa. The Poles said there were no R/T homing facilities on the airfield, so I came to the conclusion in my own mind that to make certain of our arrival at this first stop we should ideally be launched from within sight of Takoradi. We heard also from the Poles that there had been one other Hurricane party down the route before us: 73 Squadron apparently had preceded us by a month but had sacrificed a whole flight by getting lost in the middle of Africa. We needed this news to confirm in everyone the necessity of not only keeping the navigating Blenheim in sight, but also to be prepared to have an alternative plan to find our staging post destinations if we did lose the Blenheim through bad weather or other causes. Unfortunately, the Poles told us that the maps of the route were not at all good.

The Hurricanes were being serviced in the carrier's hangars by a party under a splendid RAF Flight Lieutenant engineer. Unlike those we had flown off the *Glorious*, these Hurricane 1s were fitted with long-range ranks mounted under the wings. Apparently the orders were that these tanks should not be filled for take-off from the carrier because the extra weight would affect the performance. This was plainly sensible always providing that the trip from the ship to Takoradi was a short one.

For some reason unknown to us 'passengers', the convoy went into Freetown in Sierra Leone and as we steamed up the river to the town I saw Africa at close quarters for the first time. Again no shore leave was permitted, but Captain Talbot had to make his calls ashore and invited me to accompany him. We visited the governor and the naval officer in charge of the port. I had never seen so many coloured people before and I was intrigued at these laughing folk in their bright, often garish clothes. The calls over, we returned to the *Furious* in the early evening when the lights were beginning to twinkle on shore and on the ships anchored in the river. It was quite romantic for me as a newcomer to be in such a lovely warm place and it was something of an anti-climax to contemplate dinner in the wardroom. However, as I stepped onto the deck after the Captain, the officer of the watch handed me a signal which read, "Captain Heath requests the pleasure of Wing Commander Cross's company at dinner in HMS *Vindictive*. His pinnace will be alongside at 19.00 hours." This sounded delightful but who was Captain Heath and why had he asked me? I consulted Captain Talbot as to whether it would be all right to accept the invitation and he said it would since we would not be sailing until next day and I then went to my cabin for a shower and tidy up. I was on deck at 19.00 hours when a very smart pinnace came alongside and I embarked. We sped up river in the gathering dusk and came alongside a large ship. I went up the gangway and there at the top was 'Wings' Heath of the *Glorious* whom I had last seen shortly before take-off for Narvik way back in May. He was all smiles as he greeted me and led the way below.

The two of us had a splendid dinner in his cabin, and he told me about what happened aboard the *Glorious* after I had flown away. I knew from my own observation that Captain D'Oyly-Hughes did not have the same measure of respect for John Heath that all us aviators, both Naval and Air Force, had and also of the Captain's misplaced belief that he was capable of operating the Fleet Air Arm aircraft himself, with or without Heath's assistance. I knew from my own interviews with D'Oyly-Hughes that he lacked the knowledge of operating and technical procedures necessary for this role and as a result was ordering operations quite beyond the capabilities of the ship's aircraft and aircrew. Heath had had the difficult task of reconciling the Captain's requirements with what was possible and consequently found himself in frequent disagreement. In the end on returning to Scapa Flow after launching my Squadron, D'Oyly-Hughes had dismissed Heath and requested his court martial.

The final break had come over an operation proposed by signal from the Flag Officer Narvik which "invited consideration" of the possibility of attacking enemy troops and transport "on the Mosjoen-Jamo road and Mosjoen aerodrome". To any airmen the use of just five slow Swordfish aircraft (the total on the ship at the time) in daylight on such a task was absurd. Not only did the proximity of Mosjoen airfield mean that high-performance fighters were likely to be met for which the Swordfish were 'sitting ducks', but being torpedo carriers their secondary armament of bombs and guns was insufficient to cause significant damage to enemy troops and transport. Additionally, in the absence of reconnaissance it was likely that the risks run would be for nothing if there were no such enemy troops and transport on the road. At first D'Oyly-Hughes had agreed that the operation was improper employment for Fleet Air Arm aircraft, but nevertheless Heath and his assistant Lt Cdr Paul Slessor agreed to collect such information and maps of the area as were available in the ship. Sometime later D'Oyly-Hughes changed his mind, sent for the two officers and accused them of "a marked reluctance" to prepare the orders for the operation. This was not true because Slessor was actually holding the operation order in his hand. Fortunately, the operation was not ordered but Heath was required to leave the ship at Scapa Flow. After the sinking of the *Glorious* there was no court martial and Heath was sent as executive officer to the *Vindictive*, a repair ship which at once sailed for Freetown. Later he was appointed to command the ship and promoted to the rank of Captain; and here he was.

Poor Heath—as he told all this to me it was plain that several things concerned him deeply. Firstly, was there anything he could have done, or not done, to have saved the *Glorious*? Secondly, it was essential for the Fleet Air Arm's future that such mismanagement should be known to the navy and so minimise its repetition. Thirdly, he wished to clear his name as a naval aviator. It comforted him a little that the three naval officer survivors who had been in Gleneagles Hospital with us had not the slightest doubt as to who was responsible for the sinking of the ship: the Captain—D'Oyly-Hughes.

We sailed next day and shortly after we were clear of Freetown I was sent for by Captain Talbot. He had the ship's navigator with him and a chart spread out. Talbot pointed to a cross marked on the chart and said, "On Wednesday this is where we shall be putting you off." I was horrified to see how far out into the South Atlantic the cross was. I asked the navigator what the distance was from Takoradi and he told me "about three hundred miles." I said that I thought that it was too far out for us. Captain Talbot registered surprise in the look he gave me as clearly he had not intended this to be a matter for discussion. "Why?" he demanded. I said we would have difficulty in locating Takoradi. "What", he said "can't you navigate?" "No", I replied "we have a compass and a watch but no means of either calculating drift over the sea or checking our position in the three-hundred mile flight. When we hit the coast we shall be getting low on fuel, the maps are bad and we shan't even know which way to turn."

He retorted, "There is a U-Boat reported off Takoradi, how close do you want me to go?" I thought for a moment and then said "Until we can see the place from the deck."

There was silence and I was dismissed. I called the pilots together and told them we would be taking off in two days time but did not mention the three hundred miles. I heard no more until late on Tuesday when the navigator told me that our departure point had been changed and that we would be launched within sight of land. He gave me the latitude and longitude of the new point. I called the leaders of the seven flights together, gave them the position for take-off, and as all other arrangements had been made beforehand we were ready for the next day.

Wednesday 8 January was a fine sunny day. We had stowed what little gear we had in our respective Hurricanes and were ready in our flying kit on the flight deck where the first six Hurricanes were ranged. Unlike my previous experience in the *Glorious* there was a fresh wind into which the ship had turned. Over the intercom came the message "Wing Commander Cross to report to the bridge". I hurried forward Mae West, helmet and all to find the Captain, with the navigator, Commander and several other officers clustered round him. By his side there was an enormous telescope on a stand. "Look through that" said Captain Talbot. I did and saw a collection of white buildings and some palm trees. "What do you see?" asked the Captain. I told him. "That", he said, "is Takoradi". I thanked him and hurried back to my Hurricane and climbed in.

I was again to be the first off and as I fastened the straps I realised that I had not flown a Hurricane for seven months—it had been on 8 June 1940 that I had landed on the *Glorious* from Bardufoss, Norway. I was given the signal to start engines and mine started first time. As the dispatching officer dropped his bats, I opened the throttle. This was 'it' for the second time. The *Furious* had about the same length of flight deck as the *Glorious* but no ramp as in that ship: flat all the way. I was airborne well before the end of the deck, but the extra weight of the long-range tanks made the aeroplane very sluggish to handle. By the time I had my wheels and flaps up and had turned onto the heading for Takoradi the next aircraft was already climbing up towards me and shortly afterwards all six were airborne. We were overhead Takoradi quite quickly and all landed safely on the tarmac runway, which was a new experience for most of us because up to that time we had been used to grass airfields. Shortly afterwards the other Hurricanes began to arrive and lastly Skeets Harris and his Fulmars.

Takoradi was a very busy place, mostly receiving cased aircraft which were then assembled. This included the Blenheim which was quite a big aircraft. The domestic arrangements were good. In the Mess I met 'Tiny' White, an enormous man and already a legendary Air Force figure. He was the Senior Accountant Officer and over a drink made sure that I understood how to claim for my allowances when or as he put it "*if* you make it to Heliopolis." The next day we were innoculated and then met Flight Lieutenant Williams and Flying Officer Bagnall, the pilot and navigator of the Blenheim which was to lead us across Africa. They explained the route which they had flown once before. From Takoradi the first leg over Togoland and Dahomey to Lagos in Nigeria was an easy two and a half hour trip during which all systems should be checked. There was an experienced technical party at Lagos and any faults could be rectified during our night stop. Williams warned that this would be the only "easy" day on the whole trip.

From Lagos we would make the first of many early starts to Kano in northern Nigeria, then to El Genina in Chad, El Fasher and Khartoum in the Sudan, Wadi Halfa and then Heliopolis in Egypt. Legs would be between two and a half and four hours, and sometimes we would do two legs in a day. For me who had been brought up on the premise that one hour was the maximum a fighter aircraft would normally need to accomplish its mission, this was something quite new. The long-range tanks fitted under the wings were complete with electric pumps and as the main tanks emptied as shown on the gauge, the pilots switched on the pumps and replenished them. Williams told me that most of the airfields on the route were dirt strips and that some of the accommodation was primitive. We would be departing at 10.00 hours, a gentlemanly hour, but he warned that some of the take-off times would be very early, depending on the distance to be covered in the day.

My Flight consisted of a Flight Lieutenant, three Flying Officers and one Sergeant Pilot and we were all in our cockpits in good time next morning awaiting the signal from Williams to start up. When both engines of the Blenheim were running he gave the signal and we all started. This drill and the order of take-off and landing we kept for the whole trip. The first leg to Lagos was mostly along the coast and it was hot and sticky. We flew at three thousand feet and I was glad of the water bottle I had brought with me in the cockpit. Two hours later we were overhead Lagos and followed the Blenheim in to land, with myself as the first of the Hurricanes. The others all landed satisfactorily except the last, our Sergeant Pilot. He bounced his aeroplane all over the airfield before coming to a halt, thankfully all in one piece. Nevertheless, it was a bad omen for us, facing a three thousand-mile plus flight. Lagos was remarkable for its high humidity—everything dripped!

We were airborne the next morning at 08.00 hours when it was reasonably cool and flew over jungle for the next two and a half hours. We flew at eight thousand feet and the flight was uneventful. We had no difficulty in keeping the Blenheim in sight as Williams carefully avoided the towering cumulus. At Kano the Sergeant kept up his average by overshooting the runway without fortunately doing any damage to his Hurricane. There was a great change in the climate between Lagos and Kano for though the temperature was higher, it was very dry and we found it quite invigorating. The RAF detachment on the airfield had everything well organised and we were lodged in good wooden buildings. There was to be some sort of jamboree for the local Sultan that evening with all the local Arab tribes coming in to pay their respects, and we were invited to see this exciting do.

The Sultan sat on a raised stage at the edge of an open space the size of Horse Guards Parade in London, and each chief galloped his party past. Apparently the size of each party indicated the importance of the tribe. Some were over a hundred strong and the smallest about twenty-five. Sadly we had to go to bed early for the next day we were to do two legs: Kano–Maidugari, Maidugari–El Genina, the latter the longest leg on the trip at over four hours.

We were airborne just after 06.00 hours into a lovely early morning sunrise and landed two hours later at Maidugari. The terrain beneath us had changed completely to open rolling country, much as I had read of the South African veldt. All went well except that the gallant Sergeant overshot and had to go round again, but he was successful the second time. We were off again at 09.00. Our route from Maidugari, the last stop in Nigeria, took us over the French colony of Chad and we saw the waters of the lake of that name to our left. We passed a good landmark, Fort Lamy, on our right-hand side soon after take-off and then settled down for the long trip. After about two hours the terrain began to change, with more hills and small mountains appearing. After three hours I began to notice how hard the parachute seat was, but in the last hour big mountains appeared ahead to break the monotony. We had been flying for almost exactly four hours when we arrived over El Genina, just inside the boundaries of the Sudan. The Sergeant disappeared into the bush off the end of the runway, but he was pulled out backwards and miracle of miracles there was no damage to the Hurricane.

We slept that night on camp beds in grass huts, and then were up in the dark and dressed by torchlight. At the first sign of light in the east, Williams gave the signal to start and my Hurricane fired first time. We had to taxi along a runway at right angles to that from which we were to take off, passing by a small knoll. As I passed it I saw a horseman in Arab dress sitting motionless and watching us. As I went by him I gave him a wave whereupon he tore off a salute that would have done credit to the Brigade of Guards. I got the impression that he was on our side and proud of it. I had a nice warm feeling as I turned onto the runway behind the Blenheim, ready for take-off. From my logbook I see that "we had a lovely trip into the eastern sky over rugged mountainous country," and we landed at El Fasher, Darfur Province of the Sudan in time for breakfast. It had been a short leg, just one and a half hours and at last the gallant Sergeant landed without incident!

We were airborne again at 08.40 hours, our track being east to El Obeid and then a sharp turn north-east to Khartoum. This diversion was to follow the caravan route because a course direct from El Fasher to Khartoum lay over almost uninhabited desert, and search and rescue in the event of a forced landing would have meant a major effort. Even the route via El Obeid took us over nothing but desert with hardly a sign of human life. It took three hours flying to Khartoum and we landed at mid-day in shimmering heat. Here for the first time since Takoradi we were on a first-class RAF airfield and were taken off to the cool Officers' Mess. I met Squadron Leader Wakeham, a fellow pupil on the Flying Instructor's course at Wittering in 1935. He was now Personnel Staff Officer to the Air Officer Commanding, Air Commodore Leonard Slatter, whom I remembered as CO at Tangmere, the home of 1 and 43 Squadrons, the 'other' two Fury squadrons of which my Squadron, 25, had been the third. I saw the AOC in his office that evening. He was keen to know of the fighter operations over southern England—it is interesting to note that the term Battle of Britain though used by Churchill in a speech, had not yet caught on in the RAF as referring solely to the air battle.

We were up early for the fifth and last day of our journey and airborne at 04.20 hours. Our track took us parallel with the Nile at first but contrary to my schoolboy atlas memories of this great river it did not follow a straight course to Egypt and after a short time we flew away from it and across yet more desert. We hit the river again about an hour and a half later where it was flowing from east to west, crossed it and then met up with it again at Wadi Halfa, where we landed at 07.40 hours after three and a half hours' in the air.

Up to now the ground organisation at all the staging airfields had been excellent, but at Wadi Halfa it was abysmal. We saw no officer the whole time we were on the ground, the refuelling took an age, and it was not until after mid-day that we were airborne again. This time we were in sight of the Nile for most of the trip. We were flying at 10,000 feet where Bagnall, the navigator, thought there was a favourable wind and from that height the river with its strip of vegetation appeared to be almost black in contrast to the yellow of the desert. We flew all afternoon and then as the sun was beginning to go down, we saw the white buildings of Cairo at last. Despite having been on the go for fifteen hours, seven of them in the air, the sight of Cairo and the Pyramids thrilled me and all fatigue departed. (I learnt later that the sight of Cairo had exactly the same effect on all the other Hurricane pilots.) We tightened our formation behind the Blenheim as we crossed Heliopolis airfield at the north-east corner of the city and everyone landed safely, including the Sergeant (two in a row) and we lined up the Hurricanes by the Blenheim.

We had brought the second convoy of Hurricanes 3,630 miles across Africa without loss and delivered them to Heliopolis as ordered. Nobody at our destination took the slightest notice as we retrieved our modest luggage from the Hurricane fuselages, but the NCO in the watch office did at least telephone for a truck and eventually when it arrived at the office we went to the Officers' Mess, dropping our great survivor, the Sergeant at his mess on the way. We found our rooms and after a shower met in the Ante Room to celebrate. Soon we had some dinner, over which we nearly fell asleep and so to bed. The day had lasted just twenty hours.

Next morning, we reported to the Station HQ and there I said goodbye to Williams and Bagnall and to the five Hurricane pilots, most of whom I was to meet again when they joined squadrons in Egypt or the Desert. That evening I was given a car to take me to Middle East Headquarters in the St Miramis Hotel in the centre of the city. The evening seemed to be an odd time to report, but I found later that the working hours for the Headquarters were 08.00–13.00 and then 17.00 until 20.00, or indeed until work was finished which sometimes meant the early hours. I reported to the personnel department where I was told to go and see Air Vice-Marshal Peter Drummond, the Senior Air Staff Officer, an Australian who had spent most of his career in the Royal Air Force. He received me kindly and was interested in my experience on the Takoradi route. He said the AOC-in-C was away at present but would see me on his return. In the meantime I should join Wing Commander Johnston who was the present occupant of the post I was to take over.

I went to look for Johnston whom I remembered had commanded 41 Squadron flying Spitfires at Catterick before the war. I found him sharing a large office with two other Wing Commanders, Selway and Elton the three forming the operations staff at their level. I spent most of the next three days in their office learning about operations in the Desert and East Africa. Malta also was becoming more active as a base for operations. When the AOC-in-C, Sir Arthur Longmore returned I was sent for. I had met Longmore briefly at one of Sassoon's garden parties at Trent Park but I don't think he remembered me. He said there had been a change of plan and I was to go to Alexandria to command 252 Air Defence Wing which was responsible for the air defence of the western half of Egypt. I was a bit disturbed at this news since I had rather looked forward to being at the centre of affairs at Middle East Headquarters. However, when I told Johnston, Selway and Elton about the change they quickly disabused me of the belief that being a staff officer in Cairo was preferable to being a Commander anywhere and made it plain that they thought I was very fortunate. I packed my bag and, there being no aeroplane available, was driven the half day's journey to Alexandria.

The Headquarters of 252 Wing was in a hutted camp built for the purpose by the sea on the western side of Alexandria and a few hundred yards from the Fleet Air Arm airfield at Dekheila. The Wing was really only a skeleton organisation, with a thin screen of radar stations covering Alexandria and Cairo, a good reinforced concrete Operations Room and a Filter Room at Wing Headquarters and one empty airfield at Amiriya ten miles south of Alexandria on the edge of the Western Desert.

The officer I was to take over from was Squadron Leader H A Simmons, who had distinguished himself representing Great Britain in the Olympic Games in Berlin while still at school in Southampton. I knew him from the Air Force Athletic Championships at Uxbridge in 1935 when I was in the Sealand team. We agreed on a week's takeover and he then took me to the Operations Room which was half a mile from the hutted camp. It was modelled on a Group Operations Room at home but simpler. There was no Observer Corps to plot aircraft over land so the radar screen not only plotted over the sea but also over land. The flatness of the Delta and Western Desert made this possible, and so we had very few 'permanent echoes' on our screens. There was a Gun Operations Room included in the building commanded by an Army Major and manned by a mixture of British and Egyptian Army personnel. A rudimentary arrangement for the control of fighters existed, which never functioned, and one of the first things I did on taking over was to form a Sector Operations Room for the control of the fighters which I was assured would be allotted when necessary. Up to this time, with the Regia Aeronautica as the main enemy, no serious raids had been mounted against the Fleet in harbour or against the cities of Alexandria or Cairo. But the Luftwaffe had by now put in an appearance at Tripoli some thousand miles away to the west, so I calculated that it was only a matter of time before the Germans turned their attention to Alexandria and the Fleet.

The AA gun set-up was interesting. About half the guns defending Alexandria and all those deployed around Cairo were from the Egyptian Army. Egypt was not at war with either Italy or Germany, but when Alexandria harbour was attacked a few months later, the Egyptian gunners opened up with a will when instructions were passed from the Gun Operations Room. Cairo was never attacked during the whole war, which considering it contained military HQ and other legitimate targets was extremely gentlemanly of the Italians and Germans! The head Egyptian in the Operations Room was Brigadier Schnaggi Bey, a grand man with whom it was as easy as it was pleasurable to work.

I was told by some of the staff who had been in the Wing since its formation at about the time Italy entered the war that the Italians had made some not very serious attacks on the harbour at the outset, but soon discontinued them. Things had been pretty quiet for months since the first defeat of the Italians by Wavell with O'Connor as his front runner. A good many of the officers in the Operations Room were locally enlisted and managed in a number of cases to continue to run their businesses when off watch. I found that they were a very good lot, keen as mustard on the job and amusing people off duty. The airmen were all general duties clerks trained in Fighter Command. Their soccer team easily held its own with the best of the British service teams and even with the Egyptian Army sides that were pretty hot stuff. The key to the success of our team was an airman named Maguire who had played for Wolverhampton Wanderers before being conscripted and he drilled and encouraged our youngsters so that they feared no local opposition.

A few days after Simmons departed and I was left in full command, I received a signal saying that the AOC-in-C would be landing at Dekeila on a visit to the Commander of the Mediterranean Fleet, Admiral Sir Andrew Cunningham, and that he wished me to meet him and accompany him. I had made my number with Rear Admiral Creswell, the Port Admiral and also Fortress Commander, who was my normal contact with the Navy, but I looked forward to meeting Cunningham, because he was already a famous sailor. I met Longmore and his ADC at Dekeila, the latter carrying a couple of brace of partridges for the Admiral's table. We had a couple of cars waiting and Longmore took me with him. On the way he said the Navy were uneasy at the prospect of heavier raids on the harbour now that the Luftwaffe were already in Sicily and Tripoli and would soon be in Libya. It was important therefore for me to convince Creswell that within the limitations of equipment and numbers, the defence provided by the RAF and the Army was as good as it could be.

We arrived at the quay and were met by Admiral Cunningham. It was plain to see that he and Longmore were on the friendliest of terms, and we boarded his pinnace to go to the flagship, the battleship *Queen Elizabeth*. I was not in on the meeting between the two C-in-C's but afterwards whilst having a drink in the Admiral's quarters, Cunningham said to me, "I believe you are a survivor from the *Glorious*". I confirmed that I was, whereupon he said, "Tell me about the action". I did so and he asked me several questions about the accuracy of the German gunnery. When I said that the ships were not in sight, just patches of smoke on the horizon, when the first salvoes arrived, and had hit with the second salvoe he exclaimed, "I am convinced that they have radar ranging". Later intelligence proved the Admiral to be correct, and post-war knowledge shows that German technical progress in radar was at least the equal of our own, but that the Germans had linked their research much more to the improvement of naval and anti-aircraft gunnery, than to air defence by fighter aircraft. The Fighter Command control and reporting system was well ahead of the Germans in 1940.

The 'Fortress' concept for defence was a legacy from pre-war academic Inter-Service planning, whereby some places overseas, mostly ports, were designated Fortresses and the Fortress Commander appointed from the Service predominantly concerned. In practice this generally meant the Navy. Alexandria as a fortress was clearly Naval and the Fortress Commander was Rear Admiral Creswell, a great old man who had retired from the Navy before the war and had been called back on the outbreak. In theory then, for the fighter defence of Alexandria, I was under his operational control. But my master for the air defence of western Egypt was the AOC-in-C and Alexandria was but one of the targets (though undoubtedly the most important) in my area of responsibility. Similarly the Lieutenant-Colonel commanding the AA guns at Alexandria was, as in the UK, responsible to me the airman, for operational matters generally but for Alexandria specifically he was responsible to Creswell. It was a very complicated set of arrangements but such was the goodwill between the sailor, the soldier and the airman, that all worked as well as could be expected. Of course it put a considerable extra load on me as the *de facto* Air Defence Commander because I was obliged to discuss everything I did and every change I made with Creswell. He knew nothing of the air, had never flown in an aeroplane and all his experience was based on two-dimensional movement at a maximum of thirty knots.

When the Germans started attacking the harbour at night a few weeks after I assumed command, we had no night fighters anywhere in the Middle East nor any of the GCI radars which were in use in England. So doing the best we could I gave the AA guns complete freedom of action to fire at any target located by searchlights or the gun-laying radars within their range. Outside this range we patrolled with Hurricane I day fighters in the hope of making visual contact with enemy aircraft whether on its approach to the target or on its departure from it. We had very little success with our Hurricanes, as had been the case in England. The Rear Admiral was very critical of the fighters' lack of success. I endlessly explained the difficulty of seeing a moving object in the air at night. "But" he said "they should hear them, I can hear them quite clearly standing on my balcony!" Nevertheless our defence was mostly successful. Few ships were hit and this was mainly due to the sheer volume of Ack-Ack fire over the harbour. With every ship in the Fleet firing and the shore-based British and Egyptian guns at full blast the harbour was like a volcano erupting.

Creswell's HQ was at Ras El Tin on the edge of the harbour and every morning after a raid he would call a conference for 10.00 hours. These were of little benefit to me with the constant repetition of what each and every one thought, but I had to attend and stick it out to the end, though there were far more important things to be done back at Wing HQ in preparation for the expected night activity. I think Creswell appreciated the load I as a Wing Commander of half his age was carrying and though often critical at meetings, was always kindness itself to me in private. When the conference finished he would invite me back to his beautiful villa next door to his HQ. I would try and excuse myself knowing the work still to be done, but he would not be denied. He offered me a drink consisting of half a glass of dry sherry topped up with water, always saying the same thing, "This won't put your eye out!" Although in his ignorance the Admiral was critical of almost all things concerning the Air Force, he was very proud to have a son flying as a Sergeant Pilot in Bomber Command. He was a great old salt and despite all our arguments and disagreements we remained good friends.

All the attacks from March 1941 onwards were by the Luftwaffe, always at night against the Fleet in Alexandria harbour and on a small scale, twenty to thirty aircraft at a time, with little serious damage done. So, after the Admiral's conference I would hurry back to the Operations Room to check the arrangements for the night. After a while, my staff became very expert and it was then a pleasure to find from now on that all preparations had been made before I returned.

After lunch most officers rested in anticipation of an all-night duty, but I found that I lasted better if I took some exercise, so off I went to Smouha or the Alexandria Sporting Club, both of which had eighteen-hole golf courses where I played a round with friends. I often encountered Admiral Cunningham at Smouha doing the same thing. Shortly after my first meeting with him, I received a telephone call from a Mrs Holmes who introduced herself as the wife of Judge Holmes of the Egyptian Mixed Courts. She gave me her address and asked me to call on her, saying that Admiral Cunningham had given her my name. In due course I called and so began a friendship with a most delightful family. Judge and Mrs Holmes were Irish and after qualifying as a barrister, Hugh Holmes had been appointed as a judge in the Mixed Courts in Alexandria which tried cases involving the very large cosmopolitan population of that city. They were both charming people and not surprisingly their four daughters and one son were equally delightful.

My call was the first of many and indeed the Holmes house in Alexandria became a second home for me during my service in Egypt. Mrs Holmes told me that her eldest daughter Hilary had married Lieutenant Commander Wells, the Gunnery Officer in the *Glorious* and brother of a friend of mine, Jimmy Wells. The Holmes family had received the news from Hilary who was in England that her husband was 'missing' after the loss of the *Glorious* but still clung to the hope that he was alive. It was now nine months since the ship had been sunk and I was quite unable to believe that if Wells had survived it would not have been known by now. So I was little comfort to them. It was a very sad business.

Meanwhile, the air defence of the western half of Egypt continued to function satisfactorily if not very lethally against the night raids on the Fleet in Alexandria. Against high-flying single reconnaissance aircraft, Do 215s or Ju 88s, we were very successful. The long radar warning of their approach over the sea and the perfect weather gave the Hurricanes of 274 Squadron or the Tomahawks of 3 Squadron (RAAF) a great opportunity and most intruders were shot down. These successes earned great praise from the Navy. Then the Luftwaffe switched their efforts to the eastern half of Egypt by starting what turned out to be a considerable campaign of mining the Suez Canal combined with attacks on Suez itself and Port Said. The air defence here was under the Wing Headquarters at Ismailia, commanded by Group Captain C N Lowe who as a young Flight Lieutenant had played rugby football for England and there are still many who believe he was the finest wing threequarter of all to represent his country. Unfortunately, Lowe had no experience of modern air defence and when the Luftwaffe, operating from Benina (near Benghazi), started their operations against the Canal, the Wing was found wanting in a number of ways. There were several conferences at Ismailia which I was asked to attend by HQME and eventually it was decided that the entire air defence of Egypt should be put under one commander. The Wing at Ismailia was disestablished and Lowe went off to the relative quiet of Cyprus. I was promoted to the rank of Group Captain in July 1941 and told to get on with the job.

One of the first difficulties I encountered on visiting and staying at the Sector Operations Room at Ismailia was the absence of any common operating procedures between the two Wings. Consequently there were difficulties encountered by the squadrons when moving between the two, as they were often required to do. Where there were officers from Fighter Command in the two organisations, they carried on as expertly as they had done at home, but there were also many officers who were locally recruited who were not only without air defence experience but lacking normal Air Force practice as well. It was plainly necessary for a 'Bible' of 'Battle Orders' such as we used in Fighter Command. All operations staff relied on it and so procedures were uniform.

By great good fortune I found a copy of this publication in the safe at 252 Wing Headquarters. How it got there nobody knew, but as it stated in capitals on the first page "In no circumstances to be taken outside the United Kingdom" I didn't press the need for an investigation.

It was invaluable to me and I worked eighteen hours a day adapting it for the defence of Egypt. When the adaption was complete I had it copied by an RAF printing unit and sent to all units concerned with the air defence of Egypt. I sent one to Middle East Headquarters "For Information" and was gratified a few weeks later when the new AOC-in-C, Air Marshal Tedder, visited the Wing and said he had read my 'document' and had a query about the height intervals for day fighters patrolling at night. As this was his only comment on some two hundred pages of instructions I considered I had succeeded pretty well. However, it would not be until 1942, when GCI radar stations arrived together with AI-equipped Beaufighters that we were able to punish the Luftwaffe so severely that it gave up raids on Egypt.

Air Marshal Tedder had arrived in Cairo to take up his appointment as Deputy Commander-in-Chief on 10 December, 1940 almost exactly a month before I arrived in Egypt. He had traversed the Takoradi route as I did. I had met him once before in 1932 when he commanded the Air Armament School at Eastchurch when my Squadron visited and even as a very inexperienced Flying Officer I recognised him as a charismatic man. Now eight years later I began a period in which I saw a great deal of him in Egypt, Libya, Tunisia, Sicily, and Italy and appreciated how fortunate I was to serve under such a splendid Commander-in-Chief.

Tedder had many problems to solve when he succeeded Longmore as AOC-in-C, not least of which the fact that his aircraft were numerically and qualitatively much inferior to those of the enemy. In this situation both the Navy and Army suffered at the hands of the Regia Aeronautica and the Luftwaffe and loud and often were the complaints. In addition to his command responsibilities, Tedder also had the task of "educating" his fellow C-in-Cs in the ways of air warfare. His philosophy that the presence of the Air was essential in making combined operations effective, found a ready recipient in Auchinleck but less so in Admiral Cunningham; as the commander of the historic Mediterranean Fleet, he valued his individual freedom of action. Quite often from my camp at Alexandria, situated a mile or so from the Great Pass, the entrance channel to the harbour, we would see this massive fleet of destroyers, cruisers, aircraft carriers and battleships silently putting to sea, mostly at dusk. In my 'scrambler' telephone conversation with Middle East Air Headquarters in Cairo, I used to mention that I had observed this Fleet movement and was surprised that Tedder knew nothing of it! Needless to say with the arrival of the Luftwaffe in Greece and Sicily, the Mediterranean Fleet got some awful shocks and despite the triumphs at Taranto and Matapan the Luftwaffe closed the Gibraltar-Suez route for two whole years from 21 May, 1941 until May 1943. Tedder's inability through lack of resources to cope with the Luftwaffe was not appreciated by Admiral Cunningham and complaints continued, but nevertheless as modern aircraft reached the command and our operations increased, Tedder did succeed in gaining the confidence of both the Navy and the Army. Later when the Americans entered the war and Tedder was appointed Air C-in-C under Eisenhower, he was to display a mastery of all aspects of air warfare.

He was always a welcome visitor to the squadrons and the aircrew, and his informal talks on the wider aspects of the war were greatly appreciated by those actually doing the fighting. Tedder never sought popularity from those whom he commanded but he always had their universal respect.

Periodically there were lulls in enemy activity and at these times I missed the flying practice I had been accustomed to in my Squadron and looked round to find a source from which to borrow an aeroplane from time to time. I was lucky that at Aboukir some miles to the east of Alexandria there was an RAF Depot of very considerable size and capability, engaged in repairing and servicing aircraft from all the

squadrons in the command. These aircraft had to be tested on completion, and to my delight I found that the officer in charge of the
Flight Engineering Squadron was Squadron Leader T N Coslett, an
old friend from the 1936 RAF rugby football team against the Army
and Navy. He quickly put me on his list and I was able to keep my
hand in by flying Hurricanes, Lysanders and (a special treat for me)
the Blenheim.

Norman Coslett had been serving in Egypt since before the war and
had many friends in Alexandria. He introduced me to the Savons, he
French and she Canadian. Georges was a shipping broker and he
and his wife became lifelong friends. He had offices in Alexandria,
London, Algiers, Beirut and Buenos Aires and after the war I met
him many times in London. We were all keen golfers, and operations
permitting we played many a good game at Smouha or the Sporting
Club. The Savons had a beautiful house overlooking the sea in
Alexandria, which they inhabited with their two daughters Georgette
and Jeanne, and Marie Louise's Canadian sister Gabrielle Coste threw
some wonderful dinner parties on Sunday evenings. Georges regretfully had to move his head office from Alexandria when Nasser made
normal commercial life impossible in the fifties. I once asked Georges
what became of his house when they moved out. "It was requisitioned
by the Egyptian Government and handed to the Soviet Embassy", he
said. He was never paid.

As a newcomer to Egypt I caught all the usual maladies. First,
'Gippy tummy' and following that sandfly fever. The characteristic of
the second is a splitting headache and the Wing doctor quickly had me
in the 8th General Hospital in Alexandria where I shared a room with
Captain S M Raw of the Royal Navy, who was recovering from the
same illness. He was the Captain of HMS *Medway*, the Submarine
Depot Ship for the Eastern Mediterranean. I was out in a week, but
feeling very second hand. The doctor prescribed a few days' leave and
as we seemed to be in one of our periodic lulls I agreed with him.
Coincidentally there arrived at the Wing Flying Officer Ferguson,
known as 'Fergie'. He had been a pupil in the Cambridge University
Air Squadron, had joined up on the outbreak of war and had since
survived two operational tours on bomber Blenheims, one in England
and one in the Desert. Fergie had been sent to the Wing for a rest
from operations. When he heard that a week's leave had been
prescribed for me he said "I know just the place for sick leave—
Haifa." We had a Magister light aircraft allotted to us for flying
practice and as he and I were the only qualified pilots in the HQ,
I agreed that we might as well get our practice flying to Haifa.

We set out without delay landing at Ismailia and Ramleh, near Tel

Aviv to refuel. Before leaving Alexandria, Fergie sent a telegram to a girl friend of his, Rachel, and when we arrived for lunch at one of his favourite restaurants, the Astoria, Rachel and some of her friends joined us. They were delightful girls and had already arranged a party for that evening with everyone Fergie knew in the town there. Rachel also told us that one of Fergie's squadron was around, one Gerard Glaister, and would join us in the evening. The party was a tremendous event that went on into the early hours. It was most enjoyable but I doubt whether it was quite the treatment that the doctor would have prescribed.

We stayed in the Camelia Court Hotel, spending the days on the beach and the evenings in the restaurants and night clubs of which Haifa seemed to be well endowed. Our companions were three delightful girls Rachel, Zepura and Atara, all Jewish and the daughters of emigrants to Palestine from Europe. Zepura, who became my girlfriend, came from a family which had left Russia in the thirties. The days flew past and my leave was soon over. As we flew back to Egypt I agreed with Fergie that Haifa was certainly the place for leave, and that we would come again.

The light night raids on the harbour remained infrequent, just enough to remind the cosmopolitan population of Alexandria that there was a war on. The Egyptians were active in enforcing the blackout but except for this restriction, life was much as it always was in the beautiful city. There was no rationing and the food in Pastroudis and the Union Bar, the Services' favourite restaurants, was of the highest standard. The hotels were good, the Cecil being the most popular, and the night clubs, particularly the Carlton and the Monseigneur, were first rate. Life was all very enjoyable—hard work, excitement, modest achievement and if there was spare time exercise at the sporting clubs and amusing night life.

I began to think, however, that enjoyable as life was in my present post, it was too far from the real war. That was taking place at sea, in Malta, in Tobruk and primarily for the Army and the Air Force, in the Desert west of Alexandria. I had from curiosity already visited 204 Group which worked with the Army. Its HQ was at Maaten Bagush and I wished I was part of that group. Its commander was Air Commodore Raymond Collishaw, a Canadian and an 'ace' from the First World War, and I had a talk with him in the summer of 1941. During the time I was in his office we were repeatedly interrupted by a succession of corporal clerks bearing signals from all and sundry. Collishaw would read the signals, dictate a reply, sign it and off went the corporal to despatch it. I thought it was a bit odd that none of his staff were consulted, and wondered how they knew what was going on. I heard later that Collishaw had conducted business this way whilst supporting the O'Connor advance earlier in the war, when 204 Group had very few squadrons, and had refused to change now even though the force had more than doubled.

In September 1941, it was announced that the Army, also expanding, was to have a name commensurate with its size—8th Army—and that 204 Group would likewise change its name. From now on it was to be known as the Western Desert Air Force. Air Vice-Marshal Coningham (another famous Great War ace) had replaced Collishaw at the end of July and Lieutenant General Sir Alan Cunningham (younger brother of the Admiral) was appointed first commander of the 8th Army. Early in October I returned to Maaten Bagush and immediately on landing sensed that there had been a change. Everyone from the airmen who marshalled me to the officer who provided me with a Ford pick-up to take me to the HQ were very alert and quick about the place, in stark contrast to my last visit.

At the underground HQ I saw the Senior Air Staff Officer, Group Captain Freddie Guest, whom I knew. I asked him if there were any jobs going with his expanding force. "Well", he said, "if you are keen to join I will ask the AOC when he returns from Cairo." As I could see that he was pretty busy I left and went to see another friend, Wing Commander Al Bowman, an Australian who had transferred from the Royal Australian Air Force to the Royal Air Force in 1931. He had been a Flying Officer in 33 Squadron at Bicester when my 25 Squadron had co-operated with his in the attack and defence of bombers using Harts and Furies. An outstanding pilot, Al was at that time Chief Training Officer. He briefed me about the state of squadron training and then I flew back to Alexandria.

One evening in the first week of November, while working in my office at Seagull Camp, there came a personal phone call from the Desert. There were very few lines west of Alexandria and it was with some surprise that I took the call. The voice at the other end asked "Is that Cross?" I said "Yes" whereupon the voice said, "This is the AOC Western Desert Air Force and Guest tells me that you are keen to join us." I said "Yes sir." "Well I will bear your name in mind if any post occurs," said the AOC and rang off. I was visiting Judge and Mrs Holmes that evening and told them I had had a call from 'Mary' Coningham himself (his nickname Mary came from Maori, a reference to his New Zealand nationality). "Oh Mary Coningham is a wonderful man", said Rose Holmes "we knew him well when he was a Squadron Leader blazing the trail across Africa in his biplanes. He is a very fine pilot." Two days later a signal arrived posting me supernumery to Western Desert Air Force Headquarters, and nominating my old friend Johnston from Middle East to take over 258 Wing from me.

He arrived next day and the day after (13 November) I put my kit in the Magister and flew to Maaten Bagush. I reported to Freddie Guest who took me in to meet the AOC. Coningham was an impressive man. Over six feet tall he kept himself very fit and his face was already bronzed. The look he gave me seemed to be particularly penetrating. He asked some questions of my war service and then said that the post he had in mind for me was that of Group Training Officer (Fighters), to train squadrons on how to work together, rather than training individual pilots, and as this was a Wing Commander post it would be necessary for me to relinquish my rank of acting Group Captain. I was prepared for this—better a Wing Commander in the battle than a Group Captain in the flesh pots of Alexandria—so I said nothing. He asked a few more questions and that was all. I went straight to my tent where with a pair of nail scissors I cut off one of the four stripes that had adorned my epaulettes since July.

The location of the HQ at Maaten Bagush, which incidentally was just a name on the map with no buildings or signs of civilisation, was an idyllic spot. It lay in a small bay about a mile wide with gleaming white sand and the clearest blue sea. The tents, trailers and dugout operations rooms and offices were in the sandhills bordering the bay. The work routine was as follows: starting at 08.00 hours; lunch 13.00 hours–14.00 hours followed by a swim; 15.00 hours to 19.00 hours was work again and at 20.00 hours dinner was served. The Operations Room was manned throughout the twenty four hours. At this time there was a great deal of army/air planning going on for the next advance westwards—given the name Crusader—to relieve Tobruk and the subsequent operation Acrobat—the advance to Tripoli. The Army plan was for three armoured columns of 30 Corps to cross the 'wire' (frontier) between Bir Sheferzen in the north and Fort Maddalena fifty miles to the south, then turn north west towards Tobruk. At the same time the New Zealand Division would advance westwards along the coast road. The Tobruk garrison was at a given moment to break out, join up with the advancing armoured columns and so break the siege.

Sidi Barrani was the most forward airfield for our fighters and with the increasing number of squadrons planned to be available for Crusader this one airfield was plainly inadequate. It was decided, therefore, to scratch out four new airfields and, because of the risk of torrential rain on the coast, to position them behind the line of advance of the armour. These four were to be east of Fort Maddalena and some sixty miles inland in virgin desert.

For several weeks before 18 November 1941, the planned date for the start of Crusader, the whole of the fighter force was involved in protecting the shipping supplying Tobruk. The ships sailed from Alexandria, and were therefore well within range of Luftwaffe bases in Cyrenaica during the latter part of their journey. It was always arranged that the last part of the passage to Tobruk west of Sidi Barrani should be done at night, but daylight protection meant we had to keep standing patrols over the ships. It was an essential duty but one which was cordially and universally loathed by the fighter pilots involved. The single-seat fighter is essentially an offensive tactical weapon, relying for effectiveness on its freedom of action in searching out and destroying its prey, enemy aircraft. Tied as they were to patrolling over or near slow-moving ships, our pilots were sitting ducks for the enemy fighters, consisting of Me 109Fs who knew precisely where to find our boys and using this knowledge would attack from 'out of the sun'.

Unlike at home, there was no radar along the coast from which warning of the approach of enemy aircraft could be obtained, so our fighters were entirely unaided. Not only were the losses we sustained worrying, but the effort involving all our fighters meant that training for our future offensive role in the air, which would be essential if we were to prevent the Luftwaffe attacking the army advance on Tobruk, could not be carried out, except in dribs and drabs in between convoys. So my work as Group Training Officer was greatly handicapped, and I was a frustrated spectator on the airfields for a lot of the time.

Coningham had planned a new organisation for the fighter force in the anticipated advance of some eight hundred miles to Tripoli. He expected movement to be rapid once the enemy land forces had been destroyed south of Tobruk and was therefore forming a second Wing, 263, to add to that presently at Sidi Barrani and making both mobile by providing a generous establishment of MT. The intention was that the second Wing Headquarters would remain alongside that controlling the fighters, then move forward with the Army and install themselves on the next set of airfields constructed by the Royal Engineers as the advance proceeded. As soon as they were installed they would call the fighters forward and so remain well within range of our forward troops. To prevent confusion as to who was in command, the CO of 258 Wing was to be a Group Captain and 263 a Wing Commander. The Group Captain would decide for himself which HQ he would command from. The officers nominated for these key posts were Wing Commander 'Bull' Halahan (to be made an acting Group Captain) and command 258 Wing while 263 Wing was to be commanded by an old friend from Digby days, Wing Commander Fred Rosier.

The two men were contrasting figures: Halahan was a burly man who strode about the place with an arrogant air which plainly said, "I am the boss around here and make no mistake about it." He had commanded a squadron in France in the early days and had done a short stint in Malta. Rosier had been a Flight Commander in 229 Squadron at the time of Dunkirk and in the days before self-sealing tanks were standard equipment in the Hurricane. He had been hit and when his plane caught fire, baled out but was badly burned about the face in the process and still bore the scars. He was a most intelligent man, a great character and trusted by everyone from top to bottom. Halahan on the other hand was a man who it was difficult to get to know. He was a loner. He made grandiose plans for sweeps with Big Wings and indicated that he would always lead when a Big Wing operation was ordered. When he said this to all the fighter pilots gathered for a conference to discuss Crusader, a pilot who had been with Halahan in France was heard to remark, "I will give five hundred piastres for every time that man crosses the wire."

Halahan's idea, an absurd legacy from the Big Wing sweeps at home by Fighter Command across the Channel which achieved nothing at great cost and retained Spitfires in England which were desperately needed elsewhere, was quickly quashed with the arrival in October of Air Commodore Basil Embry as the Senior Air Staff Officer to Coningham. He was, in my opinion, the most outstanding leader in the air up to the rank of Air Vice-Marshal that the Royal Air Force produced in the war. Starting in 1939 as a Blenheim squadron commander, he continued to fly on operations in each rank from Squadron Leader to Air Vice-Marshal. He was a most dynamic personality and quickly took a grip on the fighter organisation, pronouncing that even if Big Wings were an advantage, which he doubted, the difficulty of mass assembly and take-off from desert strips with their attendant clouds of dust made them impossible. Moreover having three different types, the Hurricane I and II and the Tomahawk, with different characteristics would make manoeuvre and control in the air too difficult to put into practice. He consequently paired the squadrons by type of aircraft into Small Wings which certainly proved to be a very satisfactory tactic during Crusader.

Of course nothing made up for the inferiority in performance of all the fighters in use in the Middle East in comparison with the Messer-schmitt 109F. Neither of our best, the Hurricane II and the American Tomahawk, could compete and the Hurricane I was quite outclassed. Even the Italian Macchi 202 was better than anything we had. Well might our Commander-in-Chief, Air Marshal Tedder have written in his journal "One Squadron of Spitfire Vs would have meant a lot."

In the end Halahan was not even to have the opportunity of "crossing the wire". The request to the Air Ministry to promote Halahan to Acting Group Captain was refused and Coningham had to think again. He sent for me on 11 November and explained again his planned organisation for the command and control of the fighters through the two Wing HQs, 258 and 263, then said—rather reluctantly I thought—"I want you to command 258 Wing." I was surprised at first and then delighted, even though I thought that Coningham wasn't all that certain that I was the right man for the job.

I went back to my tent to find the discarded Group Captain rings, and having given the communal batman a packet of cigarettes, asked him to sew them back on again. When I went to the Mess for a drink before dinner the buzz about my appointment had already got around and I received about an equal number of congratulations and commiserations. "Bound to be put in the bag old boy, right out in front like that" was a typical comment. My main worry was that Crusader was only seven days away and I had better get moving, to do all that I could to prepare for the coming battle.

CHAPTER XI

WESTERN DESERT

The 258 Wing Headquarters was at Sidi Barrani and how to get there was my first problem. There were no communication aircraft at Maaten Bagush so I got Embry's permission to take a Hurricane from the Maintenance Unit at Fuka. I remember him saying, "You'll cut no ice with the squadrons unless you fly on operations with them, so you will need an aircraft". On 12 November 1941, I therefore collected BD 884, a brand new Hurricane II and flew to Sidi Barrani which, being near the coast, was easy to find. On arrival I discovered that Halahan and the main part of the Wing HQ had moved to new airfields sixty miles to the south, so I had the Hurricane refuelled and then took particular care in marking my map and calculating the course to steer. This was the first time I had flown any distance inland into the Desert where there were none of the navigation aids so abundant in Britain. Here it was all dead reckoning with compass and wrist watch. However, the marvellous visibility made up for any deficiencies and people got lost on very few occasions.

The difficulty of navigation in the Desert had already been demonstrated by the enemy in September when a whole squadron of Italian Ju87s got lost and landed all over the place and mostly on our side of the lines. As a result of the Italian mis-adventure, we all had a chance to fly the Ju87, the Stuka dive-bomber. I thought it was an excellent flying machine with well-balanced controls and seemingly no 'tricks', but it's performance with a crew of two and a bomb load was low and it was easy meat for contemporary fighters.

I set off from Sidi Barrani sticking very close to the compass heading I had calculated and keeping an accurate air speed, and had no difficulty in locating the new airfields, four of them, just graded strips 1,000 yards long, marked with empty fuel drums. I circled round and had a good look. There was a collection of tents and vehicles and the two office trailers positioned on a small ridge to the south were, I guessed, the Wing HQ. There were no aircraft, the squadrons remaining at Sidi Hinaish (east of Maaten Bagush) at this time and going forward to Sidi Barrani when operating over the front, or more often covering the ship convoys making their way along the coast to Tobruk.

I landed and parked the Hurricane in the nearest dispersal area to the Wing HQ. There were no ground crew airmen about and so I unbuttoned the fuselage panel with the small screwdriver on my pen-knife, extracted my bag and camp kit and waited hopefully for some transport to come and pick me up. I immediately noticed the great silence of the Desert. On the coast, with its main road and adjoining air strips, there was always noise from vehicles and aeroplanes even at night. Here it was dead quiet, not a sound. I was sure that my arrival had been seen from the Wing HQ since I had flown over it, but after waiting a while and with no transport appearing I put my parachute back in the cockpit and, shouldering my camp kit and carrying my bag, I set off on the not inconsiderable walk to the Wing HQ. When I arrived I found the Operations Tent unmanned but in an adjacent office trailer there was a Flight Lieutenant who said he was the Camp Commandant when I introduced myself to him.

It was plain after a minute or two's conversation that he was quite unaware that I was the Wing's new Commanding Officer and was puzzled at the arrival of a senior officer flying himself in a combat aeroplane. I asked for Halahan and was told that he had gone to Fort Maddalena to inspect another set of airfields that had been built there, and which the squadrons would occupy later. He was expected to be back about lunchtime. There was not much I could do but wait. I talked to the Camp Commandant about the administrative arrangements. He said the Royal Army Service Corps had been very efficient at providing rations, fuel and water at Sidi Barrani, and in the few days in the present location it had been the same. In the months ahead I was to find supply by the RASC in every way admirable. When we were on the move or the land battle was fluid then we would probably be on hard tack, but as soon as the situation stabilised there would be an immediate improvement in the rations, and we even had green vegetables. The office trailer we were in was the Wing's administrative centre, and the other trailer was the CO's office and sleeping quarters.

At about one o'clock a convoy of station wagons pulled into the camp and Halahan emerged from the first wearing the inevitable flying boots. He asked me what I wanted and I realised that he also might not know that I had been sent to replace him. Concealing as best I could my surprise, I asked him if we could have a word in his trailer.

He agreed and we walked over to it. I said I had come to take over command of the Wing and asked him if he had not heard about it. "I heard something about it", he said, "but assumed it would not be until later". This was disconcerting. Halahan evidently resented the fact that he was to lose his important command to a younger man (there were 3½ years between us) of the same substantive rank. I asked him if he had not seen the signal from Western Desert HQ announcing the change and the date. He simply said "No".

Fortunately, I had been given a copy of the signal before I left Maaten Bagush and I pulled it from my Battle Dress breast pocket and handed it to him. He glanced at it and then said it was time for lunch which we ate with the small Wing staff at a trestle table in the open. It was an uncomfortable meal for though Halahan still did not fully accept the change in command, the staff somehow were now aware of it. It was all very awkward. During the afternoon Halahan came to the conclusion that the game was up and announced that he would be holding a farewell party in his trailer at six o'clock that evening. He said later that he thought it would be better if I didn't attend! I asked the Camp Commandant if there was a spare tent, but there wasn't so I spent the night on my camp bed under the stars.

At first light the next morning an obliging airman brought me a cup of strong tea and a small can of hot water for shaving. I accomplished the latter by feel since I had no mirror. Halahan appeared for breakfast and then left in what was now my station wagon. I still had no transport but the Camp Commandant took pity and found a thirty hundred weight 'pick-up' so at least I was mobile. The station wagon was returned some days later. I called the small staff together in what was now my office trailer and told them what I knew of the Army's intentions and of the Air Force's plan to render maximum assistance. In the air we had already started by attacking targets on the enemy supply route from Benghazi to Bardia with Blenheim and Maryland light bombers, and with Wellington medium bombers. The fighters were still fully occupied at present covering the convoys to Tobruk. This task, which required the bulk of the fighter force, had been prolonged by the Australian Government's insistence that their 9th Infantry Division, which formed most of the garrison in Tobruk, should be brought out. Despite appeals at the highest level, Churchill to the Australian Prime Minister Fadden, the Australian Government insisted on the move. Consequently, the extra convoys required to take in the relief troops and bring out the Australians meant that there was little time to train the fighters in the type of air fighting they were likely to encounter over the battlefield or in the ground attack role in support of the Army.

I explained that once the battle started our prime task as a fighter force would be to prevent the enemy air force from interfering with the Army's operations against the enemy ground forces. In Greece, Crete and earlier in the Desert, the Army had had to fight the enemy air force as well as his troops on the ground and this was believed to be the main reason for their defeats. Before leaving Western Desert Air Force Headquarters I had heard references to a request to Mr Churchill from the New Zealand Prime Minister, Mr Fraser, for an assurance that after the experience of the New Zealand Division in Greece and Crete his troops would not for the third time be committed to go into battle without adequate air support. Churchill had replied that ample air and tank strength would be available. This assurance, based on our anticipated numerical superiority, did not take into account our inferiority in performance in both fighters, and especially tanks, that made winning the battle so difficult. However, the fact that we did have numerical superiority in the air gave a filip to the morale of pilots accustomed to being outnumbered as well as out performanced. To make the most of this advantage we decided, therefore, to operate over the battle area in the largest manageable formations which after trials we found to be two squadrons, a total of twenty-four aircraft. Maintenance was not a problem and service-ability high. The Tomahawk was beautifully built but both it and the Hurricane were short of performance compared to the 109F and G.

At this time in the Desert, we had four Hurricane squadrons, four of Tomahawks, plus a naval squadron of Hurricanes and Grumman Martlets. The naval squadron was made up of aircraft and pilots from the carrier *Illustrious*, after her disablement by the Luftwaffe on a Malta convoy which necessitated her leaving the Mediterranean for repairs. Though I was not aware of it at the time, I learned later that Tedder had to contend with numerous suggestions for the organisation and operation of the air forces under his command, particularly those in the Desert. The 8th Army Commander, Lieutenant General Sir Alan Cunningham and General Sir Thomas Blamey, the Australian, were foremost in their 'requirements'. Mostly the demands were for squadrons to be allocated directly to Army formations, mostly to Corps and Divisions, but even Brigades were to have their quotas. The Squadron Commanders would receive their operating orders direct from the Generals concerned. That none of these gentlemen had ever flown an aeroplane or had the slightest knowledge of the training, operational or logistic aspects of Air Forces, did not appear to concern them at all. Fortunately, in General Sir Claude Auchinleck, Tedder had as a colleague one of the most intelligent Generals on the British side in the entire war. He saw very early on the virtues of centralised control of air forces by the Air Officer Commanding located alongside the Army Commander. Tedder and his subordinate Air Vice-Marshal Coningham made their arrangements accordingly.

The final organisation was that the light bomber squadrons and their Wing Headquarters would operate directly under Coningham's HQ and he would decide their targets according to their suitability for air bombing. Bombing would be by daylight and the Blenheims and Marylands would have to be escorted by fighters. The Wellington medium bombers located in the Canal Zone, would remain under Tedder's control, and he would choose their targets with the overall plan in mind. The one squadron of fighter reconnaissance aircraft was to work directly with 30 Corps Headquarters. The 258 Wing fighter squadrons would operate initially under Coningham, but according to the speed of the advance, 258 Wing would move alongside the forward Corps Headquarters and operate independently. It was Coningham's intention that, except in exceptional circumstances, his instructions to me as OC 258 Wing would be in the form of general directives, often verbal, and that all detailed orders to the squadrons would be my responsibility. These arrangements worked well, aided considerably by the efficiency of Operations Room staffs at both his HQ and my own. Shortly before Crusader began, Cunningham and Coningham were to move up to the Fort Maddalena area to a site not far from the four airfields we had built there.

The squadrons joined us on the airfields south of Sidi Barrani a few days before the battle was due to start on 18 November and we at once started fighter sweeps over the wire. It was hoped at Western Desert Air Force HQ that the move might not be noticed for a time by the enemy, but a patrol of five 109Fs appeared over the airfields just as No 2 South African Squadron was landing and shot down a Tomahawk that tried to climb up to engage them. Though plainly the enemy now knew our position, this was the only time we saw them over our base. We operated from these airfields until 18 November and then moved to our battle airfields at Fort Maddalena. During these days we had one enormous slice of luck. On the coastal strip the rains came, the enemy airfields at Gambut and further west at Gazala were waterlogged, and there was a complete absence of Luftwaffe aircraft when the Army rolled forward on the 18th. Nor did the Luftwaffe put in an appearance on either of the next two days, so Rommel was virtually blind as far as air reconnaissance was concerned. For our part the lack of enemy attack from the air gave the Army a wonderful start.

Of course, this non-appearance of enemy aircraft couldn't last and as the ground dried, on 24 November the 109s and Ju87s appeared. There were several engagements south of Tobruk in which we outnumbered the enemy and shot down some dive-bombers. At the same time, we were providing fighter escorts for the Blenheims and Marylands which were attacking targets in the battle area unimpeded by enemy air forces. Already congratulatory messages were coming in. Churchill in a message to Auchinleck wrote, "say Bravo to Tedder and RAF on air mastery . . ." Then after so promising a start in which the Army had reached the ground of their choosing without being seen by the enemy, things started to go wrong.

Rommel, who was apparently preparing for an attack on Tobruk, was initially surprised by the 8th Army advance, but now he quickly recovered. His two formidable Panzer Divisions, 15th and 21st, appeared on the scene and in a series of violent engagements around the ridge of Sidi Rezegh, south of Tobruk, our armour was brought to a standstill and the planned relief of Tobruk did not occur. However, 13 Corps to the north of Maddalena had surrounded the enemy at Halfaya and Bardia, and leaving some forces behind to contain them, pushed westwards to Tobruk with the New Zealand Division leading, and so it was 13 Corps that eventually joined up with the Tobruk garrison many days later.

We airmen, who had been fighting the Germans in France, Norway, the Battle of Britain and over Germany itself, had no illusions about the formidable prowess of our opponents and consequently were not often surprised by the operations of the Luftwaffe during Crusader. Operationally, we were more experienced than the Army and despite the inferiority of our aircraft we seized the initiative from the beginning and held on to it throughout. Our surprise was caused by growing realisation of the incompetence of large parts of the 8th Army. I had assumed that having chased the Italians out of Egypt and Cyrenaica, met the Germans, however briefly, in Greece and Crete and faced them for some months recently on the Egyptian frontier, the Army's organisation would be adequate to absorb inexperienced formations fresh out from the United Kingdom. I could not have made a more incorrect assumption. The first shock was the realisation that, like ours, much of the soldier's equipment was inferior to the enemy's but unlike the airmen, lack of continuous operational experience meant the Army had not learnt how to minimise these deficiencies. Many of the commanders at all levels had not fought the Germans at all in this war. This led to a crucial lack of appreciation of the importance of the most elementary essentials when facing so formidable an enemy. Nowhere was this more apparent than in the area of communications.

W/T communication from forward formations to Army HQ and vice-versa simply did not work. The result was that even the location of friendly formations was often unknown and this made planning bomber operations difficult and sometimes impossible. Despite this almost complete absence of information on the location of our troops, mercifully few mistakes in identity occurred. The most serious result to us was the under-utilisation of the light-bomber force which waited hour after hour bombed up and ready to go, but no information about targets came from the Army. Army intelligence did not pass on to us accurate locations of enemy formations even with the air reconnaissance squadron working directly under Corps HQ, as had been agreed before the battle began. But this proved to be immaterial. With our fighter sweeps and bombers continuously over the battle area the reports we received often gave us a more up-to-date and accurate picture of what was going on than was available at 8th Army HQ. This was quickly recognised and the exchange of information between Operations Rooms became rapid and extensive and benefited all.

In my frequent visits to combined Army-Air HQ I found that my old friend David Belchem from pre-war days at Lydd with the 3rd Battalion of the Royal Tank Corps, was now a senior staff officer at Cunningham's Advanced HQ and I was able by talking to him to get a soldier's impression of what was happening. As a tank man David was critical of the way our armour was being handled. He told me that the German armoured divisions did not at first concentrate to meet our offensive, and our own armour became dispersed through mishandling. Wireless communications were uncertain and Cunningham (who was fired in mid-battle on 26 November) wavered between over-optimism and undue pessimism. He was also harassed by dissension between his infantry and armoured subordinates. The muddle in the battle area meant that our fighters were unable to assist in the ground-attack role as much as we might have done. In our primary role of preventing enemy aircraft from intervening in the land battle we were almost completely successful, however.

Meanwhile, on 24 November, Rommel sent an armoured column supported by motorised infantry behind our forward troops and made a dash eastwards to the frontier wire aiming at a point near Sidi Omar. The route was right across the Army's communications from Fort Maddalena. This move was not reported by the Army, but by mid-morning our fighter leaders were reporting a column going east "lickety split behind our forward troops." 8th Army HQ at first refuted the idea that any enemy could be in such a position "behind our troops" and asserted "RAF mis-identification." I quizzed the next Wing Leader to land, personally. It was Pete Jeffrey, a very experienced and hard-headed Australian. I said, "The Army say it can't be an enemy column in that location." "Well tell them the tanks have big black crosses on them and no British column possesses flak like this one!" The next sweep due over the battlefield was by two South African squadrons who were quickly re-briefed to attack the 'soft' part of the column (ie, the transport vehicles) because their machine-guns were useless against 'hard' tanks. I decided to go along with them to see things for myself. It was mid-afternoon and before I left I gave instructions that all squadrons were to attack the column until darkness made further attacks impossible, but unfortunately there was only about two and a half hours of daylight left.

We found the column without difficulty because of the enormous cloud of dust it was kicking up by its high speed. It was led by thirty or forty tanks followed closely by some 200 MT. Up came the light flak as we approached and for some apparent reason the entire column stopped. The squadrons made their attack while I watched, and then I flew quickly back to base on my own. It was plain to me that Rommel was headed for the wire and the key question in my mind was, would he turn north to help his troops surrounded at Halfaya and Bardia, or would he turn south to attack our Headquarters and airfield area? From his present position he could reach us to the south during the night. I landed and hurried off to Western Desert Headquarters to see Coningham. He had already anticipated my fears and had asked the Army to alert the brigade assigned to airfield defence, only to be told that it had been sent elsewhere.

Of course there is nothing more vulnerable than an airfield with its aeroplanes on the ground. The vast perimeter dictated by the length of the runways makes defence an impossibility for the airmen ground crew, hence the need for ground troops to attack the enemy before he reached the airfield area. Also, the airmen ground crews were neither trained nor equipped for soldier duties. Without any defence, there were only two things to do: evacuate the aircraft to safe bases and when they had gone, send the ground crews off into the desert and hope the enemy wouldn't find them. We had no weapons for defence except rifles and pistols. Back at Wing Headquarters I sent an order for all squadrons to return to their original airfields in the rear at Sidi Hinaish "before last light". There was just about an hour and a half of daylight left and it was a measure of our operational efficiency that despite the complete surprise of my order, all service-able aircraft left promptly and were safe at Sidi Hinaish before dark.

The next step was to disperse the ground crew and equipment away from the airfields and orders were sent to proceed south for some ten miles and to camp there for the night. This move, though unpre-cedented, quite unexpected and at very short notice, was satisfactorily completed but the officers and airmen spent a most uncomfortable winter's night on 24/25 November, sleeping under their lorries. No fires were allowed, not even a cup of chlorinated tea to lessen their misery.

During the night, which I spent in the operations truck, we were full of apprehension. Would Rommel turn north or south when he reached the wire? There were no troops between us and him now. Worse still, as darkness fell, our only source of reliable information, air reconnaissance, ceased. Suddenly there came the sound of armour close to where we were and it took me a moment or two to realise that not even Rommel could have covered the distance from the point of last light sighting to our location in such a short time. I went outside to see a collection of Honey light reconnaissance tanks going by with David Belchem in the leading tank. "My, my", I thought, "we really are scraping the barrel if this is our only defence against Rommel's formidable column!" Sitting through the long night with my Wing staff, it was inevitable that the deficiencies of the 8th Army was a topic of conversation, and it was pretty critical conversation at that. Many sarcastically reminded us of the Army's queries before the start of Crusader as to the Air Force's ability to fulfil its role! The general conclusion amongst these battle-hardened airmen was that our Army partners in Crusader were a very amateur lot, particularly their Commanders. We were grateful that in Tedder and Coningham we had experienced leaders and that their subordinates had been thoroughly tested in combat against Germans and Italians in Europe and the Mediterranean.True the South African squadrons were new to it all but when teamed up with the British and Australians they learned fast, and when it came to air firing they were above average anyway.

When dawn came, pre-arranged reconnaissance aircraft from Sidi Hinaish were already over the area of the enemy column's last sighting and quickly located it on the wire south of Sidi Omar and going north. Sighs of relief all round and then, after consultation with Coningham I ordered the squadrons and ground crews to return to their airfields. During the day the light bombers, which remained undisturbed in their bases in the rear, kept up a continuous attack on Rommel's column which, having failed to dislodge the 4th Indian Division around Sidi Omar, turned west and returned to Sidi Rezegh.

But the enemy armour, though reduced in numbers by the loss of tanks in the dash for the wire, and by hard fighting in the main battle area south of Tobruk, managed to re-group and the struggle continued. The Luftwaffe tried to intervene without much success because of our presence in strength. There were a number of vigorous engagements between our fighter sweeps and German fighters

escorting dive-bombers and our own escort fighters were often hard
pressed while protecting the light bombers. Claims for victories in
aerial combat seemed to favour us, but scores were less important
than the prevention of almost any attacks on the Army. The New
Zealand Division was quick to recognise the difference now from its
previous experience in Greece and Crete. Indeed, General Freyberg,
the Division's commander meeting Tedder during the battle said, "I
want to tell you I think your chaps are simply magnificent and all
my men are saying the same."

Nevertheless the superior performance of the 109F was a continuing
headache to us. Because our sweeps over the battle area and the
bomber escorts were defensive, the Germans would sometimes
surprise us, put in an attack on our fighters and then use their superior
performance to climb away before we could reply. We very much
missed the sort of warning given over R/T by ground controllers based
on radar information as in England. There was a CHL radar set in
Tobruk, however, and we had instructed the crew operating it to
broadcast information of the approach of enemy aircraft from the
west. By our reckoning the radar ought to be able to plot the 109s
soon after taking off from their bases at Gazala, but in practice we
got very little information from this source. I discussed the absence
of warning with Fred Rosier (OC 263 Wing) and we came to the
conclusion that the crew in Tobruk did not appreciate the nature of
the information required by our fighters and that the only solution
would be to send someone there who thoroughly understood our
requirements. The problem was that the air strip in Tobruk was short,
only about six hundred yards, and was within range of the enemy's
guns surrounding the place.

In the early days of the siege, a lone reconnaissance Hurricane had
been left there when we retreated eastwards to the Egyptian border.
The Hurricane was artfully concealed in a convenient wadi with nets
stretched over the top. When it was operated it was started up still
concealed and when all was ready taxied the few yards to the runway,
where it took off, did one full circuit of the Tobruk perimeter at
nought feet and at full throttle with oblique cameras going, landed
and disappeared down the wadi before the enemy even opened fire.
This reconnaissance was invaluable to the garrison commander at
first but gradually his own observation posts could see pretty well
everything that was going on. This was fortunate because inevitably
the enemy got the form, and could lay down a barrage on the air
strip in a matter of minutes, which made life difficult for the Hurricane
pilot who had no choice but to land in the middle of the bombardment.
So in the end the Hurricane and its gallant pilot were withdrawn.

We desperately needed someone to go and state our case.

Fred Rosier volunteered for the job, bless him, and I laid on an escort of two Tomahawk squadrons for his Hurricane and off they went. Unfortunately, before reaching Tobruk the formation encountered a large number of 109s and a battle ensued in which several of the enemy were shot down. Shortly afterwards the Tomahawks began to return in ones and twos, a sure sign that they had been in action. Only one was missing, but so too was Fred's Hurricane. A signal from Tobruk in reply to our 'Most Immediate' query said he had not landed there, and none of the Tomahawk pilots had seen the Hurricane after the engagement. One pilot had seen "the Wing Commander going well on the tail of a 109" but that was all. Gloom descended on our HQ. Fred, as well as being invaluable in organising daily operations, for which his intimate knowledge of the capabilities of each squadron was especially useful, was also the most cheerful of individuals and however bad things were could always see the bright side of any circumstance and make everyone feel better. Now there was nothing for it but to report him 'Missing'. Mary Coningham was very upset when he heard the news and sent for Wing Commander H A Fenton, who, like Fred, had brought a squadron out from England after participating in the Battle of Britain. He had been promoted to Wing Commander and left behind at Sidi Hinaish to look after the reserves left there when we moved forward for Crusader.

The battle continued in what seemed to be an awful muddle and we were not surprised to hear that General Cunningham had been superceded by the Army C-in-C himself, General Auchinleck. David Belchem, back at Army HQ after his 'fling' in the Honey tanks (he never made contact with Rommel's column) was my main contact for inside information. He was plainly still unhappy at the 8th Army's performance to date. In his book *All in the Day's March*, he is quite explicit and there sums up what he was saying to me at the time. Referring to the conclusions he came to immediately the battle for Tobruk ended, he wrote "First we had no General who was a match for Rommel in a major showdown . . . the second major shortcoming was the lack of training of our Desert Army in mobile armoured operations . . . all too frequently our tanks attacked in cavalry-like charges which, against an anti-tank gun line on the ground of the enemy's choosing was often disastrous." He went on to emphasize the "inadequate performance of our radio networks", and finally, the fact that the "Senior Commanders had no conception of the vital need to evolve the systems needed for efficient army/tactical air force operation. This was exemplified during the Tobruk battle when there were at times aircraft waiting at call for target information which was not being provided to the RAF by the Army."

The two battles, one on the frontier around Sidi Omar, Halfaya and Bardia and the other south of Tobruk continued, but enemy air activity was restricted to the latter area where on 4 December six Ju87s were claimed as shot down and six more as damaged. It was now seventeen days since the start of Crusader and Tobruk had still not been relieved. We were well behind the Army's optimistic forecasts made before the battle started, but things did seem to be going better on the ground and our losses in the air from ack-ack and fighters were much less than we had anticipated. We at 258 Wing were confident we could keep up the maximum effort called for by Coningham for some time yet.

In December we had a visit from Major General George H Brett of the American Army Air Force, who was now stationed in Cairo to facilitate the flow of American aircraft across the Takoradi route and to observe and report on the whole situation in North Africa. He was with me on 8 December when the news of the Japanese attack on Pearl Harbor was reported on the radio. His reaction was, "Well we are all in it together now". What he said anticipated by days the German declaration of war on the United States but was an indication of the realisation in the American military of their inevitable participation in the Second World War.

Later that day I flew on a sweep with 274 Squadron and over Gambut airfield, which seemed to have been deserted by the Germans, I heard and felt a bang in the fuselage below my seat. All the instruments appeared normal and after checking the controls, I came to the conclusion that the bang must have been made by a stray ack-ack shell exploding nearby. We then saw that Gambut was not deserted as had been reported for two 109s appeared from under their camouflage sheets and took off. Sid Linnard, the CO of 274, detached two sections to deal with them. At the end of the sweep we returned to LG 124, the Squadron's airfield, and I decided to land there to have a word with the pilots. I came in at the end of the stream and held off for a normal landing but as soon as the wheels touched the ground the Hurricane did a forward somersault and finished up upside down in a cloud of dust with me trapped in the cockpit. I couldn't move and it was quite dark, but almost at once there was the sound of voices outside and the aircraft was lifted bodily by the airmen and pilots who had rushed to the spot in any vehicle that was handy. Sid Linnard helped me release my harness and parachute and lowered me to the ground. I thought I was alright, albeit a bit shaken, but I was helped into an ambulance as a precaution, and after a short ride arrived at a collection of tents that I learned afterwards was an Army casualty clearing station.

I was put into a bed in my clothes on rough army blankets. There were a dozen beds in the tent with some occupied by groaning patients. A doctor appeared to examine me. I had had a crack on the head when the Hurricane hit the ground and this seemed to affect my left eye, but otherwise I was in no pain although I did feel extraordinarily weak. I was told by the doctor that this was the effect of shock. I couldn't understand this since I had never had such symptoms after any of the crashes earlier in my service. Anyway, at that moment I was quite content to lie still and to be left alone though the arrival during the night of several more wounded soldiers made sleep difficult. I lay in the tent for the next two days and on 11 December I was told that I was to be evacuated by air to Cairo. Nobody came to see me from Wing HQ which I thought a bit odd, until I heard afterwards that the doctor had forbidden visits. I went by ambulance to LG75, the HQ airfield, and was by this time a 'sitting patient' with a bandage over my left eye.

The aeroplane was a small civil Lockheed flown by Captain Hunt of BOAC and there was only one other passenger, General Freyberg, the commander of the already famous New Zealand Division. We sat side by side and he was very complimentary about our efforts in "almost clearing the air completely of the enemy." I suppose we had been flying for about an hour when the co-pilot wrote down a message that he had received on his earphones. He handed it to Captain Hunt who read it and then turned round and handed it to Freyberg, who also read it and then appeared to be thinking about its contents as he looked ahead. After a while he handed me the message which read, "The Admiralty regret to announce the loss of HMS *Prince of Wales* and HMS *Repulse* in operations in the China Sea." What a terrible thing to happen. The Navy were having a very rough time indeed, and I could visualise the scene in the Air Defence Centre of my old 252 Wing HQ with urgent calls from the Naval Office at Ras el Tin imploring us to prevent any air reconnaissance of the harbour.

We landed at Heliopolis and I was taken off to army general hospital in Cairo which was civilisation indeed compared with the casualty clearing station. There were clean sheets, nurses, white-coated orderlies, iced water, everything you could wish for. Next day the doctors removed the bandages and examined my eye. Apparently the front of the eyeball had received a blow in the crash and this had made the retina bleed. The blood dripping down obscured the lower half and this meant that I had only half vision in that eye. The Army doctor was explicit. "Either the blood will absorb in which case you will be restored to full sight in that eye. Or, if it does not absorb, then your sight will remain as it is now." Rest was prescribed but after a week with no noticeable change I managed to get myself discharged on a week's sick leave, which I spent on a delightful river houseboat moored on the Nile near the Gesirah Sporting Club. I wore a patch over my injured eye. There were several other air force officers recuperating on the boat and it turned out to be an enjoyable break, but the news from the Desert on the radio and in the local English language newspaper was good, and I longed to be back with my Wing.

So at the end of the week, I went to Middle East HQ and told my friends in the Operations Branch that I was returning to the Desert. "What about your eye?" asked Wing Commander Elton. I said it would be alright in a few days and collected my meagre kit from the houseboat, thumbed a lift to Heliopolis and went straight to the watch office on the edge of the airfield. There I asked the Sergeant doing Pilot Duty if there were any aircraft going up to the Desert. He shook his head but pointing to a row of Hurricanes commented "those have to be ferried." I said I would take one up. The duty crew were sent for and they stowed my kit in the fuselage, but there was a snag: I had no parachute. Eventually one was obtained and I signed for it. The Hurricane, a new Mark II, was started and surprisingly I found my one good eye to be quite adequate. It was late afternoon by the time I was airborne and I decided to break my journey at Alexandria, so I set course for the naval airfield at Dekeila and managed to stay the night with Judge and Mrs Holmes.

The next morning, 28 December, I headed west, landing at Maaten Bagush, the location of Rear HQ of the Western Desert Air Force. There I learned that Advanced HQ was now at Tmimi fifty five miles west of Tobruk. My 258 Wing, now commanded by Wing Commander Jimmy Fenton, and the fighter squadrons were at a place called Msus right out in the Desert about sixty miles south-east of Benghazi. I flew on, refuelled at Tobruk and was at Tmimi by nightfall, reporting to Air Commodore Embry, the Senior Air Staff Officer, who gave me a warm welcome. I met Mary Coningham and the rest of the staff when they foregathered in the Mess tent that evening before dinner. Mary's manner was a bit distant, in distinct contrast to that of Basil and the rest of the staff, and I heard afterwards that it had been his intention to have Jimmy Fenton (who was more amenable to Mary) succeed me at 258 Wing and that only Basil's indignant intervention had saved me. This was the first real indication I had that I did not have the full confidence of the Air Officer Commanding.

I flew to Msus in the Hurricane next morning, a fifty-minute trip, and by concentrating on keeping an accurate compass course had no trouble finding the place. Jimmy Fenton met me. He had had a signal from Basil telling him that I would be re-assuming command of the Wing on arrival. He had no knowledge of any move to supersede me. We went to my office trailer where Jimmy gave me a run down on the current Army and Air Force situations. He told me that our Wing was now working directly with 13 Corps commanded by Lt General Godwin-Austen with Brigadier John Harding as his BGS. Their HQ was located about forty miles south-west of Msus at a place called Antelat where three new airfields were being constructed for us and to which we would move as soon as they were ready. The Army front was static at Agedabia near the Gulf of Sirte, but Jimmy said that the Army Commander, Lieutenant General Ritchie, had landed at Msus a few days before on his way to 13 Corps. Ritchie had told him that he was confident that as soon as supplies had built up through the port of Benghazi, he would advance again with Tripoli as the objective. This meant moving some three hundred miles westward. We had already travelled five hundred miles and were becoming accustomed to these considerable distances; our new-found mobility gave us confidence that anywhere the Army went we could go too.

I went over the flying programme that Jimmy had laid on for the day and then flew down to Antelat to call on 13 Corps HQ. The General was away and I was briefed by John Harding. The line at Agedabia was manned by a Guards Brigade and 22nd Armoured Brigade. A new Armoured Division from the UK, the 1st, was due to move up shortly and the 7th Armoured Division (the Desert Rats) and 4th Indian were up in the Jebel Achdar, the latter near Barce. Though Benghazi had been captured five days previously on 24 December there appeared to be no urgency to move south to where the Germans were, at Agedabia. I thought that the Corps was scattered over a very wide area, but the Army believed that Rommel was only just able to hold on at Agedabia and that as soon as we were ready to advance he would resume his retreat westwards.

The Luftwaffe had not interfered significantly since the Army had reached Agedabia, but it was quickly clear to me that our airfields at Msus were too far behind the front line, and that if we moved forward to Antelat we would have more time for sweeps over our forward troops. Having absorbed the local 'form', I flew back to Tmimi to clear the move forward to the Antelat air strips with George Beamish who had replaced Basil Embry as Coningham's SASO in January 1942. The move was completed by mid-January, but our stay at Antelat was to be short lived.

The sweeps from Antelat over the Agedabia area encountered little opposition from the Luftwaffe but as usual the flak from the enemy positions there was as hot as ever. On 17 January we had a visit from both Tedder and Coningham, in Blenheims of 45 Squadron. I got all the Squadron Commanders together and as usual Tedder was splendid in talking to and with them.

It was terribly cold in the desert at this time and by some freak to do with sun spots, wireless communication with Western Desert HQ was interrupted for long spells each lasting twenty-four hours. Since 13 Corps HQ found the same difficulty in communicating with 8th Army HQ, we were largely left to ourselves in conducting operations. I discussed with Fred Rosier (who thankfully had rejoined us after a three-day march through enemy lines) our prospect for the advance into Tripolitania and we agreed that as soon as it started we should be prepared for greatly increased opposition in the air, and the inevitable losses we would suffer since there had been no change in the situation whereby all our fighters were inferior to the latest models of the Me 109. Because the distances to our base areas in Egypt were so great and the communications so poor, we decided to bring up before the advance started the two reserve aircraft per squadron that were held in the rear supply unit way back at Maaten Bagush. With these additional aircraft we would have just over a hundred fighters on the four airstrips at Antelat and this comprised the major part of the fighter force in the Middle East at this time. Then on 20 January it started to rain.

We had no meteorological staff in the desert since forecasting was unnecessary, the weather always being flyable. Now it rained and how it rained! Most downpours lasted for about half-an-hour and the rain was heavier than anything I had experienced anywhere before. The graded dirt runways were rapidly turned to mud and unfit for take-off or landing. Many of the tracks from the Wing HQ to the airstrips became bogs and impassable for vehicles. This was a very serious situation. On the Antelat airstrips the fighter force was quite helpless, and unable to lift a finger in its own defence, let alone defend the Army. The Luftwaffe were operating from sandy strips near the coast which we knew from previous experience dried quite quickly after even the heaviest of rain. When the enemy discovered our plight, as they were bound to do sooner or later from our complete absence from the skies over the front line, we could expect our airstrips to be attacked and our aircraft destroyed. The gun defence of the airstrips provided by the Army was thin, and the light ack-ack of Bofors guns, our main defence against low-flying fighters, though good, was far from sufficient to prevent any determined attack. The long term effects of the destruction of the fighter force, if this were to happen, were appalling to contemplate. The Army, though much superior in numbers to the enemy, was only just a match for him if left alone to get on with the job. If it was to suffer air attack by an unfettered Luftwaffe as well as by the enemy land forces, then defeat as in Greece and Crete could be expected. To my great surprise, however, 13 Corps were not particularly worried when the situation was explained over the field telephone. They said that the front at Agedabia was quiet and it was believed that the first movement there would be *our* offensive to start the advance into Tripolitania.

During the afternoon of 20 January the rain mercifully eased and in discussion with Rosier and the Squadron Commanders we decided that if we could make the strips serviceable by filling the soft spots with bushes and stones, we could at least provide a token presence in the air over the front and hopefully conceal our predicament from the Luftwaffe. When I went to bed that night I prayed that the dry weather of the afternoon and evening would continue during the night. My prayers were in vain. All through the night at irregular intervals the heavens opened and down came the rain. The noise of the downpour on the metal roof of my trailer was deafening. Then it would stop and the silence of the desert would return and after a bit I would fall asleep, only to be wakened shortly afterwards by the next deluge.

When dawn came at last on 21 January I dressed quickly and went outside. My first step on what looked like firm ground resulted in my leg descending up to my upper thigh in mud the colour and consistency of chocolate blancmange. Water was lying in puddles everywhere. Because there was no lasting vegetation and therefore no root structure to hold the soil together or provide any form of drainage, the desert was waterlogged. By carefully probing the ground with a stick I reached the Mess tent fifty yards away. The cooks were busy making breakfast but were late because, like me, they had encountered problems moving from their sleeping tents to the Mess. Fortunately the field telephones continued to function despite the lines being laid on the surface. I checked with the Squadron Commanders and found that conditions with them were the same as at my Headquarters, so that all our airstrips were unserviceable. It had stopped raining, however. I called a meeting of the Commanding Officers at once. They made their way on foot as best they could, and when they were all gathered, I told them that it was imperative that we move from the Antelat area just as soon as we were able. I explained that there was an ex-German airstrip south of Benghazi, which seemed to have escaped the worst of the rain and which we would use temporarily, and we could cover the front from there. It would be a bit congested with all six squadrons on the one strip but we would have to accept that. The next problem was how we were to fly off our waterlogged strips. One of the Squadron Commanders said that his strip, though pretty bad, was not as wet as the others because it had been built on a slight ridge, and we all staggered off to look at it. It was certainly better than the others but even here, there was still the problem of the apparently bottomless holes filled with mud. There was only one thing for it—we would have to fill these holes with whatever we could find nearby, which in practice meant little scrub bushes and stones.

We set about the task, some two thousand men, everyone except the Bofors crews and the wireless operators on watch. In no time all were coated in mud from head to toe but everyone was cheerful, glad to be getting on with something constructive at last. By mid-day a strip, eight hundred yards long and forty feet wide, had been prepared and was tested by manhandling a lorry on to it and sending it up and down a couple of times. We were ready to go. Fortunately, the rain still held off and the desert was beginning to dry. Then a signal arrived from the coast that the airstrip south of Benghazi was unsuitable because parts of it had been mined by the Germans. There was no alternative now but to return to the strips we had left some days before at Msus. We knew they were dry. I sent a 'Most Immediate' signal to Beamish telling him of the change, and got a reply within the hour saying that he did not understand the reasons for going to Msus but nevertheless agreed with the change. In the meantime the order of take-off by the six squadrons had been arranged and then began the most extraordinary take-off operation witnessed in the Desert up to that time.

First, the Hurricanes. Each one was manhandled to the take-off point by thirty or more airmen under the wings and some on the tail. Then with the engine going full bore and amidst clouds of mud and water the aeroplane progressed slowly towards the end of the strip. I watched with some anxiety as the first Hurricane opened up for take-off. It went lurching down the narrow strip, the pilot rightly keeping the tail down until he had enough speed to give him some fore and aft control and then tail up and he was airborne. I breathed a sigh of relief. One after another the Hurricanes left the ground and then it was the turn of the Tomahawks. These aeroplanes were heavier than the Hurricanes but surprisingly did not sink into the mud as much; probably because they had larger diameter wheels. By nightfall we had despatched three of the six squadrons. In the meantime, my Wing HQ and the advanced ground parties of the squadrons had packed up and were ready to move back on the main desert track from Antelat to Msus. It was to take them twenty-four hours to cover the forty miles to Msus, many bogged vehicles having to be winched out by the winding gear of the accompanying ack-ack gunners. There was no rain that night and at first light on 22 January the remaining aircraft were manhandled to the strip and dispatched. The ground crews left in their vehicles immediately the last aircraft was airborne.

We had decided that Fred Rosier and a skeleton Wing HQ would remain at Antelat, keep in close touch with 13 Corps HQ and brief the fighters in the air by R/T as they passed overhead on their way to the operating area at Agedabia. My own Hurricane was at the end of the strip, but before leaving I went over to Corps HQ to tell them of the arrangements I had made. When I got there I sensed a certain uneasiness and John Harding told me that the Germans had attacked towards Agedabia during the night. He believed that the enemy move was "only a reconnaissance in force and wouldn't get far." I was startled: we had enough problems without having to cope with an enemy advance. However, the measure I had taken of moving the squadrons back to Msus, entirely because of the unserviceability of the airstrips at Antelat, proved fortuitously a move that in the event saved all six squadrons and 258 Wing HQ from being overrun by the enemy.

I hurried back to the airstrip, saw Fred Rosier, briefed him on the situation, warned him to watch closely with Corps HQ the enemy's movements and to let us know at Msus, by point-to-point R/T, of any developments. I then took off in my Hurricane and landed on a good hard strip at Msus half-an-hour later. My HQ had arrived some hours previously and had set up camp in its former location. I joined them there and was regaled with the story of their horrific journey through the night, with the frequent bogging of vehicles. However, all had arrived eventually at Msus together with the ground parties. With the ground drying rapidly, I hoped that the rear parties (those that had departed after the last aircraft had left) would travel quicker. This proved to be the case and we were all complete by mid-afternoon on 22 January. The ground at Msus was quite dry and despite the exhaustion caused by our journey from Antelat, the squadrons would be operational for first light next day, 23 January.

My station wagon had survived the move and during the afternoon I went round the squadrons. Everyone was in good heart and looking forward to resuming full operations the next morning. When I returned to the Wing HQ in the late afternoon I found the operations caravan functioning fully and contact with Western Desert Air Force HQ established. I therefore sent a brief situation report to Beamish and then asked the Operations Officer if Wing Commander Rosier had reported anything from Antelat? He said he had been unable to contact him on R/T or W/T. This was odd because I had impressed on Fred the need to keep us informed about the ground situation as interpreted by 13 Corps. No contact having been made with Rosier by 16.00 hrs, I decided to make a quick trip back to Antelat before dark to see if I could raise Fred by R/T from there.

The wintry sun was low in the sky as I flew and was directly ahead of me, making forward visibility difficult. I was over the top of Antelat almost before I realised I was there, and overshot the airfield a little. Looking back down sun, the visibility was better and I saw that the site of Rosier's Wing HQ was now empty. I was flying at 2,000 ft and I saw a column of vehicles headed by a few tanks approaching the now empty airstrips on the track from Agedabia. At the same moment the column opened up on me with a volume of light flak and I realised at once that it was the enemy. Reconnaissance in force it certainly was! It had moved fast to reach its present position. I sheered off and headed for Msus. On the way back the truth struck me. There was no Army presence between Antelat and the squadrons on the ground at Msus. What's more the desert was drying rapidly and it wouldn't take long for the enemy to cover the forty miles, which it had taken our ground parties twenty-four hours to negotiate. I was fairly certain though, that they couldn't do it during the night. I called the Wing on the R/T and told the operator to summon the Squadron Commanders and Wing staff to a meeting at the operations caravan right away. I landed just before dark and drove straight there to find that they were all already assembled. I told them of my experience over Antelat. In the meantime, I was informed that we had received no replies from our frequent calls to 13 Corps and Rosier.

There was no need for me to stress our extreme vulnerability at Msus. We would have to move further back until the Army stabilised a front somewhere. Mechili was the next airfield about eighty miles to the north-east and that was where we would have to go. There were long faces amongst the Squadron Commanders when I said the ground parties and aircraft must leave at first light, whilst the aircraft would operate forward to the Antelat area and land back at Mechili. One CO said, "Some of my chaps have only just pulled in from that dreadful march from Antelat and have had no sleep for 48 hours". "Well," I relied "If we don't leave at first light we may well be 'in the bag' by mid-day!" They all knew the truth of what I said and hurried off back to their squadrons. Though the men were near exhaustion, preparations for the departure started straightaway and then, sometime after midnight, all was quiet as everyone snatched a few hours sleep. I sent a signal to Coningham's HQ telling them what I intended. By this time I was pretty certain the situation at Antelat would be known at Tmimi, where the joint Army-Air HQ were located and they would fully appreciate the need for a hasty withdrawal to Mechili. Long before dawn I was awakened by the noise of vehicles and having dressed I went outside. All around were the lights of trucks forming themselves in columns and more and more joining from the airstrips every minute.

We had a Flight Lieutenant Young, a "hostilities only" officer, who was something of an expert in desert navigation and he had been given the task and great responsibility of leading the convoy to Mechili. At the first sign of light in the east he came across to my trailer and asked permission to start. I gave it to him and wished him luck. He went back to his vehicle, pulled out a Very pistol, fired a green light high in the air, mounted his vehicle and started off eastwards at the head of his four hundred truck convoy. As it grew lighter, the first of the squadrons was airborne and the ground crews who stayed behind to see the aircraft off, then ran to their trucks and set off to catch up with the convoy. When all the squadrons had gone I went over to my Hurricane, the airmen starting the engine as I approached. We changed mounts, the ground crew in my station wagon and me to the aeroplane. They were confident that they would soon catch the convoy up and I waved to them as I took off, setting a course for Tmimi, for it was high time I found out exactly what my superior HQ knew about what was going on.

At Tmimi I saw George Beamish in his office trailer and gave him an account of the events at Antelat and the reasons for my ordering the move to Mechili after such a short stay at Msus. He appreciated that there had been no time to consult Coningham by signal and said that both he and Coningham were very relieved when they heard that I had extricated the fighter force from such a predicament. I emphasised that it was the rain soaking the airstrips that had dictated my decision to withdraw from Antelat and that if I had depended on 13 Corps and their belief that the enemy's advance was "just a reconnaissance in force that won't get far", all six squadrons with over a hundred aircraft and the Wing HQ would have been overrun and captured. Beamish said that word had come through that 13 Corps HQ at Antelat had very nearly suffered that fate themselves and were now on their way to Msus. Mary Coningham was away from the Headquarters and George said I must stay until I had seen him. I could see this meant staying the night when I was anxious to rejoin my Wing and squadrons at Mechili, but there was no alternative.

I got a message to go to Mary's trailer after dark and found my way, stumbling over the guy ropes of the tents. The trailer looked like any other from the outside, but inside it was a tiny piece of civilisation in the wilderness of the desert. Soft-shaded lights, comfortable bench seats and the whole tastefully decorated. Mary was pleased to see me, gave me a drink and wanted to hear at first hand all that had happened at Antelat and Msus. Whilst we were talking the door opened and a worried looking General Ritchie appeared. He refused Mary's offer of a drink and held out a signal which he said he was proposing to send to 13 Corps. Mary read it and handed it back without comment. When Ritchie had gone, Mary said it was an instruction to 13 Corps to go over to the offensive. I was surprised because with my knowledge of the confusion amongst the formations that had been at Agedabia, the remoteness from Corps HQ of those around Benghazi and with the Corps Commander and his staff on the move, I believed that the best we could hope for was a withdrawal and that formations would not be attacked piecemeal in their dispersed state. Before leaving I said I would be off to Mechili at first light. Mary agreed but insisted that I return the next evening when Tedder and Auchinleck were expected.

When I arrived overhead Mechili next morning, it looked very crowded with over a hundred aircraft on the airfield. Fortunately, the Luftwaffe had been left far behind by the Wehrmacht and were out of range for we certainly were an excellent target. I landed and was met by my driver full of tales of the convoy's experiences on the way from Msus. He drove me over to Wing HQ located on a small knoll about half a mile from the edge of the airfield. Here all was functioning well. A programme of armed reconnaissance had been arranged for the fighters and had been going since dawn. Another squadron was standing by to escort Blenheims who were expected overhead by mid-morning. I was told that reconnaissance of the Antelat/Msus area showed that the enemy was in small numbers at the former but they had not progressed further east. Rosier's 268 Wing HQ was now set up at Msus and had been in contact with the recce aircraft.

It was a relief to know that Fred was safe and during the day we exchanged signals. We agreed that he would stay at Msus as long as he could to perform the same role as at Antelat—always supposing 13 Corps established themselves at Msus and had any information worth passing on to our fighters. At present our situation map at Mechili, based entirely on air recce and reports from the fighter leaders, seemed to be the only one in the Desert painting the whole picture. During our operations that day we saw nothing of the enemy air force. This absence was fortunate because the Desert east of Msus and up to and beyond Mechili was full of straggling army units heading east who plainly could not defend themselves against air attack. We were using all our aircraft forward and couldn't possibly have looked after such widely dispersed motor transport. Many of these stragglers stopped at Wing HQ asking for information about what was going on. Many had no orders and were just following the general movement eastwards.

The next day, having waited for the results of the first-light reconnaissance which showed that the enemy had not progressed beyond Antelat, and having arranged a programme for attack on targets resulting from further reconnaissance, I went off to Tmimi as instructed, to see Coningham and Tedder. There was a signal in to 8th Army HQ to say that 13 Corps was now established at Msus but as it was plain that the Corps had lost control of its formations and knew little of what was going on, 258 Wing would now revert to the AOC's command, Mary ordering our operations to fit in with the Army Commander's plans.

I said that though Mechili was satisfactory in being forward enough to allow us to operate as far west as Antelat, having six squadrons on one airfield was too much of a risk once the Luftwaffe started operating again. Coningham agreed and said he would have the ex-enemy airstrips at Gazala prepared for us. These were sixty miles further east still so he said we would have to accept the risk and stay at Mechili until the tactical situation on the ground made it necessary to move back. Now that we were directly under his control, he would give the order to move. As I flew back to Mechili I thanked my lucky stars that the Air Force commanders at least seemed to know what they were about.

On 26 January we started getting orders from Coningham's HQ for our operations. As these were based almost entirely on the information contained in our own reconnaissance reports, we had often anticipated those orders and consequently were very quickly off the mark. Fred Rosier remained at Msus even after 13 Corps had once more up-sticked and retired eastwards. We really could not see the reason for this move because our reconnaissance showed that the enemy's advance had stopped at Antelat. Later it became apparent that this pause was determined by a second enemy thrust northwards to attack the other part of 13 Corps and to recapture Benghazi, which they did on 28 January.

Coningham's HQ brought the light bombers more and more into the operations, even though no calls were coming from the Army. The Blenheims were based at Gambut (about thirty miles to the east) and we had no telephone communication from Mechili. This made detailed arrangements for escort by my fighters difficult. The Squadron mostly concerned was 14 which seemed to have been nominated to lead whenever more than one squadron participated.

It was commanded by a remarkable young man, Squadron Leader John Kenneth Buchanan. I had first met this outstanding chap in the days before Crusader when, as Group Training Instructor at Western Desert HQ at Maaten Bagush, I had been involved in exercises to determine the drill to be adopted by fighters for escorting the Blenheims and Marylands. As was usual, at the beginning of such exercises "cock-ups" occurred and at the conference afterwards the fighter squadron commanders, who were in the majority, were vociferous in blaming the bombers for all the mistakes. However when the noise died down, a small slim Squadron Leader with rather long fair hair and effeminate appearance quietly refuted the criticism of the bombers and turned the tables by explaining precisely what had gone wrong and showed that most of the mistakes had been by the fighters. It was clear to me as the arbiter in the argument that Buchanan was right and I noted that here was an exceptional leader whose judgement should be respected. I found that his crews had complete confidence in him and would follow him anywhere. Apparently he had a passion for bombing the enemy, so much so that he never missed a sortie by his Squadron irrespective of whether it was his turn or not. This procedure became so exhausting for his crew that he arranged to have two crews which he took on operations alternately.

Buchanan now brought his Blenheims up to Mechili and we made our arrangements. He would be receiving his targets directly from Western Desert Air Force HQ which would repeat the "time on target" to us. He would lead his bomber formation overhead Mechili where we would have a squadron at readiness to scramble on sight and escort him to the target and back. I thought I had better see for myself how this bombing 'maestro' operated and so joined the next escort. The target was a concentration of enemy M/T north of Antelat. When we arrived at the pin-point given, the number of vehicles were much fewer than had been reported earlier and Buchanan started a search. We fighter pilots were all the time conscious of our diminishing fuel and the possibility of the appearance of 109s. In our vulnerable position, tied to the bombers, we were sitting ducks. After what seemed an age I began to wonder how much longer we would be hanging about in this area. when a larger column of M/T was sighted and after one 'dummy run' the Blenheims hit the target fair and square. I was relieved when we turned for home, and when afterwards I remarked to the fighter leaders on the time Buchanan had taken in the target area, one said "Buck is always like that, never wastes a bomb, but he puts years on us."

13 Corps HQ stayed a few days at Msus and then moved back

again advising Fred Rosier to do the same. Fred could not see the sense in this since our reconnaissance still showed that the enemy had not advanced from Antelat and all the movement seen was northward towards Benghazi. So he ignored the Corps' advice and remained a few more days, giving such information as he could glean to the fighter sweeps as they passed overhead. On 28 January we moved to Gazala occupying the three airstrips that had been prepared for us astride the coast road. That evening Fred and I were in the operations vehicle taking stock. Between 2 and 28 January we had moved the entire fighter force of over a hundred aircraft four times. Once forward and three times back. Except at Antelat, where we had left six unrepairable aircraft, we had lost nothing, not even a vehicle. Now, with a line forming in front of us at last, it was time for 'make and mend'. Aircraft maintenance was first priority and sleep the second. However, we were now in communication with our HQ by telephone and George Beamish had other ideas. He wanted a maximum effort on "interdiction" and despite my pleas about the exhaustion of the force, he insisted. Fortunately the difference was referred to Mary Coningham who took my part, so our original programme stood. Whilst these discussions were going on some signals were brought in by a runner and placed on the bench in front of us. When we had finished our work I picked up the first signal which announced that "the immediate award of the Distinguished Service Order had been made to Group Captain Cross and Wing Commander Rosier." I handed it to Fred who read it, laughed and said "If we had been going forward instead of retreating we would probably have got VCs."

We were not long at Gazala because the defensive position being established there south to Bir Hacheim (a line more than forty miles in extent) meant that our airstrips were too far forward for safety. But whilst we were there, an unforgettable incident occurred. The Luftwaffe started operating again and a Ju88 was seen at about 18,000 ft over our airstrips. We had no radar warning of its approach and though two Kittyhawks were off the ground in double quick time we knew they had no hope of intercepting. We had a battery of 3.7 AA guns as part of our defences but for some reason that was never known to me, when the order to fire was given instead of four, only one gun fired. To everyone's astonishment this single round scored a direct hit against all odds. The Ju88 was badly damaged and crashed some distance away to the east.

We moved eastwards again, this time to a new set of airstrips adjacent to the main Gambut airfield that had already changed hands four times in just over a year. Fred Rosier set up his Wing HQ at

El Adem airfield about fifteen miles south of Tobruk. At Gazala we inherited a CHL radar which had been used up until then to provide some cover for the ship convoys going along the coast to Benghazi. We were surprised and delighted to discover that this set could detect and plot aircraft quite soon after they had taken off from Martuba (about 120 miles west of Gambut) which became the forward airfield for the Luftwaffe. This source of information was to prove most valuable as time went on.

By February 1942, the war in the Far East had begun to affect us significantly. From six squadrons with over a hundred aircraft, we were reduced by the middle of the month to just forty fighters. It was therefore just as well that the front became static with few calls from the Army for attack of ground targets. The bombers, Blenheims and Marylands by day and the Wellingtons from Egypt by night, turned their attention to the enemy's lines of communication right back to Benghazi. Our main task was now the air defence of Tobruk, the main supply port. Its importance to us was equally well known to the enemy and he brought his Ju87s up to Martuba and mounted daily attacks on the shipping in the port. Thanks to the radar set at Gazala, we had considerable success in intercepting these raids. Occasionally we missed and if we were very unlucky a ship would be hit. Mary Coningham had come to the Desert from Bomber Command and had no experience of the use of radar in air defence. Consequently, he was inclined to doubt its value and be critical of our holding the main part of the force at Readiness on the ground, dependent on its warning alone. He had thought initially that we would do better to have aircraft in the sky over Tobruk and the front throughout the day.

I pointed out that with our much-reduced force this would mean patrolling in small numbers which would not be effective against the Tobruk raids, and over the front would be extremely vulnerable to the 109s with their superior performance. After some discussion we were allowed to continue our interception policy. This meant telling the Army that the forward troops would see little of us for a time and it was agreed that, to give them the best chance to defend themselves, they were cleared to open fire on any aircraft seen without having first to identify it. Our fighter reconnaissance aircraft who were active every day, now took the sensible precaution of entering enemy territory from the sea rather than crossing our own front line.

The Luftwaffe, now in some strength at Martuba and Derna, were not slow to note our numerical weakness and rubbed it in with surprise attacks on our airfields by small numbers of 109s. We did everything we could to minimise the damage caused by these attacks by wide dispersal and building dummy airfields. These measures helped, but on one occasion 112 Squadron, under the legendary Clive Caldwell was attacked out of the blue just after landing at Gambut Main and lost half its aircraft in a matter of minutes. Mary Coningham was always splendid when we had a real disaster and was quickly on the phone with words of encouragement. In between, though, he kept niggling on about having "continuous patrols".

Once we were static, visitors from Cairo came in a steady wave to see what was going on. The Press particularly were there in force. At first Western Desert Air Force HQ attracted them but having once visited the Wing they were inclined to hang about to get first-hand stories. We were rather pleased to see some fresh faces around the place, but in one instance the presence of the Press led to an unfortunate occurrence that could have been, but thankfully was not, a very serious matter.

During my frequent visits to Mary's caravan I noticed that a Flight Lieutenant, always the same man, would bring in a sheaf of signals printed on very thin blue paper which Mary would sign for. This was Ultra. Many months later, when I became an Air Officer Commanding myself, I was indoctrinated into this most secret intelligence source, and I then realised these were the signals that I had seen Mary receiving. On one occasion Mary read one of the blue chits to me (which he should not have done) about a proposed enemy attack on Gambut at first light the next day. When I got back to the Wing, the staff were all at supper in the Mess, so finding the Duty Operations Officer, I instructed him to warn the squadrons and Ack Ack, and to have a patrol airborne to cover the first light period. Unbeknown to me, this conversation was overheard by a Reuters correspondent (in the Desert everyone dressed the same—in khaki battledress) who sent off a piece which was published in Cairo and London. I found out afterwards that all hell then broke loose in both cities, with Tedder himself demanding explanations from Mary.

I should explain that such was the importance in preserving the secrecy of Ultra from the enemy that when intelligence from this source was used to initiate air operations, elaborate cover plans were mandatory to mislead the Germans into believing we had obtained the information from another source. For instance, if Ultra told us that a supply ship was leaving port at a certain hour bound for Benghazi, then before it could be attacked by bombers or torpedo aircraft it would first have to be located by reconnaissance aircraft which would broadcast the ship's position when sighted. Only then could it be attacked. Of course without Ultra the reconnaissance aircraft might never have found the ship at all. In February 1942 I knew nothing of this secret, and in giving my instructions to the Duty Operations Officer used the same words that Mary had used to me which he had taken from the Ultra signal. It was the exact use of these words by the journalist that had caused the alarm in Cairo and London. Presumably the Germans did not spot it, for Ultra continued successfully until the end of the war, and the Reuters man, true to his profession, did not disclose his source when quizzed later in Cairo.

At about this time my driver, a very important man in the Desert, was required to take a course in Egypt. I asked the MT officer if he could recommend a replacement and he said he had a particularly good airman whom he was sure would do the job well. When I met him I found that Aircraftsman Rees was Dai Rees, the already famous professional golfer, and thus began a partnership that lasted until I went to Tunisia in 1943, and a friendship which endured until his death in 1983.

My relations with Mary Coningham remained somewhat strained. He would not go so far as giving me a direct order to introduce the continuous patrols which I believed would be ineffective, but he continued to niggle about our interception policy, particularly when we missed. For my part, I was sure we were doing the best we could with our depleted force. Despite being on the defensive in defending Tobruk, once airborne on an interception we were on the offensive and the German fighters, tied to their dive-bombers, often suffered. Mary never did give the order to change.

Now came news that the fighter force was to be built up again for the next offensive planned for the spring and for the Wing organisation to be changed. My 258 Wing was to become 211 Group and the squadrons would be paired together each under a Wing HQ. It seemed to me to be rather top heavy but in the event the reorganisation did not concern me personally because, during one of Mary's infrequent visits to Cairo, I received a signal posting me back to command my old 252 Wing at Alexandria. I was to be succeeded by Guy Carter who had once been my Flight Commander at Sealand in 1935. Guy was a delightful man, a World War 1 pilot but with no operational flying experience in World War 2.

It was a bit of a shock. No doubt my disagreement with Mary over the employment of the fighter force was the cause of my move. Well, it was Mary's air force and if he wanted a change that was it. Guy arrived and I did my best to put the old retread into the picture. Thankfully Fred was to remain as Guy's No 2 so that would ensure continuity. At the end of a week I packed my bag, stowed it in the Hurricane, gave the rest of my kit to Rees and Tommy the batman to take with them in the station wagon, arranged to meet them at Seagull Camp in Alexandria and flew off out of the Desert.

CHAPTER XII

SQUADRON LEADER I K P CROSS DFC

Ian was the youngest of our family of five children. The eldest, my sister Joyce, died of peritonitis following an operation for appendicitis before Ian was born on 4 April 1918, so I was the eldest followed by two more sisters Jean and Baba. As the youngest, Ian was the favourite and deserved our love and affection because of his splendidly cheerful disposition. He was ill for a long period while a baby, being unable to digest any form of milk. Though I was only seven at the time I can remember the gloom in the household. He was saved by the local GP at Hayling Island where we were on holiday, who recommended goat's milk which did the trick and his recovery started.

Ian was at several local private schools in Hayling and nearby Havant and then at Churchers College at Petersfield, a small public school. His initial poor health never recurred and though not as tall as his brother and sisters he grew up a sturdy boy and a considerable athlete. At Churchers he was the star in the rugby team and he won the sprints and long jump in the school athletic sports. Like all the family living near the golf course at Hayling, he became a good golfer and a competent shot, shooting duck on the marshes around the island. Academically, Ian never quite caught up from the delay caused by his early poor health but his headmaster at Churchers, A H J Hoggarth, made a point of telling my parents that he had no doubt that Ian's character would ensure success in whatever he chose to do in the future.

In 1936 Ian left school aged 18 and joined the Royal Air Force on a Short Service Commission for training as a pilot, probably because I was already in the RAF but not influenced by me in any direct way. By 1936 the menace of a resurgent Germany was becoming ever more apparent and the expansion of the Royal Air Force was underway. The college at Cranwell and the five Flying Training Schools at

Netheravon, Digby, Grantham, Sealand and Abu Sueir in Egypt were unable to cope with the vastly increased numbers of pupil pilots and initial flying training on light aircraft was therefore removed from the Flying Training Schools and given to hastily formed Civil Flying Schools. Thanks to the enthusiasm for light aircraft flying in Britain in the twenties and thirties, there were many flying clubs, the majority of which formed the basis for the new Civil Flying Schools. Ian was sent to Hanworth in West London for his initial training. He flew the Blackburn B.Q and I was pleased that his instructor was Flying Officer Rowley who had been an instructor at my FTS Grantham in 1930 and had since left the Service.

Ian went solo after ten hours' dual instruction and after completing fifty hours achieved an 'Average' assessment as a pilot and was posted to the new No 8 Flying Training School at Montrose in January 1937, to start his Royal Air Force life. His time at Montrose was a happy one for him. He had no difficulty in learning to fly the Hart and Audax service type aircraft though like his brother at this stage of training his category as a pilot remained only 'Average'. Ian made friends with local families and was often invited to nearby shoots. Consequently, he and I were hardly ever on leave together. Both his hobbies, shooting and games, were instrumental in making these new friends and this happened wherever he was stationed in the years to come. Having qualified and been awarded his wings he was posted to 38 Squadron in 3 Group, Bomber Command at Marham, a new RAF station built in the pleasant Norfolk countryside south of King's Lynn. I think it was the team aspect of bombing that appealed to him most.

The Squadron was equipped with twin-engined Fairey Hendon monoplanes. For any officer, joining his first squadron is probably the most significant event in his service to date, and it was certainly so for Ian. He was fortunate in that his first Flight Commander was Squadron Leader W H Merton, an outstanding officer and leader. 'Willie' as he was known to his friends throughout the Service, believed in leading his Flight from the front and by example both on the ground and in the air. He therefore earned the respect and affection of his subordinates and Ian learned much from his service under Willie who ended his service as an Air Chief Marshal after a splendid war record.

The Hendon aircraft was the first of a new type of monoplane bombers in Bomber Command and was a revolutionary departure from the slow biplanes which, up to that time, had equipped the bomber squadrons. However, as the initial experiment it was only partly successful, being rather underpowered. It gave the Air Force experience of flying and maintaining a monoplane aircraft, but its limitations were recognised and it was not continued as a main type, being replaced by the next generation of twin-engined bombers, the Whitley, Wellington and Hampden. Ian's Squadron was re-equipped with the Wellington in December 1938 and when war began nine months later, Ian was an established second pilot and his flying category had improved to Above Average. Unfortunately, Willie Merton was posted from the Squadron on promotion and his successor possessed few of Willie's leadership qualities. As at Montrose Ian quickly made friends amongst the locals, and was invited to shoot by the farmers and landowners and in King's Lynn was fortunate early on to meet Mr and Mrs Parker. Mr Parker was an eye surgeon and, having no family of their own, they took a special interest in the young officers of Ian's Squadron. Ian became a particular favourite and when war started they were very kind to him.

From the first day of war Ian kept a war diary of which I had no knowledge, in a large service ledger book. What his purpose was and for whom it was intended is not indicated. Perhaps it was to relieve his feelings of fear, frustration and sometimes near despair. He wrote freely and in detail and together with his flying logbook, the diary gives a vivid picture of his brief wartime service life. Sometimes it is a terrible story and I shall quote freely from it.

On 3 September 1939, Ian was a 2nd Pilot in a war crew in 38 Squadron. To understand his activities it is necessary to appreciate the state of Bomber Command at the outbreak, and for the first year, of war. It was not nearly as far advanced as Fighter Command in its state of readiness. This is surprising since the Air Staff had argued consistently for the primacy of the offensive over the defensive in the air defence of Great Britain. However, a report written by Air Chief Marshal Sir Edgar Ludlow-Hewitt on 10 November 1937 two months after being appointed AOC-in-C, was emphatic in the assessment of the command's unreadiness for war. This report to the Air Ministry was followed at intervals by pungent letters, all making practical criticisms, until Ludlow-Hewitt was relieved in April 1940. In effect, the report said the command could not find targets in a blacked-out Germany and if it did find them, could not hit them. Ludlow-Hewitt was one of the most discerning of the many distinguished airmen in positions of responsibility at the outbreak of the war and his report was not questioned, as he was a man of total integrity, total dedication, and immense professional skill. But the Air Ministry was slow to act.

From 4 September, Ian's diary records a catalogue of mismanagement. Panic signals from on high in the early hours of the morning to bomb the German fleet—"washed out" later when all bombing-up preparations had been made. So often were operations "washed out" that one outspoken Canadian pilot suggested that the Royal Air Force motto should be changed to "washed out"! Not only was there indecision at the top which was so disturbing for the squadrons but command at squadron and flight level was abysmal. Ian records that by the end of September 1939, a month after the war had started, neither of the Squadron Leader Flight Commanders had even flown the Wellington. Yet these were the men who were to order the aircrews into the unknown world of operations. The diary includes a list of the six "war crews" in 38 Squadron: neither the Wing Commander commanding the Squadron nor either of the Squadron Leaders commanding the two flights feature in the list. This 'opting out' by middle rank officers from flying, and later from operations, was not confined to Ian's Squadron.

Before the war, no provision had been made for pilots to keep in practice once they had left a squadron or other flying unit. Many overcame this deficiency by 'scrounging' some flying in squadrons commanded by friends but others, particularly the weaker characters, took advantage of the situation to regard administration as their role and abandon flying altogether. This changed as the war progressed and in Bomber Command the likes of Basil Embry set a splendid example leading their squadrons and their groups in operations against the enemy. In the meantime, Ian and his friends were often led from behind on the ground. In October, they were therefore delighted to get a new Station commander, Wing Commander Hugh Pughe Lloyd, who had already commanded a bomber Station at Honington.

I had met Lloyd when I was sent by Leigh-Mallory to interview him after the first raids by the Honington squadrons on the German Fleet at Wilhelmshaven. I was impressed at the time by his detailed grasp of all that occurred in that operation. Years afterwards I was to serve under him in North Africa where he remembered Ian as "one of the best". He had a first-class brain and a capacity for hard work that I never saw exceeded in all my service. We served together again when he was the RAF Instructor at the Imperial Defence College and I was a pupil on the first post-war course.

The so-called "phoney war" was far from phoney for the bomber crews. The weather in the winter of 1939/40 was particularly bad and operating off grass airfields and with little in the way of aids, made war anything but phoney. In this period of about eight months there was a prohibition on bombing the mainland of Germany. It was a prohibition prompted by the French who were fearful of retaliation by the Luftwaffe on France itself. This meant that the primary role of Bomber Command to attack war industries and communications could not even begin. At first therefore, operations were almost entirely confined to attacks on shipping, particularly the German Navy. These activities were interspersed with Nickel raids (dropping leaflets), which of course meant penetrating the enemy's air defences and which were just as dangerous as bomber missions proper. The phoney period did have some advantages in that with the coffers open and especially with the now rapid provision of spares, training could be increased. Also, since there was a belief that the Wellington squadrons could penetrate the defences in daylight, by flying in formation, Ian records that this essential practice began to feature in his Squadron's belated preparations for operations.

Ian's first war operation was on 3 December. "At last" is the diary comment. The other Squadron at Marham, 115, was leading and the lack of knowledge of the requirements of formation flying (a technique that should have been mastered months before the war started) was glaringly apparent, 38 Squadron having to over boost their engines to keep up. Ian noted that it was "madness to push these engines, they are our very life and should be treated with great care". The target was shipping at the island of Heligoland.

> "We turned on to attack ships lying in the harbour. At this point AA fire was opened and they got our height at once (10,000 ft) but only one burst near to shake us. I was bomb aiming and things were pretty tense. Everything went OK but made bad run up and bombs overshot by about 100 yards. Someone dropped a pretty one right alongside a ship which must have shaken loose every rivet... We were jinking hard now at 2½ boost. Fighters then attacked us, nine 109s although I only saw two.
>
> "Odoire was a bit behind and got beaten up a bit. His tyre was burst and about 20 rounds in wing. His rear gunner was saved by his quick sealing unit, a bullet glancing off. He claims to have shot one down in flames. By this time we were out of range of AA and fighters did not attack long".

The next operation came eighteen days later on 21 December, again with shipping near Sylt as the target, without any recorded result.

Ian's relaxation from the strain of continually waiting for the few operations that took place, was to get away to the golf courses whenever he could; and he saw a lot of the Parkers. He was always welcome at their house in King's Lynn and played a lot of golf with Mr Parker who was a low handicap man. Mrs Parker also organised dances and other social gatherings and introduced Ian and his friends to the daughters of their friends. Ian fell badly for a girl called Betty and recorded all the joys and doubts of this platonic friendship.

Following the engagement over Heligoland, Ian became convinced that the Wellington needed a beam gun in addition to the forward and rear turrets and he persisted in making and trying out mountings for a K Gun. His work became known at 3 Group HQ, at Vickers, and finally at the Air Ministry. Ian noted that the gun business at this level was handled by Squadron Leader Walker ("Gus", as he called him in brackets). So my old rugger captain from Twickenham days met the other half of the Cross Air Force family. Ian received letters of appreciation from Group HQ and was pleased to note that Vickers adopted his mounting although it was not generally fitted as night bombing became the only role for the Wellington from that time. More leaflet raids occurred in January, Hamburg being amongst the recipients. He kept a selection of these useless chits pinned to the appropriate page in his diary.

When Germany invaded France and the Low Countries on 10 May 1940, Bomber Command devoted its whole strength to attacking targets influencing the land battle. Ian attacked ten battlefield targets in May and June and then targets within Germany itself: oil refineries and the Junkers storage depots in Bremen, and the Blohm und Voss shipbuilding yards in Hamburg. One operation for which Ian and his crew were specially selected was a photographic reconnaissance of Stettin, on the Baltic coast, north-east of Berlin and more than 550 miles from Norfolk. This long, hazardous solo flight was carried out on the night of 11-12 July:

"Sent on a very good trip to recce and take night photographs of Stettin docks. Stettin was the place where the training took place for the landing parties that took Norway and Denmark.

"Two machines were supposed to go from Marham, one from 38 and one from 115. Felt very proud that they should choose us. Just before we left the 115 machine had a very nasty accident and a flash bomb went off on the bomb rack and the machine was completely destroyed in a few min. Hell of an explosion which shook the hangar and blew many windows out. However, we were not too late off at 20.30. This trip meant a lot of day flying over the North Sea and more when we came back, but the weather was very cloudy so didn't worry much. Climbed up to 12,000 ft and stayed there. Didn't see where we crossed the German coast as we were 10/10 and raining hard. Heavy thunder storms made things more unpleasant still. We were shot at all the way in, on and off, but not too accurate.

"Our ETA was 00.14 so at 23.50 we started to lose height down to 7,000 ft. Navigation was good and at 00.10 we came out over the lake above Stettin. No opposition for quite a time but couldn't pin-point ourselves at first. After our first run up they opened fire on us and searchlights made it very difficult to see the ground. Each approach got worse as regards flak, heavy and light. First two runs at 8,000 and second two at 9,000. After the last picture had been taken we dived to 6,000 to get up some speed and then set course for home. We were fired at for about 5 min after that. Made pretty good recce of docks and harbour.

"Had excellent trip back at 10,000 ft above and in 10/10 cloud. Very pleased to find this over Heligoland Bight!!. Weather got clear at about 100 miles out from English coast. Navigator Wildic was very good indeed. We turned on ETA and hit the coast dead on!!

"Landed at 04.30. Station Commander and Bowles on tarmac to meet us. Felt pretty tired. On the way back we took the precaution to warm our guns up every hour or so. Very fed up that three of our pictures were no good but one very good just missed the target by a few hundred yards. This night photography extremely difficult when you are being shot at and searchlights have you."

To be met on the tarmac was an indication of the tremendous scale of the operation. On 22 July Ian completed his tour of operations with an attack on the Krupps Works in Essen. Thirty was the official number but Ian had done thirty-four. On this last raid Green, his second pilot, was doing the bomb aiming and he believed he hit the large building he was aiming at near the river. "As this was my last raid", wrote Ian, "I was pretty careful not to make any mistakes!!"

"Very light moonlight and kept a keen look out for fighters. However trip went off without incident although we were a bit off track on way across sea.
P.S. Swales had his rear gunner very badly wounded by a shell from a fighter. He died later in hospital."

Ian's departure from Marham affected him deeply. He had lived there for three years, two in peacetime and one in war. Professionally, he had started as an Average 2nd pilot and had finished as an Above Average Captain. He had completed 175 hours of operational flying in a period of the war when little was known of the hazards facing aircrew, and he had survived. At Marham too he had made many friends not only on the Station but amongst the locals. He had fallen in love, fallen out of love, and he recorded it all in his diary. He was now twenty two years and three months old.

An entry on 14 September 1940 reads:

> "John Norman came over to my room to inform me that I had
> been awarded the DFC. Better still Kenneth as well had been
> given it too. Well I never thought I would live to see the day.
> The thing that has given me the greatest pleasure is the knowledge
> of how pleased the family must be. At least it is some reward
> for all their teaching all my life. I am afraid I am not very thrilled
> about it myself. Went up to King's Lynn; the Parkers were thrilled
> to death and gave me a great welcome."

Ian was next posted to No 11 Operational Training Unit at Bassingbourne as an instructor on Wellingtons and seven days later gave his
first dual instruction. He noted the change in atmosphere from the
realism of the operational station at Marham to the training unit at
Bassingbourne and particularly the lack of keeness and competence
of the ground crews. As an Above Average pilot in his Squadron,
he was distressed when he had two minor flying and taxiing accidents,
"the first I have ever had." After a while he found teaching the new
crews became more interesting though the need for better flying
weather than that accepted on an operational station, restricted flying
and was frustrating. Surprisingly, he was asked to form a crew from
his fellow instructing staff for a Nickel raid over France. This was
surprising because Bassingbourne was a training and not an operational station. It was, however, indicative of the lack of experience
of those in charge. In an operational squadron the cohesion and
comradeship of the crew who flew exercises together, before going
on operations, was an essential requirement. Ian, at very short notice,
was asked to assemble a crew for a flight over enemy territory. Not
surprisingly the trip nearly ended in disaster and Ian's description is
worth repeating.

Sunday, 10 November

"Was rung up by W/Cdr Constantine at 16.00 hrs and told that
there was to be a Nickel raid by a D Flight aircraft. A staff crew
were to be selected to carry it out. As there were very few people
in the Flight, all junior to me, I said I would take it and White
said he would come as second pilot. We were told that the AOC
6 Group would be coming with us. As the notice was so short
everything was done in a hell of a rush. We had to take a Ia which
had been flown by every ham fisted pupil on the course. AOC met
us in the crew room at 20.45 and had a hell of a game dressing
him. But he is a grand fellow and I have the greatest admiration

for him. By the time I was in the aircraft I was sweating like hell and everything seemed to go wrong. The intercom wouldn't work, the port motor was dropping 300 revs. Had hectic take-off.

"S/course Harwell, bloody awful navigation. We should have hit Littlehampton but came right over Portsmouth. All the guns in the place opened up. I felt very strange as I thought that the guns firing at me, and the bursts were very near, were most likely the guns at Hayling Island my home that I love with all my heart and which I may have to die for. If that should come I know God will give to me courage to face it like Kenneth would, like a man worthy of my dear family who mean everything to me. I went over to Shoreham and we set course for Le Havre or just west of it. We were at 16,000 ft now to get over the clouds which were full of ice. At this point the port motor began to heat up and oil temp up to 85′ pressure 60lb.

"Decided to cut the leg short and started dropping the leaflets. White my good 2nd, all over in 15 min. With bomb doors open the aircraft would not keep height at 1½ lbs boost and if I open her up any more she heats up. The strain of having the AOC on board was very wearing, we could make no mistake. Tried to jettison bombs but owing to cold the releases wouldn't work. Staggered along at 135 mph just keeping height as I daren't go through the cloud owing to ice. Ten min before ETA English coast I decided to risk it and down we came. We got iced up at once and everything seemed to give in. I kept her straight by the Turn and Bank indicator. Giro had packed up.

"When we came out at 2,000 ft over sea we found land behind us, coast running east and west. At once I thought it must be the French coast and so I steered 315°(M). On and on we went—still sea. Wireless could get no answer even to our SOS which we sent out. Long after we should have seen the English coast we were still over the sea. Things looked distinctly black. I thought of everywhere we could possibly be and at last thought we must be off the east coast so turned due west and after we had been steering that for about 4 min a hell of a yell from the W/op told he had made contact!!—030(T) from Linton-on-Ouse. In the heat of the moment and the intercom not being too good I thought he said 300°(T) but soon put that right.

"Then the long wait, my eyes nearly popping out of my head looking for the coast. At last we saw a white flashing beacon and eventually came over what must have been Lundy Island. The petrol question was OK so we cruised around looking for an aerodrome. Found several dummy flare paths and at last found

Harwell beacon. Then Abingdon at which we landed.

"What a trip. The situation was made twice as bad having the AOC aboard. He took it very well and was grand all the time. He couldn't do enough for us in the Mess. We saw him next morning and he even seemed pleased at the experience he had gone through."

Air Vice-Marshal W F MacNeece Foster, who was no youngster (he was 51 at the time of this flight), was known in the Service as a 'good 'un' and he showed his form in doing this trip, but that his staff at 6 Training Group should have allowed him to go on such a flight with a scratch crew from a non-operational unit is staggering and shows the lack of realism at Group HQ level. Nonetheless, Ian was very pleased to receive a letter from Foster written in his own hand and a signed photograph as a "souvenir of how we spent the early hours of Armistice Day 1940."

On 11 November Ian started a week's leave and came up to Watnall to see me. I was on duty the next day and arranged for him to play golf at Hollinwell with Jack Chance, one of our wartime officers in the Operations Room and a low handicap man. We had a bit of a party in Nottingham in the evening with amongst others, Rupert Leigh, a most amusing chap. We said goodbye to Ian the next day as he was off to finish his leave in his beloved Norfolk. It was to be the very last time I saw him because I left for Egypt on 8 December.

Ian's life at Bassingbourne was made pleasanter by the kindness of Wing Commander Hugh Constantine and his wife Helen. Wartime messes were impersonal places because of the large number of officers passing through, especially at a training unit. Ian mentions several times in his diary how nice it was to be invited to the Constantine's home. Several times he expresses the hope that for his next operational tour he would be posted to fly "a four-engined aircraft." He had heard that the Stirling was to be the first of the new breed to be introduced into Bomber Command and he discussed the possibility with Constantine whom he was "sure would help him". Constantine was promoted to Group Captain and posted to command a new Bomber Station at Elsham Wolds in Yorkshire. Shortly afterwards, in August 1941, Ian was also posted there. Sadly, Constantine had to tell Ian that the Stirling was not coming to Elsham and that therefore he would remain on Wellingtons. He was to be a Squadron Leader and Flight Commander in 103 Squadron, but it was a disappointment for Ian to be on Wellingtons again.

His diary records:

"After waiting a day for the signal to confirm my posting I left for

Top left: Flight Lieutenant P.G. Jameson, Officer Commanding "B" Flight No 46 Squadron, depicted by Eric Kennington. The best pilot in the Squadron and the best man I ever knew.

Top right: Air Commodore Basil Embry (left) visits L.G. 110, in preparation for Operation Crusader, November 1941.

Middle: In the misty light of dawn on the first day of Operation Crusader, I brief the Wing Staff at Fort Maddalena before the battle commences.

Bottom: With Coningham at Fort Maddalena November 1941. He is making a note for his staff at DAF Headquarters. The bottle was for decoration only!

Top left: With Fred Rosier at Fort Maddalena 1941. He had forced landed behind the enemy lines, was missing three days then turned up having walked through a German Armoured Division at night.

Top right: January 1942 at Antelat - *From the left:* Johns, Coningham, Self, Tedder, Caldwell, Morris, Gould, Linnard.

Bottom: Gambut - Western Desert. What a nice way of saying 'You're sacked!' Within three months I was back again.

Top left: Alexandria Sporting Club - summer 1942. The enemy only attacked at night so plenty of time for exercise! My partner for golf on many occasions was Admiral Cunningham.

Top right: The marvellous view from my villa at Alexandria.

Middle left: Corporals Dai Rees (left) and 'Tommy' Houghton - driver and batman from the Western Desert to the Baltic.

Middle right: Christmas 1942. The Corporal's Club at Seagull Camp. Only two officers were asked to go to their party - Norman Glover and myself - which we viewed as a great compliment.

Bottom: Churchill arrives at Cairo West by Liberator wearing an Air Force uniform to emphasise the part played by the Air in protecting the 8th Army in its retreat to El Alamein. Here he is shaking hands with Tedder. The date is 3 August, 1942.

Top: Ju 86 high-flying reconnaissance aircraft. 252 Wing, using specially lightened Spitfires Vs shot down three of these in the weeks before El Alamein. We didn't see them again.

Middle left: My personalised red Spit 9, parked in the desert.

Middle right: Trenchard and Cross, Alexandria, in the winter of 1942.

Bottom left: Winston, Alanbrooke, Coningham, Slatter, at Dekhiela airfield autumn 1942, with me appropriately marked with a cross.

Bottom right: Chez Broadhurst, Derna 1942, prior to his taking over the SASO caravan.

Top: General Spaatz USAF, Coningham, and Self , Castel Benito Airfield, Tripoli, January 1943. They were both on their way to take up their new commands in the MAAF (Mediterranean Allied Air Forces), and were rather put out that they had to fly way down south to go to Algiers, to avoid the front. Both would have taken the chance if allowed.

Middle: 242 Group at Bizerta 1943. Me in the middle front row!

Bottom: Fiesler-Storch, most sought after "capture" in North Africa. This one was found at El Aouina, Tunis and removed under the noses of the Desert Air Force by Group Captain Hugo on my instructions. May 1943.

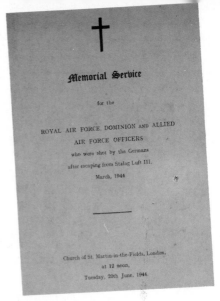

Top left: Squadron Leader I.K.P. Cross - my brother.

Top right: Memorial Service programme for the Air Force Officers shot after escaping from Stalag Luft III.

Middle and Bottom: RAF Beaufighters of the Coastal Air Force going into attack a steamer which was afterwards believed to be carrying ammunition, on 25 July 1943. The Beaufighter on the right of the picture scored a direct hit, resulting in the vessel blowing up, as photographed by another aircraft.

Top: Chatting with Beaufighter pilots just returned from a shipping strike.

Bottom: The date is 9 September 1943 and the Italian battleship *Roma* has just been hit by an FX-guided bomb launched from a Luftwaffe aircraft. The *Roma*, with the rest of the Italian fleet, was out of Genoa and Spezia, bound for Malta via Bizerta, to surrender. The Germans found out and attacked west of Sardinia. This photo was taken from another Italian ship and came into my possession when I took over an Italian floatplane squadron at Taranto at the end of 1943.

Top: A remarkable photograph of myself with Leigh-Mallory, remarkable because D-Day was only two months away and here he is in his greenhouse!

Middle: Brenda and I on our wedding day, January 15, 1945.

Bottom: Tommy Elmhirst, AOA and my friend at 2nd TAF HQ, Brussels, 19 April 1945.

Elsham. Said goodbye to everyone. The only thing that stuck in my throat was old Buck, it seemed I was leaving him."

Buck was Ian's best friend at Marham and had crashed and been killed at Bassingbourne when flying down to visit Ian.

"Arrived Elsham by air with U/T crew. Good runways, hangars only half built. Gee I felt strange, the only man I knew was Connie, and he was the station master, a great help but not much company. However I saw him and it was good to get such a grand welcome.

"Saw the Squadron CO, W/Cdr Lowe, a very nice chap I thought on my first meeting. Situation was a bit tricky as apparently things had gone a bit astray and the Sqd/Ldr I was supposed to relieve was still here and didn't want to embarass anyone so decided to attach me to B Flight (S/Ldr Lane) until things got sorted out."

Five days later, on the night of 14-15 August, Ian started his second tour of operations with an attack on a target in Hanover:

"Went on my first operation second time round so to speak. Went with a P/O Petrie in Wellington 2999. Target Hanover Railway Station. Took off at approximately 23.00 hrs and climbed to 7,000 ft by the time we crossed the coast. He flew it most of the way out—quite well I thought except that he was inclined to fly a little slowly. Weather was good but some ground haze. Crossed the Dutch coast on Track. Gee it was strange to be back at it again. I spent most of the time in the Astro Hatch. Clouds kept search-lights quiet and AA nothing to worry about.

"As we were about 50 miles away from the target at about 17,000 ft there was a very concentrated cone of searchlights away to our port about 40-50 miles. I saw a slight fire start and then it grew larger and eventually it was a machine on fire. It started to fall and at about 8,000 ft I suppose it exploded in mid air and crashed in two separate pieces. Hell of a sight, couldn't help thinking to myself there's one bunch of good chaps who will not return to their base, poor devils. I'll bet there's some broken hearts in six little homes in England today.

"Found the town OK but could see very little else. A few fires started but nothing big. I don't know whether the Bomb Aimer could, anyhow he thought he could, and down they went 3 × 500, + 1 × 100 + 1 × 250. The old Wimpey fairly leapt up as they went off. Hell of a strong wind going back and it seemed ages before we could get clear of the hundreds of searchlights around the city but the city flak wasn't too bad. Good trip back and made good landfall. Set course from Cromer for Elsham and that was that".

Between 9 August 1941 and 12 February 1942, Ian did fourteen operations on his second tour making 48 all told since the war started. He attacked targets again in Hanover, the Krupps Works in Essen, and in Berlin and had a particularly long flight to Turin. Other targets were in Le Havre, Frankfurt, Cologne, Stettin, Emden and Ostend. Of significance in light of later events were attacks on the German battle cruisers, *Scharnhorst* and *Gneisenau* in Brest, though the diary records, "results not observed—cloud". He also recorded "that the C-in-C Bomber Command came down and stayed to lunch... introduced to him and must say he impressed me". He was Air Marshal Sir Richard Peirse.

On 1 September 1941, Ian was promoted to Squadron Leader and took command of B Flight, 103 Squadron and an operation on Berlin is recorded for the night of 7-8 September:

"Target tonight was the Railway Station in the centre of Berlin. Very thrilled to have my first crack at the 'Big City'.

"Took off at 21.00 hrs in X 7665 V. It had just completed a 40-hour inspection and had the cowling treated with that paint to cover up the glow when she gets hot. Climbed in great style and were at 12,000 ft over Cromer, Set course from there to Morden on the Z. Z. and levelled out. Cloud about 8/10ths tops at 8-9,000 ft. After the Dutch coast 10/10 very good as searchlights never tried to pick us up. Climbed to 14,000 ft and stayed there. Very bright moon. Had a perfect trip to the target but got off course to the North, Saw Berlin a long way away. Only a few bombs had been dropped but when the boys got going in earnest they put up a hell of a barrage. It was, by a long way, the heaviest I have ever seen. We approached from the West instead of the SE and had just got over the outskirts of the place when they tried to get us. I started to glide but it was too late and several got right on us. We were well over the city but some miles away from the target. Several bursts came very near and one turned the old Wellington up on her nose, so decided to get rid of the bombs, and it was just as well we did. We bombed a large fire already burning and as we turned away things got hot (very). We dived like hell but they let us have it hot and strong, and to be perfectly frank I thought one moment we had 'had it', but at last we were out of range and climbed up again.

"There were more very large fires burning we could see

many miles away. The AA was really incredible and perfectly co-ordinated with the searchlights. Berlin looked the hell of a size and I was amazed the amount of detail you could see.

"On the way back just before we crossed the Dutch coast above 10/10 I saw an Me 110 going like hell in the opposite direction (thank God!) about 100 ft below us and about a mile away, but as we were against the dark sky away from the moon, he didn't see us. Hit English coast at Southwold—very good. Landed at Elsham OK."

Three days later, on 10 September, Ian was detailed to attack a target in Turin with seven other aircraft of his Squadron which all landed at Honington to top up with fuel for this very long flight. He records that he "had a bad cold and was not feeling too good":

"We took off at 20.00 hrs and set course for Orfordness. Cloud 10/10 at 2,000 ft but not very thick. Machine climbed well and we were at 12,000 ft by the French coast. Got shot at but not badly. Searchlights were ineffective owing to cloud. Climbed up to 15,000 ft and levelled out. Couldn't see anything of the ground because of cloud and haze.

"The first thing we saw was the rising ground to the North of the Alps and discovered we were in front of ETA. Altered course on ETA but after about 30 mins flying pin-pointed ourselves over Geneva and just west of the lake!! Geneva was not blacked out at all and it was great to see a city lit up as for peacetime. I was a bit worried at the time as I thought we were more off course than we actually were. We altered course for Turin and now we were off to cross the Alps.

"What a sight! Mont Blanc was about 20 miles on our port and almost on our level. I'll never forget the sight as long as I live. As far as you could see about a hundred miles of great snow-covered peaks and great valleys. It was as light as day as it was almost full moon and now no cloud. Must say I kept a very keen eye on the oil pressure and temp as it was not the place to be caught flying on one motor!!! But the 'old gal' kept going like a watch and purred away for hour after hour. We saw AA fire just before we were over the Alps giving away the position of the target. Lucky they did so as it was very hazy and we could see no ground detail except lights. AA was pitiful after the Hun's exhibitions and it all rested whether we could see anything.

"Flew over the city and saw several good fires just starting. Took one roughly in the position of our target the main railway station to the SW and let them have it. Our bombs burst to the NE about ½ mile, which was a good thing as they were sure to have hit the town. Very little AA and no searchlights. Bombed at 16,000 ft. Soon after we had turned for home. We very nearly had a head-on collision with another Wellington going in to attack—I had the hell of a scare!!

"On the way back we saw much more of the ground flying away from the moon and the machine went very well... empty!! Is a hell of a sweat keeping them up high as the slightest relaxation in flying and they fall three or four hundred feet before you can stop them. There was only ground haze now and the 10/10 stuff didn't start until about 200 miles from the French coast, which was just right as searchlights couldn't get at us. We got a bit to the left of our track by some way so decided to go home by the South coast rather than the East. Cloud broke up over the Channel and we crossed the coast at about Brighton. Homed on Abingdon.

"Handed over to Bray at English coast for first time and was ready to get out of that seat. Turned on Abingdon and s/c for Honington and landed at about 04.00 hrs. My cold had got much worse and as a result my ears were giving me agony and I couldn't hear a thing. When we got to the Ops Room we found that Petrie was missing and had had no word from him. Still no word by 07.30 so concluded he had had some bad luck. Sgt Hose had turned back with overheating motors. The rest had all got there and back.

"This was probably my most thrilling trip, not from the opposition point of view, but the flight over the Alps. I wouldn't have missed it for anything and certainly I will never forget it. Went and had some breakfast and left for Elsham at 07.35. Feeling awful so did Bray who also had a cold".

This description vividly conveys what the medium bomber pilot went through even after two years of war. Ian had flown the unstable Wellington manually for seven and a half hours before handing over to his inexperienced second pilot. Furthermore there was no auto-pilot in those days and he suffered constant anxiety over the engines, particularly the oil pressure, Despite his continuing cold, and colds that put two members of his crew out of action, Ian was operating again two nights later against a target in Frankfurt. His aircraft was holed by flak, but nonetheless, he managed to bring the damaged aircraft back safely.

After the Turin operation Ian operated regularly through the autumn and winter of 1941-42. He was not the man to lead his Flight from an office desk, as he had experienced at Marham. Up to

February 1942 his logbook records attacks on targets in Frankfurt, Cologne, Ostend, Stettin, Emden, Wilhelmshaven and Brest. The target in Brest comprised the German battle cruisers, the *Scharnhorst* and *Gneisenau*, which had arrived there on 22 March 1941. These two malevolent monsters, after sinking me in the *Glorious* in June 1940, had withdrawn to Trondheim and subsequently to their home port Kiel. On 23 January 1941, the two ships sailed from Kiel for a sortie into the North Atlantic during which twenty-two allied ships were sunk or captured, before putting in to Brest. Ian, together with hundreds of other Bomber Command aircrews, attacked them soon after their arrival until their departure in February 1942. It was a very difficult target for our aircraft of this period. No radar bombing aids had yet been developed and heavy anti-aircraft fire, the most intense in Europe, made visual bombing by day or night extremely difficult. Nevertheless Bomber Command attacked the ships at every opportunity when the weather allowed. During the period March 1941 to February 1942, the *Scharnhorst* and *Gneisenau* were each hit five times but the calibre of the armour-piercing bombs then available was insufficient to cause mortal damage, though each hit was enough to prevent the ships sailing. Ian attacked Brest twice in February but made no claim for hits on the ships.

Ians last flight began from Elsham Wolds on 12 February. His Squadron was part of the 100 aircraft ready at four hours notice to attack the German battleships if and when they attempted to break through the Channel to reach a German port. The existence of a German plan to do this was unknown at station and squadron level and the Station Commander, Group Captain Hugh Constantine, was therefore surprised when ordered to despatch twelve aircraft to attack a "convoy" in the Channel. By the time the aircraft were bombed up and ready for take-off however, the ships had already passed through the Straits of Dover and Ian and his fellow captains were given a position for the ships off the Dutch coast.

Ian took off at 14.54 on the fourteenth sortie of his second tour in Wellington Z8714, in bad weather which remained all the way to the target area. He was unable to find the ships at first but continued to search in bad visibility and low cloud. He was just about to abandon the operation, when emerging from dense cloud he found himself right over the two battle cruisers. The Wellington was hit repeatedly by gunfire from the ships and their escorts and Ian was forced to ditch about forty miles off Rotterdam. The dinghy was launched successfully and Ian and his second pilot Flight Lieutenant Phillips, Sergeant Gallop and Sergeant Eastleby scrambled in but unfortunately the dinghy parted company with the aircraft and the four men aboard suffered the agony of seeing the other two members of the crew, Sergeant James and Sergeant Holmes, drown trying to reach the dinghy as it drifted away. These details about Ian's last flight and its tragic end only became known to the Cross family after the war. At Elsham Wolds he was reported missing and my parents at Hayling Island were informed. They sent me a telegram which reached me at Gambut. Shortly afterwards, on 24 February, the International Red Cross passed on a message from the Germans that "on 13 February, S/L Cross, F/Lt Phillips, Sgt Gallop and Sgt Eastleby had been saved from the sea unwounded".

Ian and the surviving members of his crew had been rescued by a passing German convoy. They had been in their dinghy for sixty hours. Shortly afterwards Ian arrived at Dulag Luft, a transit camp and Interrogation Centre for newly taken prisoners near Frankfurt am Main. There he met a Pilot Officer, Robert Kee, pilot of a Hampden of 420 Squadron, Royal Canadian Air Force, who had been shot down by flak on the north coast of Holland on the night of 18-19 February, 1942. After his release from a prison camp in May 1945, Kee wrote an account of his experiences which is dedicated to "the memory of my friend Squadron Leader Ian Cross, DFC, and those 49 of his fellow prisoners who were shot with him by Hitler's orders on re-capture after escaping from Stalag Luft III in 1944." This book, *A Crowd is Not Company*, was published in 1947 and described by *The Times* as "Arguably the best POW book ever written." Soon after his release, Robert wrote a letter to my mother about Ian which she greatly valued and it came to me on her death. Here it is:

Dear Mrs Cross

You will have no idea who I am, so I hope you will not think it impertinent of me to write to you like this. I returned from Germany a few days ago after 3½ years as a prisoner and as I knew Ian very well there I thought I might possibly be able to fill in some gaps in your information about him.

As I have already said that he was a friend of mine I don't need to tell you what a blow it was to me when I heard of his death after the big escape from Sagan. It meant so much to me—and to all his other friends in the camp—that I am able to form some small idea of what your own sorrow must have been.

I first met Ian in late February 1942 when I arrived at the transit camp in Germany (Dulag Luft) a few days after being shot down and was lucky enough to be shown into his room. His tremendous spirit and great sense of humour—in spite of the fact that he himself had only been shot down recently and was still suffering slightly from frostbite—made all the difference to me in those first bewildering days, and we became very good friends. We later moved to Sagan (Stalag Luft III) together; from there to Schubin in Poland (Oflag XXI B) and from there back again to Sagan. I lived in the same room with him in each camp. In late 1943 he got the chance to move to another compound in the camp, he took it and moved to the North Compound from which the big tunnel was later built. I saw him only a few days before the tunnel broke so successfully—he was over in our compound playing football one afternoon—and he was in great spirits and naturally very excited about his coming escape. I have never met a man who did his duty so magnificently and managed to enjoy doing it so much at the same time.

This was of course not the first time he had attempted to escape. He had made one unsuccessful attempt with me in the summer of 1942 and I remember how amusing he made our subsequent stay of 14 days in the local jail. Then again he had escaped from a tunnel at Schubin in March 1943 and was at large for 2 days before being recaptured. By the time of his last escape he had learnt a fair amount of German by hard work in the camp and had a very good chance of getting home.

I expect the Red Cross have told you as much as is known about the recapture of him and the other officers who escaped with him. I also expect you know how and when he was shot down and that he spent sixty hours with the rest of his crew in a dinghy before being picked up. But if you have any questions to ask about this or about his last escape, or indeed anything at all about his life in camp I shall be only too glad to answer them. So do please write to me and ask me if I can be of any help at all—although I know that nothing I can say or do can be any comfort to you in your great loss.

I shall be on leave for another 5 weeks and you can contact me by letter any time at this address, or if you should be coming to London during this period I should be very pleased to meet you.
Yours sincerely,
Robert Kee
Flight Lieutenant RAF

Ian's arrival in the North Compound coincided with the decision to attempt the most ambitious tunnelling project ever in Stalag Luft III, at Sagan, about eighty miles south-east of Berlin, which is now in Poland. The project was the simultaneous construction of three tunnels 'Tom', 'Dick' and 'Harry'. It was in a way a reply to the intense efforts the Germans were making to detect the tunnelling activities of the prisoners. Among the measures taken was the burying of microphones outside the boundary wire and an increase inside the compounds of mobile guards (known as 'Ferrets') and provided with steel rod probes. Also, trenches were dug right round the camp but this latter measure was overcome by the prisoners tunnelling deeper, in the case of Tom, Dick and Harry to fifteen feet. Wing Commander Harry Day, the most experienced POW—he had been a prisoner since October 1939 in addition to imprisonment in the 1914-18 War— and Group Captain H M Massey, the Senior British Officer, checked and approved all the plans. The head man on the executive side working under the Camp Escape Committee was Squadron Leader Roger Bushell, known as 'Big X'. A barrister by profession, he had joined the Auxiliary Air Force well before the war. I knew Roger in peacetime when he served in 601 Squadron at Hendon. He and a fellow barrister friend of his, Michael Peacock, were well known to the young regular officers in the Service because they had often individually defended them at their courts martial when up on charges of unauthorised low flying—a temptation which few could resist. Roger was a remarkable man. When war came he rose rapidly in the flying game and was CO of a Spitfire squadron when shot down and captured. He spoke German and French fluently and had attempted escape several times. He had the confidence of everyone and his handling of this project was a tribute to him and his subordinate organisers, of whom Ian was one.

A major problem and one of the most difficult to solve was the disposal of the spoil from the tunnel digging. It was mostly a bright yellow sand, the slightest trace of which would alert the ever-vigilant guards. Ian and Flight Lieutenant Jimmy James were the head men in this part of the organisation. Most spoil was disposed of under the theatre which had been constructed in the North Compound as part of a momentarily more liberal policy adopted by the Germans towards their prisoners. The spoil had to be transported in long stocking-like bags under greatcoats at night and Ian and Jimmy James supervised this part of the operation. In all, some six hundred tons of sand were concealed. Every aspect of the operation—the concealment of the entrances to the tunnels, the construction, the ventilation, the lighting, and the actual tunnelling—was a miracle of ingenuity, determination and courage, all of it conducted in complete secrecy in the face of an enemy whose suspicions were thoroughly aroused. I suppose in retrospect, that with the flower of the youth of the Allied nations in the aircrew, and every one a volunteer, it should not be surprising that this miracle of achievement was accomplished.

Tom was discovered (and much photographed by Germans so delighted with their own cleverness that they felt gracious—briefly—to such skilful and determined prisoners. Dick had to be abandoned because a new compound was begun just where it would have broken surface. But Harry was safely completed on 14 March 1944. According to British sources, it was 336-360 feet long. The entrance shaft was 28 feet deep and the exit shaft 20 feet high. The breakout took place on the night of 24-25 March. The Escape Committee decided that a maximum of 200 men should take part, drawn from the 510 men who had worked on the project. The first 30, fluent in German and therefore considered to have the best chance of reaching England, were nominated by the committee. The next 70 were chosen by lot in three groups from a list of 90 key workers. The second hundred were drawn from the remaining 410 names. Ian was not in the first 30, but must have been placed somewhere between 31st and 76th because No. 80 was spotted emérging from the exit and his three predecessors, who were close by, immediately surrendered to prevent him being shot. Ian got out at some time shortly after 1am and before 4.55 am. The tunnel length had been slightly miscalculated and the exit was not as far into the surrounding trees as had been anticipated. The escape was further complicated by an air raid alert which meant that the electricity supply was cut off and light in the tunnel had to be replaced by primitive oil lamps. By morning the magnitude of the escape became apparent to the camp authorities and *Oberst* (Colonel) von Lindeiner-Wildau informed higher authority that the escape should be considered a *Kriegsfahndung* (a war-emergency manhunt). However, SS *Obersturmbannführer* Max Wielen, chief of the Criminal Police HQ in Breslau increased the scale of emergency by declaring a *Grossfahndung*—a national alert.

It seems that Ian was quickly captured somewhere east of the camp, taken to Gorlitz (about forty miles south of Sagan) and put in a civil gaol with 34 other escapees. From there, they were taken singly to Gestapo HQ for interrogation. "From about 30 March", recalled one prisoner, "a guard would go into different cells and call out names. These men would then be taken away and we did not see them again. We thought that they were being taken out for further interrogation and, when they did not return, that they had been sent back to camp." In fact, detailed instructions for the murders had been sent by tele-printer from Gestapo HQ in Berlin to the prisons in which escapees were held. They were to be driven in small groups to isolated places, ordered to walk away from the car and shot in the back "while trying to escape". The bodies of some who had actually been murdered in Gorlitz gaol were taken to be "found" in other places and so give colour to the claim that the escapees were desperados who refused to surrender when challenged.

On 31 March, three large cars drew up outside the Gorlitz gaol and ten Gestapo men in civilian clothes got out. They seized Ian and five other officers: Flight Lieutenants Michael J Casey (British), George W Wiley (Canadian), Albert H Hake and Thomas B Leigh (both Australians) and Flying Officer John Pohe, a New Zealander.

Dr Wilhelm Scharpwinkel, head of the Breslau Gestapo, was responsible for these and other murders. Wounded fighting against the Russians in the last days of the war, he was taken to the Soviet Union in May 1945 and after much diplomatic and military pressure, the Russians permitted him to be interviewed by an RAF investigator in August 1946.

"The British were brought to the headquarters", said Scharpwinkel. "As I speak English, I put one or two questions to the prisoners while they were being interrogated: were they married? had they children? etc. Lux (appointed by Scharpwinkel to head his murder squad) explained to the prisoners that by order of the Supreme Military Commander (Adolf Hitler) they had been sentenced to death. Then we drove away." Having reached a place called Halbau that was suitably deserted and near a wood, the cars stopped and every-one got out. "The prisoners were placed in position", continued Scharpwinkel. "It was revealed to them that the sentence was about to be carried out. The prisoners showed considerable calm, which surprised me very much. The six prisoners stood next to one another in the wood. Lux gave the order to fire and the detachment fired. Lux shot with them. By the second salvo the prisoners were dead."

According to another Gestapo agent, Richard Max Hansel, the murders took place in broad daylight, about midday. The airmen were kept standing on the road for five minutes before Scharpwinkel ordered them to move off into the trees. Hansel went back to his car for a sandwich and while eating he heard two sub-machine guns open fire. He ran into the wood and saw the sprawled bodies.

They were cremated and the ashes sent to Stalag Luft III, as were the ashes of the other victims. During the summer of 1944, permission was obtained from the Camp Commandant to build a stone memorial in the woods outside the compound in which the urns could be kept. The names of those who died were engraved on the memorial and it was carefully tended by the prisoners until their departure. The memorial was then damaged, but when the Germans were driven westward and Sagan became a Polish town, it was restored and respectfully tended.

I was in my wooden hut office at HQ Allied Expeditionary Air

Force at Bentley Priory when I heard the news of Ian's murder. So he hadn't been safe after all. I sat alone for some time and then the need to speak to someone, a friend, became overpowering and I walked through the grounds of the priory to another wooden hut where Air Commodore Finlay Crerar had his office and we talked for a while. Then I telephoned Hayling Island. My parents already knew the terrible news and I told my father that I was coming down. I saw Philip Wigglesworth, Leigh-Mallory's deputy, asked for a couple of days off and got a car to take me to Waterloo. My father met me at Havant station and drove me the six miles to Hayling. My poor mother was sick with grief. I suppose that Ian as the youngest of the family was the favourite with all of us. My two sisters were there. Jean, who was a Flight Officer in the WAAF, had got immediate leave and Baba, whose husband was in the Navy, lived nearby. We did our best to comfort my mother but without much success. The whole family attended the Memorial Service on 20 June 1944 at St Martins in the Fields where Portal read the lesson and the Chaplin in Chief gave the address. It was a sad day with so many old friends and heavy hearts.

It was not until later that the full extent of the atrocity became known. Group Captain Massey, the Senior British Officer in Stalag Luft III, had been earmarked for repatriation on account of ill health before the escape. His repatriation went ahead as planned and he arrived in England soon afterwards. So first hand information was available from an early date. There was widespread indignation in all the Allied countries, and when the matter was raised in Parliament the Foreign Secretary Anthony Eden spoke bitterly about this "cold bloodied act of treachery" and promising that after the war those responsible would be found and treated to "Exemplary Justice".

The first of two trials of those responsible for murdering the fifty airmen began in Hamburg on 1 July 1947. These criminals had been brought to justice by the superb work of the Special Investigation Branch of the Royal Air Force Police so graphically described in Allen Andrew's remarkable book *Exemplary Justice*. Despite Eden's statement in Parliament, once the war was over the politicians lost all interest and no resources were voted to track down those responsible for the fifty murders. A grudging concession was given that the Air Ministry could conduct its own investigation providing it did so from within its own resources. Portal and his successor, Tedder, as Chief of the Air Staff, were adamant that it was an article of faith with the aircrew that these murderers should be found, tried and punished.

At that time, I was serving in the HQ of the British Air Forces of Occupation in Germany and my chief, Air Marshal Sir Philip Wigglesworth, invited me to accompany him on several occasion when he attended the trial. In the dock sat these eighteen creatures, mostly Gestapo, whose faces were the most evil I had ever seen. Each was provided with his own German lawyer, some of them women, sitting immediately behind the dock. The court was similar to that of a British court martial with a senior officer as president and a number of other officers on the bench. All were in uniform. A representative of the Judge Advocate General was present. The Prosecutor was an Army officer whom I believe was a barrister in civil life. Each of the eighteen accused faced individual charges mostly of murder. The defence was invariably that the accused were obeying orders from higher authority. The attitude of the accused varied. Some said nothing. Others, and especially a particularly obnoxious Gestapo man Johannes Post, defiantly boasted about his crime, saying he would do the same again if ordered. After several visits I was present finally on 3 September 1947 for the verdicts. Of the eighteen, fourteen were sentenced to death by hanging, two to life imprisonment and two to imprisonment for ten years. On review, one of those sentenced to death was sentenced to life imprisonment. The other thirteen were hanged in Hameln gaol on 27 February 1948 by Albert Pierrepoint, who had flown from Northolt in a Dakota. In my opinion, he never did a better day's work in his long career. As for Scharpwinkel, he was too ill to travel to Hamburg and died in a Russian prison on 17 October 1947. Lux had been killed in Breslau in 1945, fighting against the Russians. Hansel was acquitted at the second trial, also in Hamburg, which began on 11 October 1948. The other two defendants received life sentences. Several other men who took part in the murders were brought to justice subsequently.

CHAPTER XIII

ALEXANDRIA

252 WING, with its HQ still at Seagull Camp, had come up in the world by April 1942. Its responsibility for the air defence of the whole of the Egyptian Delta had been recognised by Middle East HQ and so the Wing had been upgraded to a Group, No 219 with me in command. The rader warning network was much the same, giving cover over the south-east corner of the Mediterranean from a point 100 miles west of Alexandria to El Arish (near the Palestine border) about 230 miles east of Alexandria. What had changed, and was of great operational significance, was the arrival of Ground Control Interception Radars for the precise control of fighters by day and even more importantly, of Beaufighters equipped with airborne radars for use at night. Although these had not yet arrived, they were scheduled for Idku, an airfield we had made on the mudflats a few miles east of Aboukir.

On taking over command I did a tour round the Sector Operations Rooms at Heliopolis, Ismailia and Port Said. The last was commanded by Wing Commander "Tubby" Mermagen, a contemporary of mine from my home town of Portsmouth and who, like me, had joined the RAF in 1930 on a Short Service Commission. He was something of an athlete and we had once played together for the Air Force XV. When I flew to Ismailia I was instructed over the R/T to land at nearby Abu Sueir, the largest Maintenance Unit in the Middle East. To my surprise, I saw faces from 46 Squadron that I knew amongst the airmen manning the duty flight. The delight in our meeting was mutual and I enquired what they were doing. Warrant Officer Wyn, a real squadron character, said "we are waiting for the aircraft and pilots who are coming via Malta, and in the meantime we are giving a hand here". I thought it was odd that I had not heard a word of the move of my old Squadron from the UK and next time

I visited Middle East HQ I made enquiries which uncovered a most painful story.

46 Squadron had reformed at Digby in the summer of 1940 whilst Jameson and I were in Gleneagles Hospital after the Norwegian adventure. The ground crew was unchanged, but having lost ten pilots and with both Jameson and I out of action, the flying part of the Squadron was almost completely changed. In May 1941 the reformed Squadron, after participating in the Battle of Britain was, for the second time, ordered to take passage in an aircraft carrier and again embarking at Greenock. This time it was the small carrier HMS *Argus* and the destination was Malta. The ground crew was sent by transport round the Cape. The *Argus* reached Gibraltar on 29 May 1941 and its Hurricanes and pilots were transshipped to a larger carrier the *Ark Royal*, for the more dangerous part of the journey in the Mediterranean. I suppose that whoever ordered this move considered the extra length of the *Ark Royal's* deck necessary for the Hurricanes, which would be carrying full overload tanks, since for her own safety the carrier would wish to launch the Hurricanes as far away from Malta as possible.

When the Squadron had been transferred they were told that they were no longer named 46 Squadron and that their number had been changed to 126—the number of a squadron already in Malta! It is inconceivable to anyone at squadron level how any such thing could be ordered. To the fighting man, the Squadron is *the* unit. The pilots live together, eat together, drink together and fight together. The airmen in the Squadron live for it too, and it is only by their devoted work in servicing and launching aircraft that the pilots meet the enemy with the best prospect of success and survival. A gun failure, an R/T set on the blink, a fault in the oxygen system: any of these could mean the death of a pilot. The trust and mutual respect amongst all serving in a squadron is a priceless asset. Now 46 Squadron pilots were to be joined with the airmen of a strange squadron. Without any period of familiarisation, they were to be thrown into one of the fiercest air battles of the war. How could the Air Ministry do such a thing? I was told that it was the intention to keep the No 46 alive by reforming it as a night fighter squadron equipped with Beaufighters and to station it at Idku. At least I thought I shall be in a good position to welcome the airmen when they arrive. Shortly afterwards, J A A (Jasper) Read, my number two at 219 Group HQ as Wing Commander Ops, was posted to command the Squadron. I was very pleased. He was the very best type of Auxiliary Air Force officer and a Scot. A man of few words, good in the air, Read set, and insisted from others, very high standards. I felt sure that 46 Squadron would be a good one under Read.

Then the Beaufighters with trained aircrews started to arrive and training began at once using the GCI radar covering Alexandria. The fully trained controllers were expert in the business and agreeably surprised at the increased distance the pilots could see at night in the fine Egyptian weather, as compared with the UK. We were only just in time because the Germans had started to attack the harbour at Alexandria again at night from their bases in Crete. With plenty of warning of the approach of the enemy from the north-west, the Beaufighters were now early in position on patrol and the unsus-pecting enemy took a severe beating. On one occasion in the early summer Jasper Read was brought into visibility distance by the ground controller and his own radar operator and the Beaufighter's four 20mm cannons did the rest. Almost at once another target appeared on the radar screen and Read shot that one down too. Two in ten minutes! On this and subsequent nights the Beaufighters enjoyed steady success and it was not long afterwards that the enemy gave up their raids.

Admiral Creswell, the Fortress Commander, was still insisting on morning "wash up" conferences and I was still obliged to attend and waste valuable time because I always had plenty to do in preparation for the next night's anticipated action. I often saw Admiral Cunningham doing the same thing. The enemy invariably attempted a reconnaissance of the harbour on the day after a raid by a high-flying Ju 88. These flights were always above twenty thousand feet and were well plotted by the radar as much as one hundred and fifty miles out to sea. This gave the Hurricanes or Tomahawks from Amiriya ample time to get airborne and up to the enemy's altitude. Consequently, most of these intruders were shot down.

Whilst I had been in the Desert, Air Vice-Marshal Keith Park had taken over Air HQ Egypt from 'Tommy' Elmhirst, and I looked forward to renewing my slight acquaintance with this great New Zealander whom I had served under briefly at Northolt in 1931-2 when he was the Wing Commander CO of the station. He came on a tour of inspection very soon after I had taken over. At the end of a long day during which he inspected everything from the radars to the aircrews, and including a visit to Admiral Creswell, we had a short discussion. Park asked a few penetrating questions which confirmed the impression I had already gained that he was a complete master of air defence in every respect. In my opinion, he was the best group commander of the old school in the Royal Air Force during the war. By this I mean those who had been pilots in the Great War and had reached air rank at the outbreak of the second in 1939. He, like many others of his generation, had survived the savage reduction of the Service from over a million strong in 1918 to just over thirty thousand all ranks in 1930 when I joined. Not only had manpower been cut to the bone, but equipment and particularly aeroplanes were kept at a very low level. There were just enough aircraft to meet squadron establishments and related to this figure, the bare minimum required for training those pilots needed by the squadrons. There had been no provision of aircraft for those officer pilots who were temporarily in staff appointments. In these circumstances, it is not surprising that many senior officers failed to keep up their flying once they had been promoted out of the squadrons. The parsimony of successive governments from 1918 until the mid-1930s meant concentrating what little there was exclusively on front-line squadrons. Park had experienced these difficult times but somehow managed to continue as an active pilot, and this was an important advantage from 1936 onwards when the change over from biplanes to monoplanes opened up a whole new era in military flying.

In the Battle of Britain Park, as the Commander of No 11 Group, was often in the air in his Hurricane, flying in the battle area and listening to the R/T conversations of the squadrons in action. He thereby gained first-hand knowledge on which to base his judgement and decisions. Few other group commanders had any practical experience of contemporary military flying. For instance Leigh-Mallory never flew any of the monoplane aircraft, such as the Hurricane, Spitfire, Blenheim or Beaufighter with which the squadrons in his Group were equipped. As a result he relied exclusively on the reports from his Squadron Commanders and it was often he who spoke loudest who was listened to. (As I wrote earlier, Badar realised this very quickly and he had a very loud voice anyway.) Only one other group commander of Great War vintage other than Park made a reputation with the aircrews and that was Ralph Cochrane in 5 Group, Bomber Command. He was a man of exceptional intelligence and possessed an iron will which compensated to some extent for his lack of first-hand knowledge of current operations. Later in the war, officers who had started as Squadron Commanders found that their up-to-date knowledge led to them dominating policy in air operations. This in turn led to rapid promotion to air rank to command groups where operational experience was essential. Basil Embry in 2 Group, Don Bennett in 8 Group (Pathfinders) and Harry Broadhurst in the Desert Air Force are three examples of officers who started their war careers leading squadrons and completing an operations tour. All three were exceptionally successful as group commanders.

Park's personality was such that those serving under him recognised immediately that he was a man who knew his business backwards. No good trying to bluff this one. He had a quizzical sense of humour and his eyes sparkled when displaying it, but any nonsense and those eyes could quickly become unsmiling and icy. He seemed to be satisfied by what he saw in 219 Group and with my handling of it. Just as he was leaving to return to Cairo he said "isn't it about time you had some leave?" It was now April and my last leave, or even day off had been in December after hospital in Cairo but I was agreeably surprised and encouraged that Park had checked. "I think you deserve it. What about ten days?" I thanked him and said I would go right away. As soon as he had gone I sent for Read, who was still my number two, and told him I was off on leave the next day, and would be going up to Haifa. I had no Ferguson for company this time. He was now flying a Spitfire in the Photographic Reconnaissance Unit, but I had all his contacts and the next day I flew a Hurricane to Haifa via Port Said, and put up at the Lev Carmel Hotel high up on Mount Carmel. My girl friend of the last visit, Zepora, was away but Rachel, Fergie's pet, rallied round all our friends for a party to start off the ten days. During those days, I flew up to Beirut which now had an air defence set-up in which an old friend from Digby Squadron Leader 'Daddy' Dakin, was in charge of the Sector Operations Room.

When I arrived back at 219 Group on 30 April I found that there had been little enemy activity—only the occasional Ju 88 on reconnaissance. Shortly after my return, there was an unfortunate occurrence with the Americans. The USAAF had sent a few of their four-engined B-17s to the Middle East. I heard that it was the intention to use these high-altitude day bombers to attack Benghazi harbour. Coincidentally Intelligence warned us that we could expect to see the German long-range Focke-Wulf Condor over the Mediterranean. This aircraft also had four engines. Around Alexandria there was a 'prohibited area' extending some sixty miles seaward. It was a restriction required by the Navy and any aircraft entering it without prior warning would be treated as hostile and engaged on sight. Our own fighters involved in the defence of the fort were exempt, as they could enter the area when under radar control.

One bright morning in late July 1942, an aircraft was plotted by radar approaching Alexandria at medium height and shortly afterwards entered the prohibited area. A section of two Tomahawks had been scrambled from Amiriya on the initial detection and made a perfect interception twenty miles out reporting, on giving the "Tally Ho", that the target aircraft was four-engined. The first attack by the No 1 in the section missed which was fortunate because the pilot,

Flying Officer Waddy, saw the white star of the USAAF on the fuselage which up to that moment he had taken to be the white of a swastika. He warned his No 2 who broke off his attack without opening fire. Waddy then reported that he thought the aircraft was a B-17 though he had never seen one before. I was in the Operations Room throughout the incident and immediately it was over, complained to Air HQ about the infringement of the prohibited area and also about the fact that the movement of the aircraft had not been passed to the air defence centre as was obligatory. I also pointed out that it was only an error by Waddy that had prevented the aircraft being shot at. I asked for action by Air HQ Egypt and Middle East Headquarters to prevent a similar occurrence in the future. I thought the matter would have ended there but I was wrong. Major General Lewis H Brereton, USAAF, complained to Tedder about "the deliberate attack"... "unforgivable on an ally"... "grave international incident etc". We were surprised at this violent reaction because as the result of nearly three years experience of air war we recognised how easy it was to misidentify a target at altitude and in the heat of operations. However, no amount of explanation pacified Brereton and later in the day, Tedder ordered an investigation into the whole occurrence, and I was detailed to undertake it.

Normally such an investigation would take several days, sometimes weeks to complete. Dates convenient for all concerned have to be agreed, witnesses have to be summoned and a venue fixed. On this occasion I was anxious to get it over with as quickly as possible, since I had many more important things to do. So as soon as I received the signal detailing me, I decided it would be quicker if I went to see all involved instead of asking them to come to me. So I quickly made out a programme and telephoned those concerned giving a time when I would call on them. Next morning I landed at Amiriya at first light to see the Tomahawk pilots. Next I went to Heliopolis to see Brereton particularly to ask why we had not received notification of the aircraft movement. He swept aside this point because, as I found out later, he was unaware of the agreed procedure. It was plain that he believed the attack was deliberate and in vain I attempted to explain about misidentification. He was particularly insulted that the white star could be mistaken for a white swastika. I then went to see the crew of the B-17 who maintained that their movement had been authorised, but admitted that after several hours' flying over the sea they were not too sure of their position when nearing the coast. On my flight back I realised that if the facts of the whole business were not stated and known to everyone involved, and as quickly as possible, it could lead to a great deal of trouble and especially a loss of confidence by the USAAF in the RAF.

When I landed at Dekeila in mid-afternoon, Rees was waiting with the car and I hurried off to my office at Seagull Camp. Fortunately, there were several good stenographers amongst the airmen clerks and we started work at once. While the drafts were being typed I telephoned Air Vice-Marshal Hugh Pughe Lloyd who had now joined Tedder's staff and told him the story. He said, "I can see this becoming a big row. The Americans are new to the business and don't realise the problems of identification and the need for strict compliance with instructions on the notification of aircraft movements. What I need is a report of your investigation in writing as soon as possible. When can you let me have it?" I said I aimed to have it completed that night and would get it to him by the morning. "Good", he replied "as well as the official copy send one to me personally". We worked through the evening and it was finished by midnight. I sent copies to all concerned so that they would have them on their desks when they arrived for work next morning. It was fortunate that we did so because at Tedder's morning meeting Brereton made an impassioned speech of complaint. I heard afterwards that Tedder let him go on and when he had finished, picked up his copy of the investigation and said quietly, "Have you read this?" Though I had made certain that a copy had gone to the General's office he had to admit that he had not. "I think you had better read it", said Tedder, "and then we can discuss". Later that morning a chastened General emerged from Tedder's office and that was the end of the matter. Later Hugh Pughe telephoned to thank me for his copy. "A good investigation", he said, "but it was the speed that counted".

Meanwhile, the news from the Desert, where the Army faced the enemy at Gazala, had a familiar ring. "We are building up for an attack." But on 26-27 May the enemy pre-empted our attack with one of his own. With no first-hand knowledge I was dependent for news on the brief operation summaries issued by Tedder's HQ to all units in the Middle East Command which were necessarily rather vague on precisely what was happening. Nevertheless, at first all seemed to be going well on the ground, the Gazala Line held and the enemy attacks on Bir Hacheim, at the southern end of our defence line, were not successful. In the air the fighters, now built up to a total of twelve squadrons, and including one flight of six precious Spitfires, seemed as usual to be dominating the air over the battlefields, though inevitably the occasional raid got through to the prime target Bir Hacheim. The new Kittyhawks which had started arriving just before I left the Desert were not, in my opinion, a great improvement on the Tomahawk. However, they were fitted to take both bomb racks and Clive 'Killer' Caldwell, the CO of 112 Squadron, dropped the first bomb on the enemy in March. But there had been little opportunity for the training necessary to give the pilots the skill required for them to be effective in the new role of fighter-bombing. Anyway, the first priority for the fighters was still to prevent the Luftwaffe and Regia Aeronautica attacking the troops on the ground; a difficult task because, with the exception of the six Spitfires, we were still out-performed by the enemy fighters. From all reports we seemed to be coping well and the Free French were quick to recognise the protection from air attack they were enjoying, sending a signal to Western Desert Air Force HQ which we intercepted and read: "Bravo, merci pour le RAF!"

It was tantalising to be so far from the battle and with no first-hand knowledge of what was happening, but from the operations summaries I soon began to realise that all was not well on the ground, and when I read on 13 June that enemy tanks were reported on the escarpment overlooking El Adem airfield, I realised that the Gazala Line had gone. The Gambut airfields, less than forty miles east of El Adem, were still in our hands but when I heard on 21 June that Tobruk had been captured I knew we would have to move off them, which we did soon afterwards. The Army was now in full retreat and from discreet enquiries, I learned that it was the intention to fight a "delaying action on the Egyptian frontier at Halfaya Pass but to make the real stand on a line stretching south from Mersa Matruh", more than a hundred miles east of that pass. That the stand was being made so far back was a shock: never before had the enemy penetrated so far into Egypt. Even in 1940 when we had been very unprepared and the Italians had attacked in overwhelming numbers, they never got much past the frontier and our airfield at Sidi Barrani, only fifty miles inside Egypt, had never been captured. Worse was to follow for by 28 June, the Army had been driven out of Mersa Matruh and was in full retreat eastwards.

I was very worried. Up till now my Wing had been no more than interested spectators, but Mersa Matruh was only about 160 miles from Alexandria, no distance at all in desert warfare. My chaps continued their work quite unperturbed, a real example of ignorance being bliss. To them the Desert war had always been remote, swinging backwards and forwards but always at a distance. They found it difficult to appreciate that the war on the ground might shortly involve them personally. I heard that Auchinleck had again taken over command of the 8th Army, this time from Ritchie, on 25 June. Last time it had been from Cunningham. I was comforted by this news.

I had seen how Auchinleck had pulled the show together at Fort Maddalena in November 1941 and I believed, rightly as it turned out, that he would do it again. In the meantime, what about my 219 Group? The entire organisation, radar stations, operations rooms, night fighters and the various HQs was entirely static. Were they all to be overrun?

There was a great silence at Air HQ Egypt and it was worrying not being able to plan for what looked like a very likely eventuality. In the Desert we had learned from hard experience that whatever the Army's plans and intentions, our airfields were liable to be overrun by the enemy ground forces. We also knew that if the enemy air force gained uninterrupted control of the air over the battle area, then our Army was sunk. So whatever happened we believed it was essential for the fighters to be over the battle throughout daylight hours. The key to this requirement was the mobility of the squadrons' ground crews and their equipment. They had to be ready to move fast when the order was given. In fact, they anticipated it, by moving half the ground crews on to the next set of airfields that were within range of the current ground operations. Whether the Army moved forward or back, we must always control the air above it. This was accepted doctrine throughout the RAF in the Middle East—so much so that earlier in the year, as I have recorded, I had moved the fighter force of six squadrons back from Antelat, Msus, Mechili to Gazala entirely at my own discretion and based on air reconnaissance of the enemy's movement. Coningham not only approved the moves retrospectively but said he expected me to make them. But that was in the past, now things were different. We had, however, no common doctrine for movement in Egypt. Were we to evacuate when the enemy approached or was Alexandria to become a fortress like Tobruk? If this was the intention then presumably we should stay put.

A Lieutenant General W G Holmes came to see me. He said he was on a reconnaissance of the western side of the Delta prior to preparing a plan for its defence. I was astonished that anyone thought that a plan could be prepared at this late stage and be put into effect with the enemy just two hundred miles away. Holmes was about to set up a Headquarters in Alexandria and he told me he would need help from me in planning. I told him I had plenty to do with active air operations and didn't relish being involved in what I thought was quite useless planning and was relieved when Middle East attached Group Captain Eric Whitley for the air part of the planning.

Uncertainty was the worst part of this period and it was a positive relief when Park told me that there was no question of 219 Group HQ moving and we were to remain in operation whatever happened.

This was a tall order but strangely we all felt better at once. Now we could make our own preparations. We had a strength of about four hundred airmen to man and operate the air defence centre, mostly clerks, plotters and operators in the building. Rifles were obtained and flights formed and training started. Then, to everyone's surprise, one of the main reasons for the air defence system was spirited away. The Mediterranean Fleet began to depart from the harbour on 27 June. We were not told where it was going.

The news from the Desert was that Auchinleck intended to fight it out on a line that had been prepared at El Alamein. I had heard of this fall back position when I joined the Western Desert Air Force in November 1941 but had not taken much interest since at that time I believed we would never need it. Then I received a signal giving the location of Coningham's HQ which had retreated to a temporary camp on the edge of the Delta. It then moved on to a point on the coast at Burg-el-Arab less than thirty miles from mine at Alexandria, and I decided it was time I paid a visit to find out exactly what was going on, and what the prospects were for the future. On 2 July I went by car since there was no airfield immediately adjacent. Mary Coningham was not there, but Jock Dunning a "hostilities only" Squadron Leader and head of the operations trailer staff met me. I knew that he was Coningham's confidante and I would get an informed comment from him. I asked him at once "Can the Army hold Rommel on the El Alamein line?" Jock said that considerable order had been created out of chaos in the few days since Auchinleck had taken over and that this, together with the distance Rommel was from his supply bases at Benghazi and Tobruk, gave us a pretty good chance of holding on this line. The fact that we had completely dominated the air had saved the Army during its retreat. He thought that Rommel would attack sooner rather than later to try to keep us on the run.

The next day I flew out to the newly built airstrips south-east of Burg-El-Arab to see the squadrons and visit 211 Group HQ. I landed and went to the nearest dispersal which turned out to be that of 229 Squadron. They had just returned from a sweep and the Hurricanes were being prepared for another, due to take-off almost immediately. It was obvious that the pilots were tired. The Squadron had been at maximum effort since 26 May and it was now early July, but when I saw them start on their next sortie their air discipline was as good as ever. I made my way to 211 Group HQ, and saw my successor, Guy Carter, whose first words to me were, "So there is to be no Benghazi for me". I was surprised that his first thought should be for himself and also because we old Desert hands had long learned to regard territorial acquisition as being only of secondary importance. Our task was to be operational wherever the Army was. We had been on the "Benghazi Handicap" twice already "there and back" as Clive Caldwell put it. Plainly Guy had not yet absorbed the philosophy, which was not surprising. He was a man of the Great War not flying on operations with the present generation, and knew little of what the pilots thought.

On returning to my Headquarters on the same day (3 July) at Seagull Camp, I found a signal from Middle East transferring my Group from Park's command to Coningham's. I thought this was odd since the air defence of Egypt was a considerable commitment that Coningham would surely not wish to add to his already heavy load in the west. I spoke to Park who said the transfer had been made at Coningham's request. I said I could see difficulties ahead since Park and his staff understood the air defence organisation covering Egypt whereas it would be new to Coningham and his staff. But the order had been given and there was nothing for it but to get on with the new arrangement. Off I went again to Western Desert Air Force HQ. This time Coningham was there to welcome me to his caravan and he explained it was necessary for him to command my Group since his airfields were now all in the area covered by my radar, and that he had to be in a position to give orders for their defence. I thought that this was theory being put before practical considerations, but didn't say so. I asked if he intended giving me some squadrons to help defend his airfields but he said "No, all my squadrons will be operating offensively westward from their airfields and mainly over the El Alamein area". I was to operate defensively over Alexandria, Cairo and his airfield area. With the exception of the last task, it was what we had been doing for months so essentially it was to be very much business as usual. One advantage of the new arrangement was my being able to keep in touch with the battle for Egypt, because I was required to make regular visits to Coningham and I also attended his commanders' conferences.

Rommel's attack had begun on 1 July and met its "real breaking point" (according to Tedder) on the 2nd. But hard fighting went on in what later became known as "the First Battle of El Alamein" until the 17th. The last four days had gone very clearly in Auchinleck's favour and Rommel was obliged to break off his attack. The remarkable feat by the Western Desert Air Force in operating at maximum effort every day from 26 May until 17 July despite having to move onto four sets of airfields in the process, saved the 8th Army by preventing a retreat becoming a rout.

In England, the Air Force's efforts were being watched with intense interest and on 4 July Churchill sent Tedder a message which read, "Here at home we are watching with enthusiasm the brilliant supreme exertions of the Royal Air Force in the battle now proceeding in Egypt. From every quarter the reports come in of the effect of the vital part which your officers and men are playing in this Homeric struggle for the Nile Valley. The days of the Battle of Britain are being repeated far from home. We are sure you will be to our glorious Army the friend that endureth to the end".

Life in Alexandria amongst the civilian population, Egyptian and European, after an initial mild panic, quickly returned to normal. Some Europeans who had evacuated themselves to Cairo and Palestine returned after a few weeks. The behaviour of the Egyptians during this period of tension was admirable. Their sympathies were with the British, but as neutrals, they were not quite so apprehensive at the prospect of Alexandria falling to the Germans as were the Europeans.

Air activity in the Group area did not increase despite the proximity of the Luftwaffe at Daba barely seventy five miles from Alexandria. We received reinforcements in the shape of a Greek Hurricane squadron which arrived at Amiriya and a Yugoslav coastal recon-naissance squadron came to share Idku with 46 Squadron. They were to operate under 201 (Naval Co-operation) Group commanded by Air Vice-Marshal Slatter whose main task was to work with the Mediterranean Fleet.

Then without warning from Intelligence or from England, a new problem faced our air defence. Early one morning I had just left my house in the usual brilliant sunshine when Tommy, my batman, came running out to say that the Controller was on the telephone and wished to speak to me. I went back inside and picked up the phone. The Controller said "We have a high flying aircraft plotted seventy miles north-west and heading for Alexandria. I have a section of 274 Squadron Hurricane IIs airborne and barring changes of heading by the enemy, should make an interception some five miles out". He added as an afterthought "you should be able to see it". I asked a few questions about back-up sections and as everything seemed in hand, went outside to watch instead of going to the Air Defence Centre as I normally did. Shortly afterwards a high flying aircraft appeared to the north-west with a very big condensation trail behind it. The trail was so conspicuous that I knew the Hurricane pilots would have no difficulty in spotting the aircraft and I waited for the inevitable combat. Nothing happened and when the enemy was almost overhead I telephoned the Controller and asked "What's happened?" The Controller replied that the Hurricanes were at almost the highest they could climb to at thirty-six thousand feet, but reported that the enemy was still well above them. Our ground radars had no accurate height-finding capacity at this time, but the Ack Ack gunner's gun-laying radars which were very accurate were tracking the aircraft. I asked the Controller what height they read on the enemy, "They say he is at 42,000ft". This came as a considerable shock since the best fighter I had in the Group was the Hurricane II with a ceiling of about 36,000ft. The enemy had by this time passed over the harbour and had turned for home. This really was a problem. One photographic reconnaissance, though useful to the enemy was of limited value, but repeated reconnaissance and comparison of photographs would record movement and other changes which would enable the interpreters to build up a comprehensive knowledge of our activities and forecast with some accuracy our future intentions.

I discussed the problem with the staff at Air HQ Egypt and signals were sent to England for any information they had about this flyer. The answer was soon with us. The Air Ministry believed the aircraft to be a special high-flying Ju 86 used solely for reconnaissance. It was assumed that it had a pressurised fuselage or cabin since it remained at altitude for many hours. It was not a fast aircraft, nor was it armed, relying for its defence on flying higher than any opposing fighters. Apparently the type had made a few sorties over the United Kingdom but because of the relatively few cloudless skies had not been very successful. Nevertheless, the Air Ministry recognised the seriousness of the problem and had ordered a high-flying Spitfire which, like the Ju 86, would have a pressurised cockpit. Unfortunately the Spitfire would not be available for some time and once again, as so often in the past, we, in the Middle East Air Force would have to do the best we could with what we had. My best aircraft was just not up to the task but fortunately there were a few Spitfire Vs at Aboukir being modified for the Desert Air Force and two were allotted to us.

It was apparent to me that though the Spitfire V was superior in performance to the Hurricane II it would have difficulty in climbing above forty thousand feet quickly enough to intercept the Ju 86 before it turned for home. It was decided therefore to lighten the Spitfires by removing everything but essential equipment for this particular role. As a start, because the Ju 86 was unarmed, the heavy protective armour was unnecessary and so removed. Also, as the Ju 86 was a large aircraft it would be an easy target so the Browning guns were removed, leaving two 20mm cannons as the only armament. It was argued, rightly I thought, that with the Ju 86's cabin being pressurised, one strike by a cannon shell would be enough to de-pressurise the cabin and force a rapid descent to a lower altitude where if necessary it could be dealt with by the Hurricanes. Other items removed included the IFF responder, survival kit and Browning ammunition chutes.

In the meantime, the Ju 86 came again and completed what was to become in the following weeks a regular route. It appeared on the radar screen well out to sea from Alexandria, flew over the harbour, down the road to Cairo, across to Suez up the Canal to Port Said and then away to the north to what we guessed was its base in Crete. Such comprehensive photographic cover of every sensitive area in Egypt was plainly of great value to the enemy and would nullify any attempt we might make at deception and greatly lessen the value of camouflage. The first Spitfire was ready at last and was to be flown by one of the test pilots at Aboukir. He was soon in action. Despite his being new to the air defence business and unfamiliar with the controller's interception jargon, there was no difficulty in putting him in visual contact, the condensation trail being so easily seen from miles away. Then began the long chase and climb to get up to the altitude at which the Ju 86 was flying.

The first interceptions were failures, the Spitfire's rate of climb being insufficient to make the required height before the enemy got too far ahead. There were urgent consultations with the test pilots after each sortie. They said we must lighten the Spitfires even more. The heavy cannons were removed and two of the lighter Brownings substituted. Ammunition was limited to 150 rounds per gun, and later reduced to 50. The heavy duty battery was removed and a small radio battery put in its place. Even so, on the next sortie though the Spitfire got within two thousand feet immediately below the Ju 86, it could not get any higher and raising the nose for a long-range shot led to an immediate stall. The pilot reported that he was at 43,000ft with the '86 going away when he broke off the attack. Another problem now presented itself—the bends—the pains that occur though increase of pressure on the pilot's body when descending after prolonged flight at high altitude. In England, this was taken care of by the pressurised cockpit which would maintain a mean pressure throughout the flight. I quizzed the pilots on this phenomenon but they made light of it saying that although it was painful it didn't last long. What to do next?

We needed to increase the performance of the Spitfire somehow, so the engineers turned their attention to the Rolls-Royce Merlin engine. It was decided that the only measure within the competence of the engineering resources in Egypt was to increase the compression by taking a sixteenth of an inch off the cylinder head. I was startled by this proposal because I had flown behind Rolls-Royce engines for most of my service, the Eagle, the Kestrel and now the Merlin. I knew that Rolls-Royce were implacable where the integrity of their engines was concerned, so much so that before the war their engines were virtually sealed products which even for overhauls were returned to makers. Now it was proposed to actually change the engineering! However, it had to be done and it is a measure of the skill that had been built up over the years in the work force at Aboukir that the task caused little concern. Most of the artisans at Aboukir were civilians, the highest proportion being Maltese but there were also Greeks, Egyptians and other nationalities employed there, and had been for years. The supervisory staff were all RAF officers and senior NCOs. The job was done and with a severe restriction on take-off power—it was forbidden to open the throttle more than half way—the Merlin functioned as well as ever.

Even with this increase in power, though, it was still impossible to reach the height the Ju 86 flew at. On one attempt the pilot climbed to within a few hundred feet but with his fuel down to a few gallons he had to give up the chase. The last remaining heavy piece of equipment was the R/T set, but if this was removed how was the pilot to be directed by the ground controller to make the interception? In discussion with the pilots it was decided that the set should be taken out and that the lightened Spitfire would take off and climb in formation with a standard Spitfire until a visual sighting was obtained when the lightened aircraft would continue on its own. There was elation a few days later, on 24 August when the Ju 86, presumably unaware he was being stalked, suddenly received a burst of fire out of the blue at 42,000 ft and immediately began to lose height. Its echo faded from the radar screens and we credited it as a 'probably destroyed'. Two more received the same treatment in the following weeks but not without loss on our side. On the last occasion, the test pilot managed to reach the enemy's altitude at 43,000ft, some seventy miles out to sea and gave it a burst of fire causing the Ju 86 to go into a steep dive, once more disappearing from the radar screen, and we presumed it went down in the sea. The test pilot turned for home but his fuel gauge was already showing empty and a few minutes later the engine stopped. The pilot covered a long distance in the glide towards the shore in his feather-light Spitfire, but failed to make it and when down to a thousand feet, baled out successfully. He was rescued almost at once by an Egyptian felucca. This was the third Ju86 we had engaged and the last, as we never saw that aircraft again in the Mediterranean.

In 1960, when I was Commander-in-Chief of Bomber Command, I invited Field Marshal Montgomery to visit Cottesmore and witness a demonstration by our 'V' bombers, at that time Britain's only nuclear deterrent. Though I had met him several times before, he didn't remember me and having looked at my medal ribbons, said in his usual challenging way, "I see you wear the African Star. What did you do to help win the battle?" I thought of my three years' service in that theatre, much longer than his, but then I remembered the Ju 86s and told him that it was my Group that had stopped their daily reconnaissance of his preparations for Alamein. "My word", he said, "you did that? If that photography had gone on all my deception plans with dummy tanks would have been useless". When it came to recognising essentials there was nobody better than Monty.

Nothing much happened in the last part of July but on 3 August there was a great gathering in Cairo. Smuts came from South Africa and Wavell from India, Churchill and General Brooke (who was CIGS) arrived separately in two aircraft, Brooke first, Churchill a little later. As if to demonstrate that he recognised who had saved the Army and Egypt, the Prime Minister emerged from the aeroplane wearing his Air Commodore's uniform and ignoring everyone, including the Ambassador, Sir Miles Lampson, went straight up to Tedder and shook hands with him.

My Group was still under the command of Mary Coningham and together with other senior commanders, I received an invitation to lunch in the Desert with the Prime Minister. Coningham asked me if my Group, located on the outskirts of Alexandria, could organise the food. My chaps were delighted to be of service, particularly the locally enlisted lot, and I left it to them. Off they went with a couple of lorries into town to Pastroudis, owner of the best Greek restaurant in the place and renowned for his catering. On 5 August I arrived at the appointed spot for lunch and saw that a marquee had been dug in and that many of my fellow guests were already there. Soon after Churchill, accompanied by Tedder and Coningham, arrived. I was fortunate to be on the top table, two places from the great man and was able to study him throughout the meal. What a man! He was already in his late sixties, had been on the go all the morning visiting the Army and here he was, despite the heat and dust, full of life and conversation. We had made sure that there was some good brandy at the end of lunch and the Prime Minister had a glass but refused a second. Tedder, who was sitting next to Churchill asked him if he would like to speak to the commanders. "I would be very glad to", said Winston, so Tedder tapped the table for silence and Winston stood up.

"I don't need to tell you gentlemen of the terrible consequences if we had lost the battle of Egypt a few weeks ago. Every time you take off in your aeroplanes you see that fertile delta that you have so worthily defended". I cannot remember much of what else he said but his opening words showed how well he appreciated what his audience had done. When he had finished and was leaving the tent, he saw a fly perched on the netting by the door. He had a fly whisk with him and with a violent back-hander got the fly first time. There was a spontaneous cheer, a recognition from a collection of fighting men for another and what's more, one with offensive ideas. I was to meet Churchill again when he came to Dekeila at the end of his desert visit. At this time, we heard that there were to be changes in Army command. Auchinleck was replaced by Alexander as C-in-C and another new man from home was to replace "Straffer" Gott who had been earmarked for the job of commanding 8th Army, but was killed on 7 August by the Luftwaffe when the Bombay he was travelling in was forced down by a lone 109 and he was hit while trying to help other passengers out of the aeroplane. Shortly afterwards I heard the name of the latest commander of the 8th Army, a Lieutenant General Montgomery, and soon heard he had arrived. So once more my chiefs would have to go through the wearisome business of teaching these newcomers the best way for the air forces to be employed to further the overall aims. Tedder had already had Wavell and Auchinleck and now Alexander. The last had virtually no experience of working with air forces but apparently was keen to learn.

Mary Coningham's opposite number had been Alan Cunningham, who was sacked on the ninth day of Crusader in November 1941. Auchinleck himself took over briefly before appointing Lieutenant-General Ritchie the next 8th Army Commander and Mary Coningham had to start again. When seven months later Ritchie got the sack, Auchinleck took over again, and now there was to be a fifth change in command of the Desert Army, this time a Lieutenant General from home who had done no fighting for two years. It was trying for Mary, who had plenty to do running an expanding Western Desert Air Force without the additional task of educating a succession of Generals in air matters. I was at his HQ in mid-August and asked Jock Dunning what this new General Fellah was like. "Miserable" said Jock, "No fun in the Mess".

Numerous writers on Montgomery's Desert campaign have made much of his arrival, and how he went up to the Desert by car from Cairo and was met and briefed in the car by Brigadier Francis de Guingand, the newly appointed BGS of 8th Army. One item in the catalogue of weaknesses detailed by de Guingand which surprised airmen who served before, during and after this period was "the lack of co-ordination between army and air force"[1]. These words hardly do justice to the Western Desert Air Force whose command and organisation had proved themselves during an advance beyond Benghazi and through two retreats, the first to Gazala and the second to the El Alamein line. De Guingand had been just one month in the Desert when he expressed this opinion. In the opinion of us experienced airmen, it was not co-ordination that was the problem, but rather the inability of 8th Army HQ to provide Western Desert Air Force HQ with accurate information once the battle had been joined. This prevented our full potential, particularly our bombers, being employed. When it came to the enemy dispositions, we learnt to treat Army information with suspicion finding from experience that our own fighter reconnaissance reports were much more accurate. The Army's failure in this respect was due to a lack of appreciation of the need for accurate information from Brigades, Divisions and Corps to Army HQ, the very low standard of Army signals at all levels, and the general amateurishness of subordinate commanders and staffs. By the time of the retreat to El Alamein, the Air Force had learned how best to help the Army from its own knowledge of happenings in the battle area, based not only on the specialised fighter reconnaissance reports made at the request of the Army, but on the hourly reports brought back by leaders of fighter sweeps who become very knowledgeable from their familiarity with the areas. By now, Coningham seldom waited for requests from the Army, recognising that if he did wait a large proportion of his bomber force would remain at readiness—unemployed. The situation in the Army is accurately described on 25 June by the Commanders-in-Chief's Committee in Cairo in a report to the Chiefs of Staff in London: "Although the training of commanders had been continuous, even in the foremost area, it was acknowledged that we were still largely an amateur army fighting professionals."[2]

Again Montgomery's condemnation of Auchinleck's location of his HQ well forward behind Ruweisat Ridge and the statement "more important it was more than forty miles from Desert Air Force Headquarters"[3] conveys the impression that joint location of the two HQ was not valued much at this time. Nothing could be further from the truth. Admittedly, there were occasions when as at the first battle of Alamein, the commander needed to be close to his corps commanders, and this is what Auchinleck did with his HQ at Ruweisat. In any case, it was not the full HQ of the 8th Army, it was a Tactical HQ consisting of a skeleton staff, a practice

[1] Nigel Hamilton *Monty—The Making of a General*, page 568.
[2] Lord Tedder *With Prejudice* page 302.
[3] Nigel Hamilton *Monty—The Making of a General* page 569.

Montgomery himself adopted and used for the rest of the war. From the time I joined in November 1941, the two HQs were invariably together at Maaten Bagush, Maddalena, Tmimi, Gambut, Maaten Bagush again and then on the coast at Burg-el-Arab. So any impression that joint location was attributable to Monty is incorrect. It is odd that he and his supporters make so much of the separation at Ruweisat as a lack of appreciation by both Army and Air Force of the need to work together, a lack corrected only by Montgomery's arrival. The facts deny this claim. The agreed primary role of the Western Desert Air Force from Crusader onwards, that of preventing the enemy Air Forces from interfering with Army operations, was overwhelmingly fulfilled. This was despite the inferiority of our fighter aircraft compared with our opponents. I doubt if this success could have been achieved without the Air having an intimate, continuous knowledge of Army aims and intentions that could only be obtained by joint location of HQ.

We had many visitors to the Air Defence Centre at this time. Radar was completely new to many of the Army Generals who had left the United Kingdom before the war, and they were fascinated by its ability to observe and track aircraft up to two hundred miles away. The visit I remember most clearly was that from General Smuts. He had no difficulty at all in understanding the intricacies of the Filter Room and the organisation of the Operations and Gun Operations Rooms. We had controlled some South African fighter squadrons for a short time when on passage to the Desert and he was complimentary about our handling of them. Later on 21 October, Lord Trenchard came to spend two days with us, accompanied as ADC by Wing Commander 'Paddy' Dunn who had commanded a squadron in the Desert at the beginning of the war.

I had not met Trenchard before though like every Air Force officer, I knew of him as the founder and first Chief of the Air Staff on the formation of the Royal Air Force in 1918, and I had constant reminders in my own service of his great imagination and the soundness of his judgement. He was in office as CAS for eleven years, more than twice as long as any successor.

On the first day, we visited the squadrons at Amiriya and Idku, the Air Defence Centre and the Sector HQ in a villa on the outskirts of Alexandria. We met the Navy that evening at a dinner given by Air Vice-Marshal Slatter at his HQ looking out over the Mediterranean. It was a great success and 'Boom' charmed them all. On the second day he visited all the other units in the area, including the Allied squadrons. During the visit I was impressed by his knowledge of how everything he saw was to some extent related to measures taken by him and his colleagues in the early days of the Air Force. I realised that if their thinking had been wrong we could well have lost the Battle of Britain, might not have had Bomber Command to attack Germany and would certainly not have had the right aircraft for the Tactical Air Forces and the partnership with the Army. Wherever we went, he spoke to the assembled air and ground crews. In a few words he was able to inspire them all, from the youngest airmen to the battle-hardened pilot. Saying goodbye he said he hoped we would meet again, a wish I silently reciprocated. We did.

Within a few weeks, then, I had met Churchill, Smuts and Trenchard, three men to whom the adjective great could rightly be attached. I had already met many military figures, Cunningham, Longmore, Tedder, O'Connor, Freyberg, Dowding, Park and Coningham. I was to meet and observe at close quarters Eisenhower, Alexander, Montgomery, Bradley, Patton, Portal, Slim, Macmillan and Attlee. All were impressive men in their way but none of quite the same greatness as Smuts, Trenchard and Churchill. All very different, but all with an aura about them. There was one quality that they had in common: an instant ability to assess a situation when meeting a number of people, even an unexpected audience, and then an ability to address them with authority. They always seemed to strike the right note whether informing, warning, or encouraging. Smuts was to me the best of them. From the moment he stepped out of his car outside my underground Operations Room at Alexandria I knew I was in the presence of somebody very special. Winston, of course, was superb stumping about the Desert for hour after hour despite his age and meeting all the squadron commanders gathered together, making a short speech and giving much encouragement by his obvious knowledge of their achievements. Trenchard had an advantage, though, when speaking to an Air Force gathering; after all it was his baby grown to adulthood and it had fully justified his beliefs. He knew its strengths and weaknesses intimately and seemed always to say the right things.

Rommel launched his last major attack during the night of 30-31 August, but Montgomery resisted him strongly and the attack was called off on 3 September.

Montgomery's handling of this defensive battle at Alam el Halfa was excellent. His positioning of artillery and his refusal to let the armour pursue the repulsed Germans were entirely sensible since he recognised the need for more preparation before offensives could be risked. At this time, and for the first time, the 8th Army had tanks, 300 Shermans which were the equal of anything the enemy had, but Monty was right not to risk them at this time. Very few knew about

Ultra and Monty's positioning of his forces was attributed to his 'military genius' and, self-publicist that he was, he did nothing to contradict this belief. So that really was the end of Rommel's campaign to conquer Egypt and he now found himself in a desperate situation. His supply ships from Italy to Tripoli, Benghazi and Tobruk were under attack by ships from Malta, by submarines from Alexandria, and by aircraft of the RAF from Egypt and the Fleet Air Arm from Malta. Many supply ships were sunk. The shortest haul to the front from Tobruk by road was about 325 miles and from Benghazi was 600 miles and even these routes were not secure since whenever any long-range fighters could be spared from the battle they attacked the traffic there. Rommel's tanks were worn out, most having travelled 375 miles from Gazala, much of it on their own tracks. The Luftwaffe was outnumbered and the Regia Aeronautica seemed to have been relegated to the defence of the rear areas. The first American squadrons of the USAAF had now flown across the Takoradi route to join the Western Desert Air Force, and though the 109 was still the best fighter in quality on either side, our numbers gave us air superiority over the battlefield. The enemy air was no longer a factor which the new Army Commander needed to take into account. Indeed, after one ridiculous demand for fighter cover for his first conference of the 8th Army staff, which Coningham left him in no doubt was entirely inappropriate, Montgomery was wise enough to realise that air matters were for the AOC and he as GOC should attend to army matters. There was plenty for him to do.

Much had been written about the great victory in October 1942 at El Alamein, the first by the British Army since the relief of Tobruk in November 1941, but less has been said about the overwhelming advantages enjoyed by the 8th Army at El Alamein as compared with the 8th Army at any other period in the Desert war. The favourable comparison is even more marked when the 8th Army is compared with its opponents and tends to be ignored by Monty's admirers. Firstly, for the first time we had a tank, the Sherman, equal in its class to anything the Germans had. Secondly, the 8th Army's lines of communication were short and secure. Thirdly, despite the continuing "amateurishness" of much of the command in 8th Army, many of the troops had been living and fighting in the Desert since the end of 1940 and had learnt a lot in those years.

We airmen, who had been associated with the 8th Army from its formation in September 1941 and had seen it force a German withdrawal from the siege of Tobruk, despite the inferiority of British equipment, and the handicap of long lines of communication from Egypt, could not avoid comparing that situation with that inherited by Montgomery before El Alamein. Indeed, those flying daily over the battle area, and those organising air operations, came to the conclusion that any of the 8th Army's three previous commanders would have had difficulty in losing the forthcoming battle of El Alamein.

The battle started as planned on the night of 23-24 October. We could hear and feel the vibrations from the artillery barrage in Alexandria sixty miles away. A week went by and there was much criticism and impatience amongst us of the pedantic conduct of the operation. Finally on 3 November the front broke and the Germans making use of all the available transport, including that belonging to the Italians, departed to the west. They would live to fight another day. We felt Monty had missed the boat as he would never have the Germans in such an advantageous situation again. However, one of the unfortunate results of providing the Army with air supremacy was that the soldiers grossly over-estimated what aircraft could do.

The 8th Army, having let Rommel and the African Korps escape from El Alamein, now expected the RAF to stop the German retreat by attacking the transport on the coastal road as far west as Halfaya Pass on the Egyptian frontier, and to block the Pass. But this was three hundred miles from our airfields and out of range of our fighters. Moreover, there had been no plan for the air to stop the enemy retreat for it was not in the capability of the Air Forces to do so. Harassment, of course, but that was the limit.

So the action went away westwards and I felt rather flat in my Air Defence Group at Alexandria. The social life in the town was a poor substitute for participation in the battle. Then on 8 November we heard of the invasion of the western end of North Africa by an Anglo-American force. This meant to me that the Axis forces would now for certain be cleared out of North Africa at last. But it was to take longer than anyone expected.

Tedder had said in his correspondence with Portal that compared with fighter operations at Home ours in the Desert were "village cricket". The intensity of fighter operations over England and France were due to both combatants operating in a very sophisticated air defence environment making set battles almost a certainty when either force invaded the other's air space. In the Desert, we had little radar and no comprehensive land-line system to make it effective. In Egypt, we had a rudimentary air defence system to cover the Delta and the Suez Canal, but it was scarcely tested by the light and sporadic enemy night raids. The real air fighting such as it was, took place in the Desert, to win and maintain an acceptable degree of air superiority over the battlefield. This air fighting was dictated by what was happening on the ground. If the Army was involved in an operation, offensive or defensive, then both the enemy and our own forces became involved, protecting and assisting our respective ground forces. Such engagements as occurred in the air were not controlled from the ground and many were chance encounters. In these circumstances, there was no need to develop the complicated tactics used by Fighter Command squadrons over northern France.

However, the authorities in the UK now decided that an airman who was right up-to-date should be sent to the Middle East to spread the gospel on advanced fighter tactics. The man selected was Group Captain Harry Broadhurst. He had served in the "front line" from the start of the war as a Squadron Commander, Wing Leader, Fighter Station Commander (at Wittering) and Fighter Group staff officer. He was to succeed Group Captain Beamish as Senior Air Staff Officer in the Western Desert Air Force. Broadhurst and I had been friends since 1932 when I was Flying Officer in 25 Squadron at Hawkinge and he a Flight Lieutenant in 41 Squadron at Northolt. We met regularly at rehearsals for the Hendon displays and at training exercises held by Fighting Area. He was a good aerobatic pilot and an "ace" shot, who was always top, or near to the top, of the annual air firing competitions held at Sutton Bridge.

He arrived in Egypt after the battle of El Alamein and with the 8th Army and the Western Desert Air Force on the crest of wave and advancing rapidly westwards, Coningham was not at all anxious for his present SASO George Beamish to depart; so Broadhurst was left waiting in Cairo. Also the need for up-to-date fighter tactics did not appear to be all that urgent in the light of our domination of the Luftwaffe in the air over El Alamein. Whilst Broadhurst waited he came to stay with me in my villa in Alexandria. He was annoyed at the delay and eventually decided to go to Cairo to say that if he was not to take up the appointment he had been sent for, he would prefer to return to the UK.

This did the trick and 'Broadie' was sent up to Western Desert HQ, now at Tmimi to take over from George whose turn it was to be disgruntled. Having nothing better to do, I flew up to Tmimi a few days later to learn how the war was progressing and to see how Broadhurst was making out in his takeover from George. In the pursuit of the enemy I came to the conclusion that Rommel had got clean away. Tedder had been up to see Montgomery about the possibility of cutting off the enemy at El Agheila and was rebuffed for his approach. George had insisted that Broadhurst should serve his Desert apprenticeship in a lengthy handover period, which included sleeping in a small tent. Only when George departed would the SASO's office trailer become available to his successor.

I flew back to Dekeila wishing I was serving in the Desert, rigorous as it was, rather than in the comfort of Alexandria. My wish was not to be too long delayed. On 19 January 1943, I was in my office in the evening, when the telephone rang and a voice said, "Is that Air Commodore Cross?" "No" I replied "It is Group Captain Cross". "No", said the voice "you are now Air Commodore Cross. This is Pirie speaking". I knew Air Vice-Marshal George Pirie slightly. He was the Air Officer Administration at Middle East HQ and he went on, "You are promoted to take over command of 212 Group at Benghazi. How soon can you get there?" I said "Tomorrow I suppose, Sir. Is there a need for speed?" "Yes, Benghazi is now the main port for the supply of 8th Army and the Luftwaffe is attacking it at night with some success. You are to take over and see what can be done". I wouldn't actually be in the front line at Benghazi but it was nearer to it than Alexandria. I had had my thirty-first birthday three months before and here I was now at air rank, the equivalent of a Brigadier General. Not bad, but more important I would be catching up with the war.

I sent for Norman Glover, my Adjutant, and Milson who had replaced Read, gave them the good news and said I would be leaving at first light next morning in my Hurricane. I then went back to the house and told Dai Rees and Tommy saying I would be off at dawn and asking Tommy to pack a bag. "Do you two wish to come too?", I asked. "Yes", they said together. "Right then pick up the rest of my kit and your own and bring the station wagon to Benina airfield outside Benghazi and there you will find 212 Group". I did some telephoning that evening to say goodbye to friends in Alexandria and left Dekeila early next morning, arriving at Benina by mid-day. I was met by Air Commodore 'Bud' Rankin, very senior in the rank and another man who had served in the 1914-18 War. His forte was Intelligence, but I had got to know him during the Crusader operation when he had headed a small reconnaissance party that followed close behind the Army and chose sites for our next set of airfields. He told me that he had been the first boss of 212 Group but as he had no experience of modern air defence admitted that he was rather lost. He was therefore glad to hand over and left for Cairo by road soon after lunch.

I had a look round the Operations Room, checked that the radars were working, found that the air raid warning arrangements for the port had not functioned at first but was assured that they were now satisfactory. No night fighters had been allotted yet. Guns were in position round the harbour and in the absence of fighters had been given a free hand. I was told that there had been raids every night for the last week and that ships had been sunk, but the number of guns had now been increased. There were Hurricanes at Martuba put there to help cover the Malta convoys. I paid a quick visit to the naval officer in charge in Benghazi who knew the form, and was keeping the unloading ships as dispersed as was possible. I then went back to the Operations Room to await the night's activity. Nothing happened and at about three o'clock in the morning I went to bed. We had no activity the next night nor the next, and after a week without a raid of any sort I realised I was again in a backwater. Tripoli was captured on 23 January and would now become the main supply base: Benghazi was dead.

I made a couple of trips to Western Desert HQ, the first to Bir Dufan airfield before the capture of Tripoli and the second to Castel Benito when it too was in our hands. I enquired about the possibility of employment, but though I got a warm welcome from Mary Coningham, I received no offers. Broadhurst, having taken over from George Beamish, was also now an Air Commodore and that evening I went with the two of them to dine in the General's Mess. I was the only guest that night and was seated on Montgomery's right. The company of about twenty were all Major Generals or above except for a few ADCs. At first Monty's conversation consisted of a series of questions concerning my war service and having established that I knew a bit about the Desert, he turned to Benghazi "There have been no ships sunk there lately?" "No Sir, none since I arrived". It did not seem necessary to mention that there had been no attacks. "Good", he said. "The Navy will soon have this place working and then Benghazi will be of little importance". He was interested in the interception business and then just before the meal ended there was a moment's silence and Monty, raising his voice slightly, said "I like your pilots, they are always trying to do something". It was plain that this remark was meant for his staff as much as for me.

The next day I flew back to Benina where I found a signal telling me to report to Middle East HQ forthwith for onward passage to Algiers where I was to take over command of 242 Group, the equivalent of the Western Desert Air Force with the British 1st Army. So my tour of duty at Benghazi had lasted from 20 to 31 January, twelve days, the shortest tour of my career. I felt I could not possibly take Dai and Tommy with me this time because this posting was outside Middle East Command. I explained this to them and in the meantime Broadhurst had heard of my posting and within an hour of my departure an aeroplane arrived at Benina, swept up Dai and Tommy and took them off to Tripoli. They became Broadhurst's servants and stayed with him until the end of the war.

I had to get to Cairo quickly and was obliged to leave the Hurricane for my successor. There was a Blenheim IV parked on the far side of the airfield and I drove over to it. Two airmen were in charge, an engine fitter and an electrician. They told me that they had been sent from Egypt to work on the aircraft and it was now serviceable. They had sent a signal to that effect to their unit some days before but so far nothing had happened. I asked them how well they knew the aircraft, and they said they had worked on Blenheims for the past year since coming out from England. I had only flown in a Blenheim once before and that was a Mark II; this was a Mark IV—quite a different model. I took the two airmen into the cockpit and between the three of us we established the identity of most of the controls. I thought I knew enough to get the Blenheim into the air and said, "I will deliver this aircraft to Heliopolis and you two had better come along". The fitter said "Is Heliopolis near Cairo?" and when I told him it was both men said they would be very pleased to make the trip. I set take-off time for 09.00hrs the next day, 1 February. There would be plenty of room in the Blenheim for all my kit.

With the help of the airmen I got the Blenheim started and though I had never piloted one before, got it safely airborne and set course for Dekeila because I had left some of my kit at my old HQ. The staff were pleased to see me when we arrived and we had the usual first class steak in the Union Bar in Alexandria that evening. The next day I took the Blenheim to Heliopolis, and told the Station Commander that I had found it "lying about at Benina". I asked my two accomplices what I could do for them. They politely declined my offer of help saying they were going to take a few days leave in Cairo before reporting back to their unit. Middle East HQ told me I was booked on a Hudson which was due to go to Algiers in four days' time. I was to report to Eastern Air Command on arrival. I booked in at the Continental Hotel and relaxed for the next four days. At least I now had time to reflect on my promotion long before I had expected it. It was gratifying to feel that higher authority, particularly Tedder, believed I was able to cope with the increased responsibility. In addition, the fact that I was now a long way ahead of my contemporaries, certainly tickled my vanity.

CHAPTER XIV

THE TUNISIAN CAMPAIGN

WE LEFT Cairo West airfield at mid-day on 3 February, 1943 in a Hudson flown by an experienced crew from the newly formed Transport Operational Training Unit. There were five other passengers, only one of whom I knew and that was Group Captain Jackman, an equipment staff officer from Middle East HQ who had earned a considerable reputation as a logistic planner. I had last met him when he came to visit us in the Desert to check how his estimates of ammunition expediture were working out in practice. We were impressed at the accuracy of his forecasts. He was on his way to join Tedder's staff in Algiers. We landed at Castel Benito airfield near Tripoli to refuel and stay the night. The other passengers were taken off to the doubtful comfort of a transit camp but I was met by my ex-driver Corporal Dai Rees who drove me off to Harry Broadhurst's camp at Western Desert Air Force HQ. Broady was now an Air Vice-Marshal commanding that Air Force following Mary Coningham's departure to be the head of North-West African Tactical Air Forces which comprised my 242 Group with the British 1st Army, XII Air Support Command (USAAF) to cover the US II Corps, and WDAF, under Broadhurst, with 8th Army. I stayed in such comfort as there was to be had in Tripoli in a guest caravan, and during the evening I saw some of the 8th Army staff and learnt a little about the 1st Army front which according to them was in a mess.

The next morning we left again in the Hudson for Maison Blanche, the airfield for Algiers, avoiding the battle zone to the north by flying south into the Desert before turning west and then north. The weather was bad as we approached the mountain and we were in cloud for much of the time. I noticed that some of the passengers were uneasy, for they knew that there were no navigation aids in this part of Africa and we were relying on dead reckoning navigation only. I was a bit worried but endeavoured not to show it. As a passenger in the air (a role I avoided whenever possible) I was a fatalist. From the back of an aeroplane there was nothing I could do to influence events so on all flights as a passenger I equipped myself with a book, concentrated on it, and paid no attention to what was going on inside or outside the aeroplane. I found this worked very well up to a point, though when I found myself reading the same paragraph over and over again I realised I was more concerned with the aeroplane than I was with the book. This time our crew seemed to be quite unworried by the weather, found a gap in the cloud and decended quite close to the airfield. Maison Blanche was a French Air Force base but was now crowded with British and American aircraft, and for the first time I saw Spitfires with United States Army Air Force markings on them. We landed and were marshalled by RAF airmen to our parking place. There was nobody to meet us and whilst waiting for motor transport outside the control tower, the Air Officer Commanding, Air Marshal Sir William Welsh drove up. He recognised me which was surprising since I had only met him once before when I was attached briefly to his staff at Reading in 1940. He said he would talk to me later when I reported to his Eastern Air Command HQ. Our car arrived and we drove into Algiers. Unlike Cairo it was plain that Algiers had been considerably affected by the war. Isolated from Europe except for Vichy France, the town had a neglected look. Empty shop windows and practically no civilian road traffic. We arrived at the large Hotel Aletti which was now requisitioned by the Allied military as a transit camp. None of the good food of Cairo and Alexandria here, just British rations with corned beef and biscuits as the staples.

After lunch, such as it was, Jackman and his party went off to the Allied HQ up the hill in the Hotel St. George and I was driven back past the airfield to Eastern Air Command Headquarters located in a large building to the east of the town. I saw Welsh who knew of my appointment to command 242 Group but said that no date for my take over had yet been settled. I would have to await the arrival on 14 February of Tedder and Coningham, both of whom were on leave in England. In the meantime I had better stay in Algiers. He painted a pretty gloomy picture of the situation at the front. Only one all-weather airfield at Bône was in range of Axis positions in Tunisia for our fighters, and the strips constructed by the 1st Army were frequently waterlogged and unusable. The enemy had reacted quickly to the Operation Torch landings and had occupied Tunis and Bizerta with their all-weather airfields

El Aouina and Sidi Ahmed on which was stationed the best German fighter, the Focke-Wulf Fw 190A-4 (with tropical filters and a rack for a 550 lb bomb under the fuselage).

Our squadrons were equipped with Spitfire VBs so once more we were out performed but not so badly as we had been in the Desert. Later two squadrons were re-equipped with the Spitfire IX which was a match for the 190. From Welsh's talk, it was apparent that much of the doctrine evolved by 8th Army and Western Desert Air Force as the result of hard experience was unknown to the British Army and Air Force newly arrived from the United Kingdom. Even some long established practices at home were not being followed here. For instance in the UK, Anti-Aircraft Command was under the operational command of the AOC-in-C, Fighter Command. Control of the disposition of guns was exercised through gun operations rooms located with the RAF authority at all levels. The arrangement led to excellent co-operation between the two Services and the best use, according to circumstances, of both fighters and guns. Here, all AA guns were at first controlled by the Army and were often deployed with little knowledge of the potential air threat. Worse still, having no continuous RAF contact to record the tracks of friendly aircraft movements, the Army repeatedly mis-identified and fired on our own aircraft. It seemed to me that two years of inactivity at home had ill prepared the 1st Army for war, and it was certainly time I went up to the front to see things for myself.

The Hurricane squadron at Maison Blanche responsible for the air defence of Algiers was commanded by Tony Rook, an old friend from No 504 Nottingham Auxiliary Squadron. He lent me an aeroplane and I flew to Tingley which was the nearest airfield to 242 Group HQ in the village of Ain Seymour, and some distance away from the airstrip. I landed and was met by the CO of 322 Wing, one Pete Hugo, a young and impressive Wing Commander. Pete was a South African who had joined the Royal Air Force before the war. He had fought with distinction in the Battle of Britain from Biggin Hill and in the sweeps over France afterwards, and had risen rapidly to his present rank. He was actively flying now and was to continue to do so until the end of the war. Hugo said he received his orders from the commander of the other forward Wing, 324, located at Souk-el-Khemis in the Medjez valley where 5 Corps of the 1st Army had its HQ. He also said that it was 5 Corps who were conducting the battle, not 1st Army. I was impressed by the plainly evident efficiency of all ranks at Tingley but felt it was imperative that I go over to 324 Wing at Souk-el-Khemis to find out the exact situation. But firstly, however, I had to make my number with the AOC, Air

Commodore George Lawson at 242 Group HQ. Hugo lent me a station wagon and driver and off we set on the drive to Ain Seymour. We drove through some spectacular scenery up in the mountains, some of them snow covered, but it was a good two hours drive and I couldn't help reflecting that any Group HQ so far from the nearest airfield would have difficulty in keeping in touch with the operations of the wings. This was clearly unacceptable to my way of thinking.

We reached Ain Seymour as the light was fading. It was a small village with just one pension which had been requisitioned as a Headquarters. Neither Lawson nor his Senior Air Staff Officer, Tom Traill were in the HQ and I was welcomed by another old friend from 504 Squadron, Ken Gough. After a bath and change I went down to meet the staff for a pre-dinner drink—all very civilised compared to the tents of the Desert. It became obvious to me after a few minutes' conversation that they knew nothing of the imminent change of command and I didn't enlighten them. As far as they knew I was just a visiting officer from Algiers. I asked why the Group HQ was located at Ain Seymour and was told that General Anderson's 1st Army HQ had allocated the village to 242 Group, and taken a village a few miles away for its own HQ. I think my surprise at this information must have shown (in the Desert it was nearly always the Air Force which selected the site for the joint HQ) since one officer said that the location of all HQs was decided by the Army on the premise that the requisition and allocation of buildings was an Army responsibility. I asked why not put our HQ under canvas since tents could be pitched anywhere. This idea met with a dead silence; plainly such a solution, permitting the two HQ to be adjacent had never been contemplated. I left early next morning by car for Tingley, not having achieved my main purpose of meeting Lawson, but at least I had got the 'feel' of the Group HQ—and didn't care for it.

From Tingley I flew over to Souk-el-Arba, a grass airfield on which a strip of Summerfield tracking had been laid. I was dismayed at the sight of this tracking. I had last landed on it at Skaanland on the fjord leading up to Narvik and knew its limitations as an airfield surface. Nevertheless, I landed successfully this time and was met by Group Captain Ronnie Lees, an old friend and brother squadron commander in 12 Group at the beginning of the war. I was delighted to see him and not only for old times sake, but also because if ever there was a good egg, Ronnie was it. He had come to us before the war from the Royal Australian Air Force and was known by all of his contemporaries as a most efficient operator in everything he did. Typically, Ronnie had led his Wing into Bône airfield at the beginning of Torch shooting down a Me 109 in the process. I couldn't think of anyone I would rather have to command a wing in the Group I was about to take over, than Ronnie.

We drove up the valley to Souk-el-Khemis where several airstrips were under construction: each was a thousand yards long and again surfaced with Summerfield tracking; this time the Royal Engineers had learned their lesson and the mesh was laid on hard, impacted sand. Ronnie thought that with improving weather our problems with the airstrips were more or less over. He was right and operations were never held up again because of unserviceable airfields. The squadrons were all equipped with Spitfire VBs—a wonderful sight for me, accustomed as I had been to taking on the Germans with Tomahawks, Kittyhawks and Hurricanes.

Ronnie said that on the ground the enemy still had the initiative and were prodding away all along the British 5 Corps front. Apparently we were very short of reserves and when a minor penetration was suffered the whole line was obliged to pull back to prevent out flanking. Nevertheless the Corps were of the opinion that the line could be held despite these adjustments, forward of Medjez-el-Bab, some thirty miles from Tunis and some thirty-five miles from where we now were having the airfields prepared at Souk-el-Khemis. In the air Ronnie's 324 Wing had had a difficult time. Not only unserviceable airfields but mountainous terrain made the use of radar for air defence very difficult because permanent echoes filled the radar tubes and made detection of the enemy and any control of our own fighters very much a hit and miss business. It was no use keeping the Spitfires at Readiness on the ground as they would almost always be too late to make an interception. He had done his best to keep the air clear of the enemy over 5 Corps by frequent sweeps and patrols, but admitted that Fw 190s flying in small numbers used their superior performance to penetrate our cover, attack a target on the ground and then depart at a speed the Spitfire VB could not match. The attacks were quite infrequent—pin pricks as Ronnie called them—achieved little damage and would hardly have been noticed by the 8th Army. But this was the inexperienced 1st Army and there were complaints from all levels about the "lack of air support". I asked Ronnie what part the Group HQ played. "None so far", was his reply.

I flew back to Tingley on 8 February and spent the night with Hugo, Next morning I returned to Maison Blanche. Before leaving Tingley, Hugo told me that he had orders to move forward to Bône airfield when the Wing there moved on to Souk-el-Khemis.

When I got back to Algiers I found an empty office in Eastern Air Command HQ and wrote a short report on my visit to await

Mary Coningham's arrival. As there was a need for changes in 242
Group, particularly the location of its Headquarters, I was now
determined not to assume command until I had Mary's approval for
what I proposed. On 14 February Tedder and Mary Coningham flew
in from England in a USAAF B-17. I was at the airfield to meet
them amongst a crowd of British and American air force officers.
I managed to have a word with Mary. He told me he was off to
Tripoli at first light the next day to attend an exercise being
conducted by Montgomery. I was disappointed because I would not
have an opportunity to discuss the changes I wished to make, but
there was nothing to do but to wait for his return. I later found
out that Tedder assessed the situation on the 1st Army front and
reported to Portal in London on 18 February that Coningham was
not going to have an easy time to get rid of the "fantastic idea" of
soldiers controlling aircraft. Moreover, there was a lot to be done
to get a properly balanced force in the forward area.

Coningham arrived back in Algiers a few days later and I was at
last able to report on my visit to the front and discuss with him the
changes I proposed in 242 Group. He was in one of his cagey and
non-commital moods but he didn't veto the changes which was good
enough for me. I went straight back to Eastern Air Command to
pack my bag by which time it was mid-day. Flying was off because
the weather had closed in with cloud "on the deck", so I told my
driver to fill up the station wagon and to load the back with jerricans
of petrol. When he had done this we set off. We took it in turn to
drive and arrived at Ain Seymour at 4 am on 22 February after a
14½ hour journey. The Mess was open but of course there was
nobody about. My driver, a resourceful chap, discovered some tea
and biscuits in the hotel kitchen, and afterwards having found an
empty room for my driver, I went for a hot bath and a shave. I was
in the Mess dining room at 7 am when breakfast proper was served.
Lawson appeared shortly along with other staff officers, surprised to
see me so soon as the signal containing the order for the change in
command had only arrived the previous evening. After breakfast I
went with Lawson to his Operations Room. The reports from the
Army were disturbing. The American II Corps had recently suffered
a sharp reverse in the Kesserine Pass, largely as a result of
inexperience.

Previous to this battle, Eisenhower (the Supreme Allied Commander) had made Lieutenant-General Kenneth Anderson the
commander of all forces on the front at this time, namely 1st Army,
II Corps and the French IX Corps. Anderson sent the British 6th
Armoured Division south to reinforce II Corps and Rommel was

brought to a halt south of Thala on 21 February. But we did not know this at Lawson's HQ that morning. After the operations brief, I went with Lawson to his office where he outlined his ideas for the handover of command. He proposed that it should take approximately two weeks which would be taken up with visits to Army formations down to brigade level and to all the wings and squadrons in the Group. I said nothing and after a while he asked, "Well what do you think of the programme?" I said I thought it was too long. "Why?" "Well, George", I replied, "as I see it there's a bit of a crisis on here with Von Arnim pressing and Rommel trying to encircle the whole of our front. The air may have to play a decisive role not only in keeping the Luftwaffe off our chaps' backs but also in attacking the enemy on the ground. This means forthright action— If you and I are here together there will be doubt as to who is in charge and it will lead to uncertainty in the wings and squadrons. I think the change in command must be done quickly." "How quickly then?" asked Lawson. I said "About the time it takes you and me to draft a signal to all concerned including 1st Army notifying the change. About twenty minutes I guess". George was somewhat taken aback but passed a signal pad across his deck and I wrote it out. George read it then pressed a bell on his deck and his personal assistant came in. "Send this priority to the full distribution list", he said. He then got up, left the office and had left the Headquarters by lunchtime. I thought I had made an enemy but was mistaken. George appreciated my point of view and we remained friends until he died after the war.

As soon as he left the office I sent for the Senior Air Staff Officer Tommy Traill, at 43 a comparatively elderly Group Captain of first war vintage, whom I knew slightly. I told him that being located so far from the main airfield area made day-to-day control of operations impossible. He agreed but said (as I knew) that operations were being conducted by the senior Wing Commander Ronnie Lees, located close by 5 Corps HQ at Souk-el-Khemis, who were responsible for all British ground action. "How are we to help on the US II Corps front then?" I asked. "That's where the crisis is". Tommy had no answer. I told him "I am going up to Souk-el-Khemis and will exercise command from 324 Wing HQ, we are superflous located here". "What about 1st Army?" asked Traill. I said that as soon as I could see the Army Commander (Anderson) I would tell him that this Group Headquarters must be near its airfields and that if he placed a correct value on Army/Air co-operation he would move his own HQ up to the Souk-el-Arba—Souk-el-Khemis area alongside us. "In the meantime you had better contact your opposite number in

1st Army HQ, give him the news of our imminent move and suggest that an Army/Air reconnaissance set out at once to select a suitable site in the area". Poor Tommy was quite taken aback, for he had become accustomed to the Army initiating everything and now he was being told to tell the Army what to do. He rightly did not think they would welcome the change. "What are we going to live in?" was Tommy's final question. "Tents", I replied.

As soon as Tommy had left I asked Lawson's ADC to arrange for me to see the Army Commander at once, only to be told by the Army staff that this was impossible and that no appointment could be made for the next two days! I could not wait that long with the disturbing news from the front, so I left it to Tommy Traill to tell all of our move. Later I would have to explain the need for immediate access to the Army Commander by the Air Commander which was established practice in the Desert. I also told Traill to issue a warning order to the staff about the move and to implement it as soon as the site had been agreed with the Army. I then drove off to Bône airfield.

At Bône, Pete Hugo was already installed with his Wing and I asked him for a Spitfire to fly over to Souk-el-Arba to join up with Lees. He quickly had one ready for me. Before I left I said, "I need an ADC, can you find me one?" Hugo asked, "What sort of chap do you want?" I replied, "Well I shall be doing a lot of flying getting to know this front so he had better be a good No 2, with good eyesight. I don't want to be jumped whilst I am learning". Hugo thought for a few moments and then said, "I think I have just the one for you. I'll send him over tomorrow." That was how Tony Le Hardy joined me and we were together for the rest of the North African campaign, then Sicily and Italy. He not only had exceptional eyesight in the air: for an officer of junior rank he was possessed of great initiative and organising ability. Eventually when we reached Taranto many months later and the Group had rather a static role, Tony became a bit restless and so I sent him to command an advanced landing strip on the island of Vis a few miles off the German-occupied Yugoslav coast—a dangerous command if ever there was one. Tony did splendidly and despite his youth gained the confidence of everyone, the Yugoslav partisans under Tito, the Balkan Air Force supporting them, and particularly the 15th US Air Force whose crippled aircraft returning from lengthy sorties over Germany landed or crashed on Vis, being unable to face the crossing of the Adriatic to their bases at Foggia.

I joined Ronnie Lees at Souk-el-Khemis. He had set up his Operations Room in some out buildings of a farm a mile or so from the four airstrips. I told him to carry on just as he had been and I would "look over his shoulder" until 242 Group HQ moved into the area. I then went off to call on the GOC of 5 Corps whose HQ was at another farm a few miles away. Lieutenant General Charles Allfrey was waiting for me and we went straight to his office trailer. Tall and dignified, a delightful man but pretty suspicious, it was apparent that he thought the present arrangement of 324 Wing working direct with his Headquarters was quite satisfactory and he could see no reason for my Group taking over. I explained about the second wing at Bône now coming into the area and the need for co-ordination. Also if Coningham, now alongside Alexander at Constantine, thought it necessary for all Allied tactical air strength to be used to help II Corps, Lees did not have the staff or communications required for co-operation with XII Air Support Command (USAAF) to the south of us. I think it was the first time that Allfrey appreciated that the range of our aircraft made it possible for them to operate on other fronts than that of his own Corps. Another delicate matter I raised with Allfrey was the handling of the two Army Co-operation Squadrons, 225 and 241.

In the Desert the term "Army Co-op" had long disappeared, because it was reasoned that all squadrons were co-operating with the Army since everything they did, even bombing supply ports far behind the front, was in aid of the troops on the ground. I had learned to my dismay that 225 and 241 Squadrons were being given their instructions direct by staff officers at Allfrey's HQ and sometimes being required to attempt the most ridiculous missions. That this practice led to the loss of aircraft and crews worried the squadron commanders, who rightly believed that if their operations were co-ordinated with those of the fighter wings, then not only would losses be avoided but reconnaissance would be improved since pilots would be able to concentrate on their task rather than, as was now the case, constantly looking over their shoulders to avoid being surprised by enemy fighters.

I told Allfrey that I intended to put the two squadrons under the command of the Fighter Wing who would process his reconnaissance requests throught the fighter operations room. Allfrey was not amused and his staff were outraged but it had to de done. The presence of the Fw 190 and Me 109G over the battlefield meant we would be risking heavy losses in superbly trained reconnaissance pilots if they were operating alone, and that we could not afford. Later that day I visited the two COs of 225 and 241 Squadrons, Wing Commanders Millington and Barker. The news of the change had already reached them and both expressed relief at the new arrangement.

Both squadrons were equipped with Hurricane IICs and in addition to reconnaissance, were trained in fighter bombing though for the present the former role was fully occupying them. E G L Millington I had not met before and I was impressed by his complete grasp of his Squadron and its role. John Barker was an old friend; he had been the scrum half in the Air Force team at Twickenham with me in 1936.

There were four newly constructed airstrips in the Khemis complex and during my first day in residence in Ronnie Lees' Wing I went round them to meet the Squadron. There was the occasional face that I recognised from Fighter Command days but mostly these very young men were unknown to me. I was impressed by the air of efficiency on the flying side and as the days went by I realised that the right organisation at home in Fighter Command had resulted in a higher standard in the air than we had been able to achieve in the Western Desert Air Force. In the evening I had a long discussion with Ronnie Lees, after he had attended the BGS's daily conference at Corps HQ. We went over the day's operations in detail, and then wrote the programme for the next day. We had light bomber squadrons on airfields well back from the front but when suitable targets were found, mostly by air reconnaissance, Ronnie ordered them to attack. These light bombers were Bristol Blenheim Mk Vs. Given the name Bisley, they were slow and needed heavy fighter protection. Now having made a brief survey of my command it was essential that I met my opposite number on the ground, the 1st Army commander, General Anderson. After much telephoning on very bad lines, and not a lot of co-operation from his staff, an appointment was made for 27 February which was five days after I had assumed command of the Group. Needless to say I should have seen him on the first day, but this was 1st not 8th Army.

It took two and a half hours to motor the weary miles over poor roads to Anderson's HQ but I was shown straight to his office on arrival. The General was a tall, well built man in his fifties. He had startling blue eyes which showed some amusement when I, a thirty-one year old Air Commodore, started straight away on the changes I was making in the organisation of the Group. He showed no surprise and I guess he had already heard from 5 Corps about the moves, and made no comment other that that he had agreed to move his HQ to the Souk-el-Arba area. That was progress anyway, the Army and Air HQ would at least be together. I asked him about his future plans and was told that he could not look further than holding the line as it was at present: on the 1st Army front some ten miles east of Medjez-el-Bab.

My first impression of Anderson had been favourable. He had a sense of humour, as witness his amusement at the news of my independent decision to move my HQ; also, despite the disparity in our ages and rank he, unlike his staff, had treated me as an equal. I think that Monty underrated him when he described him as "a good plain cook", and I now prefer Eisenhower's opinion of him as "a gallant Scot, devoted to duty and absolutely selfless". I agreed with Eisenhower in his postwar assessment that Anderson was "Honest and straightforward, he was blunt, at times to the point of rudeness, and this trait, curiously enough, seemed to bring him into conflict with his British confreres more than it did with the Americans. His real difficulty was probably shyness. He was not a popular type but I had a real respect for his fighting heart. Even his most severe critics must find it difficult to discount the smashing victory he finally attained in Tunisia."[1] When I arrived back at Souk-el-Khemis on 1 March I found George Beamish awaiting me. After leaving the Desert, George had returned to the UK, but had been recruited by Mary Coningham together with Tommy Elmhirst to fill the posts respectively of Senior Air Staff Officer and Air Officer Administration in his new North African Tactical Air Force. So now these three key figures from the successful Desert campaign were together again.

I was glad to talk with George because Lawson's 242 Group HQ consisted of little more than a command post. Also, some staff posts were missing and the squadrons had suffered as a consequence. George agreed that a scaled-down establishment based on the well tried Western Desert Air Force pattern was what was needed. He said he would speak to Tommy Elmhirst on his return to Constantine. We failed to agree on one matter and that was the role of the RAF Regiment squadrons of which there were a number in the Group. In the Desert we had no need for an RAF Regiment during my time there, mainly because the airstrips with their huge perimeters were virtually undefendable against attack by ground forces and security depended on the Army holding the front line sometimes as much as seventy miles forward. If the front line broke and the Army retreated we were well practiced in moving back quickly to the next set of airfields without in any way interrupting our own operations in the battle area. As for surreptitious raids on our airstrips, the enemy never attempted to emulate the successful Long Range Desert Group and SAS operations against theirs. Now, here I found the Regiment squadrons 'guarding' the airstrips in the Khemis area.

[1] D D Eisenhower *Crusader in Europe*, Page 93.

This seemed to me to be superfluous because the real defence of the strips was, as always, the front line this time some thirty miles to the east. From my talk with Allfrey, it was clear that he was short of infantry to hold static positions in the line. I proposed, therefore that the RAF Regiment squadrons which were approximately of Army company size, should be handed over temporarily to the Army. This was revolutionary stuff to George who was always pretty conservative in his thinking, and he warned against my proposal. Nevertheless as I received no veto from his HQ, these squadrons moved up to quiet sectors of the line. The Army were grateful for this small but unexpected reinforcement. Incidentally, there was an amusing sequel later when just before the final attack that captured Tunis General Alexander, accompanied by Anderson, went up to the forward defended localities to view the ground for the attack on the morrow. Having done this, Alexander put away his binoculars and turned to go but passing some men manning a slit trench nearby, went over to them and asked the Corporal in charge what his regiment was. He was quite startled when the Corporal replied, "RAF Regiment, Sir".

A new establishment for my Group arrived from Elmhirst in forty-eight hours. There were two appointments that I insisted on making myself; the first was that of Senior Air Staff Officer and therefore my deputy. It would be he who in continuous consultation with his opposite number in 1st Army HQ would order the operations to implement agreed policy. The present occupant of the post was not up-to-date with modern aircraft and operations and would have to go. The obvious choice was Ronnie Lees who was already dealing with fighter, reconnaissance and bombing operations and doing it very well. Ronnie regretted having to move out of the Wing but agreed that it was the sensible thing to do. The other post was that of Senior Personnel Staff Officer. It was essential that the occupant of this post be able to win, and retain, the confidence of squadron commanders who, operating daily as well as administrating their squadrons, were under considerable strain. Replacing casualties in the squadrons was a particularly delicate business. Squadron commanders needed to have a say in the appointment of flight and section leaders but hitherto had not been allowed to do so by Eastern Air Command, whose own Senior Personnel Staff Officer was very jealous of his perogatives. I therefore needed a man of tact and determination and my choice was not even in the North African Air Forces, he was still in the Middle East. It was Norman Glover—the Adjutant of my old Wing at Alexandria. Every task he had been given in the Desert and in Egypt he had done well. I telephoned

Tommy Elmhirst on the usual bad line and asked if he would agree to Norman filling the post and if so could he arrange the posting? Tommy agreed but made no promise. "Remember we are dealing with another Command" (Middle East Air Force) but within a week Norman arrived, delighted to be in an active theatre of the war again. In no time at all he had made the acquaintance of all the commanding officers and gently but firmly removed executive authority from Algiers. It was a delight for me to see how quickly the not easily satisfied squadron commanders came to rely on Norman for help and advice. One more problem solved.

A site was selected near Souk-el-Arba for 1st Army HQ with 242 Group alongside and we were all installed by mid-March. We had separate messes because of size limitations, but I was a member of the General's Mess and dined in it most evenings. I was now able to meet with Anderson as and when necessary. At first he was critical of what he called the "lack of air support". As he put it, "I cannot even send a dispatch rider up to the front without him being knocked off his bike by enemy aircraft." A clear exaggeration. Although there had been an instance early on of a dispatch rider being attacked, already the reorganisation of the Air Forces, particularly the Tactical Air Forces was having its effect and the enemy was being forced to divert his resources to try and counter our air operations and had little left for ground attack. Later when Anderson realised that his troops were practically immune from air attack he became most appreciative of our efforts.

With the improving weather and our new airstrips, the Group was able to operate at an increased intensity in the battle area and with the XII Air Support Command, USAAF under Brigadier General Paul L Williams and the Tactical Bomber Force (comprising British and American squadrons) under Air Commodore Laurence Sinclair also at full bore, the beneficial change in the air situation over the battlefield was complete. We were helped in obtaining this satisfactory result by NASAF (North-West African Strategic Air Force) under the command of Major-General James H Doolittle whose bombers attacked the docks at Tunis. This had the immediate effect of forcing the enemy to devote most of his fighters to the defence of Tunis, his main supply port.

Montgomery began an attack on the Mareth Line, in southern Tunisia, on 20 March. Paul Williams and I distracted the Luftwaffe's attention from the 8th Army front by attacking airfields day and night, so permitting Broadhurst's Western Desert Air Force to devote its whole attention to direct support of the 8th Army. On 25 March, Broady's squadrons enjoyed a spectacular success, rescuing

Montgomery from a crisis. Broady thereafter was firmly established as his favourite airman, but neither allowed sufficient credit to the pilots under the command of Williams and I for occupying the Luftwaffe elsewhere. Early in April, the Americans found that with the advance of the 8th Army the enemy on its front had been forced to withdraw northwards. The Americans therefore found that they had no enemy to fight, in what looked like being the final stage of the North African campaign. This situation was unacceptable from both a political and military viewpoint. With future campaigns in mind, it was necessary to give the Americans experience of the actual fighting. Alexander decided therefore, after consultation with Eisenhower to move II Corps to the northern part of the front on the left flank of the 1st Army. This part of the front had been held defensively by a British Division which would now move south to join the 1st Army thrust up the Mejerda valley to Tunis.

The move of this very large Corps from south to north across the lines of communication of the French Corps and the 1st Army was a remarkable performance and showed the Americans at their best. The move began on the night of 12-13 April and took about a week to complete. The main road passed through Souk-el-Arba and I landed at the airfield there when the move was in full swing. Thousands of vehicles from jeeps to tank transporters were head to tail but all moving at a spanking pace. The entire move of the Corps of three Divisions over a distance of two hundred miles was made without any attack at all from the enemy air force. This was a measure of the change in the air situation since the reorganisation of the Air Forces under Tedder and particularly of the Tactical Air Forces under Coningham. Unfortunately the Commanding General of II Corps, Omar Bradley, took the air superiority entirely for granted and later when he came to write about this move in his book, *A Soldiers Story*, made no mention of the satisfactory situation in the air which alone made the move possible.

Coincident with the move, the USAAF tactical reconnaissance fighter squadron from XII Air Support Command, which worked with II Corps, was moved north onto one of our airstrips because their own in the south was out of range of the Corps' new area. As I had now learned to expect of American squadrons, its pilots were magnificently trained in the flying business but their reconnaissance reports were much inferior of those of 225 and 241 RAF Squadrons. On investigation I found that unlike the RAF, the USAAF had no Air Liaison Officer system which in the British organisation provided each squadron with Army officers trained in interpreting the Army's requirements to the pilots and in the process educating the Army in what was, and equally important, what was not achievable. These officers were invaluable to both the Army and the Air Force. There was little we could do to improve the standard of the American reports in the short term, but so that II Corps in its new area would receive some reliable reports I ordered that periodically 225 Squadron who already knew the area well, should continue to reconnoitre that front and send their reports to II Corps. With the move of II Corps to the north all was now set for the final battle of the North African campaign in which the capture of Tunis and Bizerta were the objectives.

On 15 April, 1943 Lieutentant General Dwight D Eisenhower visited 1st Army HQ. He was accompanied by Major General Carl A Spaatz, the Commander of all the Allied Air Forces in North-West Africa. It was the first time I had met Eisenhower and I took an instant liking to him; his friendly manner and the way he talked and listened made a great impression on me. He had recently returned from a visit to the 8th Army and Western Desert Air Force and was full of the part the latter had played in getting the former out of a jam while attempting to outflank the Mareth Line. He said to me "I hope you have a similar opportunity to show what the air can do on this front". I told him I doubted whether in this mountainous, wooded terrain we would be able to do what Broadhurst's pilots had done to the enemy in the open desert, but I assured him that if any opportunity occurred we would not miss it. "In the meantime", I said, "we have not done too badly in our first task—clearing the enemy air force out of the sky". Eisenhower smiled and said "I agree there!"

Three days later Mary Coningham held a conference of his subordinate commanders at Le Kef where he and Alexander had their HQ. Harry Broadhurst, Paul Williams, Larry Sinclair and I were present. The purpose of the conference was for Mary to put across to us Alexander's plan (codenamed Operation Vulcan) for the final battle. This was for an attack on all fronts, the 8th Army at Enfidaville, the French Corps to the south, 1st Army on the Medjez-el-Bab – Tunis axis and the US II Corps in the north with its objective Bizerta. The main hope for the capture of Tunis was the thrust by the 1st Army since not only was it the shortest distance, but also the ground in the Medjerda valley was suitable for armour. The attacks by the 8th Army and the French were timed for 22 April, twenty-four hours before the 1st Army started, in the hope that the enemy would react by moving reinforcements from the 1st Army front.

I was surprised at this all-round attack because with the air superiority now possessed over the battlefield, any large movement of troops by the enemy would be subject to devastating attacks from the air, and the enemy knew this. He would have to fight where he was. However, Alexander's plan was to mount the maximum sustained effort against targets on all the fronts. This was business as usual to us except for the increased effort. To guarantee that the whole force could be devoted to Army targets during the battle we began to attack the enemy airfields from the night of 18-19 April in a preliminary programme to reduce Luftwaffe interference.

The "all round the fronts" attack from II Corps in the north, 1st Army and the French in the centre and 8th Army in the south started on 22 April. There was an almost complete lack of requests for bombing from the Army, but with my experience of the Desert I had anticipated this, so Ronnie Lees and Group Captain Dudley Lewis, the bomber expert from the Tactical Bomber Force, had laid on a maximum effort programme to attack targets behind the enemy front line that had been located by our fighter reconnaissance. This meant a raid by from twelve to thirty six bombers every hour. When, as infrequently happened, a request was received from the Army, the next raid was quickly re-briefed to attack the Army target. By this means we were able to make the maximum use of our bombers. At first the Bostons and Mitchells were given a sizeable Spitfire escort but with no reaction from the Luftwaffe, this was progressively reduced, and the Spitfires freed to operate further forward. We kept this maximum effort going for six days, but by the end of April it became apparent that the Army attack had made little progress. The 8th Army was stalled at Enfidaville and the 1st Army and the French had only advanced a few miles. The American II Corps had made better progress in the north but were prevented from reaching the plain outside Bizerta by the tenacious defence of each mountain position. There was consequently a slight feeling of doubt and disappointment amongst the 1st Army staff.

I had a visit without notice from Tedder and Spaatz accompanied by Mary's deputy, Brigadier General Laurence S Kuter. (The warning signal, like so many others failed to arrive). They were concerned by the lack of progress on the ground. I was able to reassure them that everything the Army wanted from the Air Forces was being provided, and a great deal more. I explained that our bombing was not so effective in this wooded and mountainous country as it had been in the open desert because the targets were more difficult to see from the bombing height just above the light flak level. No enemy air attacks on our troops had been reported so at least "lack of air support" could no longer be produced as the reason for lack of progress. The truth was, and as was to be experienced later all the way up Italy the Germans could, and would fight a defensive battle completely without air support. After seeing Anderson, Tedder decided that we should go north to Beja to see Major General Omar N Bradley at II Corps Headquarters.

We motored off along a narrow road and found Bradley's HQ in an orchard. Some wooden kitchen chairs were produced and we sat in a semi-circle in the sunshine: Cross, Kuter, Bradley, Tedder and Spaatz. We sat in silence for a while then Tedder said, "Well General, how is it going?" "Badly", said Bradley, "on a front of this length I have only three Divisions whereas all my text books tell me I should have a second Corps". Tedder, pipe in mouth, replied, "I found my text books were out of date very early in the war and threw them away." Bradley then proceeded to give a very good description of the problems in his area and seemed to be confident that he could solve them.

Tedder then asked about help from Air. "Bad", said Bradley. I was startled, because we had kept in pretty close touch with II Corps HQ throughout the battle and had received no complaints. What was more, because the Corps' location in the north meant that XII Air Support Command's operations were being processed through my Operations Room, it was often quicker and more convenient for RAF squadrons to answer the call rather than the American squadrons. Therefore I was puzzled at Bradley's assertion. Tedder asked "In what way have the Air failed?" and Bradley told him that it was not satisfactory being divorced from XII Air Support Command, though he appreciated that with no airfields available in the north he had to accept the present arrangement. Tedder persisted, asking for specific instances of the Air's failure. "Recon-naissance", said Bradley, "is very bad", and asked an aide standing by to "bring yesterday's reports". A large bunch of reconnaissance report forms was produced. My immediate reaction was that there couldn't be any complaint about volume anyway for there must have been more than a dozen forms, each one representing a full sortie, whereas a British corps had learned to obtain all the information required from three or four sorties a day. Bradley took the bunch and passed them one by one to Tedder whilst I looked over his shoulder. "You note", said Bradley "that out of these fourteen reports only three are of any use". I looked to see which squadrons had produced the useful reports and was not surprised that all three had been the work of 225 RAF Squadron. The rest were by the USAAF reconnaissance squadron. I indicated this to Tedder by pointing with a pencil. Tedder said nothing but placed the three reports to one side. When Bradley had finished speaking, Tedder pointed out that it was only the new arrangement that had produced the three useful reports, all from an RAF Squadron. Bradley looked at the reports again and without hesitation said "Can I have them all done by the RAF then?" Tedder allowed himself a half smile and said pointing to me, "he will do the best he can for you". Shortly afterwards we left and drove back to Souk-el-Khemis where Tedder and Spaatz said some complimentary things about our efforts and then they departed for Algiers.

In my diary for Sunday 2 May 1943 appears the following entry: "It now became apparent that the offensive which has been going on for the last ten days, has failed to achieve its main objective, ie the capture of Tunis". What would happen next?[1]

The most reliable source of information for me was Harry Broadhurst who had met Alexander when he arrived at a Desert Air Force airfield and flew him up to Monty's forward HQ and was present throughout the meeting. As Broadhurst told me afterwards, it was Monty who pointed at the Medjerda Valley on the map and said it was the place to attack. Anyway, it was decided to reinforce the 1st Army's 9 Corps already in the valley with the 7th Armoured and 4th Indian Divisions and the 201st Guards Brigade. A new Corps Commander would also be required because Lieutenant General Crocker, the present commander, had been wounded and was out of action. According to Broadhurst, Alexander's choice was Freyberg of the New Zealand Division, but Monty preferred Horrocks, the Commander of 13 Corps and it was the latter who came over to our front. Before he left his Corps in the desert he had expressed some concern at leaving the 'air cover' provided by the Western Desert Air Force, but he was reassured by Broadhurst who said his friend Bing Cross would look after him. Dear Broadie, we have now known each other for sixty years and hardly a week passes without us talking. A great friend.

The 1st Army Staff eagerly awaited the arrival of these formations from the victorious 8th Army. I think they believed that they would be all "spit and polish" and would be an example to their own divisions, but they were in for a surprise for what they saw resembled more a gipsy caravan than an all-conquering army. First came the 4th Indian whom I had known so well. They had come some eighteen hundred miles from Egypt and not surprisingly their motor transport was somewhat the worse for wear. Most good vehicles had another

---

[1] When waiting in Algiers, I realised that I might be part of an epoch-making military episode so I bought a diary (in French). But, maddeningly, pressure of events prevented me from keeping it up for more than a week.

in tow, sometimes two. The dark-skinned Indian soldiery, dressed to suit individual taste in a mixture of tropical and battle dress uniform, were draped about their vehicles again according to individual preference. Some rode on top of the cab, others sat cross-legged on the running boards and some were asleep on the load. Underneath many of the vehicles were coops of chicken suspended from the chassis. So eggs were still important! Then came the 7th Armoured with their tanks on transporters and the troops dressed in an even more remarkable collection of garments than the Indians, including a fair sprinkling of civilian clothes particularly corduroy trousers. All seemed indifferent to the surprise caused by their appearance. They seemed to me to be possessed of a quiet confidence from achievement. They were a wonderful lot and I was proud that I had been associated with them.

The change in plan meant that all major action would now be on the 1st Army front and this caused Mary Coningham to reconsider arrangements for support. With the 8th Army still stuck at Enfidaville Broadhurst couldn't do much to help them. The French were not strong enough to debouch onto the Tunis plain, the Americans were making steady progress but because of the terrain the Air was unable to help them much. Only on the 1st Army front could our overwhelming tactical air power make a real impact.

Coningham decided therefore that all components of the North African Tactical Air Force should operate on that front and come under my command: XII Air Support Command (Paul Williams), the Tactical Bomber Force (Larry Sinclair) and the Western Desert Air Force (Harry Broadhurst). There was no difficulty about assuming command over the operations of Williams and Sinclair because their forces were already working closely with my operations staff. But I was apprehensive about the Western Desert Air Force. Under Coningham, it had developed an independent tradition, based on the quality and experience of its pilots and ground crews. Broadhurst had inherited and fostered that tradition. Although he and I were old friends, he was my senior in rank and experience. However, I reflected that he and I were subject to Coningham, far superior to both of us, and Broady would be unwise not to do as he was told, promptly and willingly, at a time of active operations. And, of course, that proved to be the case, even though we had one or two awkward moments.

I sent signals to Williams, Sinclair and Broadhurst inviting them to visit 242 Group HQ to go over the 1st Army plan for the final attack and our plan to complement it. Williams and Sinclair came the next day and we agreed what needed to be done. No reply from

Broadhurst, so I sent him another signal on the pretence that he had not received the first. Again no reply. Coningham checked that the arrangements with XII Air Support Command and Tactical Bomber Force were complete and was annoyed that the same was not so for Western Desert Air Force, and he sent a curt signal to Broadhurst, with a copy to me, telling him to visit me without delay. Broadhurst signalled that he would be with me the next day, landing at Thibar, the HQ airstrip. I was waiting there next morning when he arrived in his Spitfire VB with his ADC in another. As he taxied in with the hood back he gave me a broad smile as might be expected on seeing an old friend, but by the time he had dismounted the smile had vanished and ominously it had been replaced by that expressionless look that I knew from experience meant that he was going to be awkward.

Anderson was unable to be present, but the newly appointed BGS (Brigadier Macmillan) was waiting for us in my office caravan when we arrived. He ran through the Army plan on the map. When he had finished, Broadhurst asked a couple of questions and then I thanked Macmillan who left. "What are you going to do?" asked Broadhurst belligerently. Ronnie Lees and his Ops staff were waiting outside and now came in and presented our plan, giving the parts to be played by Sinclair, Williams and ourselves. When he had finished, I asked Broadhurst if he had any questions. "Are you not going to use us?" he exclaimed. I said "Just a moment please", and thanked Ronnie who departed with his staff, leaving me alone with Broadhurst. "Now Broady," I said, "you know as well as I do that you would have queried every task in detail if I had included you in my plan". Broady laughed. "You are dead right there," he said, "after all, you lot over this side are a bunch of novices compared with 8th Army and Desert Air Force". "Not all of us," I replied, "I was in the Desert long before you; what's more from my know-ledge of the Desert squadrons I believe that the squadrons in 242 group are more highly trained." "Is that so?", retorted Broady. "But you can't leave us out of the final battle". He was almost pleading now. "Of course not", I said. "I know exactly what we would like you lot to do, and it's mostly in the area which is difficult for us. I omitted it from Ronnie's presentation to avoid argument." I went to the map and ran through the part we had allotted to the Western Desert Air Force. "Well that's fine," said Broadhurst, and laughed again. "I'll send a couple of chaps over to go through the details." I said, "I have the full details here if you would like to take them with you". "OK", "where's lunch?" After lunch, when he had departed, Ronnie came in and asked if there were any changes in the tasks which we had agreed beforehand for Broadhurst's force but which, on my instructions, he had left out of his presentation. "None," I said, "Broady's happy". Ronnie laughed and turned to go. Over his shoulder he said "know your enemy *and* your friends".

On 6 May we carried out the biggest blitz of the North African campaign, with over two thousand sorties in the daylight hours mostly over the 1st Army front. The Americans in the north requested a few strikes, which were quickly arranged. For the rest there was a pre-arranged programme of bombing by tactical bombers throughout the day. At first all had a sizeable Spitfire escort but this was progressively reduced in the complete absence of enemy air resistance. By a coincidence, the rendezvous point for the bombers to meet their escort was right over 1st Army HQ and at last the Army staff could see for themselves the volume of support being given to the troops. During the day, with the exception of the Americans, there were no calls for support from the forward formations, so once more the practice of the Air deciding the targets for attack which would benefit the Army was justified. If we had waited for calls on the air support network a large proportion of the force would have been sitting on their airfield—unemployed.

There was no sign at all of the Luftwaffe in the last few days of the battle and we concluded that what was left of it had returned to Sicily. Our squadrons had complete freedom of action, and even at low level there was little light flak, presumably because of lack of ammunition. There was a general feeling of elation throughout the Group for all could see that the end was near in North Africa. The light-hearted attitude was apparent and epitomised by an incident during the morning of 6 May. 225 Squadron reported that a Fieseler Storch had been seen apparently abandoned on the side of El Aouina airfield outside Tunis. These little communication aircraft, superior to anything we possessed on the Allied side (they could land and take off on a large tennis court), were greatly prized by the Air Force commanders. Mary Coningham had obtained one before El Alamein and it had made visiting his units incomparably easier. I had used an Auster for the same purpose, but it required a strip of at least two hundred yards which restricted its use some- what. Now came a rare opportunity to acquire the ideal aircraft. There was a problem though.

The 225 pilots reported that they had seen aircraft in desert camouflage over El Aouina so no doubt by this time Broadhurst's HQ also knew of the Storch. I knew that he would spare no effort to win such a prize, it was just a question of who could be on El Aouina first, once it had been captured by the Army. The situation map showed that our forward troops were very close, and Western Desert Air Force would also know this. What's more, knowing my friend Broadhurst, I guessed what he would do. To make sure he would send at least a flight of the RAF Regiment, with a pilot of at least Wing Commander rank so that if arguments occurred then there would be plenty of seniority to ensure a satisfactory outcome. As it happened Group Captain Pete Hugo was visiting my HQ at the time and was much amused at the interest being shown by practically the whole staff in this one aeroplane. He volunteered to go with my party, rapidly being assembled, and fly the Storch back. I gladly accepted his offer. Pete, as would be expected of someone from the Veldt, was a man of great resource. As he left in his jeep he said with a gleam in his eye, "Not to worry, we'll get the Storch".

My appreciation was correct. Broadhurst's party and mine arrived on El Aouina at about the same time and an argument started, but Hugo's rank plus the fact that the airfield lay in the 1st Army/242 Group area proved enough—the Desert Air Force party left empty handed, Hugo flew the Storch back to Thibar later that day. I used this excellent aircraft whilst we were in North Africa, then took it to Sicily and on to Taranto in Italy. By that time, Broadhurst had obtained one of his own which he had with him at his HQ north of Foggia on the Adriatic coast. Unfortunately, in the early winter of 1943 an unexpected storm blew his Storch into the sea and it was wrecked beyond repair. At the time my Group was in a static role of air defence and anti-submarine defence way behind the front line, and I really did not need the Storch, so recognising Broadhurst's need I sent him mine. He was overjoyed and used it throughout his sojourn in Italy. When the time came for him to come back to England to take part in the invasion of Normandy he had the Storch dismantled, crated and brought it back with him. He found it most useful in the beach-head and beyond. Alas, after the advance to the Rhine and during the pause there in the winter of 1944, Broadhurst, at the end of a long conference in Brussels, hurried out to the airfield at Evere anxious to reach his Headquarters at Eindhoven before dark. He jumped into the Storch, started it up and took off straight away. Unfortunately in his haste he forgot to turn on the petrol, the engine cut soon after take-off and *my* Storch was pancaked onto a roof in the outskirts of the town. It was wrecked, unrepairable, but it had done its job all the way from Tunis to Brussels. Not bad. Broadhurst, as usual, escaped unhurt.

Tunis and Bizerta fell on 7 May and the North African campaign was virtually over. I felt a bit flat that evening as did most of the staff. There seemed to be no desire for a celebration party in the Mess; I suppose everyone was very tired. On 11 May I was on Medjez-el-Bab airfield with General Anderson, awaiting the arrival of Alexander and Coningham. We were to accompany them into Tunis for the official surrender of the town. As we strolled up and down, Anderson said, "I would like you to know how grateful the Army is to the Air Force for what you have done to bring about this great victory". He stopped and looked at the continuous stream of German vehicles which extended as far as the eye could see and were full of Germans on their way to Prisoner of War camps which had been set up near Beja. Then he said, "Of course the way you employed the Air was not as I would have done it", but quickly repeated that nevertheless the Army was very grateful. Anderson's career as a front-rank commander ended in Tunis and he never understood as much as Montgomery about air power.

Alexander, Coningham and Kuter flew in and we made a slow progress into Tunis by staff cars. I believed I had seen the biggest collection of prisoners I would ever see, on the desert road after El Alamein, but now as we drove past them I realised that here the numbers were vastly greater. What was surprising was the docility of the Germans. Each lorry containing thirty or forty Germans was guarded by one British Tommy hugging his rifle and wedged against the tail board by the press of his prisoners. He could have been overpowered without the slightest difficulty. Each vehicle was driven by a German following the one ahead. The procession rolled along head to tail all the way to Tunis. Afterwards I enquired of the Army whether there had been any attempts at escaping. None reported was the reply. Apparently the Germans drove to the POW camps, parked their vehicles neatly in rows and went off to the cage on their own. Strange people. Unequalled in their courage and determination when fighting in organised bodies, but once the surrender happened, just as disciplined as prisoners of war.

There was a small pompous ceremony at the Town Hall and then the party split up and we returned to our respective HQs. My chaps had been doing some air and land reconnaissance of the area around and had come up with the proposal that the best place for the final site 242 Group was right on the beach at La Marsa, a lovely little bay with the added advantage that it had an airstrip nearby. 1st Army agreed, having already found some superb villas in the vicinity. We were all installed by 13 May and I dined with Anderson in his Mess that evening. It was a cheerful gathering, though sad as well because we all knew by now that for the next operation, Husky, the invasion of Sicily, only the 8th Army of the British would be involved; 1st Army was shortly to be disbanded. Next day I went off to see Mary Coningham at his HQ at Le Kef to ascertain what lay ahead for 242 Group.

As I expected, Western Desert Air Force was to be paired with 8th Army and XII Air Support Command with the American 7th Army, so like 1st Army my Group was spare, but it was not to be disbanded. Most of the Spitfire and reconnaissance squadrons were to go to Broadhurst, whilst what was left along with the HQ would become a combined coastal and air defence group with its HQ located at Bizerta. We were to be responsible for the air defence of the Husky assembly and launching area around Bizerta and Tunis. In addition, the Group was to be reinforced with Beaufighter and Wellington squadrons for day and night attack on enemy shipping as far north as Genoa. A reconnaissance element for this strike force was provided by two squadrons, one of Marauders and the other of Baltimores. I was specifically charged with watching the Italian Fleet, now mostly in Spezia and Genoa. The Group would be under the command of Air Vice-Marshal Hugh Pughe Lloyd, the Commander of all the North African Coastal Air Forces and a man I had met and admired in my Egypt days. These were big changes, but the move to Bizerta was not to take place until 9 June—some four weeks away.

Much to our surprise, Mary Coningham said that he thought that his subordinate commanders—Broadhurst, Cross and Sinclair—deserved some leave which, exceptionally, could be taken in the UK as nothing was going to happen for sometime. It was an offer too good to refuse and Sinclair and I went off to Algiers to see what we could find in the way of air transport to England. We were fortunate for on enquiring at Allied HQ we heard that the Americans were providing a B-17 to take our Minister Resident, Harold Macmillan, back to England via Gibraltar and might take us two Air Commodores with him. Macmillan agreed and off we went. Sinclair and I found a space in the lower forward nose compartment and were welcomed by the front gunner and another US airman. The trip to Gibraltar was uneventful and we stayed the night there, Macmillan with the Governor—General Mason Macfarlane—and the rest of us in a hotel. We left early the next morning and we noted this time that the front gunner made all preparations to fire his guns, checking ammunition and loading the guns just as soon as we were airborne.

The route followed was way out into the Atlantic before turning north-east. We duly landed at Predannick in Cornwall in mid-afternoon in very bad weather. The Americans had a staging post there and soon afterwards we were told that it was impossible to go on to Heston as planned, because of fog. Macmillan listened to this unwelcome news and then said, "I think I may now be of use for the first time on this journey. I am a Director of the Great Western Railway, is there a telephone?" The outcome was that the next express train to London was stopped at the local station and we were ushered into reserved compartments, so at least we arrived in London in style.

I went to the RAF Club in Piccadilly to do some telephoning and decided to stay the night before going to see my parents at Hayling Island. I found that Lesley was doing an ENSA show somewhere in the Midlands and made a date to go and see her later. The next morning I did some much-needed shopping and in the afternoon was about to go to Waterloo for my train to Hayling, when I had a phone call from an agitated civil servant who said that the Air Member for Personnel (AMP) wished to see me. I managed to get a taxi to Kingsway and went up in the lift to the AMP's office. I was immediately shown in. Air Marshal Sir Bertine Sutton was not known to me, nor I to him and he said abruptly, "Where have you been?" I said, "North Africa". "No", he said "since you arrived in London." Before I could answer he said "the CAS wishes to see you. Did you not know that all senior officers from overseas should report to me on arrival in the UK?" I said I didn't. Sutton didn't appreciate that the last time I was in the Air Ministry was in 1940 when I was a mere Squadron Leader and during the intervening two years had risen three ranks to Air Commodore, so really there had not been much opportunity to learn senior officer's protocol.

Anyway, I went of to King Charles Street in Whitehall and found my way to the CAS's outer office and waited there. I was a bit apprehensive. I had never met Portal, but his reputation for efficiency as Chief of the Air Staff was known throughout the Service. From those who knew him I had heard that he was "a bit of a cold fish and a stickler for discipline". I didn't think he would be too pleased that a young, very much 'acting' Air Commodore, had not even reported to the Air Ministry on arrival back in the UK. Eventually Ely, the civilian secretary, (he also had a personal assistant in uniform) whom I was to know well later said, "The CAS will see you now" and he opened the door for me. I went in with a sinking feeling in my stomach.

Portal was sitting at his desk, but he got up at once and came across the room with a smile on his face and his hand outstretched saying, "I am glad to see you, you have made a reputation for yourself in North Africa. Come and sit down". To say that I was surprised at my reception is an understatement. I had no idea that this great man even knew I existed and I did not acquit myself very well when he asked me to run through my service since the beginning of the war. We talked for about twenty minutes and then he wished me luck and it was over. Cold fish, I didn't think so. He was certainly very kind to a quaking Acting Air Commodore. As I walked down Whitehall looking for a taxi to take me to Waterloo, I reflected that our Service and the country were very fortunate to have men of the calibre of Dowding, Tedder and Portal in positions of authority.

After a few days with my parents at Hayling, a visit saddened by it being the first since Ian had become a prisoner of war, I went up to Coventry to see Lesley in her ENSA show. In the process I saw something of civilian industrial life because the show was put on in an enormous works canteen in the evening. I was conspicuous in my uniform but the workers gave me a friendly welcome and the foreman in charge was particularly kind in offering me a drink before the show. Everyone was avid for news of North Africa. Afterwards I took Lesley to a rather 'thin' supper at my hotel and returned to London the next day.

Broadhurst had returned to England in a Hudson of the transport squadron that was part of the Desert Air Force and he had offered me a seat for the journey back. The Hudson was at Predannack and its passengers were to meet at the RAF Club and go down together. The captain was the squadron's CO, Wing Commander Yaxley, a splendid pilot. Amongst the passengers was Group Captain Billy Burton who commanded a wing in the Desert and Wing Commander Jackie Darwen who had a hatred for the Germans and a relentless passion for killing them. This passion stemmed from a terrible event in 1941 when a bomb hit the Cafe de Paris and killed Darwen's wife with whom he was dancing. There were several passengers whom I didn't know.

When I got to the Club, Yaxley met me in the hall and said that the Hudson was unserviceable and that the start would be delayed for twenty four hours. I was a bit upset because I had promised to be back on time and was now going to be a day late, but there was nothing for it; I had to wait. The next morning when I saw Yaxley he said the Hudson was still unserviceable and might need an engine change. I was more than upset this time—one day late I might be able to explain, but more than that would be very difficult. I rushed for a telephone and got through to Air Movements at the Air Ministry and enquired if anything was going to North Africa. The man on the other end of the phone would not answer my query but told me to come and see him.

At Adastral House I was told that one of the USAAF's new

Douglas C-54 Skymasters was leaving for Casablanca that evening and if I could get up to Prestwick in time a seat would be reserved for me. I quickly got a rail warrant to Glasgow and managed to make Prestwick in time. There on the tarmac was the first C-54 I had seen. In shape it was like a double-sized C-47 Dakota (DC-3) but it had four engines and a tricycle undercarriage. It had a very long range for those days, and was to go far westwards into the Atlantic before turning south-east for Casablanca. As an additional precaution, the whole flight would be in darkness. This was reassuring because the North African campaign had led to a considerable increase in the traffic between the UK and Gibraltar and as soon as this became apparent to the Germans, long-range Ju88 and Me 110 fighters had been moved to France and had already made interceptions of this traffic as it crossed the Bay of Biscay, shooting down several Allied aircraft. We left in mid evening.

There was no comfort in the C-54, just bucket seats and piles of mail sacks strapped to the floor. We arrived at Casablanca soon after dawn and from there I got a flight to Algiers. I reported to Allied HQ who did not even notice that I was two days late, and then went on to 242 Group at La Marsa. When I landed I was met by Tony Le Hardy, my ADC who said "I have some bad news. The Hudson in which you were supposed to be returning was shot down in the Bay and everyone aboard is missing". It took a while for it to sink in that once more my name was not on that load of Luftwaffe ammunition. Shortly after my return we moved our HQ from La Marsa to a rather bare site on a hill just north of Bizerta. There were some changes in the staff: notably I had lost Lees whose experience was to be used in the Tactical Air Forces invading Sicily. He was replaced by L F Finch, another excellent Group Captain. We set up our Operations Room in an abandoned fort next to our camp. It was the end of a chapter for me because now I was to learn about coastal operations over the sea, quite a change from tactical over land.

CHAPTER XV

NORTH-WEST AFRICAN COASTAL AIR FORCES

I HAD managed to retain my Spitfire IX in the move from Tactical to Coastal Air Force, and as soon as we had organised the Head-quarters at Bizerta I flew from the airfield there named Sidi Ahmed, to Algiers to report to Air Vice-Marshal Hugh Pughe Lloyd, the Air Officer Commanding the North-west African Coastal Air Forces. From my knowledge of him as the Senior Air Staff Officer in HQ Middle East Air Force in Cairo and from his reputation as the man who epitomised the defence of Malta I knew already that I was fortunate in my new master. Hugh Pughe, or "Huff Puff" as he was known by the airmen, was a formidable personality. He was outspoken to the point of rudeness and did not suffer fools at all. Despite this he had a great capacity for making friends and was extremely hardworking. Most of the work of his command was over the sea and relations with the Navy were close. Hugh Pughe had quickly gained the confidence of the Naval C-in-C, Admiral Sir Andrew Cunningham, which was no mean achievement for whereas the Admiral was a great sailor, he never quite grasped the full extent of air warfare and because of this was inclined to expect more from the Air Forces than we were capable of delivering.

Hugh Pughe told me that the main purpose of my new 242 Group was to provide comprehensive reconnaissance of enemy shipping movements east of a line from Genoa in the north to Cap Bon in the south, a distance of over 500 miles, paying particular attention to naval movements out of Genoa and La Spezia, where the main part of the Italian Fleet was now based. This reconnaissance would be of increasing importance during the period before and after 10 July 1943, the date set for Operation Husky, the invasion of Sicily. If the Italian Fleet emerged then my Group would have the task of attacking it in conjunction with the B-17s of Jimmy Doolittle's Strategic Air Force. I was to be responsible for the co-ordination of plans for this operation. In the interim I was to attack shipping supplying the enemy in Sicily, which travelled between Genoa, La Spezia and Palermo. I was also to be responsible for anti-submarine air operations to protect our own shipping.

For these tasks, I had two reconnaissance squadrons (one of Marauders, for low level work, the other of Baltimores for high level work), four torpedo squadrons (three of Beaufighters, one of Wellingtons), one Hudson anti-submarine squadron and two long-range Beaufighter squadrons for escort duties. I also had a flight of Walrus amphibians; the first organised air-sea rescue we had possessed in the Mediterranean, three years into the war!

In total this amounted to a considerable force of more than a hundred and fifty aircraft, to be based on airfields at present being built at Protville on the plain south of Bizerta in a new Wing, 324, commanded by Group Captain Geoffrey Tuttle, an experienced 'Coastal' officer from the UK.

Another responsibility of the Group and of equal importance was the air defence of Tunis and Bizerta, the assembly area for all the American forces in Operation Husky and also for a large part of the British. For this defensive role, one of the Spitfire wings remained in 242 Group and was to be based at La Sebala on the plain north of Tunis. The remainder of the Spitfire squadrons and the two fighter reconnaissance squadrons were transferred to the Western Desert Air Force now located around Tripoli. Later a Free French Spitfire squadron joined the Group and was stationed at Sidi Ahmed. I saw more of this squadron than most because it was located on our HQ airfield. The French idea of maintaining their aircraft was unorthodox by RAF standards as the liaison between maintenance and aircrews was not close but the Spitfires seemed to thrive on it and when it came to scrambling at the approach of an enemy reconnaissance aircraft there was no one to touch the French in speed off the ground. A radar network was already in position to cover the area, reporting to the Fighter Wing Operations Room at La Sebala where all executive interception action was initiated and sent to the Operations Room, where I was at Bizerta so that the Group staff and myself could keep in touch.

As I flew back from my meeting with Hugh Pughe I reflected that in 242 Group as now constituted we filled eight roles: high and low level reconnaissance, day and night torpedo anti-submarine, day and night fighter, and air sea rescue. All this grouping together would have been considered very unusual in the UK with fighter and coastal combined. But in North Africa, it worked well and resulted in a great deal of 'grass roots' co-operation which was to everyone's benefit.

As I flew I had plenty of time to think, the distance from Algiers to Bizerta being more than four hundred miles, which in a Spitfire at cruising speed took a couple of hours. I pondered on the enormous changes that had occurred in this theatre of war since I had arrived in Cairo two years previously in January 1941. At that time the contest was between the British (with essential help from Australia, New Zealand, South Africa and India) and the Italians. Our land forces were small and our Air Force minute. Despite this we had driven the Italians from their foothold in Egypt at Halfaya Pass westwards for four hundred miles and captured the second city of their North African Empire, Benghazi at which point the Germans had intervened and Rommel's Afrika Korps arrived to take charge. From that time (March 1941) the Germans had dominated the enemy alliance and faced us with a more challenging problem.

In the air the Luftwaffe had been a very different proposition from the Regia Aeronautica. Though never present in great numbers, the German aircraft were always superior to ours in the fight for air superiority over the campaigns and battles in the Desert. As I have said before, the 109Es, and later the F and G models were vastly superior in performance to our Hurricane I and IIs and even to the fighters we obtained from the United States, the Tomahawk and Kittyhawk. In the Western Desert from November 1941 onwards, therefore, we managed to win and maintain a precarious air superiority only by our greater numbers and through superb leadership. Tedder, Coningham, Dawson and Elmhirst had performed miracles of organisation and improvisation to overcome our deficiencies, precisely maintaining our numerical superiority. Nor should those unknown planners who had thought of the Takoradi route be forgotten, because it was by this imaginative project that most of the essential short-range aircraft reached the Middle East Command. Now in the summer of 1943 we had our powerful American Allies with us with their enormous resources and we owned the whole of the North African shore from Port Said to Algiers. What a change!

A small but significant development for us British airmen and soldiers had been the arrival in February 1943 of the first squadron of Spitfire IXs amongst the squadrons of Spitfire Vs that comprised the fighter force for the North African landings. At last we had a fighter in this overseas theatre superior to all the 109s of whatever mark. Only the Fw190 which appeared later in small numbers in Tunisia was remotely comparable to the Spitfire IX. The possession of this superb aircraft—in my opinion the best Spitfire of any from I to XXI—had an effect on the enemy fighter force far in excess of what its numbers justified. At long visual range it was almost impossible to distinguish between the IX and the V with the result that German pilots never knew until battle was joined what they were up against. Also this uncertainty put up the value of the much inferior American fighter aircraft, the P-40D, the Kittyhawk and the Airacobra, and the P-38 Lightning. Tedder's achievements in the Middle East forced recognition for the best manner of employing air forces to benefit all three fighting services. Fortunately in General Eisenhower the Allies possessed a Supreme Commander of commendable prescience. After the initial ineffectiveness of his Anglo-American Air Forces in North Africa, he learned to employ aircraft effectively. At Casablanca, Roosevelt and Churchill assisted by the Combined Chiefs of Staff decided on a new command structure for the whole Mediterranean Theatre and Tedder was appointed Air Commander-in-Chief and Eisenhower's adviser on air matters. From then on Tedder was at Eisenhower's elbow until the end of the war. This helped to ensure that the air forces, recognised by Eisenhower as an essential key to victory, were employed to the best advantage.

One other thought struck me on my flight back to Bizerta and that was the elimination of sea power as the controlling factor in the Mediterranean Sea. Despite brilliant victories by our Mediterranean Fleet over the Italians at Taranto in November 1940 and Matapan in March 1941, which should have ensured mastery and a free passage for our naval and merchant shipping, the Allies did not secure effective control of major sea routes until November 1942. How was it that with the Italian Fleet beaten and confined to port the Mediterranean remained closed as a major shipping route? The answer was that enemy air power in the shape of Luftwaffe units in Sicily and North Africa had replaced sea power represented by the Italian Fleet and had closed the through passage to our shipping. Our Mediterranean Fleet, despite its victories, was powerless. It was probably the clearest demonstration of the dominance of air power over sea power that occurred during the war. Now at last we had the air bases on the African shore with the range to counter the Luftwaffe in Sicily and 'Eureka' the Mediterranean was open. It also meant that my role in general operations over the Mediterranean was now more important than if the Navy had been the controlling factor. Before landing at Sidi Ahmed I flew down to La Marsa and went to say a final farewell to General Anderson. He had no news of his future but 1st Army was to be disbanded and he assumed he would return to England.

In due course the three Beaufighter torpedo squadrons from the UK arrived at Protville and were joined there by the two Beaufighter escort squadrons from the Middle East. It was intended that the latter would attack the destroyer escorts to the Italian battleships and engage their flak gunners, thus giving the torpedo Beaufighters a better chance to aim their weapons accurately. These fighter Beaufighters would also escort the torpedo squadrons in attacks on the enemy shipping supplying Sicily. The Wellington squadron also arrived at Protville from the Middle East, as did Group Captain Tuttle who quickly had everything under control. The Wellington squadron was to prove a most useful part of our anti-shipping force. It had already done great execution to enemy shipping in the eastern Mediterranean operating from Egypt; it operated at night and together with the Fleet Air Arm Swordfish countered the enemy's efforts to traverse the most dangerous parts of his routes under cover of darkness. Also the Wellington had an advantage over the Beaufighter in that it carried two torpedoes instead of one. The Squadron was commanded by an excellent South African leader, Lt Col Mackenzie, who after the war went into politics in Kenya and became the only white member of Jomo Kenyatta's Cabinet. Mackenzie and his Squadron were a little impatient at first not understanding why they had been moved from the Middle East where they had been operating so successfully, but as soon as we mentioned the location of the Italian Fleet in Genoa and La Spezia, he and his crews quickly understood the significance of their redeployment. Mackenzie also quickly recognised the high quality of the shipping reconnaissance reports provided by the Marauder and Baltimore squadrons.

That these reconnaissance reports were so good can be partially credited to the use I made of Ultra intelligence. The interception and decoding of the enemy's wireless traffic has been much written about in recent years, but it was in the Mediterranean Theatre that it bestowed its greatest benefit on the Allies. The reason for this was that all urgent messages from Germany to Africa and vice versa had to be transmitted "over the air". Indeed almost all operational communication was by W/T because no cable was available and so no teleprinter. All this traffic was listened to at Bletchley Park and there decoded and sent to selected recipients in our theatre. Ultra's value in shipping strike operations was immense.

I would receive a decoded message giving the time of departure of a single ship, or convoy from Genoa, La Spezia or Naples, bound for Palermo. It would have been simple to mount an operation at once by the torpedo Beaufighters to intercept and attack the ship or convoy, but such an operation would inevitably risk making the enemy suspicious that his wireless traffic was being read. To counter this possibility, instead of sending a Beaufighter strike, a high level reconnaissance would be added to those already programmed covering the route and timing of the Ultra information. When this reconnaissance aircraft spotted the target, it would report the sighting in clear language over its radio, as was standard practice to save time. The enemy of course also heard this transmission and believed, as we heard later, that our reconnaissance was more widespread than in reality it was. From repeated use I was well placed, therefore, to appreciate the value of Ultra and also the absolute necessity of keeping it secret. As a measure of this all-important security only one officer other than myself in my Headquarters was 'in the know'. Since the Ultra secret was disclosed in 1974 there has been a tendency to overrate its great value, to the detriment of those on the spot soldiers, sailors and airmen who were making the decisions and doing the fighting. When Ultra is thus overvalued, I always point out that however useful it was in finding the enemy and revealing his intentions, in the end he had to be fought. In our anti-shipping operations we had many successes, it is true, but nevertheless we did lose a number of splendid aircrews in the process, mainly because the flak from any of these convoys was seldom less than intense. Incidentally, despite my knowledge of Ultra, I was never forbidden to fly on Ops which was very strange from a security standpoint and especially as Broadhurst later told me he had been briefed not to participate in Ops precisely because he also shared the secret.

Observing the Italian Fleet in La Spezia and Genoa was the special responsibility of the low level Marauders of 14 Squadron. Up to the invasion of Sicily, that Fleet had shown no sign of emerging from these two ports, but we had a good plan if it did come out whatever time of day or night. Together with Ultra and our high and low level reconnaissance, we were confident we would know if it did move. If it emerged by day then the combined B-17/Torpedo Beaufighter strike would begin. If by night, the Wellingtons would attack individually throughout the hours of darkness. It was fortunate that by this time I had got to know the American commander concerned, General Doolittle, and got on well with him. Indeed since joining the Algiers end of the Mediterranean Allied Forces in February 1943, I had worked often with Americans and had always found them excellent partners. NACAF was an Allied formation and my Group included USAAF units and, not unnaturally, there was some friction between the two nationalities but really we were all airmen and our common 'trade' bred understanding from the first.

Far to the east of Sicily, Force H (Vice-Admiral A U Willis), comprising four battleships, two fleet carriers, six light cruisers and eighteen destroyers, had concentrated in the Ionian Sea to protect the east flank of the landings from Italian ships based on Taranto. As part of the cover plan, it feinted towards the west coast of Greece on 9 July and then closed the assault area by dawn on D-Day. Force Z (Captain C H L Woodhouse), consisting of the battleships *Howe* and *King George V*, two cruisers and six destroyers, lay to the west of Sicily as a reserve. Force K (four cruisers, six destroyers under Rear-Admiral C H J Harcourt) provided close fire support for the landing of the Eastern Task Force under Montgomery.[1] These dispositions meant that our Beaufighters, Wellingtons and Doolittle's B-17s would have an opportunity to attack the Italians long before the Navy could intercept. Also the Navy's experience of trying to protect the Malta convoys from Gibraltar had given it a healthy respect for the Luftwaffe and made it unwilling to go far in this part of the Mediterranean.

During the period of preparation for Husky at Bizerta and Tunis, our air defences were little exercised by day except against the persistant attempts at reconnaissance by single high flying Ju88s. After the radar chain had been calibrated and the operators became more practiced, we had considerable success in intercepting and shooting down these intruders. The Spitfire was very competent for this task and the French squadron at Sidi Ahmed excelled in this role. At night it was a different story and the enemy made frequent small attacks, using twenty to thirty aircraft against shipping assembling in the inland water behind Bizerta but, as at Alexandria, night bombing of dispersed shipping was ineffective in the face of a heavy barrage of ship- and shore-based light and heavy AA guns. Few ships were damaged. The Beaufighter night-fighters took a steady toll in these night raids.

It was during this build-up phase of Husky that we had our first experience of the use of "Window" by the enemy. Window was the codename given by the British to strips of tin foil dropped by attacking aircraft to blind and deceive the ground radars as to the exact position and numbers of attacking aircraft. It was first used by Bomber Command in the attack on Hamburg beginning on the night of 24-25 July 1943, two weeks after Husky began, and naturally we had no knowledge of it in Tunisia. The Germans, however, had been quick to recognise the value of this tin foil and used it against us in a raid on the harbour at Bizerta. To say that our radar operators were nonplussed would be an understatement. They were completely confused. The warning of the raid was given in good time as was normal, but after that I received no concise information at all. The

[1] Correlli Barnet, *Engage the Enemy more Closely*, pp. 638-9

controllers said that the radar tubes were "obscured" and that it was impossible to plot the enemy aircraft through the "haze". There was one report of parachute troops, afterwards known to be the radar readings on slowly descending strips of tin foil, and there was much in the way of conjecture from all levels in the reporting and control system. None that night guessed the correct answer and in the early hours when the raid was over, our report went to Algiers disclosing our confusion. Unusually and unfortunately, one of the hundred or more ships at anchor was hit and sunk. Later that morning I received a message that Hugh Pughe was on his way to see me and I was on the airfield when he landed in his Hurricane. I was driving the jeep myself and as soon as we were alone he said, "What's all this nonsense about parachute troops?" I said it was an operator's deduction from what he had seen on the tube. "Nonsense", said Hugh Pughe, "you are likely to become a laughing stock if you go on like this". He then asked why I had not recognised the phenomenon as Window and was astonished when I told him that neither I, nor anyone on my staff, had ever heard of the term, let alone what it meant. Needless to say, we were fully briefed later that day and were prepared for its use by the enemy on future raids. I never discovered where the breakdown occurred in transmitting this essential information, though I suspect it was in Algiers rather than London.

My 'opposite number' in the Navy, Commodore G N Oliver, had his HQ in Bizerta and he took a keen interest in our shipping strikes. Sadly, he was now required for other duties in connection with Husky and left us, to be replaced by Rear Admiral Sir Gerald Dickens. He was a full Admiral resurrected from the Retired List serving in the lower rank and found it difficult to understand air operations. This caused problems later on. Tedder had established an Advanced HQ at our old idyllic site at La Marsa and he visited me in late June. He seemed satisfied with our plans for the attack on the Italian Fleet and with our current reconnaissance and strike operations. In early July, however, Hugh Pughe Lloyd told me that he intended to attach himself to my HQ over the period of the Husky landings. I didn't like this proposal at all and said "Well Sir, if you are up here running the show there won't be much for me to do so I might as well go off and do something useful with one of the squadrons". Hugh Pughe told me to calm down saying that he had no intention of interfering with my conduct of operations and to emphasise this he said he would never enter the Operations Room unless I invited him. He explained that with Tedder and Spaatz at La Marsa he would be out of touch if he stayed in Algiers. I still didn't like the idea because I thought that his presence might cause confusion with the staff and with the commanders of the wings, but in the event everything worked out very well, particularly the discussions which my senior staff members and I had with him each evening in his trailer over a glass of his whisky. Hugh Pughe was as good as his word and never interfered. He normally went to see Tedder at La Marsa in the forenoon, visited an airfield in the afternoon and was with us again by tea time. It was a good arrangement and we were all sorry when he returned to Algiers, after the success of the landings in Sicily.

As the date for Husky approached and our preparations were complete, at last I had a little time to think about the wider aspects of the Sicily landings, the first opposed landings since the Dardanelles in 1915. Would we be able to get ashore and stay there, or would we suffer another disaster?. This didn't bear thinking about. I should have realised that the great difference between then and 1943 was the vast development of air power which now dominated operations on land and at sea. During the Sicily invasion, air power would severely limit the movement of enemy reinforcements to the beachheads, strangle the supply lines to the enemy *in situ*, and provide our troops with overwhelming firepower. But what about the Luftwaffe and the Regia Aeronautica? Surely despite the hiding and losses they had suffered in North Africa they must now make an all-out effort to prevent the first major invasion of Fortress Europe? In this I was to be an interested spectator as my Group had no part to play in the preparatory air action against the enemy air forces in Sicily. This was the task of the Strategic Air Forces, British and American and more intimately the Tactical Air Forces under Coningham's command. Much of it was now based under the operational control of that very experienced commander Air Vice-Marshal Park. He would provide protection from enemy attack over the beachheads and attack ground targets for the land forces as appropriate. In the meantime the enemy airfields in Sicily were under relentless attack by the Allied Strategic Air Forces, the USAF B-17s by day and the RAF Wellingtons by night. The effect of these attacks and the added effort by the Tactical Air Forces was the almost complete elimination of the enemy air forces as a significant factor in the impending invasion.

So there was not to be a second Dardanelles though I did not know this as I watched the convoys sail from Bizerta on 8 July. In the event the ships were not attacked at all on the 9th and 10th, but there were some reports of bombing on the 11th and 12th. In the whole period of the passage and assault by more than two thousand ships, only twelve were hit by bombs of which three were sunk including that on the Window raid at Bizerta. Despite this overwhelming success in the passage and assault leading to the whole of Sicily being cleared of the enemy in less than six weeks, there was to be the usual grizzling to all and sundry by Admirals and Generals on the theme of lack of air support, which could not but affect the performance and morale of my Group and others.

Having seen the ships off to Sicily, our main reconnaissance task was the continuous watch on La Spezia and Genoa. So far there had been no sign of the emergence of the Italian Fleet. The campaign in Sicily was going successfully and I received a warning order from Hugh Pughe to be prepared to move a USAAF Air Defense Wing under Colonel Stone into the Bocca di Falco airfield at Palermo as soon as it was captured. The Wing's task would be to defend the port. Though this was Stone's first experience of operations, as it was also for his men, they coped quite well, helped by the light scale of Luftwaffe operations in that area.

My role as an Allied Air Commander was eased by Lloyd's deputy in Algiers being an American, Brigadier General Elwood R Quesada, 'Pete' as he was known to everyone. When he first joined Coastal Air Force he was excessively pro-American, almost anti-British, but in a very short time working together, and working very hard, he became completely 'Allied' and was a great help to me when I was commanding USAAF units. Palermo was captured by the American 7th Army on 22 July. Three days later we heard of the fall of Mussolini, but his successor Marshal Badoglio made known his intention to fight on at the side of the Germans so fighting continued. However, Stone's Wing disembarked from one of the first landing ships into Palermo harbour and were installed and operational with their radar by 2 August, when I flew into Bocca di Falco from Sebala. Having checked first with Stone, I flew over to the eastern side of the island, landing at Lentini the nearest airfield to Broadhurst's HQ.

Broadhurst was his usual realistic self, not surprised at the slow progress of the 8th Army up the east coast towards Messina. "The terrain", he explained, "is ideal for defence and the Germans are making the most of it". This also applied to his air attacks on the front line which he said "were much less effective than in the open desert". There was little enemy air activity by day, but at night Broadhurst's airfields had been attacked with some success. The man commanding the Luftwaffe bombers opposite us was a certain Generalmajor Dietrich Peltz, whose name I already knew and would get to know better still when we encountered him in Italy and then in North-west Europe.

I flew to Palermo several times in the next few weeks, on one occasion doing a survey by jeep of captured enemy airfields, to check out their possible use by ourselves. I was accompanied by Pete Quesada. Up to then, my experience of attacking enemy airfields with the relatively small bombloads carried by our light and medium bombers led me to believe that it was an unprofitable business. The bomb craters could be filled in quite quickly and after a small delay the airfield was ready for use again. Aircraft if widely dispersed, as they invariably were, escaped damage more often than not. On this trip on 7 August, however, we drove to Trapani to inspect the airfield there. This had been attacked by B-17s before the Allied landings and was the most completely destroyed airfield I had ever seen. Inside the perimeter boundary the whole area was covered by bomb craters—big craters that could not be easily filled and with red earth piled up all around. Pete and I abandoned our jeep and scrambled over the churned-up earth. After a while Pete said, "We are wasting our time here. It would be quicker for the engineers to make a new strip instead of trying to repair this one". So we drove back to Palermo, collected our aircraft and flew back to Africa to report. The Americans had disposed of another myth, long believed in the Desert, that airfield bombing was not worthwhile. It was the weight and pattern of bombing employed by the USAAF heavy bombers together with their extreme accuracy that made all the difference. Later, American medium and light bombers would disprove another long-held belief: that small targets such as bridges could only be hit from low levels.

By 16 August all enemy opposition had ceased in Sicily, the American 7th Army first and the British 8th Army second having reached the Straits of Messina, though both armies failed to prevent the evacuation of the enemy land forces to Italy. The air forces did their best but were thwarted for the first time in the Mediterranean theatre by intense and concentrated heavy and light anti-aircraft fire. The volume and accuracy of this Ack-Ack fire was such that in penetrating it, aircraft losses would have been unacceptably heavy. Our air defence of Palermo proved to be effective, however, since despite its importance as the major port in Sicily, the Luftwaffe did not attempt any daylight raids. At night small attacks were made but the combination of well directed Ack-Ack fire and night-fighters under radar control prevented any significant damage to the shipping or the port.

When I returned to Bizerta I checked immediately on our reconnaissance of Genoa and Spezia and found that there still were no signs of the Italian Fleet moving, and that our torpedo squadrons were maintaining their normal high state of readiness. I then received notification of the projected operations against the Italian mainland after the capture of Sicily.

On the night of 2-3 September, men of the 8th Army crossed the Straits of Messina and landed at Reggio to secure the Toe of Italy. Then, on the morning of 9 September, more 8th Army men landed at Taranto to secure the Heel. During that same day, Operation Avalanche began at Salerno, under Lieutenant General Mark Clark, commander of the US 5th Army which was divided into two corps, the American VI and the British 10th. As soon as Naples was captured I was to install my 242 Group HQ there and provide air defence and coastal operations for the area. I therefore took a keen interest in the air plans for Avalanche particularly because of my need for airfields to be acquired and secured very quickly after the capture of Naples. There was an enemy airfield at Montecorvino inland from Salerno and we intended to construct airstrips in the beach-head, as soon as the enemy had been pushed back. There was another airfield in the Naples area, Capodichino, which from air photographs I could see was very small.

Eisenhower and Tedder had decided that Salerno was the nearest point to Naples that could be covered by fighters from Sicilian airfields. Alexander (who was Deputy C-in-C) agreed. As Coningham emphasised, the enemy was bound to make a special effort when the landings occurred, even with his weakened air forces. This meant continuous air defence by our fighters over the beach-head, particularly by day. This was to be provided by the British and American Tactical Air Forces operating from airfields in Sicily at Milazzo, Lentini, Gerbino and Catania, the whole effort being co-ordinated by Broadhurst. It was 160 miles to the Bay of Salerno from these airfields and this put the Spitfires at extreme range but the American Kittyhawks, P-38 Lightnings and A-36 Mustangs (with Allison engines) possessed a larger fuel capacity and were thus able to remain on patrol over the beach-head for a longer period. All were confident that the priority task of denying the air to the Luftwaffe and so preventing it from interfering with the landings, was well within the capabilities of the battle-hardened Allied squadrons.

As part of the Avalanche force, four escort carriers and one aircraft repair carrier (Force V) were required to keep 22 Seafires (the naval version of the Spitfire) on patrol over the beaches throughout daylight hours. Force V would in turn be guarded to seaward by the heavy covering Fleet named 'Force H' consisting amongst other ships of the fleet carriers *Illustrious* and *Formidable*, my old friends from Alexandria. Force H would therefore play no direct part in the landings, the Fleet Air Arm effort being confined to the 106 Seafires of Force V. Their offer of reinforcement encouraged the planners but after initial euphoria, doubt was expressed by some hard-headed wing and squadron commanders of the Allied fighter force. They pointed out that unlike the Anglo-American squadrons which had been fighting the enemy daily for months, the Naval squadrons had only very limited operational experience. Some had participated in the landings in North Africa during Operation Torch against negligible opposition from the French Air Force but had not taken any part in the real thing, the landings in Sicily. How effective would these Fleet Air Arm squadrons be at Salerno when faced with the Luftwaffe?

The final consensus was that the Seafire sorties should be rated as a bonus to the vast number of sorties to be flown by the Anglo-American squadrons, and it was on this basis that the air planners included them in the plan. Additionally the Seafires would have an advantage in the initial stages of the assault in being under control of the radar-equipped fighter direction ship *Palomares* whereas the land-based fighters would be on their own and no guarantee could be given by the Army as to when the RAF's own radar could be established ashore. In our discussions during the planning stage, it was emphasised repeatedly that the Sicily experience showed that heavy attacks on enemy airfields by strategic bombers, the Wellingtons by night and the B-17s and B-24s by day, had virtually eliminated opposition by Sicilian-based enemy aircraft and it seemed reasonable to expect the same result from the attack on Italian mainland airfields, in relation to the Salerno operation. Our Intelligence discounted any significant reinforcement of the Luftwaffe from Germany because the campaign by Bomber Command and the USAAF 8th Air Force from the United Kingdom was now large enough to oblige the Luftwaffe to concentrate on home defence.

Much of the assault shipping sailing for Salerno from Bizerta was routed west of Sicily and my Group was responsible for the anti-submarine protection of these ships using the squadrons based at Protville, and also for the fighter defence from the north-west tip of Sicily until the ships reached a distance of fifty miles off Salerno, at which point Broadhurst's tactical air forces would then take over responsibility. My fighters would operate from Bocca di Falco for these operations.

On 5 September I was summoned to Algiers by Hugh Pughe. I flew there in a borrowed Spitfire V, landing at Maison Blanche, and drove to his HQ in the town. When we were alone in his office he said, "The Italians are going to give in. They have signed a document which means that all Italian forces will surrender wherever they are on the evening of 8 September". I was startled to hear this news for we had had no inkling of such an event. I asked at once, "How does this effect our plan to attack the Italian Fleet if it emerges from La Spezia and Genoa?" "It means you don't", he said. "You continue your reconnaissance of the two ports and if the Fleet comes out you shadow it by day and night and be ready to attack it. Similar instructions have gone to Doolittle for the B-17s. When it is certain that the Italians have capitulated you will be informed and your instructions to attack will be cancelled, but in any event the Fleet is to be shadowed just as long as it is at sea."

I considered the implications of this news on the flight back to Bizerta. Geoffrey Tuttle and his Wing would be the most affected. Since his arrival in June, he had been busy successfully attacking the shipping endeavouring to supply Sicily from the Italian west coast ports; but he and his commanders and crews always knew this was interim work, their real purpose being to attack the Italian Battle Fleet. Now only the reconnaissance squadrons would see the Fleet. It was bound to be a disappointment as well as a relief. Back at Bizerta I called the principal staff officers to my trailer: Finch the Senior Air Staff officer, D E Finlay the Operations Officer and sharer of the Ultra secret with me and 'Daddy' Hawes the Senior Officer Administrative and told them the news. We decided that only those who "needed to know" should be informed at this stage. I asked Tuttle to come over from Protville and briefed him. Despite the anticipated timing of the announcement for the day before the landings at Salerno I reminded him that there were still German submarines around so that his anti-submarine tasks would continue uninterrupted.

When all this had been done I had a long session with my Chief Intelligence Officer, Lieutenant Colonel Rogers, USAAF. He was a 're-tread' from the First World War and in civilian life a prominent businessman in Philadelphia. He had decided when the United States entered the war in 1941 to volunteer for the US Army Air Force and had been directed to Intelligence. He and a fellow American, Major Reeves, had been sent to join 242 Group on the conclusion of the Tunisian campaign, and I quickly appreciated that these two Americans were first class at their work. Rogers particularly was adept at extracting from the mass of information we received, those parts relevant to us. When he first joined, I noticed that amongst his Great War medal ribbons two were British and I asked him how he had come by them. "I served with the British Army in France and afterwards at Archangel", he replied. I asked how he came to be serving with the British again. "Volunteered," he said and then by way of an afterthought, "On the whole the British are better at it (*war*), they get more practice". I asked him what he thought the German reaction to the Italian news would be. "Well," he said, "with the number of Divisions he has in Italy he won't pull out; I think he will take over the country." A correct forecast as it happened. "What about the Italian Fleet?" I asked. "Like Vichy and the French Fleet he will try to grab it but presumably time will have been given in the Instrument of Surrender for the Italians to get away and sail to a port under our control". He was right again.

In the meantime, the convoys for the Salerno landings left Bizerta covered by our anti-submarine Hudsons. My responsibility ended well short of the Salerno area and no ship was lost during our escort, but one was torpedoed subsequently by a German submarine. Attention was now focussed on the Italian Fleet. My Marauder and Baltimore squadrons were still keeping a close watch on La Spezia and Genoa and reported no movement. Then I received a signal from Hugh Pughe telling me that at 3am on 8 September the battleships *Roma, Italia* and *Vittorio Veneto*, would sail from La Spezia and would be joined the same afternoon by cruisers and destroyers from Genoa. The route given to the Italians by Admiral Cunningham was southward to the west of Corsica and Sardinia until the North African coast was sighted when they would be met by the *Warspite* and *Valiant* and escorted to Malta. I duly received a reconnaissance report from a Marauder when the battleships emerged from La Spezia and another later to say they had been joined by the cruisers and destroyers from Genoa.

From then on we had regular routine reports from the shadowing Marauders on the Fleet's progress south and there was some excitement in the Operations Room at Bizerta when it was reported that the Fleet had changed heading to the east and would pass through the Straits of Bonifacio between Corsica and Sardinia. This was not according to plan and immediately we saw the possibility of the Italians making a dash towards Salerno to attack our shipping in the area. We had maintained a high state of readiness in the torpedo squadrons and the prospect that they might after all, be required to attack the Italians was in everyone's minds. However, once through the Straits the ships turned south again, but before that occurred the Luftwaffe took a hand in the proceedings by attacking their erstwhile Allies. At Istres near Marseilles was stationed the 3rd Group of Bomber Wing 100, commanded by a Major Bernhard Jope. His Staffeln were equipped with Dornier Do17s, each aircraft armed with the first air-to-air missile: the FX-1400 radio-controlled armour-piercing bomb. Unknown to the Italians, the Germans had learned of the plan to surrender and had prepared accordingly. The Do17s consequently attacked the Italian Fleet in the Straits of Bonifacio and obtained a hit on the battleship *Roma* which blew up and sank. Another battleship, the *Italia*, was also hit and though badly damaged managed to keep going and eventually reached Malta. The shadowing Marauder reported this attack to us at Bizerta and also photographed the *Roma* as she broke up and sank.

While this now ex-enemy Fleet was heading for Malta, I went out in a Spitfire to take a look at it. The 'duty' Marauder was still shadowing, the last to maintain unbroken surveillance over the long voyage from northern Italy. A Hudson was also in the vicinity. Shortly after sighting the North African coast, the Italians turned east and were then met by Force H consisting of the battleships *Warspite* and *Valiant* and accompanying destroyers. This meeting was reported to Lloyd's HQ and we were told to discontinue our watch on the proceedings. Within an hour of taking over from my escorting aircraft the *Warspite* received a signal from Cunningham congratulating her on her proud and rightful position at the head of the line. The aircraft of my Group that had been in charge of the Italian Fleet for 550 of its 820-mile journey to Malta received no congratulatory signals, nor did we expect any. Reconnaissance, shadowing and strike were routine business for us and in this instance we had successfully accomplished the first two and it was a pity that the Luftwaffe had provided the third. The heavily-escorted Italian Fleet reached Malta on 11 September, an event marked by the inevitable emotional signal this time to the Admiralty: "Be pleased to inform their Lordships that the Italian Battle Fleet now lies at anchor under the guns of the fortress of Malta." The sailors are strong on sending congratulatory signals and I remembered that this habit was a very old one; an ancestor of mine on my mother's side, Admiral Collingwood, who was with Nelson at Trafalgar was reported as having said just before the battle commenced "why does Nelson send so many signals? We all know what to do".

The landings at Salerno were expected by the Germans. Field Marshal Albert Kesselring, the Commander-in-Chief, had correctly deduced that landings would be made south of Naples, and as usual the German Army proved to be a tough proposition. Both assaults went well at first, with the British in the north of the bay and the Americans in the south, but once the enemy convinced themselves that these were major landings opposition stiffened and progress inland was slow. As we had anticipated, attacks on the beach-head by the Luftwaffe were insignificant from the Army's point of view.

The attacks by the Strategic Air Forces on the enemy fighter airfields at Pomigliano, Capodichino and Grazzanise just before the landings meant that these airfields were almost entirely inoperative throughout. Monte Corvino, the airfield inland from the Salerno beaches, was spared from attack because we planned to use it ourselves as soon as it was captured. The Anglo-American tactical air forces encountered a few Fw109s and claimed four destroyed for the loss of two of their own aircraft. Ineffective night raids by the Luftwaffe were punished by our Beaufighters which shot down seven in the first three nights. Monte Corvino airfield was captured on 10 September, but enemy artillery fire made it unusable for some time.

The invasion on the ground remained a desperate struggle with both the British 10th Corps and the American VI Corps establishing themselves on the beaches but the Germans never gave in easily and on 13 September counter attacked at the junction of the two Allied Corps down the banks of the Sele river. In this critical situation the only reinforcement available that could act swiftly was the Allied Air Forces which intervened in the battle on a gigantic scale attacking the enemy on the river banks throughout the daylight hours. In addition, US B-17s and British Wellingtons attacked targets immediately in the rear of the battlefield by day and night. It was too much even for the Germans and, coupled with the threat from the south provided by the advance of the 8th Army, the enemy halted their attack and by the end of the day on 15 September began to pull out.

A few days later I flew to Salerno and landed at the captured airfield at Monte Corvino. A Desert Air Force Wing commanded by Group Captain Green was already installed with Spitfires, Beaufighters and a GCI, the last of which was the most important for the night Beaufighters and because of which the only appearance of the Luftwaffe in the battle area comprised a few ineffective attacks under cover of darkness. Green confirmed to me that except at night there was practically no enemy air activity against our troops and that consequently almost all our flying had been ground attack in support of the troops. He was, of course, always prepared to switch to aerial combat if the Luftwaffe tried to take a hand in the ground battle. So, as far as the beach-head area was concerned, a satisfactory situation had been achieved but for the ships standing off-shore it had been a different story. However, they were not my concern and their operations are fully recorded elsewhere.

By 16 September, the Germans had recognised that holding their position at Salerno meant certain defeat and began to pull out, fighting a tenacious rearguard action as they went. It was not until

1 October that the first Allied troops entered Naples. Capodichino airfield took a week to de-mine and clear of the debris caused by the Allied bombing but finally on 7 October it was safe for me to land there. The 242 Group HQ advance party under the leadership of Colonel Rogers and Major Reeves had followed the Army into the city and had taken over the accommodation previously occupied by the Gestapo. We were to find subsequently that the Gestapo always requisitioned the best buildings in any captured city. It was now decided that the USAAF would be responsible for air operations on the western coast of Italy and the RAF for the east, thus aligning the air forces with the land forces of the American 5th Army and the British 8th Army. My Group was to be responsible for air defence of the base areas behind the 8th Army and for anti-submarine operations in the Adriatic. The Navy were to have their HQ in Taranto under Rear-Admiral R R McGrigor and I was told to set up my Group HQ alongside him.

Off went Rogers and Reeves to "bag" us some accommodation again. Benefiting from their experience in Naples, they put in a bid for the Gestapo building and we were again fortunate in obtaining a splendid Operations Room on the edge of the harbour with a block of flats opposite, ideal for a Mess and living accommodation. A similar block was requisitioned for the NCOs and airmen. The Admiral had already occupied the Italian Naval building adjacent to the harbour and allocated us two complete floors which was more than adequate for my small staff. It was agreed that the maritime air operations were to be controlled from an Operations Room next to that run by the Navy, but air defence was to be conducted from the Operations Room on the edge of the harbour. Later, with the arrival of Group Captain Rees Jones to command the Fighter Sector covering the area from the Toe of Italy up to Foggia, it was found to be more convenient for the Operations Room to be located at the main fighter airfield at Grottaglie. Maritime activity was now much reduced; with no shipping to strike in the Adriatic the torpedo squadrons were withdrawn, but the anti-submarine squadrons remained. With the Italians having by now changed sides, I gained a floatplane squadron which operated from the inner harbour at Taranto, a most welcome addition indeed to our reduced maritime force. When inspecting this new force, I visited its photographic section and the Italian CO showed me some very good photographs, including a magnificent picture (reproduced here in this book) taken from an Italian warship of the exact moment that the battleship *Roma* had been hit by one of Major Jope's guided bombs.

The Group was now in something of a backwater. The Luftwaffe airfields were hundreds of miles away in the north of the country. The Desert Air Force lay between us and the enemy on airfields around Foggia, where they were joined by Doolittle's bombers (now formed into the 15th Air Force) in December. There was little or no activity from enemy bases on the other side of the Adriatic in Albania, Greece or Yugoslavia. Nevertheless it never paid to underrate the Luftwaffe, as we would learn at Bari. By December 1943, Bari was our main supply port for both the Army and the RAF, including materials for the construction of new airfields around Foggia. But Bari lacked any real defence. The American heavy bombers based at Foggia were of no defensive use and no RAF fighter squadrons were based at Bari. Ground defences were neither adequate nor efficiently organised. General Major Dietrich Peltz planned an attack with 100 Ju88s that was perfectly executed on the evening of 2 December. At 7.25pm, two or three German aircraft approached at low level then circled the harbour at 10,000 feet, dropping Window to confuse the signals received by ground radars. They also dropped flares, though these were hardly needed because the port was working at full pressure and there were lights every-where. Due to an operating error, the air raid warning was not given. Fourteen merchant ships laden with 34,000 tons of cargo were destroyed, three more carrying 7,500 tons were sunk (but later salvaged) and six others were damaged. The port was closed for three weeks, with serious effects on land-air operations. One of the Allied ships destroyed was the *John Harvey* which had been carrying 540 tons of mustard gas in the form of 100-pound bombs. Many of the bombs broke open, releasing a deadly poison that spread across the harbour. The *John Harvey* had been brought to Bari because the Germans had threatened to use gas against Italy and the Allies, in turn, threatened to retaliate against Germany. Over 600 soldiers and sailors died, as well as an unknown number of Italians, in the worst shipping disaster suffered by the Allies since Pearl Harbor. We tried to conceal the extent of the disaster by a standing patrol of Spitfires to prevent aerial reconnaissance.

As the Air Defence Commander I had called on the Naval Officer in charge of the port and warned that lack of dispersal made the ships a tempting target and I suggested moving the ships double and treble banked at the quays out into the open harbour. He had said he was under great pressure to unload the cargoes, particularly the aviation petrol and the pressed steel planking for the airfield runways at Foggia. I had sensed that he thought it was a bit of a nerve for this Air Force Officer to be telling the Navy what to do!

There was a small sand airfield at Taranto and my Spitfire IX and the Fiesler Storch were brought there. I kept in flying practice in the IX and visited the various stations in the Storch; and Broadhurst flew down from his HQ at Vasto welcoming the change from his caravan to the relative luxury of hot baths and a centrally heated Mess and admiring my Storch, a newer model than his.

There was one frustrating operation that autumn of 1943, though. I learned from Ultra that a German submarine in the north of the Adriatic at Pula (on the tip of the Istra Peninsula) was preparing to make a break for the open Mediterranean. We were given its date of departure and knew from the data we had on this type of submarine that it could not complete the journey from Pula to the Straits of Otranto at the Heel of Italy, entirely submerged. It would be forced to surface once and probably twice to charge batteries. Ultra, in due course, signalled the time and date of departure and the route to be followed, and we planned to cover the whole route with our anti-submarine aircraft. To do this we needed every aircraft in the Group, including the Italian float-planes. All went well on the first day with complete coverage of the route for all twenty four hours. On the second day, we received a sighting report from the Italian on patrol and giving his intention to attack. Then silence. The Operations Room thought that the float-plane must have been hit by gunfire. About an hour later we received a message to say that the floatplane had landed safely back at his base and that a report was on its way by messenger.

Shortly afterwards, the Italian Colonel commanding the unit arrived at my office and it was plain to me that he was in a highly emotional state. He spoke quite good English and burst out that his pilot had made a perfect attack diagonally across the submarine and placed two bombs accurately on each side, but horror of horrors, he had forgotten to fuse them! The submarine had promptly crash dived. The Colonel said that of course the crew would be court martialled and as they were plainly guilty would be shot. I thought that this was rather drastic treatment for what in the Allied Air Forces would be regarded as an operational error, and I said so to my distraught subordinate. But no—the Colonel was determined— court martial and shooting, particularly the latter. I asked him to wait outside and sent for Finch, my number two, and told him of my problem. He said, "I think this is a matter for Rogers. He speaks a bit of Italian and his wise old head might help". Later I heard that a court martial had been arranged but that sentence would have to be decided by the highest air authority concerned—this of course was me, and in due course the crew were given a gentle reprimand and that was that.

At this time, we were asked to help the Dakotas dropping supplies to Tito and his partisans by escorting them with our Spitfires. Though the mainland on the eastern side of the Adriatic was in enemy hands some of the islands off the coast were held by partisans and one of these, Vis was conveniently situated on one of the main Dakota routes. I sent a reconnaissance party there by night in a destroyer and as a result it was decided to build a refuelling strip and so extend the range of the Spitfires. I selected an ADC of mine (until December 1943), Tony Le Hardy, for this task because I knew from my experience of him both as an ADC and as a No 2 in the air that he was exceptionally resourceful and chock full of initiative. So off he went with a party of Army airfield construction engineers, signalers and a generous supply of cash with instructions to report immediately the strip was ready to receive the Spitfires. Within weeks it was prepared and Spitfires were refuelling in quick time. It was never the intention to base Spitfires there permanently, as we felt that this would attract a major attack by the German ground forces only a few miles away on the mainland. Much later, when it was decided to step up the air support for Tito, a Balkan Air Force was formed on 7 June 1944 with its HQ at Bari and the Vis airstrip was transferred to its control. It proved useful not only in its intended role but also as an emergency landing field for 15th Air Force aircraft that had been damaged in combat over the Balkans and staggered back as far as Vis to land or crash land on the strip. Most could not have reached Italy, two hundred miles away across the Adriatic.

After the excitement of the German submarine, things were pretty quiet in the Heel and Toe of Italy, and in December 1943 I began to hear rumours of moves for the senior air commanders in our theatre. Tedder, at Winston's request, was to accompany Eisenhower as his Deputy when he moved to England as Supreme Commander. His replacement with us was to be Air Marshal Sir John Slessor, probably the foremost intellectual in the Service. He came from commanding Coastal Command which, at last equipped with long-range Liberators, had played a decisive part in preventing the U-boats from winning the Battle of the Atlantic. I knew him slightly and liked what I knew. Coningham went home to command 2nd Tactical Air Force and Broadhurst joined him as commander of 83 Group. Coningham was to be succeeded by an American—General Joe Cannon, who had been his deputy. I was pleased to hear of this appointment as Joe had won, and kept, the confidence of all airmen, British and American. Broadhurst would be replaced in the Desert Air Force by Bill Dickson who had expected to lead 83 Group across the Channel in the liberation of Occupied Europe. It must have been a disappointment to be relegated to what was now a secondary theatre but he showed no sign of it when he arrived, and it was of course sensible policy for the Air Ministry to send a rising star such as Bill to benefit from the experience of commanders who had succeeded in the invasions of Sicily and Salerno.

Jack Slessor visited me at Taranto in January 1944 and was much interested in the combined air defence and coastal role of my 242 Group, "very economical compared with the UK", he said with a smile. Before he left, he asked me how long I had been in the Mediterranean theatre and when I told him three years, he continued, "Any hurry to go home?" "Yes. I feel I am getting out of date with the technical advances in England. People out from home talk GEE, GEE-H and Oboe and I don't know what they mean. I believe its about time I went and found out". I think Jack was a little bit disappointed that I wished to leave his command, but he agreed with me at once and a few weeks later a signal arrived appointing Air Commodore George Harcourt-Smith to command 242 group and posting me back to England. I did a quick tour of the squadrons to say goodbye and then handed over to Harcourt-Smith. Humphrey, my ADC, had borrowed a Beaufighter, since I couldn't get all my kit into the Spitfire, and we took off from Grottaglie for Algiers on the first leg of the journey home.

In Algiers I stayed with Hugh Pughe in his villa and he kindly arranged for me to travel onwards with General Spaatz who was returning to England in a C-54. My fellow passengers were all American Army Generals. We staged through Casablanca staying the night in a luxurious villa on the outskirts of the town. I was told that it had belonged to a Romanian tycoon before the war. We had an uneventful night flight home and landed at Heston on a cold February morning in 1944. I thanked General Spaatz for the ride and was given a car to take me up to London. My word, it all looked pretty bleak after the Med. This time I was determined not to make any mistakes and phoned the Air Ministry from the Club. I was told that I could take two weeks leave and then report to the HQ of the Allied Expeditionary Air Force at Bentley Priory. I knew this was Leigh-Mallory's command and was pleased to know that I was wanted. I telephoned my family at Hayling and gave them the time of arrival of my train and they met me at Havant station. It was a sad homecoming since it was the first time I had seen any of them since Ian had been taken prisoner, but we consoled ourselves with the thought that at least he was safe. How wrong we were.

During my brief leave at Hayling Island I had time to see the effect that four years of war had had on my family. My mother, who was a very stout egg indeed, and always keen on us children doing our duty, now worried continually about Ian in his prison camp in Germany. My father now worked for the War Office doing endless surveys. My sister Jean was a Flight Officer in the WAAF and my brother-in-law Bibbs Sparkes was in the Navy. Our home, Eastoke Lodge on the edge of the sea and opposite the Isle of Wight, had its dugout on the lawn which my parents had often occupied during the Blitz on Portsmouth six miles to the west. As the Luftwaffe often missed their target by quite this distance the family dug out was clearly necessary. The family had many friends on the island and the farmers amongst them saw that we were never short of vegetables. However, my leave was soon over and I went off by train to Bentley Priory in March 1944 to report to HQ Allied Expeditionary Air Force.

CHAPTER XVI

HOME AGAIN

HQ Allied Expeditionary Air Force (AEAF) was sharing Bentley Priory at Stanmore with Fighter Command HQ, now renamed the Air Defence of Great Britain. Both HQs were over crowded despite the addition of numerous wooden office huts in the grounds. AEAF was commanded by Leigh-Mallory with an American deputy, Major General Hoyt S. Vandenberg. I went straight to Leigh-Mallory's office and after a half hour's wait was ushered in. He was pleased to see me and quickly launched into a dissertation about all his command was to do in the forthcoming invasion and the preparations already in hand. I was to fill the Air Commodore Training post on his staff. Leigh-Mallory seems always to have seen me as a training man when what I really enjoyed were operational commands.

After my interview I wandered off among the wooden huts to find the Training Department, locating it at last on the extreme edge of the hutted area and from its position surmised that its importance did not rate very highly. It was a joint department, USAAF on one side of a central passage and RAF on the other. Brigadier General Martin was the USAAF head and Group Captain Atcherley who I was to replace, the temporary RAF head. 'Batchy' as he was known, was the same Atcherley I had met in Norway when he was Wing Commander at Bardufoss and again when he was an acting Air Commodore in Western Desert Air Force at Tripoli in 1943 when I was passing through on my way to Algiers. He had a reputation as a brilliant, if unpredictable, pilot. In the piping days of peace before September 1939 he had been a Central Flying School Instructor and had participated in the Hendon Air Display and was then invited to perform aerobatics at the Chicago Air Races which was at that time the biggest air show in the United States. On arrival, Dick found he was one of several pilots from other countries who likewise had been asked to perform. He had quickly appreciated that he would be unable to compete successfully in aerobatics with these aces in their specially-built machines because his mount was a standard British-built civil light aircraft. So he persuaded the organisers that he could best entertain the crowds by an exhibition of crazy flying. Crazy flying had been an item in the Hendon Display for several years and consisted of low flying in a very erratic manner. The crowd was told that the pilot of the aeroplane was a pupil not yet fully qualified. After some debate it was reluctantly agreed that he should try, and his first performance was a sensation. Many believed that at any moment he was bound to crash. The next day the Press was full of Dick and his act that quite eclipsed the aero-batic aces. So successful was he during the week that he was invited back the following year and when he had difficulty in obtaining an aeroplane the race organisers provided one for him.

At Tripoli his unpredictability had caught up with him, however, when he crashed a new Kittyhawk and I was not surprised to hear later that he had left the Western Desert Air Force as he hardly possessed the reliability insisted on by the newly appointed com-mander, Air Vice-Marshal Broadhurst. So here he was—a Group Captain having lost his acting Air Commodore rank on leaving the Desert. He was to remain in the Training Department as my deputy. Dick explained that the task we had been given was to convert the RAF and USAAF fighter squadrons in Fighter Command and the American 9th Air Force from air fighting to ground attack to enable them to play their part in helping the ground forces in the liberation of Europe. The task had been tackled by setting up a Conversion Unit at Milfield in Northumberland and putting the squadrons through a short course in dive-bombing, front gun and rocket firing against ground targets on a nearby range. It all seemed to be going well with Dick and General Martin working closely together. I said I would like to go up to Milfield and it was arranged for the next day, when we flew in a couple of Spitfires from the Communication Flight at Northolt.

Milfield was a wartime airfield with good approaches and the usual three runways. We were met by the Station Commander and taken to the Officers' Mess for lunch. Here the Atcherley touch was at once apparent. The entrance hall was arranged like an hotel reception area and manned entirely by WAAFs wearing coloured overalls over their uniform. This change from the normally austere Mess plainly went down well with the American officers, some of whom were from a newly arrived Thunderbolt squadron 'signing in' and chatting up the girls in the process. After lunch we did a tour of the squadrons, both

USAAF at this time, and armed with the P-47 Thunderbolt. I asked if I might fly one and the Squadron Commander willingly agreed and supplied a splendid Lieutenant to brief me on the controls. The P-47, as I expected from its long range, was very heavy in comparison with the short-range Spitfire, but as usual with American aircraft the cockpit was well laid out with everything where the pilot would expect it to be. I flew it for an hour and was impressed with its manoeuvrability despite its size and weight. We returned to Northolt the next day and I congratulated Dick on his achievement in organising Milfield so well. It struck me that my experience with him in Norway and the Desert had revealed his limitations as an operational commander, but when it came to training he was quite first class.

Having seen the business end of the Training Department's responsibility, apparently with everything well in hand, I now had time to think about the role and organising of the Allied Expeditionary Air Forces and its HQ.

Allied policy had accepted since 1941 that when the liberation of the continent of Europe began the support of this immense operation would be a priority commitment for all the British and American Air Forces based in the United Kingdom. This meant that on the British side were Bomber, Fighter, Coastal and Transport Commands and the 2nd Tactical Air Force, the last specifically formed for the close support of land force operations. On the United States side there were the heavy bombers of the 8th Air Force, supported by their own fighter wings, and the fighters, medium bombers and transport of the 9th Air Force. In total, the Allies had about 9,500 combat and transport aircraft available for D-Day, of which some 5,800 were American and 3,700 British. In addition to this enormous armada, we had 1,200 gliders—all but 100 of them British. The need for an overall Commander and an organisation to co-ordinate the operations of this vast force was recognised and hence the formation of the Allied Expeditionary Air Force or AEAF.

The operational need to concentrate so many aircraft over the relatively small area of the Normandy beaches pointed at once to the Fighter Command control and reporting system. This was because since the end of the Battle of Britain in 1940 the command had been conducting operations daily across the Channel with its own aircraft and also co-ordinating operations with other commands, including the Americans. Effectively Fighter Command possessed the only aircraft movement system in the United Kingdom, and valuable experience had been gained in the years since 1940 in monitoring the operations of all the commands based in the UK. It was sensible therefore that the Commander of the new Allied Expeditionary Air Force should be a man who thoroughly understood the business of moving large numbers of aircraft from their bases in the United Kingdom and, just as important, returning them on the completion of their missions. Air Chief Marshal Sir Trafford Leigh-Mallory, as a previous commander of No 11 and 12 Groups and the current Commander-in-Chief of Fighter Command, was an obvious choice. The responsibility of Leigh-Mallory *vis-à-vis* the participating commands, was limited to the specification and co-ordination of operations. All the other commanders remained responsible for everything else in their respective commands.

Sitting in my office in a wooden hut, I pondered how these new arrangements would work out in practice. How would the great 'Bomber' Harris take to having his operations decided for him by Leigh-Mallory? Likewise Sholto Douglas at Coastal Command, Mary Coningham at 2nd Tactical Air Force? How would the Americans react? Generals Spaatz, Doolittle, Brereton and Vandenberg were all powerful men used to making their own decisions. I knew from my experience in North Africa that the co-ordination of the various RAF and USAAF formations for the invasion of Sicily, Salerno and Anzio had been aided by good relations between the commanders involved and their staffs. Now, as I considered the personalities at the morning meetings held at Bentley Priory, I was not encouraged.

Leigh-Mallory was a theoretical rather than a practical airman. His honesty and integrity compensated partially for this deficiency but he had not helped himself by his selection of staff, few of whom had any experience of working with land and sea force in an invasion. I was aghast at one key appointment—that of Air Vice-Marshal Philip Wigglesworth as his Senior Air Staff Officer—even though he had experience of invasions, having served on Tedder's staff in Algiers. He was a blunt Yorkshireman quite without charm but extremely hardworking. Like Leigh-Mallory, he was a theoretical airman and had not flown an aeroplane for years.

Leigh-Mallory's American deputy, Hoyt Vandenberg, was the nephew of the powerful Senator, Arthur Vandenberg. He was a quiet man, easy to work with and with an ability to sort out the important matters in conference. I realised very soon that Vandenberg could not tolerate Wigglesworth with his long-winded manner. On the lower levels in the staff, relations seemed to be good and my opposite number Brigadier Martin couldn't have been more helpful to me, the new arrival.

On 27 September, 1943 I was awarded an American decoration, The Legion of Merit—Degree of Commander, signed by Secretary of State Stimson and General Eisenhower, and I was summoned to a presentation ceremony at Bushey Park near Kingston where General Eisenhower's HQ was located. It was an impressive and friendly occasion. Among the recipients were Coningham and Broadhurst, and Tedder was present with Eisenhower on the dais. The General was his usual charming self, and he knew the names of all those he decorated, which was a considerable feat of memory. Afterwards we were all invited to lunch and I had the good fortune to be seated opposite General George Patton whom I had only met briefly in Africa. His performance in Sicily in command of the 7th Army had proven him to be a first-class fighting man. Patton was unlike many Generals and Admirals who, prior to the Mediterranean campaigns, had little or no experience of combined air, land, and sea operations and whose concept was limited to using aircraft as long-range artillery if they were held up anywhere. His philosophy was quite different—"If you can keep the enemy air off my back I can deal with the Kraut on the ground". He had certainly done so in Sicily and was to do so again in Normandy. When the meal ended Eisenhower made a short speech on the theme of 'Brothers in Arms' and suggested that we stand for a minute in remembrance of those who had been with us in the Mediterranean and who had lost their lives. We duly stood. As we sat down Patton muttered to himself "I hope in three months time nobody is standing up for me!"

It soon became apparent to me that there was little work for the Air Commodore Training. The task of converting the USAAF and RAF squadrons from air fighting to ground attack was just about complete. All the other British and American commands that would be controlled by Leigh-Mallory had specialised training staffs and even if I had been qualified to help, which I was not, they would not welcome any participation from anyone in AEAF. Sitting in my wooden hut office, I pondered what to do next. Of course I had hoped for an active command in 2nd TAF when I returned from Italy but its four Groups, Nos 2, 83, 84 and 85 were all Air Vice-Marshal posts and were already commanded by Basil Embry, Harry Broadhurst, Leslie Browne and Charles Steele so there was no hope there for a jumped-up Acting Air Commodore. So I only had one option if I was going to get in the battle. I would have to do as I had done in the Desert: drop a rank or two. Having come to this conclusion I asked for an interview with Leigh-Mallory.

I saw Leigh-Mallory at the end of May 1944 and explained that there was no real work for me as Air Commodore Training, and asked if I might be posted to an active post, if necessary in a lower rank. He was most upset, mainly I believe at the thought that anyone should wish to leave his staff. "Well", he said, "if you feel like that I must tell you that Portal has been asking for you and I will now tell him that you are available". This was a shock. Portal was Chief of the Air Staff and serving him could only mean Whitehall, further away still from the action! I left Leigh-Mallory's office and hurried off to the Senior Personnel Staff Officer. He, of course, knew nothing but said he would contact me as soon as he knew anything. A couple of days later he phoned to say that I was to take over the Directorate of Overseas Operations in the Air Ministry. I asked what rank the appointment rated and was told, "Air Commodore of course, the same as you are now". What a blow, the Air Ministry in wartime?! I should have kept my mouth shut. Out of the frying pan into the fire! Instead of moving nearer the action I was moving further away. The signal notifying my appointment in the Chief of Air Staff's Department required me to be there on 12 June. As it happened, I was therefore still at AEAF for the long-awaited D-Day, the Normandy landings of 6 June.

I continued to attend the morning meetings of the Commanders concerned. Leigh-Mallory was in the chair with Tedder on his right and Vandenberg on his left. Round the table were Harris, Spaatz, Doolittle, Sholto Douglas, Coningham, Roderic Hill and Lewis Brereton. It was an imposing gathering. Each gave a brief account of his command's operations for the previous twenty four hours and then they went on to discuss the immediate future. Tedder's presence, representing the Supreme Commander Eisenhower, kept everyone in order. I do not think that Leigh-Mallory would have made the same progress on his own. I recall that these meetings had a serious atmosphere but one which was alleviated occasionally by some sharp wise-cracks, generally from Doolittle or Sholto Douglas.

Meanwhile, Atcherley, with his usual initiative, had persuaded an American Airfield Engineer Regiment which was waiting for the invasion, to fill in their time by making a light aircraft strip in the grounds of Bentley Priory. He had anticipated objections since it was green belt land so he built it without reference to anyone and the Americans with characteristic energy and competence completed the job in a couple of days, so that all the protests that flooded in came too late. We stationed a couple of Austers there and the Americans did the same with their light aircraft. Air Marshal Harris particularly appreciated the strip, when flying over from High Wycombe each morning for the conference.

The great day arrived at last and the commanders moved to Eisenhower's HQ at Southwick near Portsmouth. I spent a part of the day in the Fighter Command Operations Room watching the picture on the table. Thousands of movements of Allied aircraft were plotted and during the time I was there not one hostile plot appeared. Of course the Luftwaffe had been forced off the French airfields and were now almost entirely concerned with trying to oppose the 8th Air Force and Bomber Command in their attacks on the heartland of Germany.

The orderly performance of thousands of Allied aircraft operating in a congested area over the Normandy beach-head was a triumph for Fighter Command (or Air Defence of Great Britain, as we were now supposed to call it) and a credit to its current commander, Air Marshal Sir Roderic Hill and his predecessor Leigh-Mallory, and the staffs of the commands concerned, particularly that of the Allied Expeditionary Air Force. However, once the soldiers were safely ashore and airfields constructed, the tactical air commanders set up their HQ in France and HQ AEAF became superfluous. I was glad that I had left before this happened, even if it did mean going to the dreaded Air Ministry.

Leigh-Mallory and Wigglesworth were not finished. Mountbatten asked for Leigh-Mallory as Air Commander-in-Chief for the Far East theatre and Wigglesworth went onto the staff of the Deputy Supreme Commander, Tedder.

As the Director responsible for Overseas, I was especially interested in Leigh-Mallory's appointment, though in the light of my previous experience of serving twice on Leigh-Mallory's staff and my experience in the Desert and North Africa I wondered whether Leigh-Mallory had the flexibility of mind to cope with the vast variety of problems that occurred when working with an Army. I heard that he had been allotted a personal York aircraft and would be leaving from Northolt. I decided to be there to see him off, but as so often happened in Whitehall, I was detailed to attend a meeting and had to content myself with a 'phone call to him while he was waiting in the VIP lounge. "Ah well Bing," he said, "it looks as if the war will soon be over in Europe and then maybe you'll join me in the Far East." Sadly, Leigh-Mallory never took up his appointment, as his York hit a mountain in the French Alps and all aboard were killed. Historians seem to me to have underrated Leigh-Mallory. He was not a great commander in comparison with Portal, Tedder and Harris, but he was a very good commander and an expert in his speciality, air defence.

Then, the time came for me to leave Bentley Priory, and I duly collected my gear from my comfortable billet in a nearby house and took a room in the Royal Air Force Club in Piccadilly. There were few members using the Club at this time and it would have been convenient to stay permanently but the expense was more than I could afford. I intended to look for a flat when I had time. The second morning of my stay in the Club I was awakened by Ack-Ack gunfire and was surprised because for a long time the Luftwaffe had found it too expensive to attack London in daylight. I went out onto the balcony in my pyjamas and looking eastwards towards the City I saw bursts at a surprisingly low level and flying through the bursts a very small aircraft. I realised at once that this was the 'flying bomb'. The launching sites for this formidable weapon in northern France had been under attack for months past by the Anglo-American Air Forces. The first flying bomb was followed by another at about a ten-minute interval and then a procession at irregular intervals, mostly to the east over the City. I had a nasty sinking feeling in my stomach when I realised that the dense barrage put up around these horrors meant absolutely nothing to unmanned vehicles. There was always the consolation that with manned aircraft even near misses gave the crew a fright—but these 'phut-phut robots' were completely unaffected: only a direct hit was any good.

The morning meeting, normally chaired by the Assistant Chief of the Air Staff, Air Vice-Marshal Bill Williams was attended this day by both the Vice Chief Douglas Evill and the Deputy Chief Norman Bottomley. They, like a good many others round the table, had an intimate knowledge of these weapons from Intelligence sources. One complete phase of the enemy plan to bombard southern England and especially London had already been delayed by the continuous bombing of the launching sites in France. In this second phase the weapons were launched from mobile and concealed sites, though the numbers fired were very much reduced from those planned. The commanders of the defences against the flying bombs were Air Marshal Sir Roderic Hill (head of ADGB) and General Sir Frederick Pile (head of Anti-Aircraft Command). The defences were arranged in two zones: firstly over the sea, plotted by radar and inland tracked by the Royal Observer Corps, was fighter territory. The second zone was immediately around London and was entirely the responsibility of Ack-Ack guns and balloons. It quickly became apparent that this arrangement did not permit the best exploitation of the guns. Here at last was the gunners' dream, a target on a steady course and speed, maintaining constant altitude throughout its course.

Up to this time it was universally agreed in the 'trade' that in most circumstances the fighter was the best weapon for the destruction of aircraft and the flying bomb was essentially an un-manned aircraft; so, as usual, the guns deferred to the fighter. Hill and Pyle soon recognised that this was is different and with immense courage altered the whole deployment of the guns in quick time and on their own authority. The guns (reinforced from all over Britain) were moved to a belt running along the coast and for some miles inland. There, with a clear field of fire over the sea and accurate radar plotting to help them, the guns showed an immediate improvement in the number of bombs shot down. The fighters continued to operate well out to sea and in the zone inland behind the guns and in front of the balloon barrage, and their success rate remained the same. The decision was made with the approval of Duncan Sandys (chairman of a committee set up by the Prime Minister to study missile threats) and against Air Ministry advice. It was made very clear to Hill that he would be personally held responsible if the experiment failed. The next great improvement came when the Americans made available their latest SCR 584 radar sets and proximity fuses (shells so fused that burst automatically when close to their target). From then on the guns situated on the coast were the main defence, accounting for a high proportion of the flying bombs before they crossed the coast.

Sitting in our offices in King Charles Street off Whitehall the sound of an approaching bomb distracted attention from one's work. If the engine was running as it passed overhead all was well. If the engine cut out when it was still approaching then we were at risk. If it cut out after it passed some other poor souls were likely to receive the diving robot. I shared my office with my deputy director, Group Captain 'Sparrow' Lewis, and he was very susceptible to these signals and on occasion took the precaution of moving into the well of his desk. The nearest explosion we experienced was a direct hit on the Guards Chapel in Wellington Barracks, only some six hundred yards from King Charles Street, and even our massive building shook.

In August there was a reorganisation of the Operations Directorates. There were six Operations Directorates in the Assistant Chief of Air Staff (Operations) Department, representing the main operational functions of the service—Bomber, Air Defence, Coastal, Transport, Tactical and one which covered all functions, Overseas. The task for each Directorate was to monitor the activities of their respective commands and to issue instructions and directives on behalf of the Air Council or the Chiefs of Staff Committee. George Lawson had been appointed Director of Air Defence and as soon as I could I went along to see him. He was very kind and explained the working of the ACAS (Operations) department. In the days and weeks that followed George was my mentor. I believe he wanted to show that there were no hard feelings over my abrupt take over of 242 Group from him in North Africa. Overseas Operations was abolished and its responsibilities shared by the other functional Directorates. I thought I might escape but found I was to take over Tactical from Donald Hardman, a very senior Air Commodore. In my new post I was responsible for Tactical Air Force policy, the 1st in the Mediterranean, the 2nd in Europe and the 3rd in the Far East in Burma. By far the most demanding task was looking after 2nd TAF in Europe; it was larger in terms of aircraft than the other two put together and being close at hand business was brisk. I frequently visited 2nd TAF particularly when the front stabilised on the Rhine and the HQ was in Brussels. My old Egypt master, Tommy Elmhirst, was administering and I always made a point of calling on him as early as possible in my visits as I found from experience that he had a better feel of the command than anyone else. All the groups in 2nd TAF under Coningham were commanded by friends: Embry, Broadhurst, Steele and (from November on) Teddy Hudleston in 84 Group. On my first visit I stayed with Mary Coningham, who had set himself up in a mansion and was living in great style with servants galore and food that wasn't exclusively service rations. It was a contrast to the austerity at home and I enjoyed my couple of nights, but on reflection I wondered whether such luxury was appropriate in an operational command.

On subsequent visits I arranged my itinerary so that my night stops were at one of the groups, more often than not 2 Group, where Basil Embry had set up his HQ in a cavalry barracks also in Brussels. Here it was quite different with all activity centered around the bombing operations of the Group. Nevertheless, the domestic arrangements were adequate: the bedrooms bare but clean and the Mess comfortable with well cooked service rations. The one 'luxury' was a well-stocked bar where all the staff from the AOC downwards met before dinner to discuss the day's work.

I enjoyed staying with Basil, everything was so much more realistic than at 2nd TAF. On one of my visits I got stuck in Brussels with fog covering all England and Belgium. Flying was impossible but I was keen to get back because I knew work would be piling up in London. Tommy Elmhirst also had a meeting in London and said there was nothing for it but to go by car, boat, and train so I begged a lift. At the last moment Tommy had a call from Prince Bernhard of the Netherlands also asking for a ride. So I had a very enjoyable journey, car to Calais, boat to Dover and train to London, mostly listening to interesting conversation. I thus got a very good first-hand impression of the Prince, particularly his knowledge of and interest in the operations of 2nd TAF.

In King Charles Street the weekly routine included a meeting with the CAS in his office with all the Operations Directors: Sidney Bufton (Bomber), George Lawson (Air Defence), C W Dicken (Coastal), 'Duck' Jordan (Transport) and myself (Tactical), together with the Assistant Chiefs of Operations (Bill Williams) Intelligence (Frank Inglis) and Signals (Victor Tait). The purpose of the meeting was for the CAS to go through his notes in preparation for his weekly meeting with the Cabinet. Portal was an ace at condensing reports of the immense number of operations by the British and American Air Forces, and I found that he never missed anything of importance and of interest to Ministers.

Seeing Portal once a week regularly and quite often alone on Tactical Air Force matters, I had plenty of opportunity to appreciate the exceptional calibre of the man. After the war, Churchill would describe Portal as "the accepted star of the Air Force". Between April and October 1940, Portal had been head of Bomber Command and I remember my brother Ian telling me that he somehow made his presence felt even in such a large command.

Portal had a distinguished record in the Great War and fortunately for the RAF, he chose to make his career in our Service. He advanced swiftly to senior rank in the Twenties and Thirties and was among those who foresaw a renewed war with Germany long before it began. Portal had trained himself to work very long hours. He was believed to be a hard man and certainly he demanded the highest standard of work from the Air Staff. Producing the CAS's brief for the weekly meeting was quite a performance involving all sections of my Directorate: collecting, collating and checking, up to the last minute when the papers were due 'upstairs'. He may well have deserved his reputation as a hard man but on several occasions I saw what an understanding man he could be, most notably when my brother was murdered by the Gestapo. His thoughts were never far away from the aircrew and their arduous tasks.

He remained as Chief of the Air Staff for more than five years until December 1945 and was the longest serving Chief of Staff after Trenchard. Perhaps the best assessment of Portal's outstanding service, and one with which I wholeheartedly agree, is given by Lord Ismay who served at the centre of affairs throughout the war as Churchill's Personal Staff Officer with a seat on the Chief of Staff Committee. He was asked on one occasion "I know it is a very difficult question to answer, but who do you consider to have been the greatest Commander on our side during the war?" Ismay's reply was: "It isn't a difficult question to answer at all. The answer is Peter Portal—quite easily."[1]

[1] Denis Richards, *Portal of Hungerford* p 183

My contact with the Defence Committee and with the daily meetings of the Chiefs of Staff Committee—often chaired by Churchill himself—gave me an insight into how the affairs of war were conducted at the highest level. The minutes of these meetings were masterpieces of clarity and brevity. The efficiency of the Defence Committee and particularly of its Chiefs of Staff Sub-Committee owed much to Churchill who was fortunate in his servants: Hastings Ismay, his Personal Staff Officer; Leslie Hollis, Secretary of the COS Committee and Ian Jacob, Secretary of the Office of the MOD.

The feeling of optimism, that the end of the war was in sight, spread soon after the breakout from Normandy and the gallop to Brussels got going, though this feeling was not shared by the old hands from the Desert. Too often the winning of a battle in Libya had led to optimism of 'Tripoli next stop' only to find that Rommel, having retreated in good order and extended the British lines of communication, would turn and administer a sharp "bloody nose" as the soldiers called it, preparatory to another advance. Many airmen who had served in the Desert, taking the fighting qualities of the German soldier into account, believed he would not be beaten until we reached Berlin and marched down the Unter den Linden. Our doubts were reinforced on 16 December 1944 when the 'beaten' Germans launched a quite unexpected offensive through the Ardennes.

The German secrecy was virtually complete in moving 5 and 6 Panzer Armies to Western Germany. Ultra reported some movements of Army and Luftwaffe units without correctly interpreting the purpose of these moves. It was supposed that the panzers were preparing for a last-ditch defence of the Ruhr whereas the German objective was in fact to burst through the Allied lines, swing north-west, and recapture both Brussels and Antwerp. The enemy was aided by the weather: fog covered not only the battlefield and its approaches but all the airfields in the United Kingdom, France, Holland and Belgium initially preventing the Allied Air Forces from participating at all. Not for some years had the Wehrmacht enjoyed the luxury of fighting only against land forces.

Captured German records show that the Luftwaffe had collected every available fighter and had planned to attack simultaneously all the airfields of the Tactical Air Forces but because of the fog they too were unable to operate. Over confidence at all Allied HQ (as well as ground) which spread downwards, discounted any possibility of a German offensive, and it is now known that the plan was Hitler's and that he forced it through despite opposition from the German

Generals. As can be imagined, the initial success of the German advance caused extreme disquiet at Eisenhower's HQ and when Bradley's Army Group was split in two by the enemy, Eisenhower placed the northern part under Montgomery's command.

The fog persisted and the only assistance the air could give was in Bomber Command bombing 'blind' with their extremely accurate radar bombing aid 'Oboe'. Harris bombed targets on General Hodges' US 1st Army front which elicited a signal of congratulations from Eisenhower. Tedder in his memoirs quotes the reply from Harris thanking the Supreme Commander and ending, "you can count on us in any weather short of the impossible", to which Eisenhower minuted, "Goddamit, they have already achieved the impossible."[1] The fog began to clear and the Air Forces were able to help and at the same time the US 1st Army with a little help from the British attacked the Ardennes 'Bulge' and drove the Germans back. The Anglo-American tactical air forces supported the ground forces admirably.

On 29 December I went on a routine visit to Brussels. There was a sense of anticipation in 2nd TAF HQ because it was known that Montgomery was due to attack the north side of the Bulge on 1 January 1945 (he was actually delayed until the 3rd). I had arranged to complete my visit to the HQ that day and having talked at length about current operations with Air Vice-Marshal Victor Groom, the SASO and only briefly with Coningham, departed in the evening for 2 Group to stay the night and to be ready for my appointment with Basil Embry the nexy day. I was up good and early and was having breakfast in the Mess soon after seven when the noise of low-flying aircraft began to increase to a point where it could no longer be ignored. I said to Wing Commander Peter Wykeham-Barnes, who was on the staff of 2 Group HQ that "the boys seem to be in good form this morning". "Yes" he replied and got up to go to the window. "Those aren't Spitfires" he yelled "they are 109s!" We all rushed to see and sure enough there were 109s and some 190s all over the place. We heard later that all the airfields in the Brussels area had been attacked and also many further afield in Belgium and Holland. This was the attack planned by the Luftwaffe to coincide with the Ardennes offensive but which had been post-poned by the fog.

Later I went with Basil Embry to Evere airfield, home of one of his Mitchell bomber wings. It was a sorry mess, lopsided Mitchells everywhere, where tyres had been punctured by cannon and machine-gun fire. Strangely and fortunately none had caught fire,

[1] Lord Tedder, *With Prejudice* p 627

Some had been badly damaged, others had escaped lightly and were already repaired. Supremacy in the air which the Allies had enjoyed from Normandy onwards had led, I felt, to a relaxation of the wide dispersal of aircraft on the airfields and concentration to aid reduction of turn round time. This helped the enemy in his attack. Basil Embry was intent on mounting a bombing effort as soon as possible and called his wing and squadron commanders together. I could see that now was not the time for a staff officer from the Air Ministry to hang around and I excused myself and returned to 2nd TAF HQ.

Full reports on the attacks had not yet reached the Operations Room but it was clear that not only 2 Group airfields had been attacked. 83 Group seemed to have borne the brunt as nearly all its airfields had suffered. I was due to visit 83 Group and I reckoned that by the time I got there they would have sorted themselves out, so I flew up to Eindhoven where Harry Broadhurst had his HQ in the local Golf Club. I was met on the airfield by my old driver from Egypt, Corporal Dai Rees, still driving for Harry. Rees was very solemn. I said "I hear you had a rough time this morning?" "Yes, Sir", he said "very bad". I left it at that and was soon in Harry's office. Apparently, among other things that had delayed his fighters getting airborne at first light as normal, was ice on the runways and only part of his force was in the air when the Luftwaffe arrived. A great many aircraft were attacked on the ground and like the Mitchells at Evere suffered varying degrees of damage. Fortunately, casualties amongst the airmen groundcrew and the pilots were few. Moreover, the enemy, having used their ammunition, were vulnerable on their return journey and if intercepted were easy prey. So some of Broadhurst's squadrons that were in the air over Germany were called back and did well as did the American fighters whose airfields to the south missed most of the attack.

Broadhurst was hopping mad. His first reaction was to disguise the success of the operation from the enemy by flying overtime every aircraft that had been spared and every reserve he could muster so that the enemy would see the same number of sorties over them that they had the day before. His attitude was quite different to that of 2nd TAF HQ where going on the defensive was initially advocated by Coningham whilst the overall effect of the attack was assessed.

Broadhurst told me, "I never had any warning. Not a squeak from Ultra or the Y Service. If I had I would have given him such a hiding". I asked him who was commanding the Luftwaffe lot opposite him. "I don't know", he said "they are always changing". He called up his Chief Intelligence Officer and asked him. "I think its a

General Major Peltz". I couldn't but let out a whistle! "Good Lord. That's the chap who did me at Bizerta and Bari and you on your airfields in Sicily!" Broadhurst was silent.[1]

Having completed my visit to Brussels, I returned to Whitehall and was sent for by Portal. He already had a preliminary report of the raid but asked me to give him a first-hand account. When I had finished he said "Well between us, we and the USAAF have lost some two hundred aircraft but no aircrew. The enemy lost a hundred and forty four aircraft *and* crews. We can easily replace our aircraft but he cannot replace his aircrew quickly. I think we shall find that this is the final throw of the Luftwaffe". Portal was right in that neither the bomber nor fighter forces of the Luftwaffe were capable of any major effort of the rest of the war.

But in another respect the Luftwaffe had an unpleasant surprise for us when the Me 262 jet fighter and the 163 rocket fighter made their appearance. It is an astonishing fact that the Me262's first flight with turbojet engines took place as early as July 1942. Luckily for us, the German Air Ministry took little interest in it until the following year. We were even luckier that this marvellous fighter was in fact a bomber. Thanks to German bungling, the Me262 went into production in April 1944 and fewer than 100 actually saw service. The Me 262 was first encountered by the 8th Air Force in its operations over Germany, fortunately in small numbers, but its astonishing performance caused immediate concern amongst the aircrew and the hierarchy of the USAAF because even its best fighter, the P-51 Mustang, was quite unable to match the speed and climb of this jet aircraft. The small numbers of the Me 262 meant that they were in no way decisive in preventing the American bombers accompanied by their swarms of long-range fighters from reaching their targets. However, losses of bombers and fighters, having been much reduced, now began rising again.

The situation brought about by the advent of the Me 262 was under review daily and sometimes hourly in the Air Ministry. So far, though it was reported several times, the rocket-propelled Me163 seemed to interfere less than the Me 262. The Air Ministry's immediate action was to accelerate the programme to produce our own jet fighter, the Gloster Meteor. Inevitably the 2nd TAF fighters sighted the Me 262 in its operations over Germany and Mary Coningham went rather overboard in stressing to anyone who would listen, the threat that this new aircraft posed to the Allied Air Forces. Needless to say, this threat had been well appreciated in Whitehall

---

[1] It is worth recording that I was actually to meet Peltz at a gathering at the Staff College, Bracknell, on 26 March 1993.

and Washington from the outset. Coningham though only marginally affected by the Me 262, kept up his warnings, especially to MPs. They in turn bombarded the Secretary of State with questions. Portal explained to Coningham that everything that could be done was being done and asked him to tone down his warnings.

The Germans, having lost their launching sites in northern France, now tried launching their V1s from Heinkel 111s off the Dutch coast. All told about 1,200 bombs were launched by air at night and many of those caused severe damage. Then a new threat appeared which was much more serious: the V2 rocket. The double 'bang' as this monstrosity broke through the sound barrier and descended on London became a constant worry. Between 8 September 1944 and 27 March 1945, 1,115 V2 missiles landed in the United Kingdom. There was no direct defence against these weapons but the scale of attack was much reduced by the constant attack on launching sites by Allied aircraft when they could be located. These launching sites were mobile and when one was found in the wooded area of Haagsche-Bosch on the eastern outskirts of the Hague, on 3 March 1945, the medium bombers of 2 Group were instructed by 2nd TAF to mount a raid. Their aiming point was incorrect and the bombs killed at least 520 Dutch civilians as well as causing massive damage. Commander Moolenburgh, representing the Dutch government, called on me next day to give me details. Churchill was furious and told Portal that the incident "reflects upon the Air Ministry and the RAF in two ways. First, it shows how feeble have been our efforts to interfere with the rockets and secondly, the extraordinarily bad aiming which led to this slaughter of Dutchmen."

I was sent for by Portal and told to go at once to Brussels and find out from Coningham the answer to the question "Was it an error in bombing or an error in briefing?" As always he was very precise. An aeroplane was arranged at Northolt and I was in 2nd TAF HQ within three hours of leaving Portal's office. Coningham was not in the building but was expected back shortly. I said I would wait but was then sent for by Air Vice-Marshal Groom. I told him the purpose of my visit and was treated to a tirade about my neglect of 2nd TAF's interests in Whitehall. He ignored my question about the bombing. I waited until evening but Coningham had not returned and as was my custom I went off to 2 Group to stay the night in their cavalry barracks. I said I would be available if Coningham could see me that evening and if not I would be back first thing in the morning. Basil Embry and his staff were gathering in the Mess for their pre-dinner drink when I arrived. "What are you doing here?" asked Basil in his usual direct way. I explained and Basil said "There is an investigation going on and already it looks as if a mistake was made in the map reference". I went back to 2nd TAF HQ the next morning and saw Coningham and Victor Groom together. Before I could even state my mission, Coningham said "Victor had told me what you have come for but I am writing direct to the CAS about it so there is no point in discussing it here". I was then ushered out. I returned to Whitehall and wrote a short minute to Portal giving the information I had obtained at 2 Group. He sent for me and said "So it was an error in briefing? The AOC-in-C agrees?" I explained that Coningham would not discuss it with me and was writing direct. I then experienced the Portal chill as it was known in King Charles Street, though it seemed to me to be more like an Artic "frost" and I was dismissed. I did not see Portal's reply to Winston but I heard that Portal spoke to Coningham before writing it. Anyway, we heard no more about it but I believe that Coningham's stock had sunk a bit on the fifth floor. I learned later that Portal informed Churchill on 21 March that the cause of the incident was "a most unfortunate lapse by one or more officers concerned in the briefing" and court marshal proceedings were likely to follow. Arrangements were made to drop leaflets over The Hague, carrying the text of an explanation and apology. Churchill accepted these actions and the Dutch did not raise the matter again.

Life returned to normal on the third floor. I had a visit from Group Captain Leonard Cheshire whose feats in Bomber Command, culminating in the award of the Victoria Cross (not to mention three DSO's!), we all knew about. He had been taken off flying after surviving three tours in Bomber Command and was posted to Air HQ in Calcutta in September 1944. He said, "As you are the Director of Operations Tactical and almost all the operations in the South-East Asia theatre are tactical, I thought I should call on you and find out what went on". I ran over the organisation of the command and went through the daily operations reports. When he left, I knew I had been in the presence of a quite remarkable man. A month or two later Cheshire was again in my office. I was surprised and said "I thought you were in Calcutta". "I am", he replied "I am just back here on a visit with Mountbatten". "Good," I said, "now you can tell me about South-East Asia". He gave me an amusing account of his first few weeks in the command. Having made his number with the AOC-in-C and having moved into his office, he thought that the first thing he should do was to visit the front in Burma. "Quite unnecessary," his immediate superior said "we have a satisfactory reporting system and visits are not encouraged". Plainly this staff officer underestimated Cheshire who within a week visited 224 Group which was supporting the 14th Army. He was given a warm welcome by HQ staff, who told him that he was the first visitor from Calcutta that they had had for months. He asked if he could borrow an aeroplane to look at the front and a single-seat fighter was arranged and off he went flying at eight thousand feet to be above the worst of the light flak and below the best operating height of the heavy stuff and keeping a mile or so off-shore. When he got to where the front was marked on his map, he edged in to the coast and descended to get a better view. He was not shot at all nor could he see any signs of the enemy. When he returned to Akyab he told the staff of his experience but was not believed. "The Japs are playing possum", he was told.

I now thought it was time for me to visit the more distant Tactical Air Forces overseas. My request to go to Burma was turned down owing to the length of the trip, but that to the Middle East and Italy was approved. Transport Command arranged a Hudson and off I went via Gibraltar to Termoli on the east coast of Italy, north of Foggia, where Desert Air Force HQ was located. AVM William 'Dickie' Dickson, an old friend from 25 Squadron days in the 1930s, had taken over from Broadhurst and I had a long talk with him. The situation on the front right across Italy was in our favour with the Germans completely on the defensive. When attacked, they held onto their positions until the last moment and then withdrew to their next very well prepared position. What was remarkable was that they conducted this defence despite complete Allied air superiority—the Luftwaffe by this time were almost completely absent. In these circumstances, Dickson used his fighter-bombers as additional artillery on targets in the front line, mostly directed by forward RAF controllers. That the fighter-bombers were merely an additional aid and not decisive was a tribute to the fighting qualities of the Wehrmacht.

We airman had often been told by soldiers of varying ranks that providing the Air Force could prevent the enemy from interfering in ground operations, the Army could handle the situation. When we could not do this, in numerous campaigns early in the war when the Luftwaffe was still strong, the Army usually blamed us for its defeat; we had failed, it said, to provide adequate air support. But here was an Army—the Wehrmacht—totally without any air support fighting a successful defensive battle yard by yard up the length of Italy! The truth was that the German was the best soldier on either side throughout the war and the Wehrmacht had a significant advantage over the Allied armies in the volume and accuracy of its light flak. The Allied Tactical Air Forces were well qualified to compare the two flaks since Allied soldiers never really solved the aircraft identification problem and right up the Rhine crossings, frequently fired on our aircraft. "Fire first and identify later" seemed to be the soldier's (and indeed the sailor's) motto.

Dickie Dickson recognised that turning the Desert Air Force into flying artillery might have dangers for Army/Air arrangements in the future. It had taken a long time in the Desert to educate the 8th Army in the most effective methods of accepting help from the air, particularly when the enemy had a strong air force. Quite often nothing could be spared for direct support of the ground forces. Monty's over simplified statement "The air battle must be won first before the air can participate in the land battle" helped but such sayings are apt to be quickly forgotten. Certainly in Italy, the Tactical Air Forces never had to face serious air opposition, so participation in the land battle became the major employment for the Desert Air Force. Broadhurst had recognised in Sicily that the air supremacy he enjoyed, mainly as the result of the efforts of the North African Strategic Air Forces against the Luftwaffe airfields, obliged the Desert Air Force to improve their ground-attack capability for the good of the cause. He introduced as a start the 'Rover David' innovation: an experienced operational pilot on the ground with an R/T set who briefed the aircraft on the target to be attacked when they arrived overhead. This procedure was immensely popular with the soldiers and was largely responsible for the reputation Broadhurst gained for being the 'Army's friend'! It is ironic that the Army's greatest friends, Tedder and Coningham, were never popular with the soldiers. Nevertheless credit is due to Broadhurst. He arrived in the Desert after the battle of El Alamein, when the air battle had long been won and almost all the problems of Army/Air operations had been solved. He profited from the new situation and changed the emphasis from air fighting to ground attack, at which the Desert Air Force had not been conspicuously successful up to that time.

From Italy I flew to Cairo to visit Middle East HQ which was still responsible for the administration of the Desert Air Force, then on to Alexandria and stayed a night with my good friends Judge and Lady Holmes and their three beautiful daughters. Lady Holmes was a most understanding woman. She had appreciated the effect that Ian's foul murder would have on our family and her memorable words "He is not dead as long as he is always in your thoughts" gave me some comfort. When the time came to return home, France had been cleared of the enemy and the Hudson captain was delighted to tell me that the trip would be considerably shortened as it was no longer necessary to go the long way round via Gibraltar. We refuelled in Malta and then flew straight to Northolt.

The war dragged on through the winter of 1944-5. One of my responsibilities as Director of Operations Tactical was the policy for employing Army Airborne Forces from an Air Force aspect. This meant working closely with the War Office. I was fortunate that the Director of the Department of Air was Major General Sir Kenneth Crawford. Soon after we met we had a mild argument about the number of gliders needed for the Airborne Forces, and when we left the meeting I went with him to the door in King Charles Street and he said to me "I have no doubt that we shall disagree many more times, but it is essential that we don't fall out". We never did, even though with resources diminishing everywhere in the fifth year of war, we had many long and sometimes acrimonious discussions. There were bound to be differences when one department—the Air Ministry—was providing from its resources for another, the War Office. Indeed the appetite of the commander of the British Airborne Corps, Lieutenant-General F A M Browning was insatiable.

'Boy' Browning, as he was known to everyone, was a tremendous enthusiast and demanded everything. Even the Vice-Chief of the Air Staff said once in a moment of exasperation, "when he was a Major-General he wanted a parallel RAF Group—now he is a Lieutenant-General he wants a second Group, and if he becomes a full General he'll want an RAF Command!" The Vice-Chief was referring to No 38 Group which had been formed in 1940 to provide airlift for a parachute force demanded by Mr Churchill shortly after becoming Prime Minister. Browning's ambitions were only partly fulfilled when a second Group, No 46, was given additional airborne responsibilities to its main role as a Dakota-equipped group in Transport Command.

One November morning I was rather drearily mounting the steps into the King Charles building wondering when the war was going to end when I met Group Captain J R A 'Johnnie' Peel whom I knew as an outstanding fighter squadron commander and who was now a deputy director. He was all smiles and said "I'll cheer you up . . . we sank the *Tirpitz* yesterday!" So at last the Royal Air Force had sunk a battleship and I remembered Tedder's words at Bizerta when we were preparing for the expected opposition from the Italian fleet that never materialised. "Every Air Force has sunk a battleship except us, so we had better use this opportunity now we have it." But the Italians cheated us and changed sides. Now we had done it and disproved once more the pre-war Naval theory that the battleship was impervious to air bombardment.

At Portal's weekly meeting Bufton, the Director of Bomber

Operations, gave an account of the operation on 12 November 1944 by thirty Lancasters of 617 and 9 Squadrons, flying from Lossiemouth, in northern Scotland. The raids were led by Wing Commander J B Tait and the bombs were 12,000 lb tallboys, plus some 4-500 lb mines. They finished off the *Tirpitz*, but the decisive attack had actually been made on 15 September by 27 Lancasters of these two squadrons flying from Yagodnik (near Archangel) to Altenfjord, in northern Norway. The German ship was too badly damaged to make seaworthy again and so she had been moved south to Tromso for use as a coastal defence battery. Even so, it was wonderful to know that she had finally been despatched by RAF bombers. The photo-reconnaissance Mosquito that followed the Lancasters reported that the *Tirpitz* had capsized. Portal said, "I believe that there was a film camera man aboard and that we now have the film". Bufton confirmed that this was so and that it was in the small cinema in the basement. "Let's go and see it", said Portal and the dozen or so of us sitting round the table got up and trooped down there. The film, which ran for only a matter of seconds, clearly showed the *Tirpitz* and particularly well the decisive hits. The lights went up and Portal said, "Let's see it again." We were all delighted and when the lights went up again for the second time we hurried away to our respective departments to tell the others about it.

One of my pleasant responsibilities in the last months of the war was a weekly call on Lord Trenchard in his flat in Kensington. I was to report on the main events of the week and this led to discussion. It was quite remarkable what a clear understanding he had of all these modern air operations and I was fascinated to hear his opinions. He had kept abreast of events ever since the war began and his mind remained as sharp as ever. He was extremely kind to me, never condescending to a much younger man, and our friendship continued until he died in 1956. When I commanded a station he came to stay and my wife and I were regularly asked to lunch at the Kings House at Burhill. He was a wonderful man and an inspiration to me.

One day in December 1944 I was early for the morning meeting in the War Room and sitting in my place at the table I saw a WAAF officer marking up the situation map from the night's signals. She was very beautiful and her face had a noble look about it as well. I had difficulty in dragging my thoughts back to my brief as the room began to fill with the other directors and staff officers. That afternoon I had cause to go to the War Room again and the beautiful WAAF was still there. I found out her name from the ancient Group Captain who minded the place and introduced myself on some pretext. We talked for a moment or two and I learned that she was Brenda Powell the daughter of a Wing Commander. Then, greatly daring, I asked her if she would have dinner with me that evening. She laughed and said she would. We went to the Savoy Grill, a favourite for the Air Force in wartime. I saw her every day after that. We were engaged in a week and married within a month.

My austere flat in Artillery Mansions was no good for a married couple but Brenda found a flat in Chelsea, the first of many homes she was to find us during the next forty five years. The war dragged on but it was wonderful to be no longer alone in London. Brenda and I had one sadness in common. We had both lost a favourite younger brother killed flying in Bomber Command. My Ian and her David flying his Hampden from Scampton. He was only eighteen. Brenda continued her work in the underground War Room but when she was off duty and in the flat every flying bomb and V2 was a worry.

The spring came and with it the final great land operation of the war, the Rhine crossing. It began on 23 March, 1945 on a two-army front, between Rheinberg and Rees: the US 9th Army on the right and the British 2nd Army on the left. The communication centre of Wesel and crossing point near there would be secured next day by an airborne assault, Operation Varsity. The lessons of the disastrous attack and failure of the last airborne operation at Arnhem had been well learnt, particularly the unsound command arrangement. At Arnhem, the entire 2nd TAF was withheld from the operational area and fighter support was arranged from England. It proved inadequate and for this reason, together with unexpectedly strong German resistance and over-confidence among the paratroops and ground forces, Operation Market Garden (as it was called) failed.

As a result of this failure, the next airborne operation—Varsity—was planned at Coningham's HQ in Brussels with the co-operation of all the air and ground commanders concerned. Harry Broadhurst, Britain's most experienced tactical air force commander, was made responsible for the co-ordination of all the air aspects of the operation. All 2nd TAF fighters were now based within easy range of the projected dropping zone and the land forces that were to join up with the airborne drop were already crossing the Rhine. At Arnhem the final cause of failure was the inability of the advancing land forces to link up with the paratroops. This time they were accompanied by many gliders carrying jeeps and light artillery so that they would be mobile and able to defend themselves promptly. I formed the opinion that as far as any operation in war could be called a 'certainty' then this was it. This opinion was shared by my uniformed superiors in the department but not by the politicians. After Arnhem there was apprehension at the very mention of airborne operations.

I was therefore summoned to the Secretary of State's office to give a description of the operation. Sir Archibald Sinclair had soldiered with Winston in Flanders in World War I and had been an admirable Secretary of State for Air from the time Churchill became Prime Minister. The Deputy Chief of Air Staff, Norman Bottomley and the Assistant Chief of Air Staff, Bill Williams were in Sinclair's office when I arrived and I quickly ran through the plan of Operation Varsity. I then answered questions as well as I could, at the same time endeavouring to convey the confidence of the commanders concerned. Despite this and the apparent confidence of the two senior members of the Air Staff, Sinclair still seemed to be uneasy. I was sent for several times subsequently by him and his staff to elucidate specific points. Eventually, he indicated his intention of going to the HQ airfield of No 38 Group in Essex to observe the take-off. I immediately protested to my boss Williams, emphasising the fact that for the launching of this enormous operation, the commanders and staffs at all levels would be fully employed especially in the hours prior to take-off. Williams agreed and explained this to Sinclair but he was adamant, saying he would require no special attention and no senior officer escort from 38 Group. He would take me along to explain technicalities to him!

No 38 Group HQ was at Marks Hall airfield near Earls Colne and was commanded by an old friend from Alexandria days, and the best man at my wedding Jim Scarlett-Streatfeild. When I told him of Sinclair's intention he protested vigorously that he would be fully occupied and could not 'look after' the S of S. I told him that we had done our best to prevent the visit but had no success. "Well", he said, "you will be on your own, and what's more you will have to come the evening before because once the briefing is given to the crews all the airfields are closed and nobody, repeat nobody from ten on will be allowed in or out". Archie Sinclair was a very pleasant man and I think that by this time he realised that he was being a bit of a nuisance to the uniformed part of his 'empire'. However, he could on occasion be every inch a Minister at the Head of a Department of State and this was such an occasion. I was imperiously waved to my seat in the limousine waiting to drive us to Earls Colne but as soon as we started he was his usual charming self again.

We duly arrived at Marks Hall and were directed to Jim's bungalow on the edge of the airfield. Jim had relented and actually seemed pleased to see us. He knew that Sinclair had accepted his conditions to be present for the launch. He told us that the preliminary weather report was good but there would be a full weather briefing later in the evening, after which the final decisions would be made. We had dinner with Jim and then went with him to the briefing. It was a large gathering; in addition to the hundred or more pilots and navigators, there were the key people from the Station and the Group staff. The weather forecast confirmed that given earlier, and the decision to go was taken shortly after.

Marks Hall was one of nine airfields in Suffolk and Essex used by 38 Group for the operation and were all allotted to the glider part of the operation. The enormous Hamilcars capable of carrying a light tank were there in small numbers but the main body comprised a smaller glider, the Horsa. Boy Browning was to go in one of the leading Horsas. No earthbound General was he!

The launching of this glider force was a remarkable operation in itself. We positioned ourselves at the side of the runway to watch at Earls Colne. The tugs, Halifaxes and Dakotas, were lined up on one side of the runway at an angle and the gliders similarly on the other side. This array of some thirty tug aircraft and gliders made a most impressive sight. On a given signal, the tug aircraft moved forward trailing its towing line which was quickly hooked onto its glider, pulling it forward onto the runway. As soon as the tug and glider started their take-off, the next pair moved into position and the whole lot were airborne in a very few minutes.

When the last pair had left the end of the runway, Jim said to the Secretary of State, "I am going to follow the stream for a while in my Dakota, would you like to come?" Sinclair accepted with alacrity. I pondered my responsibility as conducting officer and the risk involved, but consoled myself with the thought that Jim was a whole rank senior to me and was now plainly in charge, though of course I must still accompany the S of S. We joined the stream of tugs and gliders over Southend on a southerly course and Jim, who was flying the Dakota himself, slowly overtook what seemed to be an endless procession. The track we were making good meant that we would cross the coast in the Folkestone area and on reaching the French coast turn onto the final heading for the Rhine at Wesel. Jim was now flying faster than the stream and eventually we reached the leading pair where we settled down to formate at a safe distance. The stream turned east and I began to wonder when Jim would turn back.

Soon Brussels appeared on our left and I then began to be concerned. Any minute now we would be reaching the battle area and say a stray Me 109 should shoot down the Dakota with the Secretary of State aboard!? It had happened before in Egypt when 'Strafer' Gott had been shot down in a Bombay behind the line at El Alamein leading to Montgomery's appointment to command the 8th Army. If Sinclair was shot down, would I, the conducting officer be held responsible? As casually as possible to conceal my anxiety, I got out of my seat next to Sinclair and wandered slowly forward to the cockpit. Closing the door behind me I said quietly to Jim, "When are we going back?" "In a few minutes," he replied. From the cockpit I could see far ahead and shortly afterwards I saw bursts of flak on the horizon. I think that even the imperturbable Jim was impressed by this and shortly afterwards he turned away and set course for home. When we landed I was alone with Jim for a few minutes and said, "Were we not taking a bit of a risk going that far with the S of S?" "Not really" he said calmly "we had monitored that area for weeks and not a single enemy aircraft had been reported." Poor Jim—he was killed a few weeks later when flying into Oslo to take the surrender of Norway and hit a mountain letting down through cloud.

The airborne crossing of the Rhine was a great success in complete contrast to the Arnhem operations. The Anglo-American armies quickly joined up with the airborne divisions and formed bridgeheads from which the final assault on the German heartland could be launched. Now, at last, the end of the war was in sight and it came on the evening of 4 May 1945 when German armed forces in Holland, North-west Germany and Denmark surrendered to Montgomery. On 7 May, surrender documents were signed at SHAEF HQ in Rheims and ratified next day in Berlin.

In the Air Ministry the work tempo decreased considerably. Brenda and I took a day off and wandered around London mingling with the happy crowds. We saw Winston twice: once sitting on the back seat of a small car driving slowly down Constitution Hill and escorted only by two mounted policemen, and then later when he appeared on the balcony of the Ministry of Health building at the bottom of Whitehall to wave to the cheering crowds.

My thoughts went back to eleven o'clock on 3 September 1939, when I walked out of the darkened Operations Room at Hucknall and looked up at the bright blue sky with apprehension expecting that at any moment it would be filled with the ominous shapes of Luftwaffe aircraft. Now it was all over and victory was ours but at what a cost. Brenda and I had both lost beloved younger brothers and of my close Air Force friends nearly all had been killed. Kenneth Ferguson, the Sherborne boy with his fair hair and blue eyes that so captivated the gentler sex, who seemed to be good at everything he did whether it was skiing, flying or making a hundred at cricket, had kicked aside his safe staff post for command of a Whitley bomber squadron. He had twice been forced to ditch in the North Sea returning from raids over Germany, once in a minefield, but having survived all that, was lost on a subsequent raid. Denys Field, my foursomes partner, and my closest friend, insisted in leaving a staff post to command a Hampden squadron at Scampton just in time for the battle starting in France. He flew six sorties in quick time and was shot down over Hamburg on the seventh. John Fletcher, the tennis and squash champion, lost leading his Blenheim squadron. Jim Scarlett-Streatfeild, Caesar Hull, the exceptionally gifted South African killed leading 43 Squadron as a Squadron Leader having joined it as a 'new boy' Pilot Officer a few years before. 'Tubby' Badger, Dicky Reynell from Australia, Kenneth Campbell whom I had taught to fly in the Cambridge University Air Squadron, shot down torpedoing the *Gneisenau* in Brest harbour, winning a post-humous VC in the process, Harry Burke, the bright one in 25 Squadron with his 'E' Star grading as an engineer, killed in a Torquay hospital during a Luftwaffe Baedeker raid. Derek Ward, that splendid little New Zealander, shot down over Gambut. Yaxley and Burton killed in a Hudson over the Bay of Biscay. The eight lost in the *Glorious*, Frost, Stewart, Mee, Shackley, Knight, Taylor, Bunker, Cowles. The list went on and on and on. Perhaps I should be grateful for my friends who survived and had covered themselves in glory. Harry Broadhurst, Douglas Bader, Pat Jameson, Jimmy Fenton, 'Tap' Jones, 'Tommy' Thompson, Jasper Read. Also, I was still alive and felt I had contributed a little to the victory. I had started the war as a twenty-seven year old Squadron Leader, had commanded a squadron in battle, and two operational wings and four groups all in active operations. I had rapid promotion to fill these posts and nearly always I was the youngest occupant of the rank in the service. Wing Commander at 28; Group Captain at 29 and Air Commodore at 31.

Now the war was over and very quickly the Treasury asserted itself. My acting rank was removed and I became a Group Captain again. It didn't matter much, I had the happiness of marriage and shortly afterwards I was selected for the first post-war course at the Imperial Defence College, the top educational establishment for all three Services. I heard that the Commandant was to be General Slim, the great commander of the 14th Army in Burma and that the senior Air Force staff member was my old boss from the Mediterranean, Hugh Pughe Lloyd. Brenda and I found a house to buy at Sunningdale and were in good heart, all set to endure the rigours of peace.